HOLOGRAPHY AND PHILATELY

Postage Stamps with Holograms

Hans I. Bjelkhagen
Hansholo Consulting Ltd
2017

The postage stamps in this book are reproduced with permission from the issuing countries. The following copyright statements are listed here as requested by the involved postal authorities:

© 2000 Åland Post
© 2000 Australian Postal Corporation
© Austrian Post AG
© Bhutan Postal Corporation Limited
© 1992-2011 Canada Post
© Česká Pošta
© Correios Brazil
© Correios de Macau
© Correios del Ecuador
© Correios de Portugal
© Deutsche Post
© Hellenic Post
© Hong Kong Post Office
© India Post
© Isle of Man Post Limited
© Israel Post
© Jersey Post Limited
© JP Post
© La Poste France 1999, 2010
© Lietuvos Paštas

© Magyar Posta
© Mongol Post
© NAM Post
© NIPOST 2010, 2012, 2013
© Poczta Polska
© POS Indonesia
© POS Malaysia
© 2005 Posteitaliene
© Posti-Finland
© PostNL
© 2001 Royal Mail
© Serpost El Correo del Perú
© Singapore Post
© South Africa Post
© Swiss Post
© 2003, 2005, 2006, 2011 U.N.
© USPS 1989, 1990
© 2000, 2006 United States Postal Service

'Reproduced with the permission of New Zealand Post Limited'.

Copyright © 2014 by Hans I. Bjelkhagen.

All rights reserved. No part of this book may be reproduced or transmitted in any form or by any means, electronic or mechanical, including photocopying, recording, or by any information storage and retrieval system, without permission in writing from the copyright owner.

The marks SCOTT and SCOTT'S are the copyrighted property of Amos Press, Inc., dba Scott Publishing Co. and are used here under a licensing agreement with Scott. The marks SCOTT and SCOTT'S are Registered in the U.S. Patent and Trademark Office, and are trademarks of Amos Press, Inc., dba Scott Publishing Co. No use may be made of these marks or of material in this publication which is reprinted from a copyrighted publication of Amos Press, Inc., without the express written permission of Amos Press, Inc., dba Scott Publishing Co., Sidney, Ohio 45365, USA.

Contents

CHAPTER 1

INTRODUCTION 4

CHAPTER 2

EARLY PHILATELY-RELATED HOLOGRAPHY 8

CHAPTER 3

HOLOGRAMS ON POSTAGE STAMPS 13

CHAPTER 4

HOLOGRAM STAMPS IN GERMAN YEAR BOOK OF STAMPS 291

CHAPTER 5

ADDITIONAL POSTAL AND PHILATELIC ITEMS WITH HOLOGRAMS 296

CHAPTER 6

3D IMAGING THECHNIQUES, HOLOGRAMS AND HOLOGRAM STAMPS 316

Concluding Remarks 330

References 331

SECOND EDITION

In this second edition, the many color illustrations throughout the first edition are all included and the printing quality is still very high in this reduced-priced publication. I hope people in holography as well as philatelists around the world will enjoy learning about postage stamps with holograms issued since 1988.

Since first published in 2013, several new postage stamps and souvenir sheets with holograms have been issued. A list of the most important and interesting ones issued between 2013 and 2016 are presented at the end of the book starting page 361. *-The Author*

***

CHAPTER 1
INTRODUCTION

In the middle of the 19th century many countries around the world introduced postage stamps. Not long thereafter people started to collect stamps. Today philately is a large, worldwide business and a popular hobby. It is common among philatelists to collect stamps by *topical* subjects. Topical collecting is the forming of a collection of philatelic material selected and arranged by subject, theme or design, rather than by country of issue. For example, Spira published a paper titled: *Photographica on Postage Stamps* [1] which lists photography-related stamps issued until 1979. In another publication Miller covers the *History of Optics* as featured on stamps. [2] Over the last two decades *holograms* have become a new topical subject in philately. It is now 25 years since a presentation stamp folder with a hologram was issued in Peoples Republic of China. The following year, in 1988, the first *definitive postage stamp* with a hologram was issued in Austria. Since then many countries have issued hologram stamps or souvenir sheets, some of them on more than one occasion.

Up until 2014 about 80 countries have issued holographic stamps and the total amount of different postal items with holograms is about 450. There was a peak in hologram stamps issued during the millennium 1999/2000 celebrations.

In the beginning it was common that holograms contained *3D images*. After 2000, hologram stamps began to be covered by *holographic diffractive foil* containing stars or other repeatable patterns. Sometimes the foil is cut in the shape of a figure, such as for example, an angel, a fish, or a sculpture. In addition, clear *transparent holographic foil* has been applied to stamps carrying images of butterflies and bugs. This type of foil can also be cut in the shape of any desirable figure to be featured on the stamp. In both cases, this means that the actual pattern within the hologram area of the stamp *varies* between stamps in a particular issue. It is generally assumed that all stamps in a particular edition are identical. Stamps with a variance (color, misprint, etc.) found in one or more stamps in a given issue are regarded especially collectable, and may represent a very high value to stamp collectors. Stamps with figure-shaped holographic foil patterns vary from stamp to stamp and should not be regarded as variations. There are, however, also hologram stamps with production errors, for example, a *missing hologram* on a multiple-stamp sheet with holograms. The hologram can have been *misplaced on a stamp* during the production process (hot-stamping technique is used to attach holograms). The cut out of the hologram image from the holographic foil (kiss cutting) can occasionally have gone wrong, resulting in slightly *different holographic images* on the stamp. This should not be confused with the above-described contour-cut holographic foil of random diffractive patterns. More information about hologram stamp variations and errors can be found in Chapter 6.

It should be pointed out that postage stamps to which a piece of *shiny foil* (without diffraction) has been attached are not included here, nor stamps with shiny gold or silver dots or letters, for example. Such stamps are sometimes wrongly described as "a stamp with hologram". A postage stamp to which a hologram is attached or where the entire stamp is holographic must create *diffraction of light* when correctly illuminated. A holographic 3D image or 2D/3D images or a random pattern of repeated features should be visible upon correct illumination. When illumination and observation directions vary, the hologram shows color variations. Some postal items have only holographic foil numbers or text attached. Such items are included in the book as long as they produce diffraction upon illumination. Stamps with *iridescent ink* which behave like holograms are also included here even though technically they are not holograms.

HOLOGRAPHY AND PHILATELY

When illuminating a stamp with iridescent ink, color shifts are observed depending on illumination and observation directions, like holograms.

Lenticular images are often described as "holograms" by philatelists who are not familiar with the different techniques (See Chapter 6). A lenticular image is based on a completely different technique used to create 3D images or moving/switching 2D images. Such a stamp is covered with a rather thick plastic raster with fine groves. Postage stamps covered with the plastic raster are not really nice, nor are they easy to attach to an envelope or possible to be properly cancel. Lenticular stamps are not included in this book. Hologram stamps are, on the contrary, very thin, like normal paper stamps that can be attached to envelopes and they can be cancelled without problems. After all, the purpose of a postage stamp is to be used for sending postal items.

Provided in this book is a *chronological review* of worldwide issued postage stamps and souvenir sheets with holograms. A description of each stamp is provided together with color photographs of all postage stamps. This goes also for miniature and souvenir sheets. In addition, official and special first-day covers (FDCs) are presented and described. It is common that a *cachet hologram* has been attached to an envelope (FDC or commemorative one) when normal postage stamps are issued. Such FDCs are also included. The majority of issued philatelic holographic items are included, but some cards or other printed items with a hologram attached to them may have been overlooked. Other documents or items with holograms, for example, telephone cards, tax stamps, revenue stamps, etc., are not included.

The use of holograms on postage stamps seems to be more of a new and attractive decoration rather than a security measure. They have often been issued in connection with stamp exhibitions or other philatelic events. Stamps with holograms have already become a new field of philatelic topical interest. In this book the emphasis is placed on the holograms and their different types, on the hologram images, the producers and the story behind them. The holograms have been recorded with the help of correct illumination (spotlight at a certain angle) and a high-resolution digital camera with a macro-lens. In addition, holograms of the *two-* or *multi-channel* type have been illustrated with a number of photographs revealing the individual images stored in the hologram on the stamp. It is not possible to scan the stamps and souvenir sheets, since the scanner's illumination cannot correctly replay the holographic image. However, some of the illustrations in this book have been recorded using a scanner, for example to reproduce FDCs, which means that the hologram image on them is not correctly shown. In many such cases a separate, correctly recorded photograph of the hologram has been provided next to the scanned FDC illustration. In Chapter 6 more information is provided on how to illuminate hologram stamps and take photographs of them.

From a philatelic point of view this review lacks some details as regards, for example, detailed printing information concerning paper used for the stamps, conventional printing techniques applied, watermarks, etc. Nevertheless, this book may be valuable to philatelists who are interested in hologram stamps. This publication is completely focused on holograms on stamps and FDCs providing correct reproduction of the holographic images, including multi-channel holograms. The extensive information provided here cannot be found in any other philatelic publications or any publications listed among the references.

For those who are not very familiar with the *philatelic terminology* the following definitions are provided:

Block is an unseparated group of stamps, at least two stamps high and two stamps wide.

Cachet is a design on an envelope, usually on the left side. Cachets are most commonly found on first day covers and are typically illustrations and or texts relating to the subject of the stamp or event being commemorated. There are many examples of cachet holograms.

Cancellation (or **cancel** for short) is a postal marking applied on a postage stamp or postal stationery to deface the stamp and prevent its re-use. Cancellations come in a huge variety of designs, shapes, sizes and colors. Cancellations can affect the value of stamps for collectors, positively or negatively.

Postage stamps with holograms are rarely used, which means that cancelled hologram stamps are not very common with the exception of those used on FDCs.

Cinderella stamps are many different types of stamps, for example, commemorative stickers, stamps issued by non-recognized countries or governments, Christmas seals and local stamps as well as purely decorative items created for advertising or amusement.

Definitive stamp is a postage stamp issued as a regular stamp for the country or territory in which it is to be used.

Denomination is the value of a postage stamp as printed on the face of the stamp. Denomination is not the same as the value of a stamp on the philatelic market, which is usually different.

Error on postage stamps is normally a failure in the stamp printing process which results in stamps not having the intended appearance. Errors include the use of wrong colors, wrong denominations, missing parts of the design, misplaced or missing design elements, such as holograms, etc. They are prized by collectors, with some fetching prices thousands of times higher than the normal stamp of their type.

FDC stands for First Day Cover. FDCs are normally issued on the day when new postage stamps are issued.

Gutter is the space left between postage stamps, which allows them to be separated or perforated. Some sheets are especially designed where the gutter remains in the finished sheet and gutters may, or may not, have some printing in the gutter.

Miniature sheet is a small group of postage stamps still attached to the sheet on which they were printed. They may be either regular issues that just happen to be printed in small groups, or special issues often commemorating some event, such as a national anniversary, philatelic exhibition, or government program. Miniature sheets or souvenir sheets are often similar. But miniature sheets most often contains definitive stamps.

Overprint is an additional layer of text or graphics added to the face of a postage stamp after it has been printed.

Postage stamp is a small piece of paper that is purchased and displayed on a letter or any other postal item as evidence of payment of postage. Typically, stamps are made from special paper, with a national designation and denomination (price) on the face, and a gum adhesive on the reverse side.

Postal stationery is a stationery item, such as a stamped envelope, postal card, lettercard, or aerogram, with an imprinted stamp or inscription indicating that a specific rate of postage or related service has been prepaid.

Selvage is the margin around the sheet of postage stamps. The selvage may include the plate number, copyright, and other markings. There are examples of holograms being attached to the selvage area of stamp sheets.

Se-tenant stamps or labels are printed from the same plate and sheet and adjoin one another. They differ from each other by design, color, denomination or overprint.

Sheets of stamps are sheets of large amount of stamps, the number of stamps are often ten or more. Compare, blocks, miniature - and souvenier sheets.

Souvenir sheet is one or a few postage stamps attached to a sheet on which they were printed. They may be regular issues printed in small groups, or special issues often commemorating some event, such as a national anniversary, philatelic exhibition, or government program. Stamps on a sheet may be perforated or imperforated. The margins or selvage of the sheet may have additional printing, for example, a statement of the occasion being commemorated. The margins of the sheet may have ornamental designs, emblems and logos which are not part of stamp(s). Both the stamps and the entire sheet are valid for mailing, although they are almost always sold above face value and kept in mint collection by collectors. Hologram stamps are often issued as souvenir sheets.

Tête-bêche (French for "head-to-tail", lit. "head-to-head") is a joined pair of stamps in which one is upside-down in relation to the other, produced intentionally or accidentally.

For those unfamiliar with *holography* and *holograms* the following information is provided in brief:

Holography was invented in 1948 by Dennis Gabor who was awarded the 1971 Physics Nobel Prize for his invention. Holography was convincingly demonstrated after the invention of the laser in the early 1960s. Emmett Leith and Juris Upatnieks from the USA demonstrated a *transmission hologram* with a monochrome 3D image in 1964. More or less at the same time, in the former USSR, Yuri Denisyuk demonstrated a slightly different type of a hologram which was a *reflection hologram*. Since then, several holographic techniques have been developed. Applications of holography are found in 3D display techniques, scientific high-resolution imaging, in recording diffractive optical elements and other optical components. One important application is the use of holograms as an *optical variable device* (OVD) on documents as a security measure. Most well-known here is the use of *embossed, mass-produced holograms* on credit cards and banknotes. This type of hologram is also the type which is used on postage stamps. These holograms are known as *rainbow holograms* or *Benton holograms,* named after the inventor and MIT professor Stephen Benton. The advantage of Benton's technique is that it is possible to view the image in ordinary white light. (The laser is only needed for the recording of the hologram). Another advantage of rainbow holograms is that they can be produced in very large quantities, using *embossing* techniques. They are attached to documents, banknotes or postage stamps by *hot-stamping* techniques. The majority of holograms for postage stamps are attached by hot-stamping to printed paper stamps, but some embossed hologram postage stamps have been issued as *self-adhesive* stamps. Since the embossed rainbow hologram is actually a transmission hologram, they have to be *mirror-backed* to be able to view and illuminate them from the same side when attached to documents or stamps. This explains why holograms on stamps have a reflecting coating (looking sometimes just as a piece of reflecting foil). The reflecting layer is also included in credit card holograms. Chapter 6 provides more information on holography and holograms, in particular how to illuminate them correctly to be able to view the image. The reader can also find books on holography in the list of references. [3 – 5]

The author on the tab of the *two-channel* hologram
on the personalized Australian Millennium stamp.

CHAPTER 2
EARLY PHILATELY-RELATED HOLOGRAPHY

This Chapter provides a review of how holograms have been used in connection with postage stamps or other philately-related applications where holography has been introduced. This includes an account of the state of affairs in this field before the first *definitive stamp* with a hologram was issued in 1988. Before that holograms have only been used on cards or on the cover of a stamp exhibition catalog. P. R. China was the first country to use a hologram on the cover of a stamp presentation folder in 1987.

Fig. 2.1. The Swedish crown stamp.

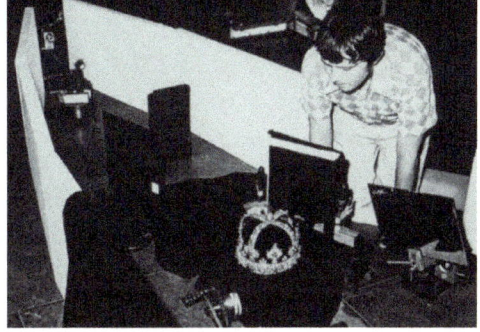
Fig. 2.2. Recording of Crown hologram.

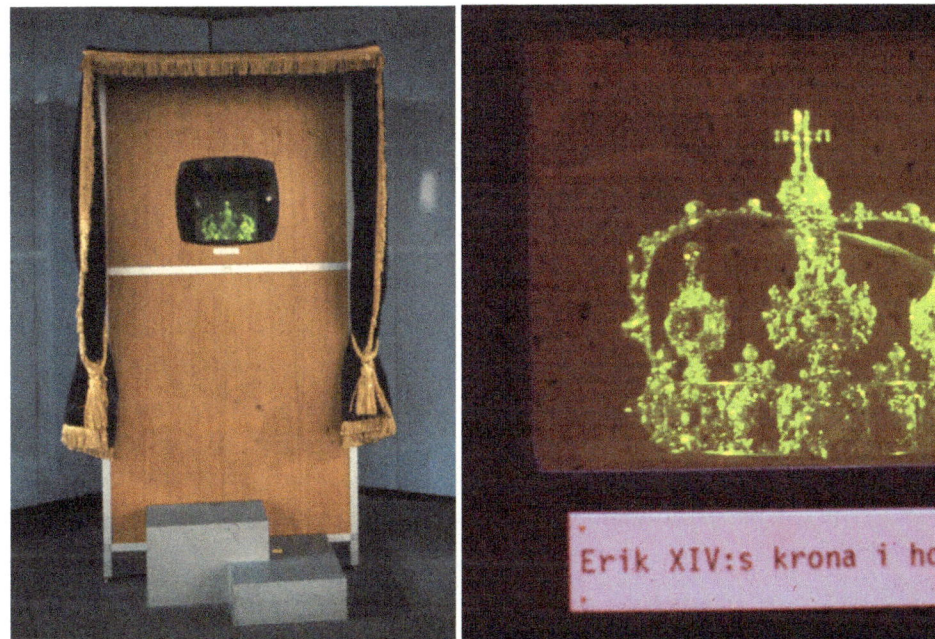
Fig. 2.3. Display case. **Fig. 2.4.** *Crown* hologram.

The first time philatelists were able to see a hologram was probably in **1974** in **Sweden**. At the international stamp exhibition STOCKHOLMIA'74, a hologram of the *Coronation Crown of Erik XIV* (from 1561) was on display at the show. On October 20, 1971, the Swedish Post issued a series of five stamps featuring the Royal Treasuries, including the Crown, shown in Fig. 2.1. Since it was not possible to show the real Crown at the stamp exhibition, a hologram of the Crown was produced. The recording of the 8" by 10" *off-axis transmission* hologram was performed in the cellar under the Royal Castle in Stockholm. During the night of August 20, 1974, the Crown was moved from the Treasury down to a room in the cellar. Figure 2.2 shows the author next to the hologram-recording setup arranged directly on the floor.

At the show, the recorded hologram was installed in a special display case in which the hologram was illuminated with yellow-filtered light from a mercury-arc lamp placed at the bottom of the display case. Figure 2.3 shows the display case with a close-up view of the Crown hologram in Fig. 2.4. The show took place between **September 21** and **29, 1974**, at the Älvsjö Exhibition Center, south of Stockholm. The hologram was a main attraction at the show and people were waiting in a long line to be able to get a glimpse of the holographic Crown. As a matter of fact, many people came to the stamp show just to see the hologram.

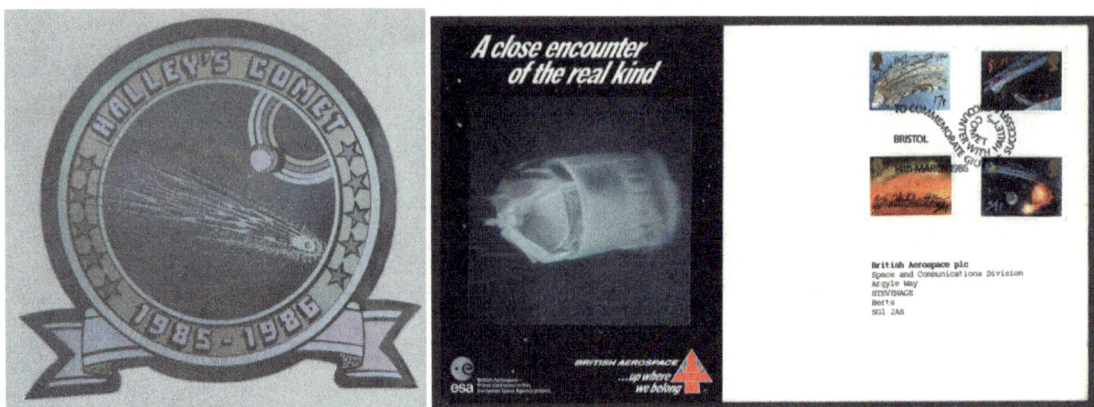

Fig. 2.5. *Halley's Comet* hologram and the *Giotto* hologram on a British Aerospace cover.

Commemorative covers were issued with holograms for the 'European Robotic Spacecraft Giotto – Mission' to study the comet Halley - Perihelion of the comet Halley. On the day of the perihelion, February 9, 1986, **Germany** issued an FDC with a cachet hologram with cancel 'OSOC - Operations Centres of ESA – Darmstadt'. During the night between March 13 and 14, 1986, ESA's Giotto spacecraft encountered Comet Halley. After a cruise of eight months and almost 150 million km, the spacecraft's instruments first detected hydrogen ions from Halley at a distance of 7.8 million km from the comet on March 12, 1986. The spacecraft was travelling at a speed of 68 km/s relative to the comet. Giotto encountered Comet Halley about one day later. When Giotto entered the densest part of the dusty coma, the camera recorded the brightest objects. The European Space Operations Centre in Darmstadt, Germany, received the first images and data which came in, and later the Centre came up with a preliminary analysis. The ESA – British Aerospace envelope with the *Giotto* cachet hologram and the Bristol cancel **March 14**, **1986**, has the Halley comet stamps: 'Dr Edmond Halley as Comet', 'Giotto Spacecraft approaching Comet', 'Maybe Twice in a Lifetime' and 'The Comet orbiting Sun and Planets' issued in **Great Britain** on **February 18**, **1986**. The *Halley's Comet* and the *Giotto Spacecraft* cachet holograms are shown in Fig. 2.5.

A *Statue of Liberty* hologram was attached to the exhibition catalogue for the US stamp exhibition, AMERIPEX'86, in Chicago, which took place between **May 22** and **June 1, 1986** (Fig. 2.6). A different version of the same hologram was used for a French – American postcard, jointly issued on **July 4, 1986**, for the 100-year- anniversary of the Statue of Liberty (Fig. 2.7).

Fig 2.6. The *Statue of Liberty* hologram and the AMERIPEX'86 cover.

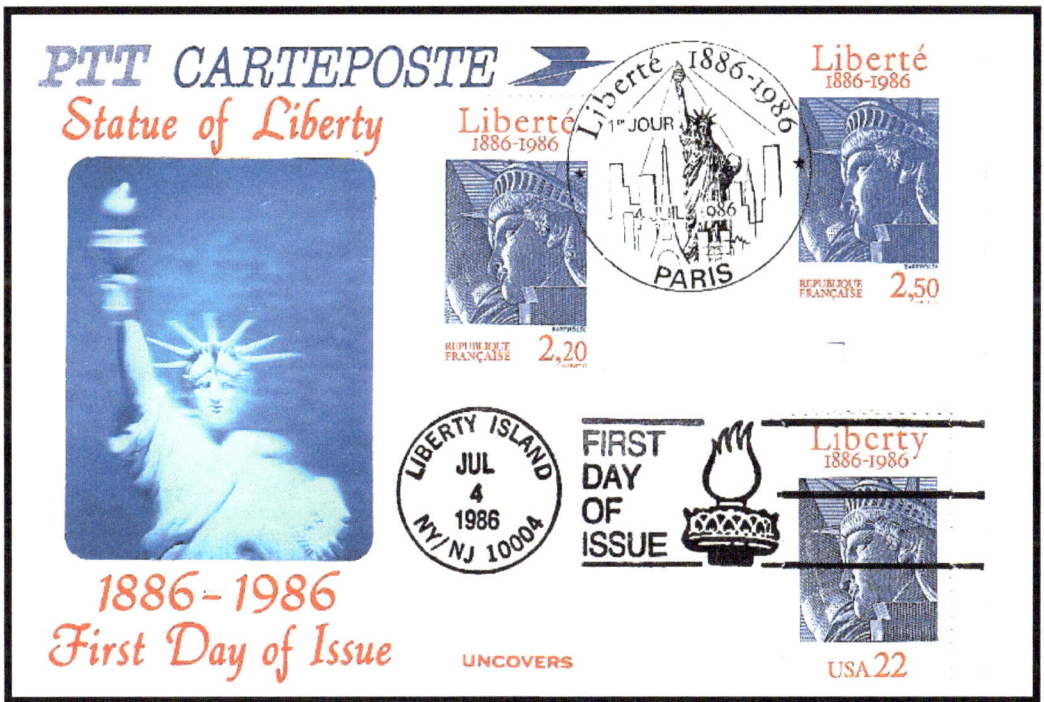

Fig. 2.7. Postcard with the *Statue of Liberty* hologram.

Fig. 2.8. The first 1987 Chinese presentation folder with the *rabbit* hologram, the hologram is on the cover (left) of the folded card, the New Year Message and the stamps (right).

In the **Peoples Republic of China** (**P. R. China**), starting in **1987**, China National Philatelic Corporation has issued every year until 1999, usually on **January 5**, a New Year Presentation Folder with an embossed hologram of the animal of the year. The first folder was issued in 1987 one containing a square 3D hologram of a *rabbit*. The hologram, produced by Qingdao Qimei Picture Co. Ltd, was attached to the cover page of the folder. There are four ordinary Chinese stamps attached to the right inside page of the folder. This card and the other issued Chinese New Year hologram cards are listed in **Table 1**. The 1987 card with its *rabbit* hologram is shown in Fig. 2.8. The folder was designed by Lu Tianjiao. In addition to this New Year card, a special postcard with a hologram was issued for the 'Topical Stamp Exhibition' held in Beijing between July 20 and 29, 1987.

CHAPTER 3
HOLOGRAMS ON POSTAGE STAMPS

This Chapter features holograms attached to postage stamps, souvenir sheets or to the margin area or selvage of stamps or sheets of stamps. Included here are also other philatelic items with holograms. Holographic stamps have been issued by different postal authorities around the world. Many *definitive* stamps have been issued. The most commonly issued holographic stamps are, however, *souvenir sheets*. All holograms on stamps and souvenir sheets are photographically reproduced. However, since the size of the illustrated stamps varies, they have not been reproduced using the same scale factor.

To reproduce holograms it is necessary to photograph them using the correct technique, for example, a camera with a macro-lens. In addition, the hologram has to be illuminated by a spotlight positioned at a certain angle and distance from the hologram stamp in order to obtain a sharp image. A scanner, which is normally used in reproducing conventional postage stamps, cannot be used for the correct reproduction of holographic stamps. In this Chapter photographs of holograms are presented, together with scanned copies of envelopes or other philatelic items in order to correctly illustrate the image in holograms on stamps and souvenir sheets.

More details about the items described, such as, size, identification numbers (Scott numbers), denomination, perforation and edition (if known) can be found in **Table 2**. In this Chapter each described stamp or souvenir sheet with a hologram is given a number which corresponds to the number found in Table 2. The table lists only the definitive stamps, miniature, souvenir sheets and some Cinderella issues, not including items such as FDCs with an attached cachet hologram, presentation folders or other items with holograms. In **Table 3** all the stamps issued in different countries are listed (countries in alphabetic order) with the same numbers as provided in Table 2.

The description of the holographic image is written in *italics*. Almost all of the embossed holograms on stamps are produced on foil and are hot-stamped in position. Some stamps are produced on self-adhesive foil. A large number of embossed holograms for postage stamps issued in different countries have been produced by three British companies: Applied Holographics plc (now OpSec), De La Rue Holographics Ltd and Light Impressions Europe Ltd. Holographic Systems München (HSM) GmbH (now Dausmann Holographics GmbH) and Leonhard Kurz GmbH in Germany are responsible for several other stamps. American Bank Note Holographics, Inc. (now OpSec) has produced several holograms for US stamps. In France, Hologram.Industries S.A. is also a producer of several hologram stamps. Many hologram producers responsible for the holograms used on postage stamps are listed in **Table 4**. In **Table 5** the security printers which have produced many of the postage stamps issued in different countries are found.

As regards holographic images, quite a few of them are space-related, including, for example, Earth, Moon, Jupiter, Sun (solar eclipse), satellites, space crafts, space station, gamma radiation, and cosmonaut images. Some hologram images are of the *two-channel* or *animated* type. In this category, butterflies and birds with moving wings can be mentioned. Some of the holographic 3D images are very beautiful, but to appreciate the quality of the image it must always be correctly illuminated. The Polish 1991 butterfly souvenir sheet hologram, the large 2007 Hong Kong 'A Symphony of Lights' souvenir sheet and the 1999 Malaysia Petronas Twin Towers are examples of such beautiful hologram images. A recent very nice hologram stamp is the 2012 stained glass window hologram on the *Presbyterian Cathedral* stamp issued in Brazil. A few images of the animated type are unique, but philatelists are often unaware of this feature and unable to correctly view these stamps. Here one can mention the Netherlands-Antilles 1998 solar eclipse animation stamp and the German 1999 Cosmos hologram stamp in which a comet collision with Jupiter is recorded. A more recent high-quality hologram stamp is the Jersey 2012 hologram achromatic 3D portrait of *Queen Elisabeth II*. This is the first time a holographic 3D portrait has been used on a postage stamp. Other hologram portraits on stamps have been of the 2D type.

3-1. Hologram stamps and souvenir sheets issued in 1988

The first time that a Post Authority in a country issued a *definitive* stamp with an embossed hologram was 1988. This happened in October that year in Austria, and this event marked the birth of a new topical subject within philately. Only one hologram stamp was issued in 1988. As already mentioned, China started to issue New Year stamp folders with a hologram on the cover in 1987. The second folder was issued in 1988. Hungary honored the inventor of holography, Dennis Gabor, by issuing a stamp (without a hologram) in a series of Hungarian Nobel Prize laureates.

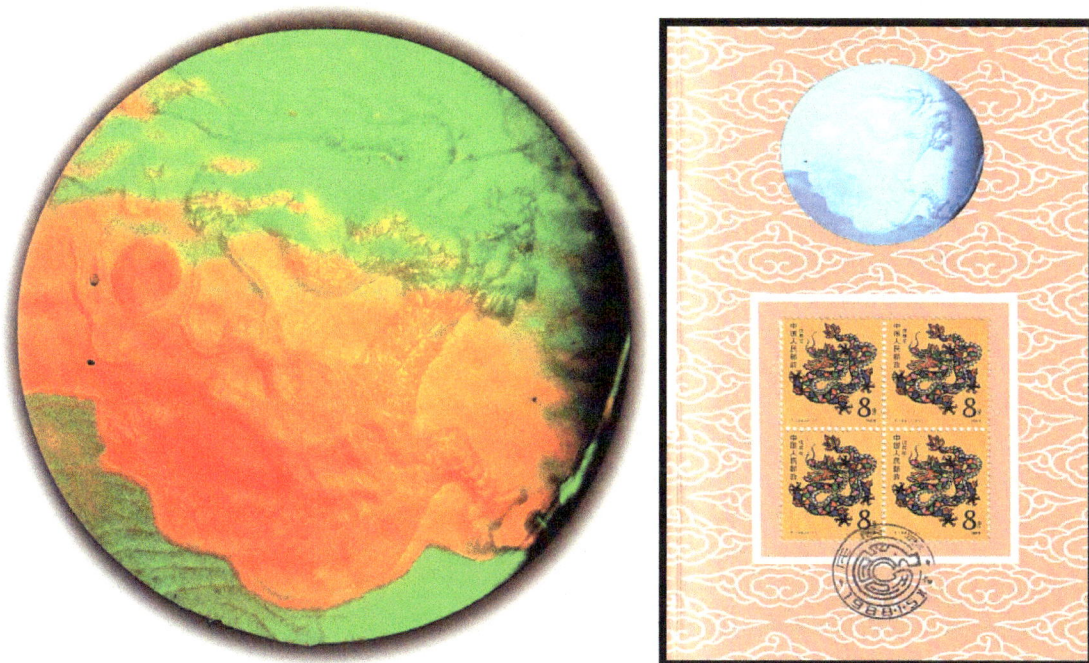

Fig. 3-1.1. The *dragon* hologram and the 1988 Chinese new year card.

The second New Year Presentation Folder in **P. R. China** was issued on **January 5, 1988**, by China National Philatelic Corporation. The folder has a circular 3D *dragon* hologram attached to the left inside page, produced by Qingdao Qimei Picture Co. Ltd. A folder with a square *dragon* hologram was also issued. Four ordinary Chinese stamps are attached to the same side as the hologram. More information about the folder is provided in **Table 1**. The front cover page has a colorful embossed relief picture of a dragon. The folder was designed by Zhou Nanhui and is shown in Fig. 3-1.1 next to a photo of the hologram.

At a stamp exhibition, EXPO'88, in **Australia**, a souvenir cover had a hologram version of the EXPO'88 stamp attached to the envelope, which was issued on **April 30, 1988**, the opening day of the exhibition shown in Fig. 3-1.2. The Stamp World-Expo was held in Brisbane and the theme of the expo was: 'Leisure in the age of technology'.

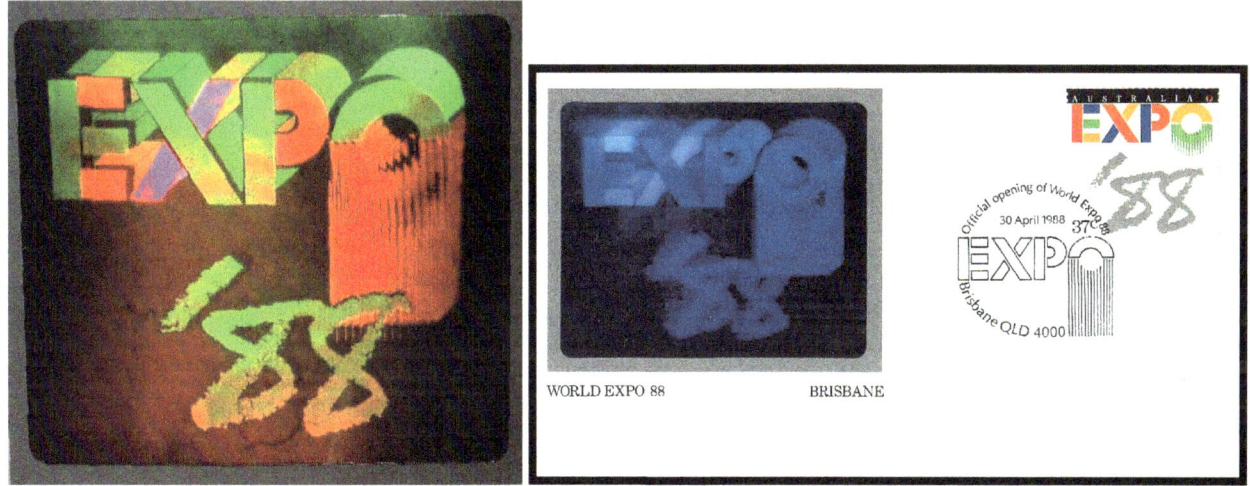

Fig. 3-1.2. *EXPO'88* hologram and the FDC envelope with the attached hologram.

Fig. 3-1.3. First definitive hologram stamp. **Fig. 3-1.4.** FDC with a cancelled eight-hologram stamp sheet.

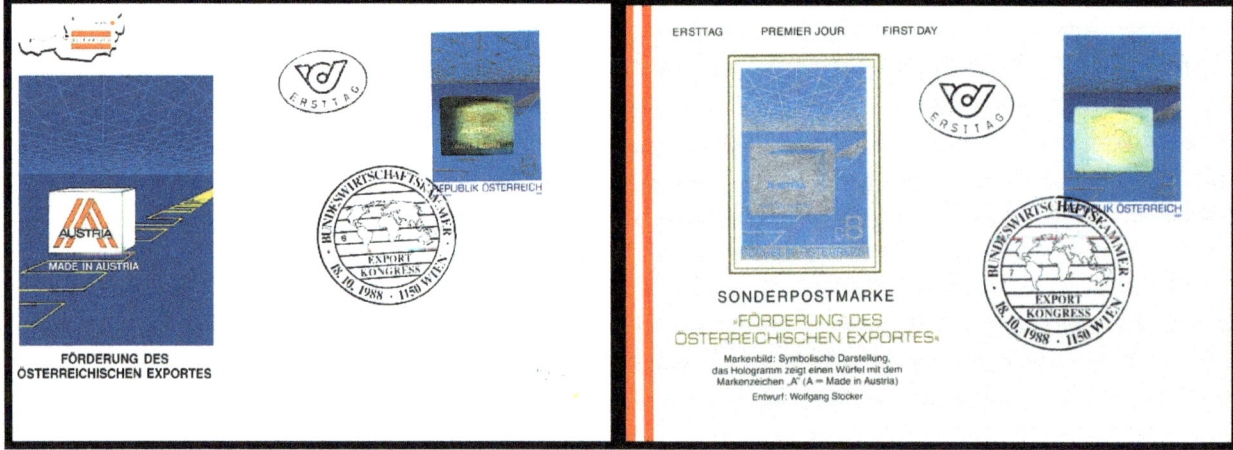

Fig. 3-1.5. FDC envelope with the hologram stamp. **Fig. 3-1.6.** Another FDC envelope hologram stamp.

On **October 18, 1988, Austria** issued the first *definitive* postage stamp with an embossed hologram (**No. 1**). The hologram features a 3D image of a *shipping crate* which floats behind a 2D graphic which combines a capital '*A*' and '*Made in Austria*' to highlight Austrian export (Fig. 3-1.3). It is an eight-schilling stamp issued in panes of eight stamps. In Fig. 3-1.4 a FDC with a canceled eight-stamp sheet is shown. An edition of 3.04 million stamps was issued. Two other different FDCs are shown in Fig. 3-1.5 and 3-1.6. The hologram stamp was issued at the '1988 Export Convention of the Chamber of Commerce'. The stamp was designed by Wolfgang Stocker. The design of the hologram for this stamp was made by 3D AG in Switzerland in cooperation with Günther Dausmann at Holtronics GmbH, Germany, where the master was recorded. Leonard Kurz GmbH, Germany, produced the embossed holograms. Austrian Bank Note Printing Company attached the holograms to the stamps as well as printed the stamps. The 380,000 eight-stamp sheets sold out in less than four hours. It is believed that not many of these hologram stamps were actually used on letters.

Fig. 3-1.7. Hungarian stamp honoring Dennis Gabor, the inventor of holography.

Hungary issued on **November 30, 1988**, a 6-Ft stamp (without hologram) honoring *Dennis Gabor**, the inventor of holography. The perforated and imperforated stamps depicted in Fig. 3-1.7, (Scott 3159) are from a series of Hungarian Nobel Prize winner stamps. Gabor received the 1971 Physics Nobel prize for his invention of holography, an imaging technique which he had invented and published already in 1948. Not until the early 1960s, when the laser had been invented, was it possible to demonstrate the potential of Gabor's remarkable 3D imaging technique. Hungary has been issuing many souvenir sheets with holograms over many years.

---

* Dennis Gabor was born in Budapest, Hungary, on June 5, 1900. In 1933 Gabor was invited to Britain to work at the British Thomson-Houston company in Rugby, Warwickshire. He became a British citizen in 1946, and it was while working at British Thomson-Houston that he invented holography in 1947. He died in London on February 2, 1979.

3-2. Hologram stamps and souvenir sheets issued in 1989

The two main events in 1989 were the issue of a souvenir sheet in Brazil and the issue of a large volume of US postal stationary with holograms. The US application is the largest production of holograms so far, requiring millions of embossed holograms. A few cachet holograms were used on FDCs, and the third Chinese New Year presentation folder with a hologram was issued in 1989.

Fig. 3-2.1. The *snake* hologram and the third Chinese card issued in 1989.

The third New Year Presentation Folder in **P. R. China** was issued on **January 5, 1989**, by China National Philatelic Corporation. The folder has a circular 3D *snake* hologram attached to the left inside page, produced by Qingdao Qimei Picture Co. Ltd. Four ordinary Chinese stamps are attached to the opposite side as the hologram. More information about the folder is provided in **Table 1**. The front cover page has a colorful embossed relief picture of a dragon. The folder was designed by Zhang Shiyong and is shown in Fig. 3-2.1 next to a photo of the hologram.

USA issued the first Priority Mail stamps on **July 20, 1989**. With this issue the United States Postal Service achieved two objectives: It promoted Priority Mail service, which promised two-day delivery between all major markets and three-day delivery elsewhere and it celebrated the 20th Anniversary of the Apollo 11 voyage to the Moon. The $2.40 Priority Mail Stamp depicts N. Armstrong and B. Aldrin on the Moon with the US flag. The stamp was designed by Chris Calle, Ridgefield, CT. The Uncovers FDC, shown in Fig. 3-2.2, has a cachet hologram of an *Astronaut on the Moon*. The hologram was produced by Light Impressions, Inc.

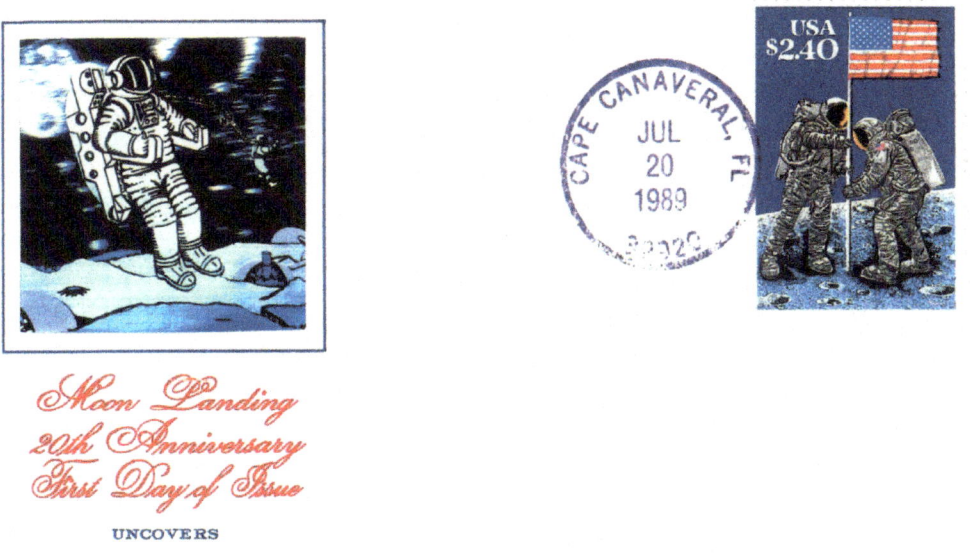

Fig. 3-2.2. The *Astronaut* cachet hologram on the Uncovers FDC.

Fig. 3-2.3. The *Barapasarus* hologram and the DINOSAURS FDC.

When the 'PREHISTORIC CREATURES - DINOSAURS STAMPS' were issued on **October 1, 1989**, in the **USA**, a *barapasaurus* cachet hologram was attached to one of the FDC envelops. A pre-historic dimension was added to stamp collecting when the Postal Service issued a block of four 25¢ dinosaur stamps. The stamps feature four of the more well-known dinosaurs: the tyrannosaurus, the pteranodon, the stegosaurus, and the brontosaurus. The cachet hologram and the FDC produced by Uncovers are shown in Fig. 3-2.3. The attached holograms on the FDCs were produced by Light Impressions, Inc. in 1984.

The three-stamp hologram sheet, shown in Fig. 3-2.4, is a souvenir sheet (**No. 2**) which was issued on **October 14, 1989**, in **Brazil**, at the 20th Biennial International Art Exhibition in São Paulo. [6] The upper part of the NCz$ 2.00 stamp depicts a painting 'Limoes' by Danilo di Prate. Upper part of the NCz$ 3.00 stamp shows a sculpture 'O Indio E A Suacuapara' by Victor Brecheret, and the upper part of the NCz$ 5.00 stamp, a photograph of Francisco Matarazzo, founder of the São Paulo Exhibition. The lower parts of these stamps contain the hologram which extends into parts of the margins. Several '*20*' are floating above the surface of the hologram intersected by the 2D holographic *Biennial logotype*. The hologram was produced by Fernando Catta-Preta and Marcelo Cunha, Holografica Producoes ltda in Brazil. The stamp was designed by Carlos Horcades and Brazilian State Mint printed the souvenir sheet. The FDC is shown in Fig. 3-2.5.

Fig. 3-2.4. Hologram across the lower part of the sheet. **Fig. 3-2.5**. FDC with the souvenir sheet.

Fig. 3-2.6. FUTURE MAIL TRANSPORTATION FDC with cache *space* hologram.

Fig. 3-2.7. FUTURE MAIL TRANSPORTATION *space* hologram.

USA issued a space-related 45¢-stamp souvenir sheet on **November 24, 1989**, during the 20th Universal Postal Congress in Washington D.C. which took place from November 13 through December 14, 1989. The FUTURISTIC MAIL DELIVERY SOUVENIR SHEET BLOCK of four FDC. The cover has a First Day of Issue hand cancel of Washington DC dated November 24, 1989, on the set of four imperforated stamps in a block of four. The stamps show these manned space vehicles: Futuristic winged spacecraft; air-suspended Hover Car; Moon Rover and the Space Shuttle. The souvenir sheet has a descriptive text to the left of the stamps. The special FUTURE MAIL TRANSPORTATION FDC has a large cachet *space* hologram, shown in Fig. 3-2.6 and the colorful cachet hologram in Fig. 3-2.7. Ken Hodges of Los Alamitos, California designed the Future Mail Transportation Block and the Souvenir Sheet. The attached hologram on the FDC was produced by Light Impressions, Inc. in 1984.

Fig. 3-2.8. *Space* hologram attached in the upper right corner of the US envelope.

USA issued on **December 3**, **1989,** during the 20th Universal Postal Congress in Washington D.C., a postal stationary item, a prepaid 25¢ envelope, (#9 size), with an embossed hologram (**No. 3**) [7, 8]. The 2D/3D hologram shows *the space shuttle preparing to dock at an orbiting space station*. The hologram foil (size: 2" by 2") was applied to the inside of the envelope through a die-cut window at the upper right hand corner (Fig. 3-2.8). Printed in blue on the envelope is 'USA 25' just to the left of the cutout. According to Gordon Morison, Assistant Postmaster General, who mentioned: "Customers have been telling us they would like to see more colorful and innovative philatelic designs. This hologram concept is a unique approach to satisfying that demand." Richard Sheaff, design coordinator of the Postal Service's Citizen Stamp Advisory Committee provided the overall design of the hologram. The artwork was done by Ken Hodges of Los Alamitos, California. The hologram was produced by American Bank Note Holographics, Inc. and the U.S. Envelope Division of Westvaco was responsible for the printing of the envelopes. The hologram was attached (not hot stamped) to the interior of the envelope so it is visible through the cutout. In addition there is tagging (visible under UV light) attached to the paper which is fluorescent. There are a few types (A – E) of envelopes used. On the back of the envelope under the flap is printed: ©USPS 1989. There exist two copyright notices; envelopes with wider and a lighter 1989 (first printing and the most common envelope); and envelopes with a narrow and darker 1989.

When new stamps are issued in the USA it is common that private companies produce FDC envelopes with different cachet designs. Sometimes the FDCs are issued in limited editions containing unique hand-made art work. Several different FDCs were issued, for example, the 'Hologram Space Envelope' by NASA artist Chris Calle, which is shown in Fig. 3-2.9. 'The first of its kind issued by the United States Postal Service' is printed under the text on the envelope. Four other special FDCs should be mentioned: - The 'WORLD STAMP EXPO'89' Hologram. The cover has a multicolor COLORANO silk printed cachet showing space crafts, each cover has this text: 'World Stamp Expo '89, First Day of Issue' and is reproduced in Fig. 3-2.10; - A very limited-edition hand-painted cachet showing an orbiting space station. The cachet is signed by Karoline Remmick and produced by KAROLINE'S CACHETS. Only 20 covers were produced. This FDC is shown in Fig. 3-2.11 and in Fig. 3-2.12; - The *1989 World Stamp Exhibition logo* as a holographic cachet; - The COLLINS 'Apollo-Soyes Docking' FDC is reproduced in Fig. 3-2.13. The FDCs mentioned here are only a few examples of many issued by different companies in the USA.

Fig. 3-2.9. The Hologram Space Envelope FDC with the US *space* hologram stamp.

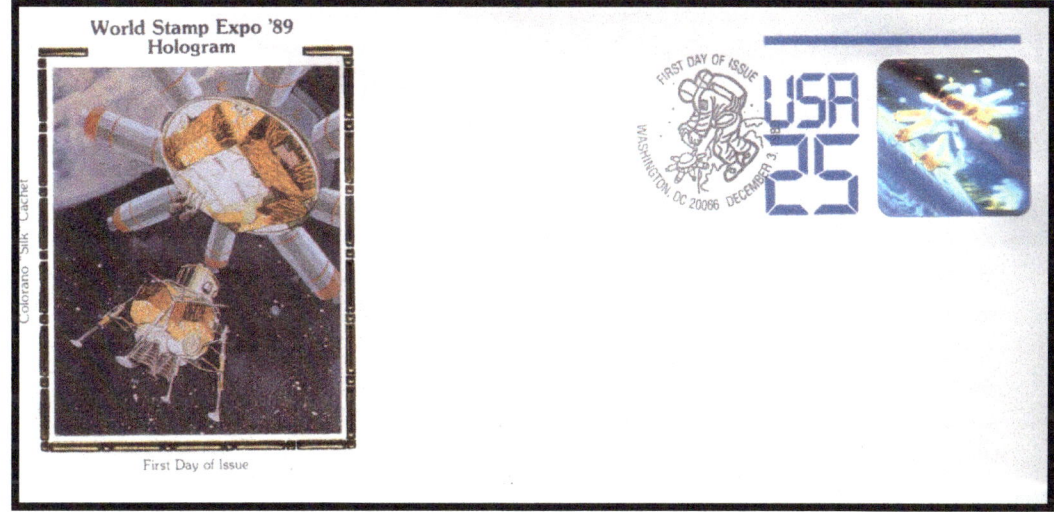

Fig. 3-2.10. The 1989 World Stamp Exposition Colorano Silk FDC envelope.

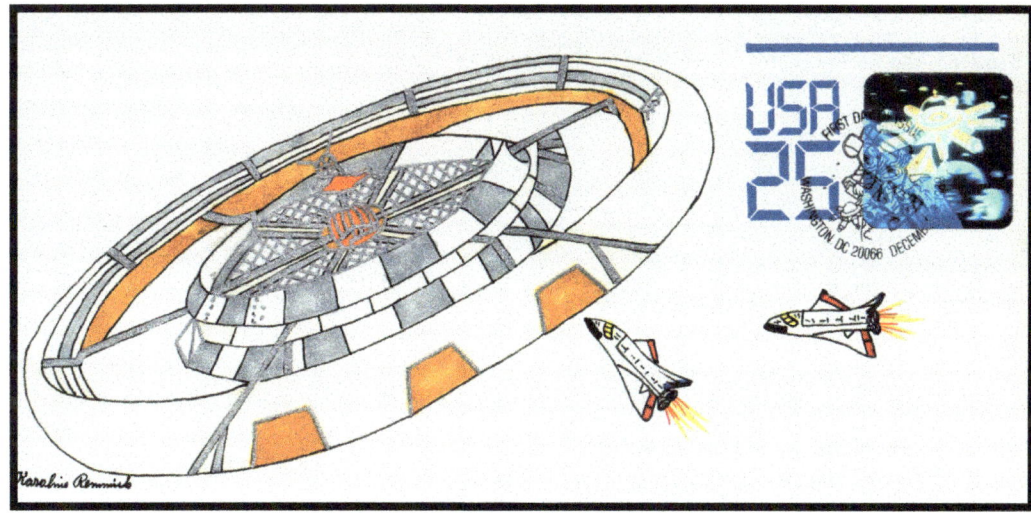

Fig. 3-2.11. The limited-edition (19/20) hand-painted Karoline's Cachets' FDC envelope.

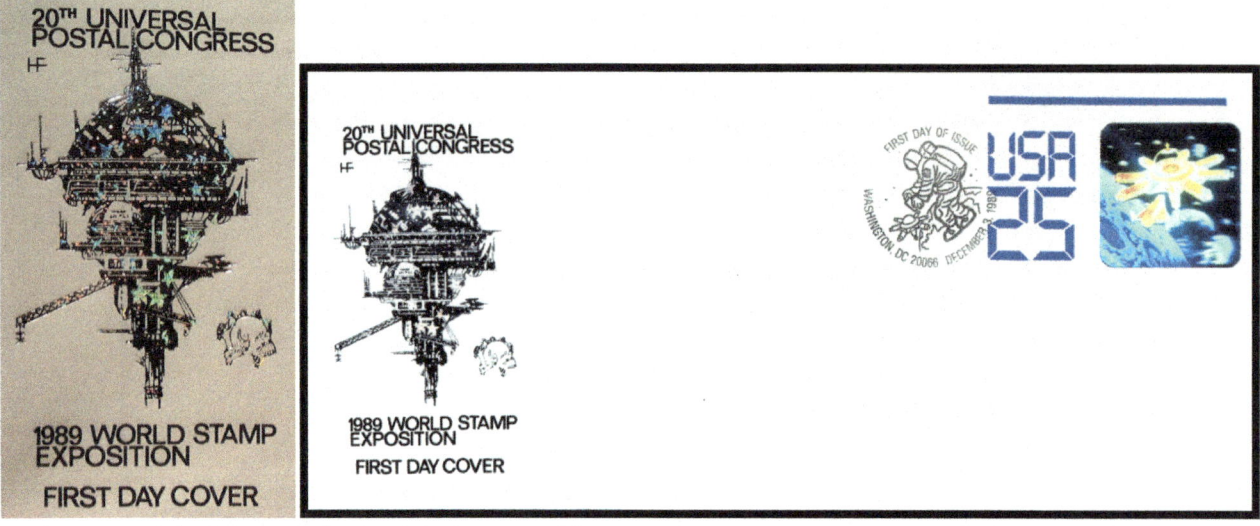

Fig. 3-2.12. The *holographic* logo and the '1989 World Stamp Exposition' FDC envelope with the US hologram stamp.

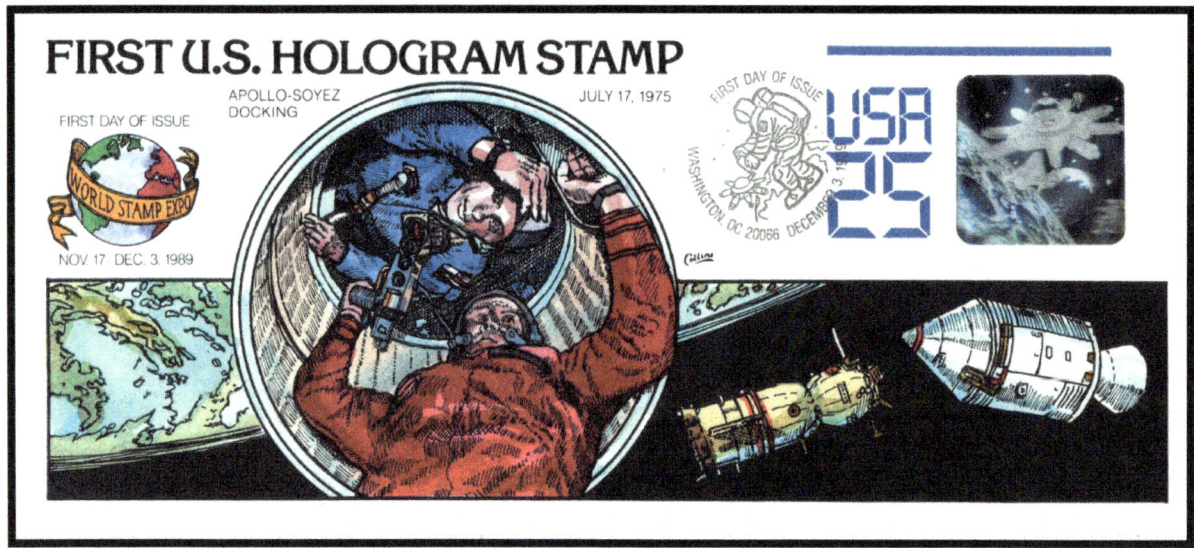

Fig. 3-2.13. The 'Appollo-Soyez Docking' FDC with the US *space* hologram stamp.

3-3. Hologram stamps and souvenir sheets issued in 1990

Two *definitive* hologram stamps were issued in Finland in 1990. In addition USA issued another postal stationary this year, which was the second US prepaid envelope with a hologram. This American-football-related issue required a large volume of embossed holograms, which were provided by American Bank Note Holographics, Inc. Another interesting holographic application appearing in 1990 was the FDC with a full-color 3D image of a circus clown in the form of a cachet hologram. The FDC, produced by Undercover Cachets, featured circus wagon stamps issued in the USA. China continued the traditional New Year stamp folder with a hologram.

Fig. 3-3.1. The *horse* hologram and the Chinese card issued in 1990.

The fourth time a New Year stamp presentation folder was issued on **January 5, 1990**, in **P. R. China**. The folder was as usual produced by China National Philatelic Corporation. The folder has a large rectangular 3D *horse* hologram attached to the left inside page, produced by Qingdao Qimei Picture Co. Ltd. Four ordinary Chinese stamps are attached to the opposite side as the hologram. More information about the folder is provided in **Table 1**. The folder was designed by Wang Huming and is shown in Fig. 3-3.1 next to a photo of the hologram.

Finland was the next country to issue definitive hologram stamps on **January 19, 1990**, Finnish Post issued two different stamps both having the same circular embossed hologram attached. [9] The stamps were issued for the privatization of the postal & telecommunication services in Finland. The stamps feature Päijänne lake, above which there is a circular hologram which shows the *Postal and Telecommunications emblem over the Earth*. The photographs were recorded by Matti Poutavaara. The Fmk 1.90 stamp is yellow/brown (**No. 4**) and the Fmk 2.50 stamp is blue (**No. 5**). The sheet is marked: 'The link to the laser area - Post-Tele.' Pirkko Vahtero designed the stamp and Applied Holographics Plc produced the holograms. Setec Oy in Finland attached the holograms and the Bank of Finland Security Printing House printed the four-color offset stamps, featured in Figs. 3-3.2 to 3-3.4.

Fig. 3-3.2. Finland's first two hologram stamps.

Fig. 3-3.3. Information folder.   **Fig. 3-3.4.** FDC envelope with the Finnish hologram stamps.

The Department of State in the **USA** issued on **March 17, 1990**, two passport envelopes; one was the 45¢ two-once rate and the other one was 65¢ three-once rate envelope. The two FDCs have the *American eagle* hologram produced by American Bank Note Holographics, Inc., which was first used on the cover of the 1984 National Geographic March issue in which the holographic imaging technique was presented by H. John Caulfield. The hologram is shown in Fig. 3-3.5 and the two envelopes in Fig. 3-3.6.

Fig. 3-3.5. The *American eagle* hologram.

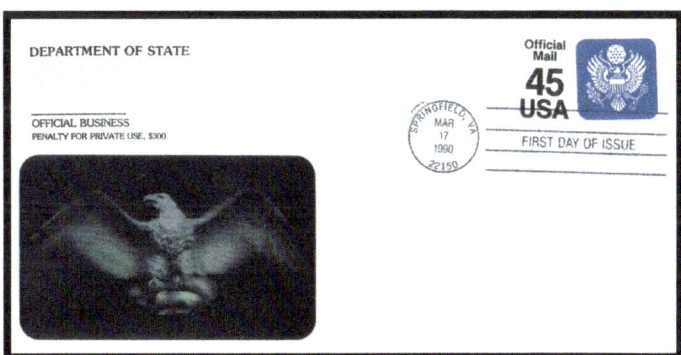

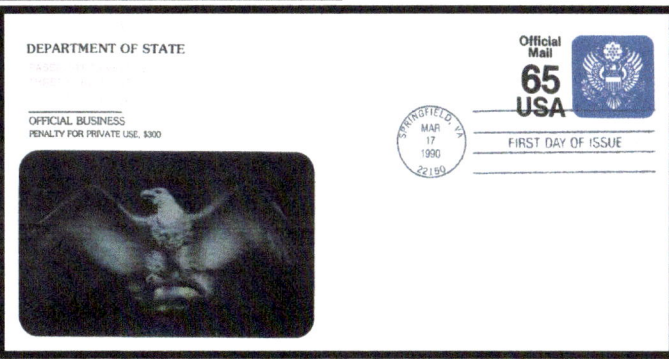

Fig. 3-3.6. The two US passport FDC envelopes with the *American eagle* hologram.

Fig. 3-3.7. The *Penny Black* hologram stamp and the Chinese 1990 World Stamp Exhibition envelope.

Several **Chinese** FDC envelopes have had holograms attached as cachet decorations. An interesting FDC, issued on **May 6, 1990**, is the one with a reproduced hologram version of the famous *Penny Black* stamp attached (Fig. 3-3.7). It was attached to the Sir Roland Hill commemorative envelope issued by the Beijing Stamp Co. for the 150th anniversary of the very first stamp in the World (The British Penny Black issued May 6, 1840). Sir Roland Hill is credited with originating the basic concepts of the modern postal service, including the invention of the postage stamp. On the envelope is a holographic *Penny Black* stamp together with the 8-yuan stamp of a horse issued on January 5, 1990. This cover marked B.J.F.-50, was released for the World Stamp Exhibition in London, May 3-13, 1990.

USA issued on **August 31, 1990**, the Circus Wagon 1900s stamps. On the FDC, by Undercover Cachets, is an embossed full-color 3D hologram of a *Circus Clown* produced by Ken Haines at American Bank Note Holographics, Inc. This hologram is interesting since it shows a full-color 3D image when illuminated at the correct angle and perpendicularly observed. Most rainbow holograms are not showing correct-color images. The cachet hologram and the FDC are shown in Fig. 3-3.8.

Fig. 3-3.8. Full-color cachet *Clown* hologram and the Circus Wagon stamp FDC.

Fig. 3-3.9. *Football* hologram attached in the upper right corner of the US envelope.

Fig. 3-3.10. Cache *football* hologram attached in the upper left corner on the 'Football Gridiron Glory' FDC envelope.

Fig. 3-3.11. NFL limited-edition (1/69) FDC hologram stamp envelope.

A second postal stationary item was issued in the **USA** on **September 9, 1990**, to which an embossed hologram was attached. [10] It was a prepaid 25¢ envelope, (#10 size), and was issued to celebrate the 25th anniversary of the Super Bowl (**No. 6**). The hologram features the NFL Lombardi Trophy and football players as a 2D image with spectators in the stands in the background (Fig. 3-3.9). Like the first US postal item, the hologram was applied to the inside of the envelope through a die cut window at the upper right hand corner. Printed in red on the envelope is 'USA 25' just to the left of the cutout. On the back of the envelope under the flap is printed: ©USPS 1990. Spectratek and Light Impressions Inc. in the USA produced the hologram. The designer was Bruce Harman and the envelope printed by Westvaco, the US Envelope Division. One issued FDC was the 'Football Gridiron Glory' FDC envelope with a cachet hologram attached, shown in Fig. 3-3.10. Even at this event several private companies produce FDC envelopes with different football-related cachet designs. For example one limited-edition (69) and hand-painted FDC was issued, which was signed by David Peterman, Custom Creations in Wisconsin. The (1/69) NFL-FDC is shown in Fig. 3-3.11. Several similar football FDCs were issued, using the new prepaid hologram stamp envelope.

Fig. 3-3.12. The *panda* hologram and the Chinese '1990 Beijing 11th Asian Games' FDC envelope.

A **Chinese** envelope, with a cache hologram, is the commemorative cover issued for the Inauguration of the 1990 Beijing 11th Asian Games which were held between September 22, 1990 and October 7, 1990. The stamps were released by the Ministry of Post and Telecommunications of the PRC. The cover marked PFN-37 was designed by Lu Dehui and was issued on **September 22**, **1990**, by China National Stamp Corporation. The *panda* cache hologram and envelope are shown in Fig. 3-3.12.

A joint **USA – USSR** issue was issued on **October 3, 1990**, with the following four 25¢/25k whale stamps: Killer Whale, Sea Lion, Sea Otter and Dolphin. In the middle of the FDC is a *dolphin* hologram. The FDC was by Uncovers Cachets. On **October 3**, **1990**, a joint 'USA-USSR MARINE MAMMALS' stamp issue was released. To the right side of the envelope there is one set of four US 25¢ stamps of a killer whale, sea lion, sea otter and a dolphin. The same four 25k USSR stamps are on the left side of the envelope. In between the stamps is a hologram of *dolphins* produced by Light Impressions, Inc. The hologram and the envelope produced by Uncovers Cachets are shown in Fig. 3-3.13. In addition to this FDC there were four separate FDCs issued one for each of the four USA-USSR stamp pairs.

Fig. 3-3.13. The *dolphin* hologram and the joint USA – USSR Marine Mammals FDC.

Fig. 3-3.14. Hologram on the cover of the card and the Freedom print.

Fig. 3-3.15. The inside of the folded card with two stamps.

Germany issued a folded souvenir card on **November 9, 1990**, containing two stamps (one of Brandenburg Gate and the other of the Berliner Wall with an opening in it). They were issued on the one-year anniversary of the opening of the border between East and West Germany. (The stamps were issued on November 6; the card was issued on November 9). On the cover of the card is a hologram of a *chip from the wall*. There is silver printing at the bottom of the card cover. The hologram on the cover of the folder is shown in Fig. 3-3.14 with the silver-printed text. The inside of the folder is depicted in Fig. 3-3.15.

3-4. Hologram stamps and holographic items issued in 1991

There were no *definitive* hologram stamps issued in 1991. Instead two important souvenir sheets were issued, one in Hungary and the other one in Poland. The Hungarian sheet was issued in several limited editions and the 1000-edition souvenir sheet is one of the more expensive hologram stamps ever issued. The Polish souvenir sheet has a very beautiful animated butterfly hologram attached. P. R. China continued issuing the traditional New Year stamp folder with a hologram. In addition, another Chinese folder with several hologram stamps was issued that year. Many FDCs with cachet holograms were issued in the USA.

Fig. 3-4.1. The *sheep* hologram and the Chinese card issued in 1991.

The fifth New Year presentation folder in **P. R. China** was issued on **January 5, 1991**, by China National Philatelic Corporation. The folder has a circular 2D/3D *sheep* hologram attached to the left inside page, produced by Qingdao Qimei Picture Co. Ltd. Four ordinary Chinese stamps are attached to the opposite side as the hologram. More information about the folder is provided in **Table 1**. The folder was designed by Lei Hanlin and is shown in Fig. 3-4.1 next to a photo of the hologram.

In addition to the traditional New Year Presentation Folder, **P. R. China** issued on **January 5, 1991**, a special folder to commemorate the first complete series of '*Animals of the Year Stamps.*' In this folder all twelve stamps are embossed hologram reproductions of all the animal stamps issued between January 1980 and January 1991. The twelve holographic stamps are in two sets of six, however, not postal valid. The card was designed by Lei Hanlin. Shenzhen University and the Institute of Reflective Materials in China produced the holograms. This folder is listed as card No. 6 in **Table 1** with the other Chinese New Year presentation folders. The twelve hologram stamps are shown in Fig. 3-4.2.

Fig. 3-4.2. The twelve hologram stamps in the *Animals of the Year Stamps* folder.

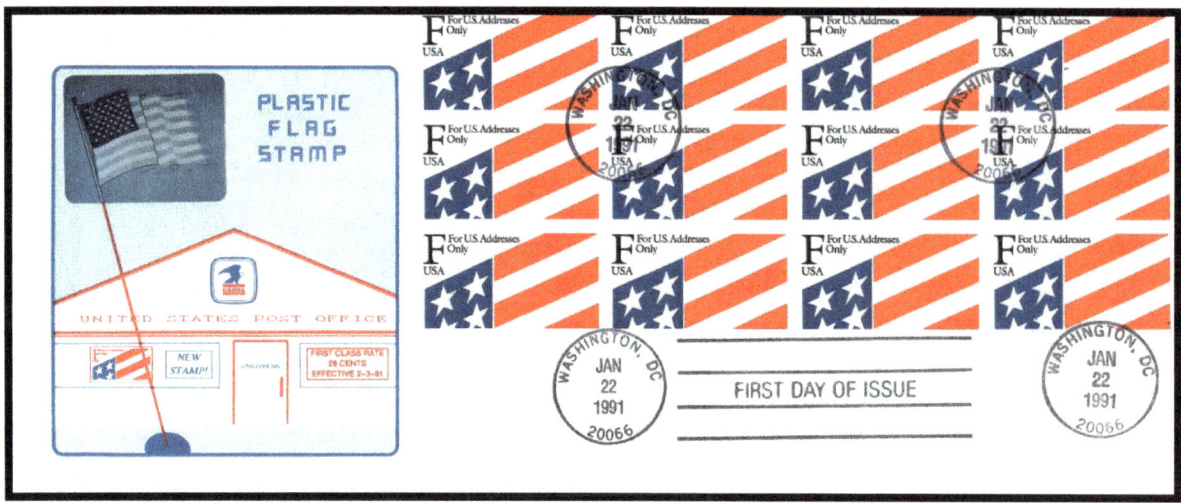

Fig. 3-4.3. The plastic stamp FDC with the *US flag* cachet hologram.

Fig. 3-4.4. The *US flag* hologram.

On May 18, 1990, in the USA, a six-month marketing test to sell stamps through Automated Teller Machines (ATMs). To meet the strict engineering requirements of ATMs, the stamps were made of a specially formulated polyester film. The panes of 12, which were the same size and shape as a dollar bill, were dispensed from the ATMs just like cash. In addition to offering customers the convenience of round-the-clock access to stamps, the ATM issues also offered the ease of peel-and-stick application with no licking or tearing. The first 25¢ denomination stamps were issued in 1990. On **January 22**, **1991**, a second version of this stamp was issued in the **USA**. This time it was marked '**F**' for domestic addresses only. Although the **F** stood for Flower on the regular non-denominated stamps, it was purely coincidental that it also stood for Flag on the experimental ATM stamps. Shown in Fig. 3-4.3 is the FDC with an attached *US flag* embossed cachet color hologram. When correctly illuminated it display a nice 3D image of the *American flag* as shown in Fig. 3-4.4. This hologram was also used on other US FDCs issued later in 1991. (See Fig. 3-4.9).

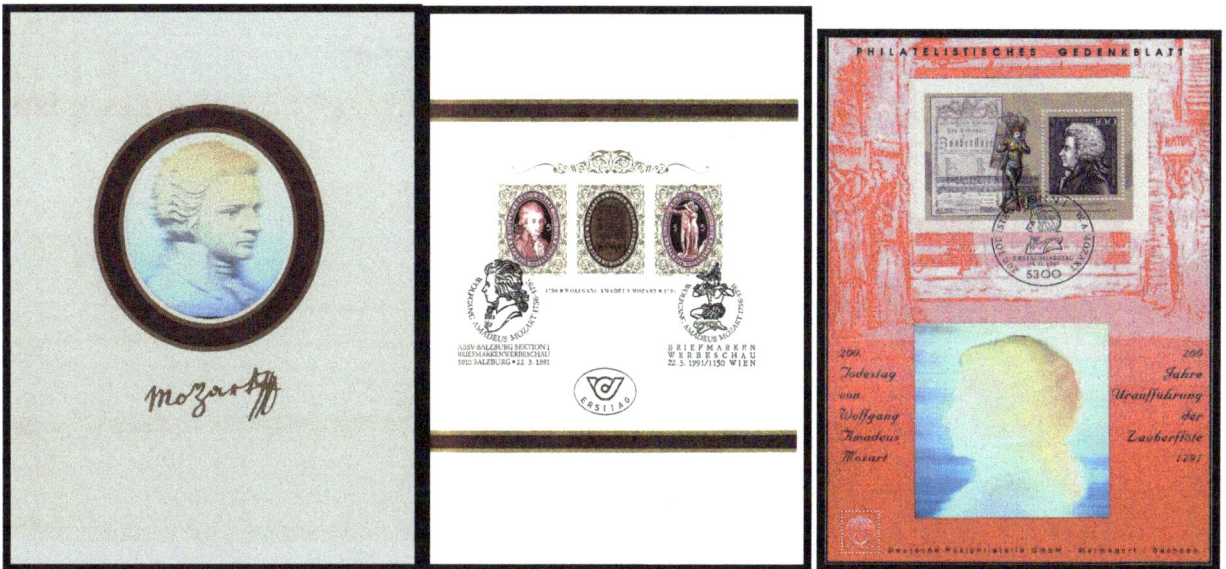

Fig. 3-4.5. Cover with *Mozart* hologram.   **Fig. 3-4.6**. Mozart stamps.   **Fig. 3-4.7**. *Mozart* hologram on German card.

Holograms of *Mozart* appeared on two different philatelic folders in 1991. One was issued in **Austria** on **March 22, 1991** (Fig. 3-4.5 and 3-4.6). A folder with a set of four ordinary 5-schilling stamps was issued 200 years after the death of Wolfgang Amadeus Mozart (1756 - 1791). The other folder was issued in **Germany** on **November 5, 1991**, to both commemorate his death and the premiere of 'The Magic Flute.' On this folder is, in addition to the hologram, a normal 100- pf stamp with a picture of Mozart (Fig. 3-4.7). The card was issued by Deutsche Postphilatelie GmbH in Wermsdorf/Sachsen.

USA issued a Cardinal stamp FDC with a Bill Norton cachet hologram of the *St Louis Baseball Cardinal Logo* on **June 22, 1991**, shown in Fig. 3-4.8. The hologram was produced by Upper Deck Co. and recorded by Lasersmith, Inc. in Chicago.

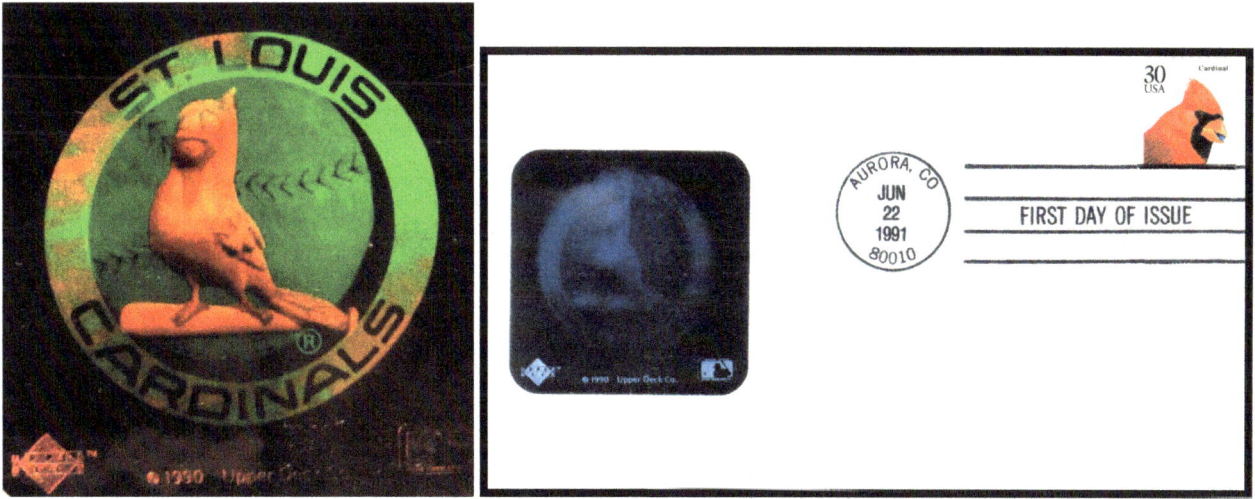

Fig. 3-4.8. The *St Louis Baseball Cardinal Logo* cachet hologram and the FDC with it attached.

Fig. 3-4.9. The *US flag* cachet hologram on the two 'Victory in the Gulf' FDC envelopes.

To celebrate the VICTORY IN THE GULF, **USA** issued on **July 2**, **1991**, a 29¢ 'Honoring Those Who Served' stamp. Two different FDC envelopes by Uncovers Cachets with the same *American flag* hologram as was shown in Fig. 3-4.4. The two FDCs are shown in Fig. 3-4.9.

On **August 28**, **1991**, **USA** issued a 29¢ basketball stamp which commemorates the 100th anniversary of one of the world's most popular sports. The other stamp on the FDC is a 4¢ stamp, issued in 1961, which commemorates James Naismith (1861-1939), the inventor of basketball. The cachet hologram of *two basketball players* was produced by Light Impressions, Inc. The FDC with the hologram is shown in Fig. 3-4.10.

Fig. 3-4.10. *Basketball players*' cachet hologram on the FDC.

Fig. 3-4.11. The *space ship* hologram.

Fig. 3-4.12. STAR TREK FDC with *space ship* hologram.   **Fig. 3-4.13.** UFO–Andromeda FDC with *space ship* hologram.

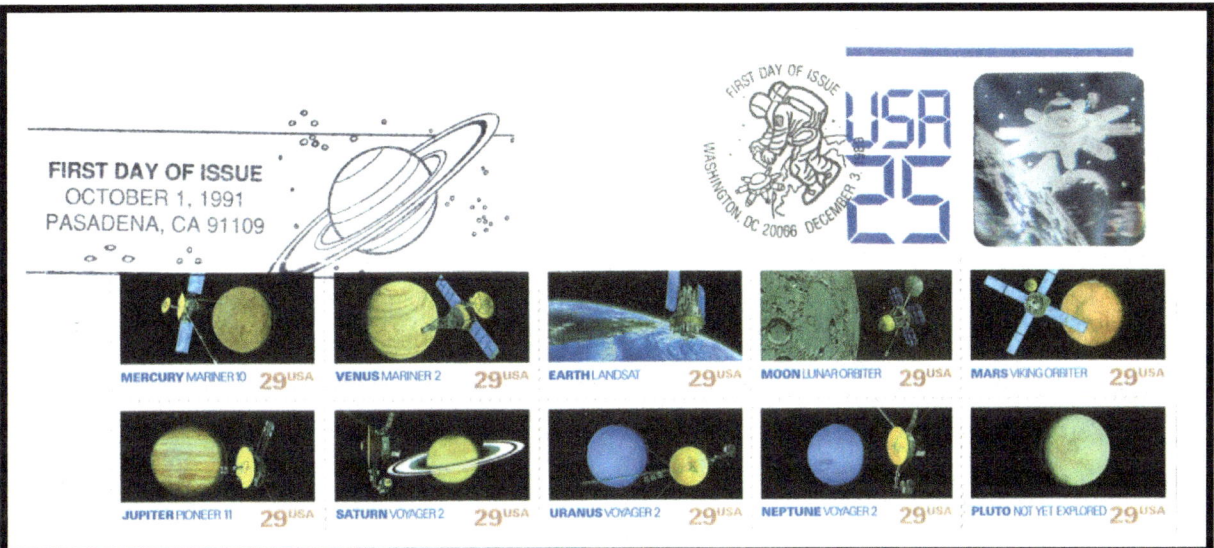

Fig. 3-4.14. The 10-stamp 'Space Exploration' FDC.

Another cachet hologram produced by Light Impressions, Inc. is a hologram of a *space ship* (Fig. 3-4.11) which was used on two FDCs issued in the **USA**; one is on the STAR TREK FDC, issued on **September 8, 1991**, with the US 45¢ 20th Universal Postal Congress Moon Rover stamp (Fig. 3-4.12). The other one is on the official First Day Cover by Spaced-Out Covers was co-sponsored by UFO Abductees, Inc. and Andromedia First Day Cover Society. It was issued on **October 1, 1991** and the stamp on it was the Neptune Voyager 2 US 25¢ stamp (Fig. 3-4.13). Also on **October 1, 1991**, when the ten 29¢ 'Space Exploration' stamps were issued in the **USA**, the FDC used was the 1989 envelope with the space hologram stamp (Fig 3-4.14). Each of the nine known planets in our solar system is represented, along with Earth's moon. The promotion of the stamps was tied to the annual October celebration of National Stamp Collecting Month, with the theme 'Journey to a New Frontier...Collect Stamps'.

Hungary issued a 20-Ft souvenir sheet with a hologram on **November 15, 1991**. The first Hungarian hologram stamp was based on a regular stamp: 'Coat-of-Arms of the Republic of Hungary' issued on August 17, 1990, shown in Fig. 3-4.15. The new hologram stamp is shown in Fig. 3-4.16 and the sheet in Fig. 3-4.17. 'Magyar Köztársaság Címere' features the new *Hungarian national 'small crown' coat-of-arms* (**No. 7**). The hologram stamp is surrounded by eighteen coat-of-arms of those used since the era of the Árpád-House and ending with the 1949 Hungarian People's Republic. Three editions exist: 1-7500, numbered in **black** on the back of the stamp, (Fig. 3-4.18, *left*) 1-3500, numbered in red, (Fig. 3-4.18, *right*) and 1-1000, numbered in red at the front bottom and marked at the top '**Magyar Posta ajándéka**' (Gift of the Hungarian Post), shown in Fig. 3-4.19. The hologram stamp was produced for and was included in *Collection of Hungarian*

Stamps'90, a book with all issued Hungarian stamps in 1990. More information about the album is provided in Chapter 5, Section 5-3. The sheets with the black numbers were inserted in the book. The hologram stamp was printed in a quantity of 200,300 perforated and 4000 imperforated. József Vertel designed the stamp, Tibor Balogh, Artplay Studio, recorded the hologram which was embossed by Kolbe Druck GmbH in Germany. State Printing House, Budapest, printed the stamps. Since this souvenir sheet was issued, Hungary has issued several stamps with holograms. One reason for producing several Hungarian hologram stamps may be that Dennis Gabor, the inventor of holography, was born in Hungary.

Fig. 3-4.15. 1990 Coat-of-Arms block. **Fig. 3-4.16.** *Crown* hologram stamp. **Fig. 3-4.17.** The 18 Coat-of-Arms with the *Crown* hologram in the middle.

Fig. 3-4.18. The reverse side of the two different Crown stamp editions. **Fig. 3-4.19.** Edition limited to 1000 stamps. *Left*: 7,500-edition, marked in **black**; *Right*: 3,500-edition, marked in **red**.

One very beautiful hologram souvenir sheet was issued in **Poland** for the international stamp exhibition 'PHILA NIPPON '91' in Japan. The souvenir sheet was issued on **November 16, 1991**. The two-channel hologram shown in Fig. 3-4.20, of a *butterfly 'Aporia Crataegi'* is attached to one stamp while an accompanying non-holographic stamp of the se-tenant pair (Fig. 3-4.21) shows the Phila Nippon'91 logotype (**No. 8**). The hologram is interesting with the butterfly's flapping wings and color shift when the stamp is tilted. Ovidiu Opresco designed the souvenir sheet and the hologram was produced by Light Impressions, Inc., USA, and printed by Speciality Printers of America. Poland's FDC of the First Holographic Issue is shown in Fig. 3-4.22 and the 'PHILA NIPPON '91'FDC in Fig. 3-4.23. Please note that on January 15, 1994, this block was withdrawn by the Polish Post by the administrative order #96, dated November 30, 1993. [11]

Fig. 3-4.20. The *butterfly* hologram on the souvenir sheet.   **Fig. 3-4.21.** The PHILA NIPPON'91 souvenir sheet.

Fig. 3-4.22. The FDC with the 'PHILA NIPPON'91' sheet.

Fig. 3-4.23. The special 'PHILA NIPPON '91' FDC.

3-5. Hologram stamps and souvenir sheets issued in 1992

In the USA the Postal Authority issued new postal stationary with holograms, which was brought about by a domestic rate increase from 25¢ to 29¢. The same 1989 space hologram was used on the envelopes. In addition, a few cachet holograms were used on FDCs issued in the USA. During 1992 Finland issued three definitive hologram stamps. This was the second time Finland issued hologram stamps. Another country to issue its first definitive stamps was Canada. China continued issuing the traditional New Year stamp folder with a hologram.

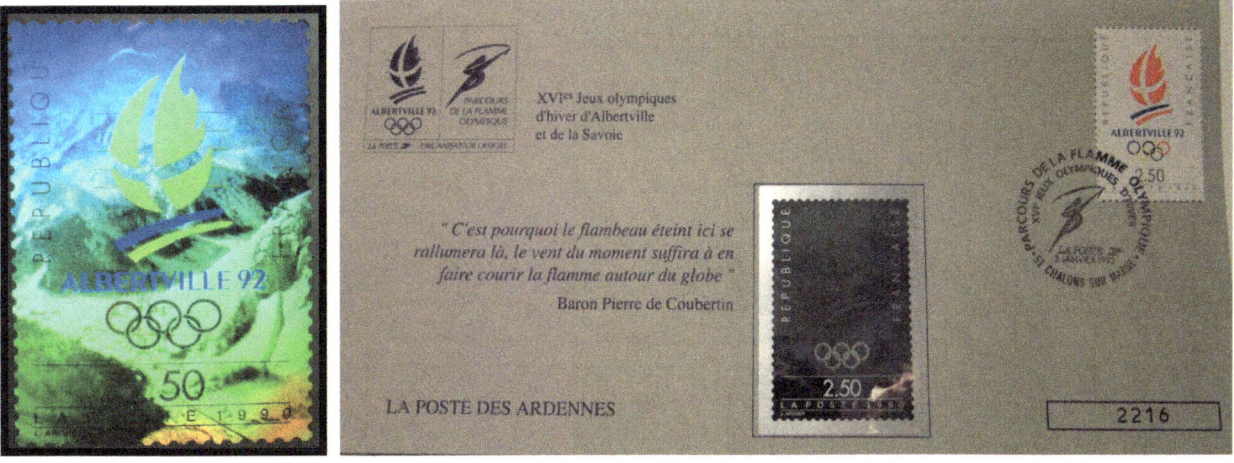

Fig. 3-5.1. Philatelists' Winter Olympic'92 hologram stamp and folder page with the stamp.

France issued on **January 3, 1992**, a special self-adhesive limited-edition philatelists' hologram stamp for the Albertville'92 Winter Olympic Games (Fig. 3-5.1). The hologram stamp was based on the Fr 2.50-stamp which was issued on February 8, 1990. The hologram stamp, designed by L. Arquer, was attached on the inside page of a Winter Olympics folder. The hologram stamp was produced by the French company Hologram Industries, S.A. The size of the stamp is 50 mm by 32 mm.

The New Year presentation folder in **P. R. China** was issued on **January 5, 1992**, by China National Philatelic Corporation. The folder has a circular 2D/3D *monkey* hologram attached to the left inside page, produced by Qingdao Qimei Picture Co. Ltd. Two sets of four ordinary Chinese stamps are attached to the opposite side as the hologram. More information about the folder is provided in **Table 1**. The hologram was designed by Liu Dun and the folder by Zhang Shiyong, both shown in Fig. 3-5.2.

Fig. 3-5.2. The *monkey* hologram and the Chinese card issued in 1992.

Fig. 3-5.3. The *skier* cachet hologram on the XVI Olympic Winter Games FDC.

On **January 11, 1992**, **USA** issued a 29¢ skiing stamp for the Albertville'92 XVI Olympic Winter Games. This stamp was designed by Lon Busch and printed by J.W. Fergusson Co. The other stamp on the FDC is the 15¢ Downhill Skiing stamp, issued on February 1, 1980, for the 1980 XIII Olympic Winter Games in Lake Placid, New York, USA. The cachet hologram of a *skier* was produced in 1987 by Light Impressions, Inc. The Uncovers' FDC with the hologram is shown in Fig. 3-5.3.

When the rate for a first class letter increased to 29¢, **USA** reissued on **January 21, 1992**, a new #10 envelope with the same *space shuttle* hologram [12,13] as was previously shown in Fig. 3-2.6 (**No. 9**). However, this time it was a #10 size envelope. Printed in green on the envelope is 'USA 29' just to the left of the cutout. Even for the 1992 envelopes on the back under the flap is printed: ©USPS 1989. Westvaco, US Envelope Division printed the envelopes. Reproduced in Fig. 3-5.4 is the same FDC cache Hologram Space Envelope by NASA artist Chris Calle which was re-used, now with 'USA 29' and "Magically producing three dimensions from one, creating a multi-hued image of the final frontier" printed under the red text on the envelope. Another FDC is shown in Fig. 3-5.5, which has a cache hologram attached. The 1984 Light Impressions, Inc. *space* hologram (Fig. 3-5.6) is on an envelope marked 'Universal Spaceship Cancellation Society, Bermuda Triangle, West Indies'. The back of this envelope has a yellow 'Intergalactic Mail' stamp with 'Universal Spaceship cancellation, Jan 21, 92', shown next to the envelope. The yellow stamp features an Earthling and the nomination is 3 zerks. The back of this beautiful hologram envelope is marked 'Space-Out Covers'92'. In Fig. 3-5.7 is a limited-edition hand-painted Cache FDC, 'Visions of Another Time' signed by the artist. Only 50 covers were produced by Wild Horse Cachets. Pugh Cachets issued also a limited-edition (125) signed FDC shown in Fig. 3-5.8. Another interesting postal item is the re-ordering envelope with the *space* hologram for obtaining the new 29¢ printed envelopes in quantities of 50 or 500, shown in Fig. 3-5.9. The FDCs mentioned here are only examples of many different issued.

Fig. 3-5.4. The 'Hologram Space Envelope' FDC with the re-issued US hologram stamp.

Fig. 3-5.5. The 'Official 3-D FDC' envelope with the printed 'Intergalactic Mail' stamp on the reverse side.

Fig. 3-5.6. *Space* hologram on the Official 3-D FDC.

Fig. 3-5.7. 'Visions of another time' FDC (31/50).

Fig. 3-5.8. 'Space Station Hologram Envelope' FDC (71/125).

Fig. 3-5.9. 29¢ re-ordering promotional envelope.

A series of baseball FDCs all with cachet holograms of the team logos were issued on **April 3, 1992**, in the **USA**. The US Postal Service saluted the game of baseball in its first year as an Olympic medal sport with a 29¢ commemorative stamp designed by Anthony DeLuz of Boston, MA. The Postal Service was a worldwide sponsor of the 1992 summer Olympic Games in Barcelona where the game was played as an official sport for the first time. It was also issued to commemorate the Braves in Atlanta, Georgia, the 1991 champions of baseball's National League. All the US National League Baseball Team Logos were featured as cachet holograms on the FDCs. The FDC with the *Chicago Cubs* logo is depicted in Fig. 3-5.10. The Upper Deck holograms were produced by Steven Smith at the Lasersmith Inc. in Chicago.

Fig. 3-5.10. The *Chicago Cubs* cachet hologram on the Baseball FDC.

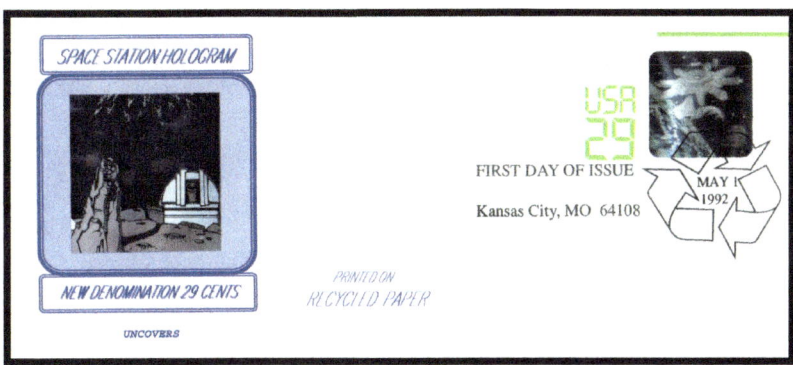

Fig. 3-5.11. The *Space* cachet hologram on the 29¢ hologram stamp FDC.

On **May 1, 1992**, Uncovers in the **USA** issued the 29¢ hologram stamp envelope with a *space* cachet hologram on the 'NEW DEMONOMINATION 29 CENTS' FDC shown in Fig. 3-5.11. The hologram was produced by Light Impressions, Inc.

On **May 8**, **1992**, **Finland** issued for the second time holographic definitive stamps. This time it was a set of three different stamps. The hologram design shows a *river* and *five trees* (*three coniferous, two deciduous*) with the background of the *Aurora Borealis*. The word '*High Tech*' is incorporated in *ASCII code*. The hologram attached to the Fmk 2.10-stamp (**No. 10**) honors Finnish patents 1842-1992 and depicts a blowing machine and fractal. The Fmk 2.90-stamp (**No. 11**) with triangles and microcircuits notes Finland's chair-country status of EUREKA, European Technology Cooperation. The third stamp, the Fmk 3.40 one (**No. 12**) celebrates the 50-year-anniversary of VTT, the Technical Research Center in Finland. Pirkko Vahtero designed the stamps and Applied Holographics Plc produced the holograms. Setec Oy in Finland attached the holograms to the stamps. The same hologram was used on all three stamps, which is shown in Fig. 3-5.12. The FDC is shown in Fig. 3-5.13 and the three stamps in Fig. 3-5.14.

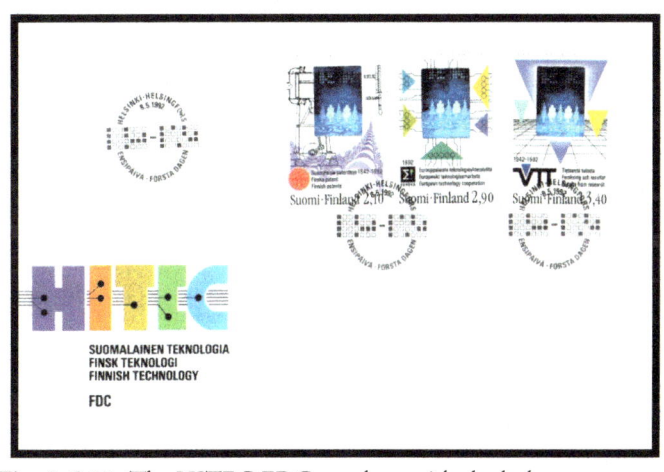

Fig. 3-5.12. The hologram.   Fig. 3-5.13. The HITEC FDC envelope with the hologram stamps.

Fig. 3-5.14. The three stamps from Finland issued on May 8, 1992.

On Columbus Day **May 22, 1992**, **USA** issued at 'STAMP EXPO'92' in Chicago, Illinois, a series of 'The Voyages of Columbus 1492 - 1992' stamps. The stamps are attached to eight different envelopes by Uncovers Cachets: two 'The Voyages of Columbus' envelopes with eight different stamps. The *Earth* hologram is reproduced in Fig. 3-5.15 and one of the envelopes is shown in Fig. 3-5.16. In addition there are six envelopes with different souvenir sheet stamps: 'Christopher Columbus', shown in Fig. 3-5.17, 'Seeking Royal Support', 'First Sighting of Land', 'Claiming a New Word', 'Reporting Discoveries', and 'Royal Favor Restored'. All envelopes have the *Earth* cachet hologram attached.

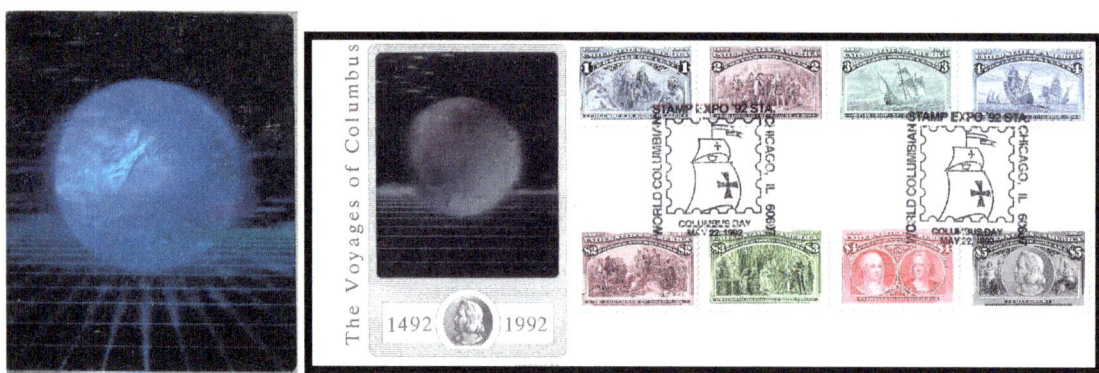

Fig. 3-5.15. *Earth* hologram.   **Fig. 3-5.16.** Columbus STAMP EXPO'92 FDC.

Fig. 3-5.17. The Christopher Columbus STAMP EXPO'92 FDC with the cachet *Earth* hologram.

Fig. 3-5.18. The 'Space Accomplishments' FDC with a cachet *Earth* hologram.

Another *Earth* cachet hologram was used on another FDC with the 'Space Accomplishments' 29¢ stamps issued in the **USA** on **May 29, 1992** (Fig. 3-5.18). These space se-tenant stamps were a joint issue with the Soviet Union and design collaboration between US and Soviet artists. The design represented a broad spectrum of space exploration. The stamps reflect the significant world space achievements of the last 25 years. Note the cancellation: Russia, Ohio.

On **July 31, 1992**, ESA Philatelic Club, Washington, D.C., **USA**, issued at Kennedy Space Center a special version of the first US prepaid 25¢ envelope with a hologram. The hologram shows *the space shuttle preparing to dock at an orbiting space station* (the 1989 one, Fig. 3-2.16). It was issued for the **EU**ropean **RE**trievable **CA**rrier, EURECA, and ESA, mission specialist Claude Nicollier and has a Kennedy Space Center Cancellation. The envelope is shown in Fig. 3-5.19.

Fig. 3-5.19. EURECA, Kennedy Space Center hologram envelope.

Fig. 3-5.20. The Dunhuang Frescoes FDCs with the cachet holograms.

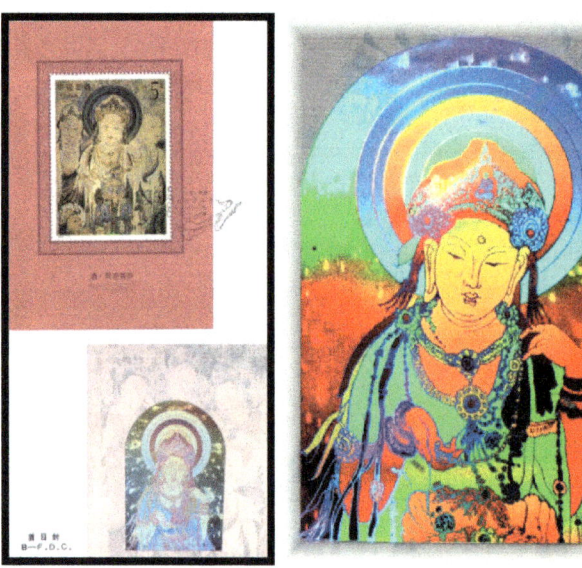

Fig. 3-5.21. The Dunhuang Frescoes souvenir sheet FDC with the cachet hologram.

On **September 15, 1992**, the Dunhuang Frescoes stamps (4th Series) were issued in **P. R. China** by the Ministry of Posts and Telecommunications. The Dunhuang Frescoes are from the Tang Dynasty (618-907) and are regarded the summit of Chinese Buddhist art. Four stamps from the Dunhuang Grottoes were issued, the 20-fen stamp - a Fresco of Bodhisattva, the 25-fen stamp – a Fresco of musical performance, the 55-fen stamp – a Fresco of a flight on back of a dragon, and the 80-fen stamp – a Fresco of appointment of the envoy for the western Regions. In addition to the stamps a 5-yuan souvenir sheet was issued. It depicts the Fresco of Avalokitesvara – Bodhisattva. The Bodhisattvas in painting of the Tang period are generally rich and grand in color. They wear sparkling jewelry, gold ornaments and embroidered dresses. The souvenir sheet depicts a detail from the illustration of the Buddha Amitabha preaching the law located on the southern wall of Cave 57 of Mogao Grottoes. The three FDCs have different 2D/3D cachet holograms attached. The souvenir sheet FDC has a beautiful cachet hologram of *Buddha Amitabha preaching the law*. The other two cachet holograms, used on the two-stamp FDCs, are the *Fresco of musical performance* and the *Fresco of a flight on back of a dragon,* holograms. The holograms were produced by Qingdao Qimei Picture Co. Ltd. The FDCs were designed by Zhang Yong and Wang Zhongfang. The two-stamp FDCs are shown in Fig. 3-5.20 with the cachet holograms next to them. The Souvenir sheet FDC is shown in Fig. 3-5.21 with the *Buddha Amitabha preaching the law* cachet hologram.

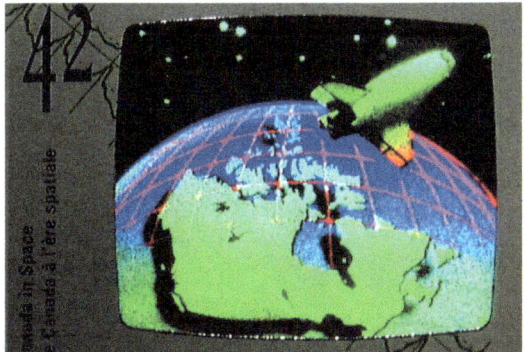

Fig. 3-3.22. The hologram on the Canadian stamp.

Fig. 3-5.23. The se-tenant stamp pair from Canada.

Fig. 3-5.24. Upper and lower viewpoint of the hologram.

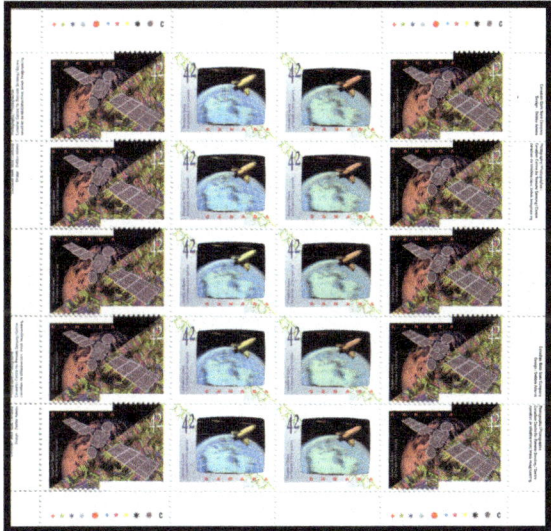

Fig. 3-5.25. The 20-stamp sheet from Canada.

The first holographic stamps issued in **Canada** appeared on **October 1, 1992**. The stamps commemorate Canada's first astronauts (Marc Garneau in 1984, Roberta Bondar and Steve MacLean, both in 1992) on a US space shuttle (**No. 13**). [14-17] The hologram (Fig. 3-5.22) of a *space shuttle above Canada* is attached to one stamp of a se-tenant pair (Fig. 3-5.23). Printed across the stamp is a human cardiogram. The printed se-tenant stamp features a communication satellite and photographs from space taken on board Anik E2. The embossed hologram is cut in somewhat of an old TV screen shape. In Fig. 3-5.24 two viewpoints of the hologram are illustrated. The stamps were designed by Debbie Adams and the tiny model was made under magnification of a microscope by George Sivy. Bridgestone Graphic Technologies Inc. in the USA recorded the holograms. The Canadian Bank Note Corporation printed the stamps. The 20-stamp sheet is shown in Fig. 3-5.25. Three small folders (Fig. 3-5.26) were produced describing the stamp hologram project and presented the three astronauts: *Folder 1*: Marc Garneau; *Folder 2*: Roberta Bondar; and *Folder 3*: Steve MacLeander. Each folder contains also tables about THE SPACE AGE, PLANETARY FACTS, and THE UNIVERSE, each folder both in English and French. On the cover of each folder is the same hologram as on the stamps, but slightly larger than the stamp holograms. The FDC is shown in Fig. 3-5.27. Variations of this particular hologram sheet and sheets with missing holograms have been reported as described in Chapter 6.

Fig. 3-5.26. Three space hologram information folders with the *space* hologram on the covers.

Fig. 3-5.27. The Canada FDC issued on October 1, 1992.

Four Christmas stamps, depicting antique Christmas toys, were issued on **October 22, 1992**, in the **USA**. The four toys, all on wheels, were a race horse with jockey, a locomotive with coal car, a horse-drawn fire pumper, and a steamship. The cachet hologram on the FDC, shown in Fig. 3-5.28, is a nice hologram of a *steam locomotive* produced by American Bank Note Holographics, Inc. The stamps were designed by Lou Nolan and the FDC was produced by Uncovers Cachets. The same cachet hologram was also on the FDC (Fig. 3-5.29) with the eighteen locomotive stamp booklet. The FDC was issued at the POSTAL ADMINISTRATION DAY, for the 'Postage Stamp Mega Event' by American Stamp Dealers Association in New York on **October 28**, **1992**.

Fig. 3-5.28. The Christmas 1992 FDC with the cachet *locomotive* hologram.

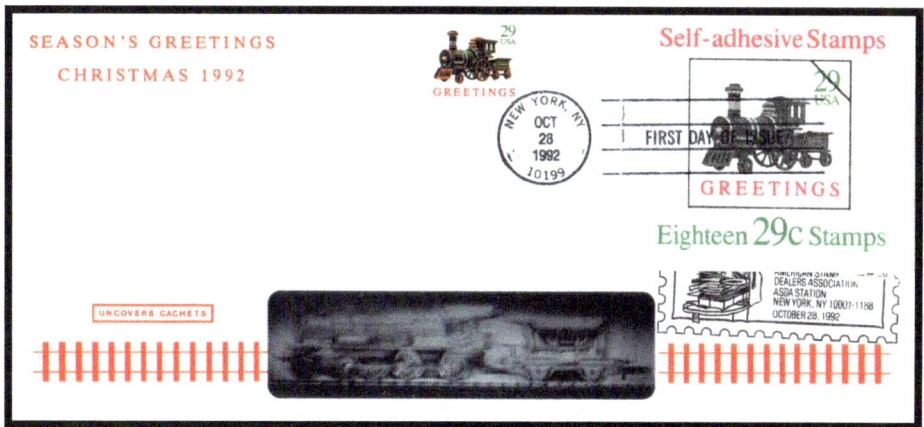

Fig. 3-5.29. The 'Postage Stamp Mega Event' FDC with the cachet *locomotive* hologram.

During stamp events or charity events in **Germany**, it is common that postcards and souvenir cards with holograms are issued. An example of such a postcard, issued on **December 15, 1992**, is the 'Zeppelinpost' card with a *dirigible* cachet hologram. A Ferdinand von Zeppelin (1838-1917) German stamp is attached to the card. On September 18, 1997, a new chapter in the history of airship aviation began with the maiden flight of the Zeppelin NT. It was not only traveling in airships that was brought back to life, but also the Zeppelin mail – much sought-after by collectors – was resumed, as the Zeppelin NT carried 'Kinderdorf Flugpost' on its first flight. Since then, the Zeppelin NT has carried airmail commemorating various social and political occasions. The income from the sale of the Zeppelin mail collectibles is used to support the Pestalozzi children's village in Wahlwies. The 'Kinderdorf Flugpost' has many customers e.g. the world leader in Zeppelin mail, the Hermann E. Sieger GmbH located in Lorch in Germany. The hologram on this card is the same which will be used on the Mongolian hologram stamp to be issued in 1993. (See Fig. 3-6.10). The hologram and the card are shown in Fig. 3-5.30.

Fig. 3-5.30. The 'Zeppelinpost' card with a *dirigible* cachet hologram.

3-6. Hologram stamps and souvenir sheets issued in 1993

During 1993 only a few hologram stamps were issued. Finland, the country interested in holographic stamps, issued four different prepaid postcards with hologram stamps. Souvenir sheets were issued in two countries, San Marino and Mongolia. China continued issuing the traditional New Year stamp folder with a hologram.

Fig. 3-6.1. The *roster* hologram and the Chinese card issued in 1993.

The traditional New Year stamp presentation folder in **P. R. China** was issued on **January 5, 1993**, and produced by China National Philatelic Corporation. The folder has a circular 2D/3D *roster* hologram attached to the left inside page, produced by Qingdao Qimei Picture Co. Ltd. Two sets of four ordinary Chinese stamps are attached to the opposite side as the hologram. More information about the folder is provided in **Table 1**. The hologram was designed by Wang Tao & Ke Chonglai and the folder by Zhang Shiyong & Liu Dun, both shown in Fig. 3-6.1.

A souvenir sheet was issued for the inauguration of the TV communication satellite in **San Marino**. These three-set stamps were issued on **March 26, 1993**, to commemorate the inauguration of state television. The first stamp in the set is an ordinary stamp and features the finishing line of the men's 100 m at the Tokyo 1991 Olympics on August 25. The second stamp offers a panorama of Monte Titano, San Marino City by night. The attached circular hologram (Fig. 3-6.2) features a *TV satellite* (**No. 14**). The third stamp shows Neil Armstrong saluting the USA Flag on the lunar surface on July 21, 1969. The photographs were provided by Fotocronache Olimpia, Milan. Franz Ramberti of Studio Expansion RSM designed the stamps and Pirkko Vahtero, Setec Oy, Finland was responsible for the design of the hologram. Applied Holographics Plc produced the embossed holograms and Setec Oy printed the stamps and attached the holograms. The souvenir sheet and the FDC are shown in Fig. 3-6.3 and Fig. 3-6.4. The souvenir sheets were issued by Azienda Autonoma di Stato Filatelica e Numismatica. The idea behind this set is that the greatest events of history are brought to us live by television.

Fig. 3-6.2. The San Marino *TV satellite* hologram.   **Fig. 3-6.3.** The three-stamp-set souvenir sheet.

Fig. 3-6.4. The souvenir sheet FDC.

On **May 5, 1993**, a special presentation folder was issued in **Germany** with a hologram on the cover. It was the 'EUREGIO Bodensee' folder with a 100-pf stamp which depicts the restored paddle steamer Hohentwiel and the flags of the three countries Austria, Germany and Switzerland. The Euregio Bodensee is the region crossing over multi-national borders and consisting of the combined border regions of these neighboring countries. The region of the Bodensee is described as 'one of the most relaxing nature regions in Europe'. The folder with the *EUREGIO Bodensee* cover hologram is shown in Fig. 3-6.5 with the issued stamp inside the folder.

Fig. 3-6.5. The EUREGIO Bodensee folder with the cover hologram and stamp.

Fig. 3-6.6. Hologram on the FINLANDIA postcards.

Fig. 3-6.7. Postcard No. 1 for NORDIA'93.

Once again **Finland** issued postal items with *holograms*, shown in Fig. 3-6.6, (**No. 15**), which happened on **May 6, 1993**. This time it was a set of four postcards issued at the Nordic stamp exhibition: NORDIA'93. *Card 1* is Mr. Lindberg's stamp collector membership card from 1918, (Fig. 3-6.7), *Card 2*, pictures owls in a forest, *Card 3*, shows water reflections and *Card 4* an aerial photo. The hologram stamp attached on these cards shows the *postal and telecommunications emblem appearing over the Earth*. The hologram is similar to the hologram used on the two 1990 Finnish stamps. The stamps were issued to advertise the stamp exhibition 'FINLANDIA'95' in Helsinki in May 1995. The Finnish artist Pirkko Vahtero designed the stamps, Applied Holographics Plc with Setec Oy in Finland were responsible for the hologram on the cards.

Guernsey Post Office issued on **July 27, 1993**, a commemorative FDC when the 'Thomas de la Rue stamps' were issued (Fig. 3-6.8). Thomas de la Rue, born 1793, was a pioneer in bank note and stamp production. John Stephenson designed the cover and Amblehurst/Thomas De La Rue Co. Ltd., England, produced the hologram. The five non-holographic stamps are on the envelope with a nice cachet hologram of *Thomas de la Rue*.

Fig. 3-6.8. Guernsey Thomas De La Rue FDC with hologram.

Fig. 3-6.9. The *Eagle* cachet hologram and the Eagle Scouts of America FDC.

On **August 4, 1993, USA** issued a 29¢ Eagle Scout stamp together with the FDC with a large cachet hologram. This was to honoring 'Eagle Scouts of America' and for the Boy Scouts of America National Jamboree at Fort A. P. Hill, VA, between August 4 and 10, 1993. On the FDC it is stated that Neil Armstrong was the first Eagle Scout to walk on the Moon. The famous American Bank Note Holographics' *Eagle* hologram is attached to the FDC which is reproduced in Fig. 3-6.9.

A souvenir sheet, 'Homage to Hugo Eckener' was issued in **Mongolia** on **August 27, 1993**, in connection with an international hot air balloon race. The *dirigible* 3D hologram in Fig. 3-6.10 is of a *dirigible* over Ulan Bator (**No. 16**). The stamps were issued in blocks of four stamps with a decorative selvage showing hot air balloons in the sky over the Mongolian countryside (Fig. 3-6.11). G. Radnaabazar designed the stamp.

Fig. 3-6.10. The *dirigible* hologram on the Mongolian stamp.

Fig. 3-6.11. Four-stamp souvenir sheet.

Fig. 3-6.12. Cachet hologram on FDC with Christmas stamps.

The Contemporary Christmas stamps FDC, issued in the **USA** on **October 28, 1993**, has a *Seasons Greetings* cachet hologram attached to the UNCOVERS envelope. This set of four self-adhesive stamps was issued for Christmas 1993 and features a jack-in-the-box, a reindeer, a snowman, and a toy soldier. Shown in Fig 3-6.12 is the American Bank Note Holographics' cachet hologram and the FDC with the holiday stamps.

3-7. Hologram stamps and souvenir sheets issued in 1994

Several hologram stamps were issued during 1994. Guyana, Isle of Man, New Zealand, Bhutan and Tonga issued their first hologram stamps that year. Elvis Presley was featured on the stamps from Guyana, whereas New Zealand, Bhutan and Tonga issued space-related hologram stamps. The Isle of Man's Queen Elizabeth II definitive hologram stamp is the first stamp where a portrait photo has been converted to a 2D hologram. Another Queen Elizabeth II hologram stamp appeared on one of the two prepaid postcards issued in Hong Kong. China continued issuing the traditional New Year stamp folder with a hologram.

Fig. 3-7.1. The *dog* hologram and the Chinese card issued in 1994.

The eighth New Year stamp presentation folder in **P. R. China** was issued on **January 5, 1994**, produced by China National Philatelic Corporation. The folder has a circular 2D/3D *dog* hologram attached to the left inside page, produced by Qingdao Qimei Picture Co. Ltd. Two sets of four ordinary Chinese stamps are attached to the opposite side as the hologram. More information about the folder is provided in **Table 1**. The hologram was designed by Liu Dun and the folder by Liu Dun & Zhang Shiyong, both shown in Fig. 3-7.1.

Guyana issued hologram stamps on **February 10, 1994**. These stamps were issued for Elvis Presley's 60-year-Birthday Anniversary. The stamp depicts an embossed photo of Elvis in the middle of the $300 stamp in front of a *colorful holographic foil background*. Two versions of the stamp exist, one with a silver foil jacket (Fig. 3-7.2) and one with a gold foil jacket (Fig. 3-7.3). **No. 17** is the perforated stamp and **No. 18** is the imperforated stamp. In addition to four-stamp sheets (Fig. 3.7.4), a postcard with his pink Cadillac, his Harley Davison motor-bike and a guitar in front of his Graceland home was issued, shown in Fig. 3-7.5. The postcard has the stamp in the upper left corner. The *Elvis* gold jacket stamp FDC is shown in Fig. 3-7.6. The four-stamp sheets are numbered as well as the postcards.

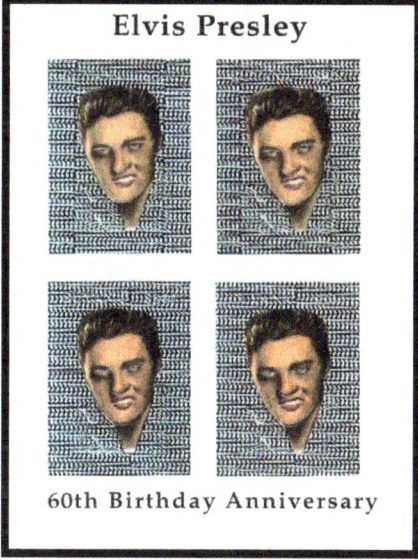

Fig. 3-7.2. *Elvis* hologram stamp.   **Fig. 3-7.3**. Gold jacket version.   **Fig. 3-7.4**. The four-stamp sheet.

Fig. 3-7.5. The card with the *Elvis* stamp.

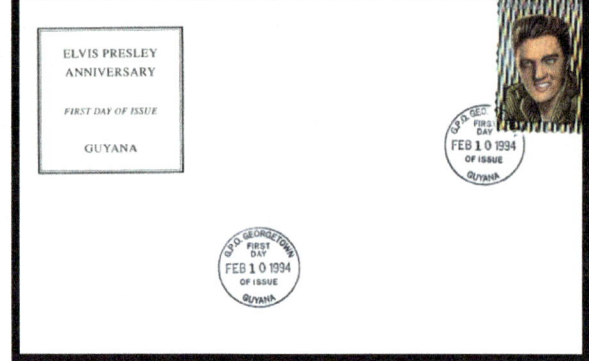

Fig. 3-7.6. The FDC with the *Elvis* gold-jacket stamp.

Hong Kong issued two postcards on **February 15, 1994**. These cards were issued to commemorate HONG KONG'94 Stamp Exhibition held between 18 and 21 February 1994. Holographic stamps are attached to the front page of the two postcards. *Postcard 1*, the first hologram (Fig. 3-7.7) is of the *1865 Queen Victoria* 96-cent definitive stamp (**No. 19**). The stamp is attached to a postcard shown in Fig. 3-7.8, which shows the Hong Kong waterfront circa 1920. *Postcard 2* has a hologram (Fig. 3-7.9) of *Queen Elizabeth II* $1 definitive stamp and is shown in Fig. 3-7.10 (**No. 20**). The stamp is attached to the postcard featuring the Hong Kong waterfront 1993. (YANG Catalogue #PP2-3.) These cards and stamps were designed by Arde Lam. Applied Holographics Plc produced the holograms.

Fig. 3-7.7. Postcard No.1 hologram.

Fig. 3-7.8. The 1994 Hong Kong postcard No. 1 with hologram.

Fig. 3-7.9. Postcard No. 2 hologram.

Fig. 3-7.10. The 1994 Hong Kong postcard No. 2 with hologram.

Fig. 3-7.11. The 1994 CeBIT folder with two holograms of *floating numbers*.

An exhibition of hologram stamps were arranged during the Hannover Messe CeBIT'94 in **Germany** which took place between March 16 and 23, 1994. Günter Tölcke's hologram stamp collection was on display containing the stamps issued up until 1993. To promote the exhibition 'Faszination der dritte Dimension Holographie' and the CeBIT event, a presentation folder was issued on **March 16, 1994**. It has two 'Die *neue* Post' Cinderella hologram stamps on the cover. The holograms display *numbers* floating both in front of and behind the hologram stamp surface. The folder with the holograms is shown in Fig. 3-7.11. People who attended the 'POSTDIENST' show got a card which they could use should they require more information. The card has also the same hologram on the cover and a normal stamp inside, which depicts the Niedersachsen Coat of Arms.

USA issued stamps on **May 26, 1994**, for 'World Cup Soccer 1994'. On an envelope by Uncovers Cachets, there is a hologram of *two football players* attached (Fig. 3-7.12).

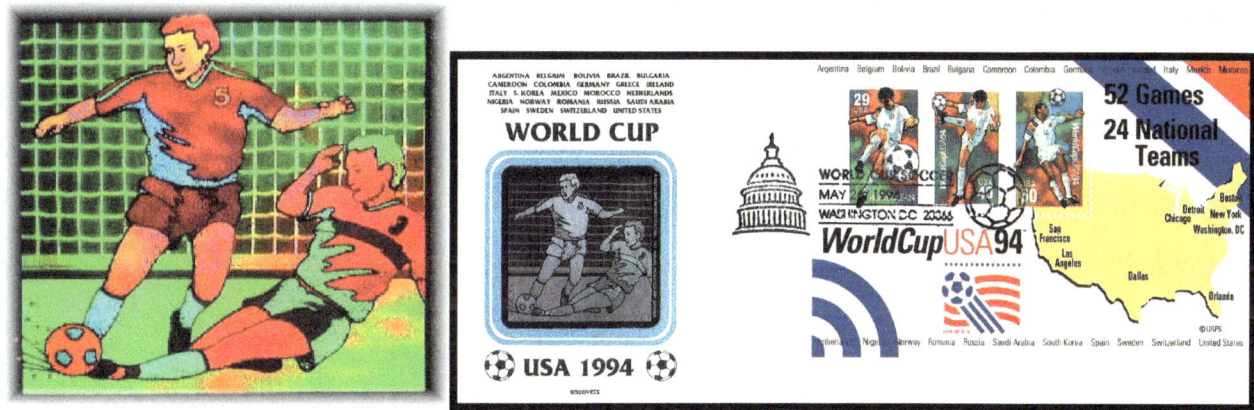

Fig. 3-7.12. The 1994 World Cup Soccer FDC envelope with cachet hologram.

Fig. 3-7.13. *Statue of Liberty* cachet hologram on the FDC.

Another Uncovers FDC envelope release was for the 'Statue of Liberty' self-adhesive 29¢ stamps issued in the **USA** on **June 24**, **1994**. In addition to being issued in sheetlets and strips, this stamp was also the first self-adhesive to be sold in full coils. The FDC is shown in Fig. 3-7.13 with a small version of the *Statue of Liberty* hologram.

Queen Elizabeth II appears on another hologram stamp shown in Fig. 3-7.14, this time on a definitive postage stamp from **Isle of Man,** which was issued on Tynwald Day **July 5**, **1994**. The hologram is produced from a photo of the Queen. The *Royal Cipher* and *Three Legs of Man* are in the background behind the Queen. This stamp was issued to celebrate Isle of Man Post Office's 21st Birthday (**No. 21**). A large cachet hologram of the Queen is on the FDC in addition to the cancelled postage stamp (Fig. 3-7.15). The same photo, provided by Alpha Photo Press Agency in London, was used for the cachet hologram. The stamp was designed by Colleen Corlett and Applied Holographics Plc produced the holograms. Walsall Security Printers Ltd in England printed the stamps. A limited-edition (500) Benham Ltd. FDC with a cachet Queen portrait was also issued, shown in Fig. 3-7.16. The sheet of ten £5 stamps marked with the plate number **1A** on the right selvage side is shown in Fig. 3-7.17. The sheets in Fig. 3-7.18 which are marked **1B** represented the majority of issued sheets.

Fig. 3-7.14. *Queen Elisabeth II* hologram.

Fig. 3-7.15. FDC with the *Queen Elisabeth II* cache hologram.

Fig. 3-7.16. A limited-edition (12/500) FDC by Benham Ltd.

Fig. 3-7.17. Sheet of ten stamps marked **1A** with a hologram of *Queen Elizabeth II*.

Fig. 3-7.18. Sheet of ten stamps marked **1B** with a hologram of *Queen Elizabeth II*.

Fig. 3-7.19. *Man on the Moon* hologram stamp. **Fig. 3-7.20.** Ten-stamp sheet.

Fig. 3-7.21. The New Zealand FDC with the hologram stamp.

New Zealand issued its first definitive hologram stamps on **July 20, 1994**. They were issued to commemorate the 25th anniversary of Man landing on the Moon (Fig. 3-7.19). The 2D/3D hologram shows *Neil Armstrong on the Moon and the Earth in the background where New Zealand is highlighted in yellow-red* (**No. 22**). The photograph for the hologram was provided by Woodmansterne Ltd in England. Brand New Ltd and Alan Hollows, Wellington, designed the stamps. New Zealand Post and Southern Colour Print, Dunedin, designed the hologram. Applied Holographics Plc in England produced the holograms and the stamps were printed by Southern Colour Print. The ten-stamp sheet is shown in Fig. 3-7.20 and the FDC in Fig. 3-7.21.

Fig. 3-7.22. Hologram of the *Vizsla dog* on the stamp. Fig. 3-7.23. Hungarian souvenir sheet.

On **August 8, 1994**, **Hungary** issued a Cinderella stamp for the International Stamp Exhibition 'PHILKOREA 1994' in Korea. The embossed hologram (Fig. 3-7.22) is of a *dog*, ('*Vizsla*', Hungarian breed), which is attached to a large stamp with a color print of a pagoda (Fig. 3-7.23). Black circles are printed around the hologram to simulate perforations (**No. 23**). The hologram stamps were issued in three limited editions: 45,000 on normal paper, numbered in black; 1,000 on thick paper, numbered in red; 200 on thick paper printed in black only and numbered in red. Pál Varga designed the stamps and Hologram Kft (Miklós Varga) was responsible for the project. Light Impression Europe Ltd produced the holograms. Hungarian Bank Note Company printed the stamps issued by Philatelia Hungarica Kft, Budapest,

Deutsche Bundespost in **Germany** issued on **September 8, 1994**, a philatelists limited-edition postage stamp in a folder with a cover on which a hologram of a *dinosaur* is attached to a HoloCard®. The stamp was issued as a limited edition (2000 cards) stamp for children (Figs. 3-7.24 through 3-7.26). Stamp size: 32 mm by 55 mm, hologram size: 70 mm by 70 mm. AHT Holografie Fachstudio in Germany was responsible for the hologram. The folder contains also a random-dot stereogram which is a free-view stereo image.

Fig. 3-7.24. *Dinosaur* hologram. Fig. 3-7.25. German Dinosaur HoloCard® (401/2000).

Fig. 3-7.26. The German Card 'FÜR UNS KINDER' stamp.

On **October 3**, **1994**, four stamps were issued in the **USA**. To encourage young people to join in the educational and entertaining hobby of stamp collecting, the Postal Service kicked off 'National Stamp Collecting Month' with four 'Wonders of the Sea' 29¢ stamps. Dubbed the 'fanta-sea' issue, this block of four stamps formed a single underwater scene. At the Postal Service's request, four underwater themes were shown: recreation, scientific research, exploration, and commercial fishing. The first day ceremony for the stamps took place off Hawaii's Waikiki Beach, 80 feet below the surface of the Pacific Ocean in a submarine. Held at a shipwrecked site, the ceremony marked the first time a US stamp was cancelled underwater. Each of the Uncovers FDCs has a cachet *underwater* hologram by Light Impressions, Inc., as shown in Fig. 3-7.27 through Fig. 3-7.30.

   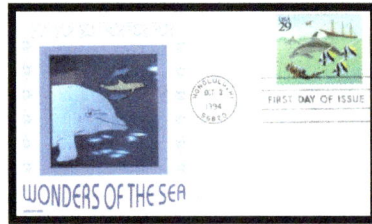

Fig. 3-7.27. Wonders of the Sea FDC No.1.   **Fig. 3-7.28.** Wonders of the Sea FDC No.2.

Fig. 3-7.29. Wonders of the Sea FDC No.3.   **Fig. 3-7.30.** Wonders of the Sea FDC No.4.

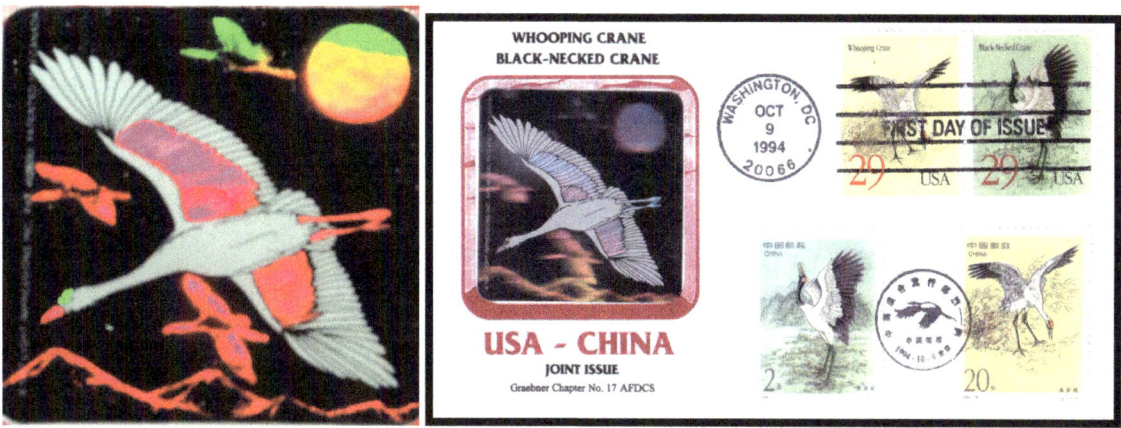

Fig. 3-7.31. The *crane* cachet hologram and the joint USA – China FDC.

On **October 9, 1994**, the 'Whooping Crane – Black-necked Crane' stamps were issued. It was a joint **USA – CHINA** issue with two 29¢ US stamps and two Chinese stamps, one is a 2-Yuan stamp and the other is a 20-Yuan stamp of the two cranes. Graebner Chapter No. 17 of the American First Day Cover Society was responsible for the FDC. The cachet hologram, by Light Impressions, Inc., and the USA – China FDC with the attached hologram are shown in Fig. 3-7.31.

Another country to issue space-related stamps in 1994 was **Bhutan**. The two-stamp souvenir sheets were issued on **November 11, 1994**, also issued for the 25th anniversary of man's first step on the Moon: 'Mankind's Milestones in Space'. One holographic stamp shows an *astronaut standing next to a rock on the Moon's surface* and the other stamp, *the space shuttle, the Earth and the Moon in a starry sky* (Fig. 3-7.32, **No. 24** and **25**). Light Impression Europe Ltd produced the holograms and Walsall Security Printers Ltd printed the stamps. A hand-made FDC is shown in Fig. 3-7.33.

Fig. 3-7.32. The hologram souvenir sheet.

Fig. 3-7.33. Hand-made 'Mankind's Milestones in Space' FDC.

Fig. 3-7.34. The *TONGASTAR-1 satellite* hologram stamp.

Fig. 3-7.35. The Tonga booklet with the hologram stamp.

Fig. 3-7.36. The 'SPECIMEN' hologram stamp.

On **December 14, 1994, Tonga** issued the first self-adhesive hologram stamp depicting the *TONGASTAR-1 satellite* launched in 1989. The T$2 stamp was issued at the 25th anniversary of the world's first full-scale production of self-adhesive stamps by the Postal Administration of the Kingdom of Tonga (**No. 26**). The booklet front cover depicts planet Earth photographed from the space. The hologram stamp (Fig. 3-7.34) is shown through a cut-out opening in the cover page of the T$10 booklet (Fig. 3-7.35). The booklet presents the history of self-adhesive postage stamps. The booklet contains a 60s scout stamp with similar design to the 25s and T$2 stamps in the Rotary and scouting set of 1980, which was the very last freeform self-adhesive commemorative issued. Another pane has nine stamps with similar design to the Queen Mother - Girl Guide stamps of 1985, all with denomination 45s. This was the last perforated self-adhesives to be issued. CPA Consultants Ltd designed the stamp, Light Impressions Europe Ltd produced the holograms and Walsall Security Printers Ltd printed the stamps. One version of the booklet exists with a hologram stamp on which 'SPECIMEN' is printed across the hologram surface (Fig. 3-7.36).

3-8. Hologram stamps and souvenir sheets issued in 1995

Finland issued again definitive hologram stamps, this time as a booklet with eight different hologram stamps. Australia issued two hologram-like definitive stamps with exelgrams attached. In the USA the Post Authority issued postal stationary with holograms for the third time. This new issue was occasioned this time by the domestic rate increase from 29¢ to 32¢. The same 1989 space hologram was used on the envelopes. China continued issuing the traditional New Year stamp folder with a hologram.

Fig. 3-8.1. The *pig* hologram and the Chinese card issued in 1995.

The New Year Presentation Folder in **P. R. China** was issued on **January 5**, **1995**, by China National Philatelic Corporation. The folder has a circular 2D/3D *pig* hologram attached to the left inside page, produced by Qingdao Qimei Picture Co. Ltd. Two sets of four ordinary Chinese stamps are attached to the opposite side as the hologram. More information about the folder is provided in **Table 1**. The hologram and folder are shown in Fig. 3-8.1.

For the fourth time, **Finland** issued definitive hologram stamps. It happened on **January 30, 1995**, when a little booklet (With Friendship) was released (**No. 27** to **35**). The holographic images are different cartoons of *dogs* (Fig. 3-8.2). The holograms have 2D images of many different characters from 'Dog Hill' children's books by Mauri Kunnas. The animals appear *in front of a set of concentric hearts*. The following eight holograms feature: *Dog writing a letter in bed, Receiving mail from postdog, Cat writing letter, Delivering mail to Moon, Spaceman, Winter scene at mailbox, On bus, Fan Mail and Dog Baby drawing*. The hologram is attached to the upper part of the stamp featuring the same characters sending or receiving mail. Applied Holographics Plc produced the holograms and Setec Oy attached them. Figure 3-8.3 shows the booklet with the tête-bêche stamps, Fig. 3-8.4 the front and back of the booklet, and Fig. 3-8.5 the FDC.

Fig. 3-8.2. Hologram on stamp.   **Fig. 3-8.3.** Booklet from Finland with eight stamps.

Fig. 3-8.4. Front and back of the booklet.

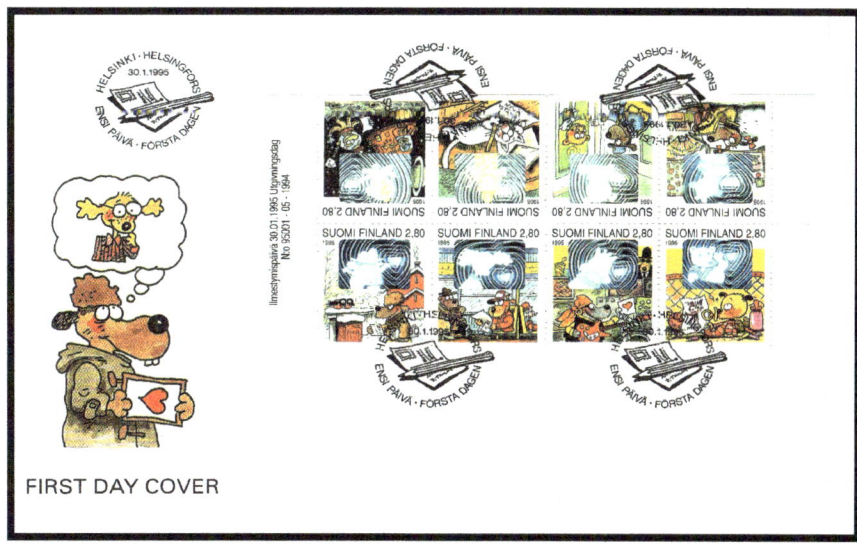

Fig. 3-8.5. Dog Hill children's booklet FDC envelope.

On **April 5**, **1995**, **Australia** issued two stamps with *exelgrams* to commemorate the importance of opals in Australia's mineral wealth. An exelgram is not exactly a hologram but similar and looks more or less the same as a hologram. It is produced by a coherent electron beam. The opal is represented by an oval exelgram in grey-scale overprinted in translucent ink. The AU$1.20 Opal Light (Fig. 3-8.6, **No. 36**) and the AU$2.50 Opal Black (Fig. 3-8.7, **No. 37**) stamps in the National Gemstones edition have different exelgrams. Sue Passmore designed the stamps and CSIRO in Australia recorded the masters using an electron beam. Leonhard Kurz GmbH in Germany produced the embossed exelgrams. Figure 3-8.8 shows the Opal FDC.

Fig. 3-8.6. *Opal Light* stamp.   **Fig. 3-8.7.** *Opal Dark* stamp.

Fig. 3-8.8. Opal FDC issued in Australia on April 5, 1995.

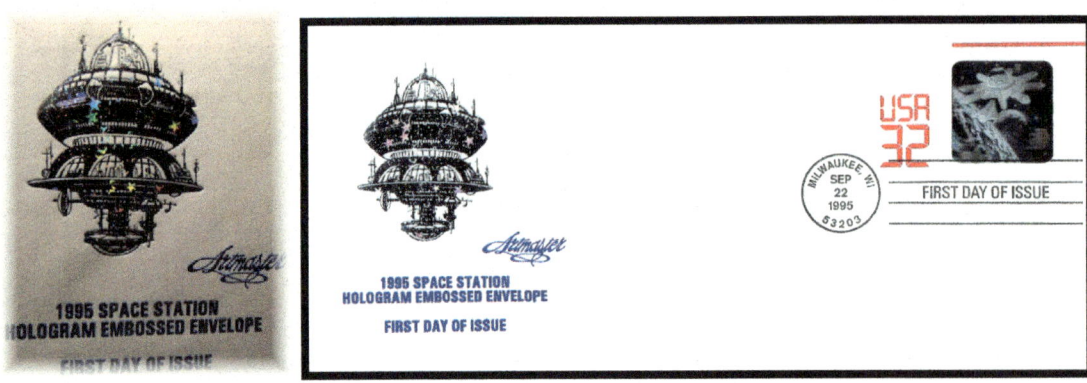

Fig. 3-8.9. FDC envelope with the first US stamp re-issued when the postage increased to 32¢.

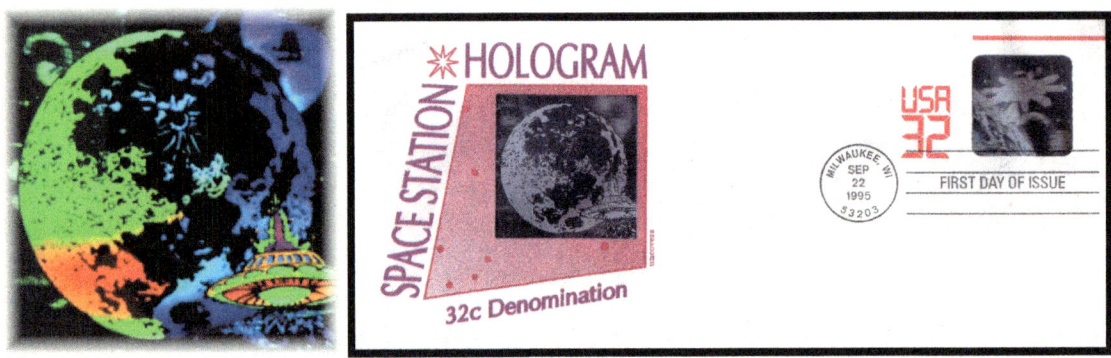

Fig. 3-8.10. The *space station* hologram and the FDC envelope with the cachet hologram.

Fig. 3-8.11. Hand-painted 'Space Station' RKA FDC (19/43). **Fig. 3-8.12.** Hand-painted 'Space Station' RKA FDC (42/85).

A new hologram envelope (#10 size) was issued on **September 22, 1995**, in the **USA**. This was caused by a rate increase to 32¢ for a first class letter. The same *space shuttle* hologram was used on the envelope as before in 1989 and 1992 (**No. 38**). Printed in red on the envelope is 'USA 32' just to the left of the cutout. Even for the 1995 envelopes on the back under the flap is printed: ©USPS 1989. This is the third time the same embossed hologram was used on postal stationary in the USA. The '1995 SPACE STATION HOLOGRAM EMBOSSED ENVELOPE' with the cachet logo FDC is reproduced in Fig. 3-8.9. Another *space station* cachet hologram on an Uncovers FDC is shown in Fig. 3-8.10. Two limited-edition hand-painted 'Space Station' RKA's Cachets FDCs are reproduced in Fig. 3-8.11 (edition of 43) and the Dynamite Cover in Fig. 3-8.12 (edition of 85). Ralph and Diane Achgill in Lafayette, IN, are producers of the RKA's Cachets.

Fig. 3-8.13. Cachet hologram on FDC with Christmas stamps.

In the **USA** Christmas stamps were issued on **September 30, 1995**. The FDC UNCOVERS envelope has the same *Seasons Greetings* cachet hologram as was used in 1993. This set of four self-adhesive stamps was issued for Christmas 1995 and features Santa Claus entering a chimney, a child holding a jumping jack, a child holding a tree, and Santa Claus working on a sled. The cachet hologram is an American Bank Note Holographics Inc. hologram used on the 1993 Christmas stamps FDC which was shown on Fig. 3-6.12. Once again the same cachet hologram was used in 1995 when the 'Midnight Angel' stamp was issued on **October 19, 1995**. The stamp designers were John Grossman and Laura Alders.

In **1995** three postcards were produced in **Hungary** of Budapest landmarks (Fig. 3-8.15). Each card has a hologram on the picture side. The postcards and the 2D/3D holograms depict the *Parliament Building*, the *Chain Bridge*, and the *Royal Palace (Buda Castle)*. BUDAPEST is printed in the sky behind the buildings in the holograms. The pictures on the cards are from 1910s Budapest. The holograms were produced by Varga Miklós and issued by Philatelia Hungarica Kft.

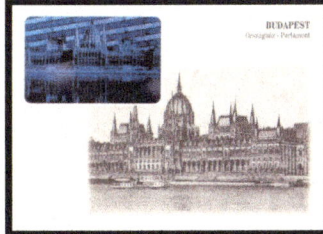 

Fig. 3-8.15. The three Budapest postcards with the holograms.

3-9. Holographic stamps and souvenir sheets issued in 1996

A variety of philatelic items were issued during 1996. In addition to several souvenir sheets issued in Malaysia, Hungary and China, the first definitive hologram stamps were issued in Thailand. Australia also issued definitive stamps, this time with another type of diffractive foil, so called foiltex stamps. For the second time Hong Kong issued a set of six prepaid postcards with beautiful hologram stamps. China continued issuing the traditional New Year stamp folder with a hologram. In addition, many souvenir sheets were issued in China during 1996.

Fig. 3-9.1. The *rat* hologram and the Chinese card issued in 1996.

The New Year Presentation Folder in **P. R. China** was issued on **January 5, 1996**, by China National Philatelic Corporation. The folder has a circular 2D/3D hologram of *two rats* attached to the left inside page. The hologram was produced by Qingdao Qimei Picture Co. Ltd. Two sets of four ordinary Chinese stamps are attached to the opposite side of the hologram. More information about the folder is provided in **Table 1**. The hologram was designed by Liu Dun and the folder by Shen Peinong & Zhang Shiqi, both shown in Fig. 3-9.1.

Another country to issue its first holographic stamp was **Malaysia** which issued on **January 13, 1996**, a souvenir sheet. The holographic image depicts *the East Asia Satellite MEASAT-1*, (Pelancaran Satelit Pertama) from Malaysia *over the Earth covered with isobars and where Malaysia is highlighted* (Fig. 3-9.2, **No. 39**). The stamps were issued to celebrate the launch of the new satellite onto geosynchronous orbit (91.5 degrees East) 36000 km above the equator. The stamp is included in a set of four stamps. The souvenir sheet with the hologram was issued in a limited edition, individually numbered (Fig. 3-9.3). The holograms were produced by Applied Holographics Plc and Southern Colour Print in New Zealand printed the stamps which were designed by Nerve Center Associates. The FDC is shown in Fig. 3-9.4.

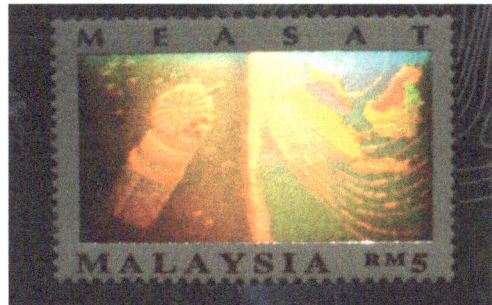

Fig. 3-9.2. The *MEASAT* hologram stamp.

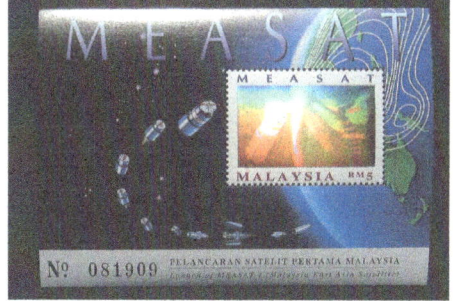

Fig. 3-9.3. Hologram souvenir sheet.

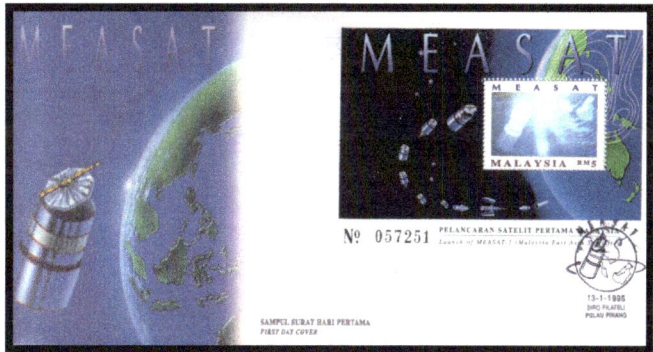

Fig. 3-9.4. The FDC with the hologram souvenir sheet.

Fig. 3-9.5. Two-channel hologram with the *rat* in the two positions.   **Fig. 3-9.6.** IX Asiatic Exhibition sheet.

Fig. 3-9.7. The back of the 6,000 edition sheet.

Fig. 3-9.8. Imperforated edition.   **Fig. 3-9.9.** Black edition.

In 1996, **Hungary** issued two very similar souvenir sheets for two International Stamp Exhibitions: 'IX and X Asiatic Exhibitions'. The first one (**No. 40**) took place in China (red lettering) and was issued on **April 25**, **1996**. The embossed two-channel hologram in Fig. 3-9.5 is of a *rat* (Chinese year of the Rat) which jumps up and down when the stamp is tilted horizontally. The hologram is attached to a large souvenir sheet with a color print of a dragon. Next to the hologram stamp is a regular 60-Ft stamp of a panda. The souvenir sheets were issued in four limited editions: 45,000 on gummed paper, perforated, with red numbers (Fig. 3-9.6); 6,000 on thick paper, perforated, with red numbers and printed: '**A PHILATELIA HUNGARICA AJÁNDÉKA**' [Gift of Philatelia Hungarica Kft] on the back. The text on the back of this sheet is shown in Fig. 3-9.7; 1,000 on thick paper, without perforation, without numbers (Fig. 3-9.8); 200 on thick paper, printed in **black** and without perforation but with red numbers (Fig. 3-9.9). This stamp (the 6000 edition) was included in *Collection of Hungarian Stamps'97*, a book with all issued Hungarian stamps in 1997. Pál Varga designed the souvenir sheets for the two exhibitions with Hologram Kft responsible for the project. Light Impression Europe Ltd produced the holograms. Hungarian Bank Note Company printed the souvenir sheets and Philatelia Hungarica Kft, Budapest, issued them.

Fig. 3-9.10. *Panda* hologram on the Chinese sheet.   **Fig. 3-9.11.** Chinese souvenir sheet with hologram in the margin.

Fig. 3-9.12. Numbered souvenir sheet.   **Fig. 3-9.13.** The HONG KONG'96 FDC with the bamboo sheet.

On **May 10**, **1996**, **P. R. China** issued a souvenir sheet for the Stamp Exhibition 'HONG KONG'96'. A small circular embossed hologram (Fig. 3-9.10) of a *panda holding a bamboo* is attached to the selvage of the souvenir sheet (Fig. 3-9.11) which is marked PJZ-3. A souvenir sheet marked with black numbers in the upper left corner was also issued (Fig. 3-9.12). The sheet depicts a green bamboo plant (**No. 41**). The 'Mao Bamboo' souvenir sheet, without the hologram, was first issued on July 15, 1993. It was designed by Xiao Rong. The 'HONG KONG'96' FDC is shown in Fig. 3-9.13.

Thailand issued on **June 9**, **1996**, its first definitive hologram stamps. To celebrate the Golden Jubilee 1996, the Communications Authority of Thailand (CAT) issued a 3-Baht holographic stamp in support of the rain-making project to alleviate the drought problem in Thailand. The stamp features a picture of an airplane seeding clouds. A circular embossed hologram portrait of *His Majesty King Bhumibol Adulyadej with a background of clouds* is attached to the stamp (Fig. 3-9.14). The hologram stamp was issued in two formats: a sheet of 25 (**No. 42**), and as a souvenir sheet with the holographic stamp and five ordinary stamps (Fig. 3-9.15, **No. 43**). The stamps were designed by Thaneth Ponchaiwong and printed by Thai British Security Printing plc, Thailand. The five stamps illustrate King Adulyadej's development intentions: the prevention of soil erosion by growing Vetiver grass, the improvement of water quality, the rain-making project, the survey project for natural water resource development, and the reforestation campaign in commemoration of the Royal Golden Jubilee. The FDC is shown in Fig. 3-9.16. A very nice A4 Golden Jubilee presentation card is shown in Fig. 3-9.17 with the hologram stamp and a wide 9-Baht stamp of a Long Tail Boat.

Fig. 3-9.14. Circular hologram on the stamp.   **Fig. 3-9.15.** Golden Jubilee stamps from Thailand.

Fig. 3-9.16. Golden Jubilee FDC envelope issued in Thailand on June 6, 1996.

Fig. 3-9.17. Golden Jubilee presentation card.

Fig. 3-9.18. German Olympic 1996 booklet with the *Deutsche Sporthilfe* hologram logo.

Germany issued on **June 13**, **1996**, a six-stamp booklet 'Für den Sport' for the 1996 Olympic Games in Atlanta. It was the 100-year-Olympics-Anniversary issue (Athen 1896 – Atlanta 1996) shown in Fig. 3-9.18. It was also issued to honor Josef Neckermann (1912-1992) who was a German equestrian and Olympic champion. He won Olympic medals at four different Olympics. The 100 +50 pf stamp in the booklet depicts Neckermann on a horse as illustrated on the booklet cover. The front and back sides of the booklet are covered with the Van Leer HoloPRISM® foil produced by the AHT Company in Bad Rothenfelde.

For the second time in 1996, **P. R. China** issued a souvenir sheet on **July 18**, **1996**, for the 22nd Stamp Exhibition in China. The stamp shows a sculpture of figures flying around a globe. The area around the stamp is a drawing of airmail envelopes, an airplane, a ship and trucks (**No. 44**). A small circular embossed hologram (Fig. 3-9.19) of the sculpture mentioned above, which is *the UPU emblem,* is attached to the selvage of the souvenir sheet, not on the stamp itself. The sheet designed by Zhao Junlong and Wu Jiankun is marked PJZ-2 (Fig. 3-9.20). A similar souvenir sheet, without hologram, was issued on October 9, 1994, to commemorate the 120th anniversary of the founding of the Universal Postal Union (U.P.U.).

Fig. 3-9.19. Small circular UPU hologram. **Fig. 3-9.20**. Souvenir sheet with hologram.

Fig. 3-9.21. Two-channel hologram with the *rat* in the two positions.   **Fig. 3-9.22.** X Asiatic Exhibition sheet.

Fig. 3-9.23. The back of the 2,000 edition sheet.

Fig. 3-9.24. Imperforated edition.   **Fig. 3-9.25.** Black edition.

On **August 12**, **1996**, **Hungary** issued the second souvenir sheets, this time for the 'X Asiatic Exhibitions' (**No. 45**) which took place in Taipei (blue lettering). The embossed two-channel hologram (Fig. 3-9.21) is of a *rat* (Chinese year of the Rat) which jumps up and down when the stamp is tilted horizontally. The hologram is attached to a large stamp with a color print of a dragon. Both the rat and the dragon are facing right on the IX sheet (Fig. 3-9.5 and 3-9.6) and left on the X sheet (Fig. 3-9.21 and 3-9.22). The Taipei souvenir sheets were issued in four limited editions: 16,800 on gummed paper, perforated, with blue numbers; 2,000 on thick paper, perforated, numbered and printed: 'A PHILATELIA HUNGARICA AJÁNDÉKA' [Gift of Philatelia Hungarica Kft] on the back. The text on the back of this sheet is shown in Fig. 3-9.23); 1,000 on thick paper, without perforation, without numbers (Fig. 3-9.24); 200 on thick paper, printed in **black** and without perforation but numbered in red (Fig. 3-9.25). This stamp (the 2000 edition) was included in *Collection of Hungarian Stamps'97*, a book with all issued Hungarian stamps in 1997. Pál Varga designed the souvenir sheets for the two exhibitions with Hologram Kft responsible for the project. Light Impression Europe Ltd produced the holograms. Hungarian Bank Note Company printed the souvenir sheets and Philatelia Hungarica Kft, Budapest, issued them.

Fig. 3-9.26. *Cultured Pearl* stamp.

Fig. 3-9.27. *Diamond* stamp with exelgram.

Fig. 3-9.28. A card with the Diamond stamp.

Fig. 3-9.29. Pearls and Diamonds FDC.

Two hologram-like stamps were issued in **Australia**. The previous Australian stamps had exelgrams on them, this time the stamps have so-called *foiltex* stamps which are of Australia Pearls and Diamonds. These stamps were issued on **September 5, 1996**. The 45¢ *cultured pearl* stamp (Fig. 3-9.26, **No. 46**) has a circular foil looking like a pearl, but is not holographic. The AU$1.20 *diamond* stamp (Fig. 3-9.27, **No. 47**) has an embossed diffractive foil (foiltex) with facets. CSIRO in Australia together with Leonhard Kurz GmbH in Germany produced the foiltex labels. Diamonds and pearls are both found in Australia's north, products respectively of the earth and the sea. The stamps were designed by Janet Boschen at Australia Post Graphic Design Studio. A first-day-of-issue *Diamond* card is shown in Fig. 3-9.28 and the Pearls and Diamonds FDC in Fig. 3-9.29.

On **October 8, 1996**, four 32¢ 'Christmas Family Scenes Stamps' were issued in the **USA**. A *Flying Santa Claus Sleigh with the Moon in the sky* cachet hologram is attached to a limited-edition (32) INFO GOLD FDC. The stamps were issued for use on holiday mail. The four stamps pictured families enjoying the holidays and showed a father and two children enjoying the glow of a fire; a mother and daughter Christmas shopping; a father and two children decorating a Christmas tree; and a little girl dreaming of Santa. In Fig. 3-9.30, the hologram inside a gold frame is shown next to the FDC with North Pole Alaska cancellation.

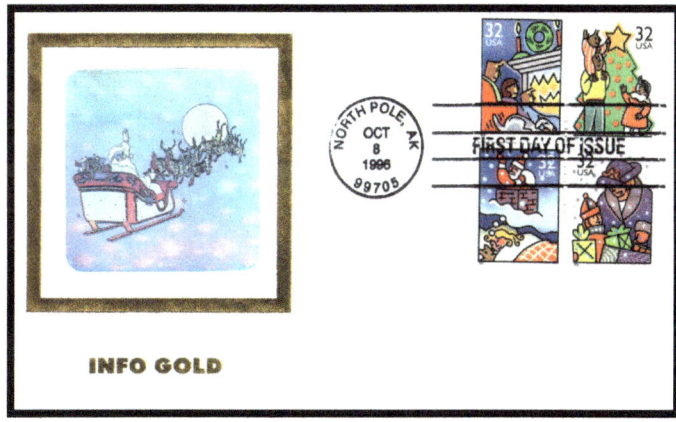
Fig. 3-9.30. The cachet hologram and the INFO GOLD (2/32) FDC shown.

 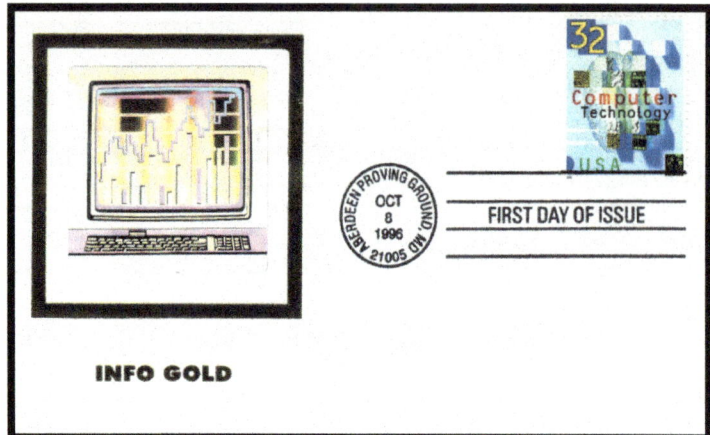

Fig. 3-9.31. The cachet hologram and the INFO GOLD (64/100) FDC shown.

Another FDC was issued in the **USA** on **October 8**, **1996**, with the 32¢ 'Computer Technology' stamp. A *computer with a 3D screen* cachet hologram is attached to a limited-edition (100) INFO GOLD FDC. With the onset of World War II, the ballistic research laboratory at Aberdeen Proving Ground was in need of a more advanced way to prepare firing and bombing tables for the Army and Army Air Corps. The plan was to produce the world's first "true" computer, which resulted in the ENIAC (Electronic Numerical Integrator And Computer), completed in 1946. Used to calculate firing tables, as well as conduct top-secret research in the development of the hydrogen bomb, ENIAC ushered the world into the computer age. The commemorative stamp was issued for the 50-year-anniversary of the ENIAC. The stamp image is a high-technology graphic design featuring a brain partially covered by small blocks containing parts of circuit boards and binary language. The stamp was the work of Nancy Skolos and Tom Wedell of Boston. In Fig. 3-9.31, the hologram inside a gold frame is shown next to the FDC with Aberdeen Proving Ground, Maryland cancellation.

A third holographic souvenir sheet was issued during the same 1996 year in **P. R. China**. The souvenir sheet (**No. 48**) is attached to a presentation card issued on **October 9**, **1996**. China issued jointly with **Singapore** these cards for the two simultaneous Stamp Exhibitions in Su-Zho, China and in Singapore which took place between October 9 and 13. A small circular embossed hologram of a *walking panda surrounded by bamboo leaves* is attached to the selvage of the souvenir sheet (Fig. 3-9.32). The stamp on the souvenir sheet depicts two panda bears (Fig. 3-9.33). The souvenir sheet, marked PJZ-4, is attached to the upper part of a card with printed information about the stamp exhibitions. Souvenir sheets with black numbers were also issued (Fig. 3-9.34). On the back of the card is a reproduction of the stamp. The 'Giant Pandas' souvenir sheet (T-106) without a hologram was previously issued on May 24, 1985. The sheet was designed by Han Meilin and Deng Xiqing and printed by Beijing Postage Stamp Printing Works.

Fig. 3-9.32. Souvenir sheet *panda* hologram.   **Fig. 3-9.33.** Chinese card.   **Fig. 3-9.34.** Sheet with black number.

HOLOGRAPHY AND PHILATELY

Fig. 3-9.35. The different hologram stamps on the six Hong Kong cards.

Hong Kong issued a set of postcards on **November 27, 1996**, to advertise HONG KONG'97 Stamp Exhibition which took place between February 12 and 16, 1997. Different stamps featuring Hong Kong landmarks are attached to the six prepaid postcards. Each card has a 2D/3D hologram stamp on the front and a printed one with the same image on the back: **Postcard 3**, (**No. 49**) *Surfing board and the Queen*; **Postcard 4**, (**No. 50**) *Mass transit railway map*; **Postcard 5**, (**No. 51**) *Convention and Exhibition Centre*; **Postcard 6** (**No. 52**) *Wan Chai Post Office*; **Postcard 7**, (**No. 53**) *Wong Tai Sin Temple*; **Postcard 8**, (**No. 54**) *Hong Kong by night*. (YANG Cataloque #PP5). De La Rue Holographics Ltd in England produced the holograms which are of a very high quality. The cards were issued by Hong Kong Post Office's Philatelic Bureau. The six hologram stamps are shown in Fig. 3-9.35, the cards in Fig. 3-9.36 and the address side of postcard number 3 in Fig. 3-9.37.

Fig. 3-9.36. The six postcards with hologram stamps.

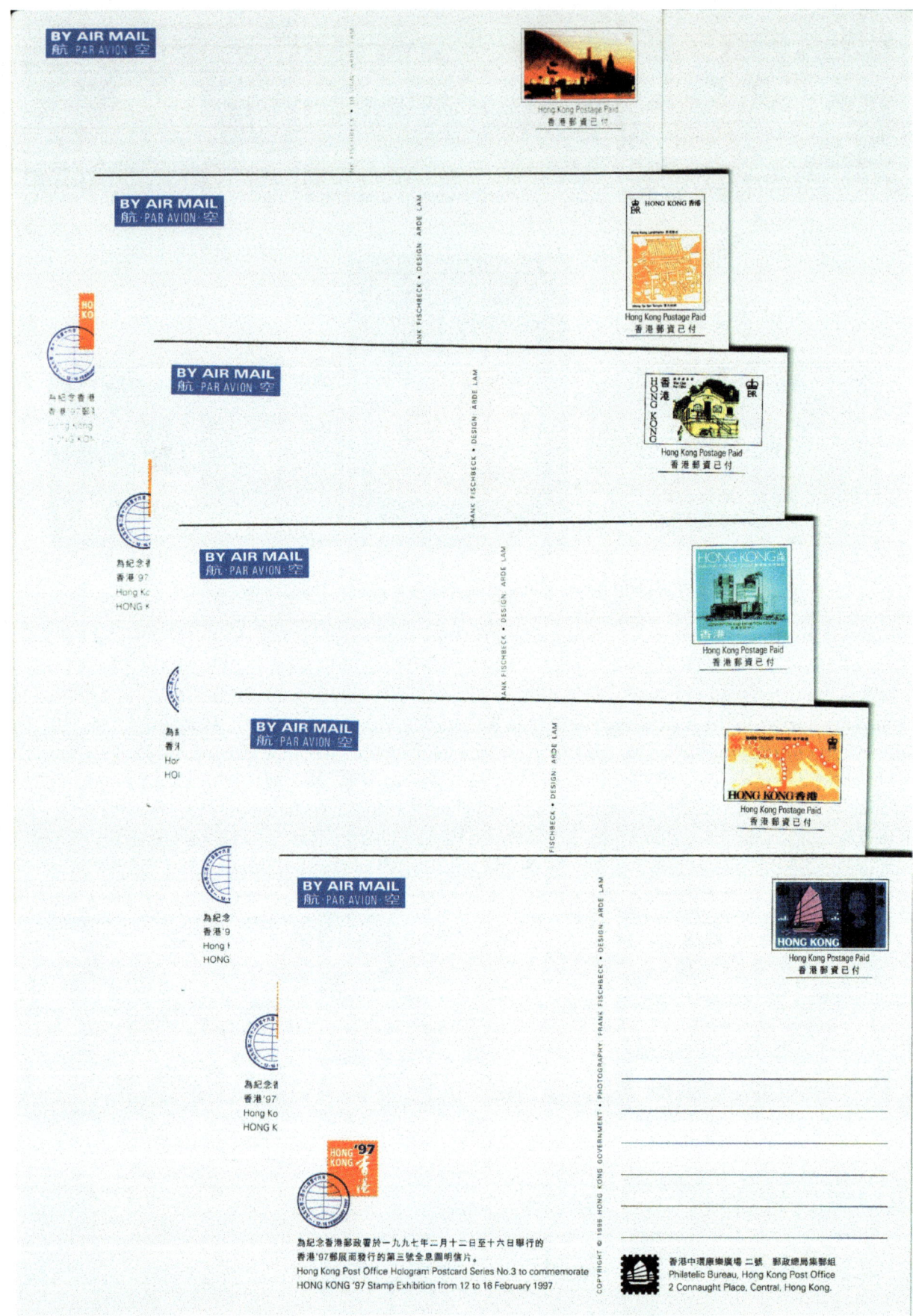

Fig. 3-9.37. The address side of the six prepaid postcards.

3-10. Holographic stamps and souvenir sheets issued in 1997

The main hologram stamp event in 1997 was when Åland issued a souvenir sheet with a two-channel hologram in June. Several FDCs were issued in the USA, with cachet holograms on the covers. On one of the 'WORLD OF DINOSAURS' FDCs four small photopolymer reflection holograms were attached. They are unique, since normally only embossed rainbow holograms are used on stamps and FDC covers. China continued issuing the traditional New Year stamp folder with a hologram.

Fig. 3-10.1. The *ox* hologram and the Chinese card issued in 1997.

The New Year Presentation Folder in **P. R. China** was issued on **January 5, 1997**, by China National Philatelic Corporation. The folder has a circular 2D/3D *ox* hologram attached to the left inside page, produced by Qingdao Qimei Picture Co. Ltd. Two sets of four ordinary Chinese stamps are attached to the opposite side as the hologram. More information about the folder is provided in **Table 1**. Liu Dun was responsible for the design of both the hologram and folder, shown in Fig. 3-10.1.

USA issued two 32¢ stamps on **March 13, 2007** during the 'Pacific '97 Stamp Exhibition': 150th Anniversary of United States Stamps. It was the Triangles Set of two, the Stagecoach and Ship stamps. Two FDCs by Uncovers with the same cachet hologram of a *ship* were attached to both the ship stamp FDC and the stagecoach stamp FDC. The *Ship* hologram shown in Fig. 3-10.2 was produced by American Bank Note Holographics, Inc. The two FDCs are shown in Fig. 3-10.3.

Fig. 3-10.2. The *ship* cachet hologram.

Fig. 3-10.3. The two Pacific'97 FDCs with the *ship* cachet hologram.

Fig. 3-10.4. Three FDCs with different embossed cachet holograms of *dinosaurs*.

Fig. 3-10.5. Four small photopolymer cachet holograms and 'THE WORLD OF DINOSAURS' FDC.

USA issued on **May 1**, **1997**, several FDCs for 'THE WORLD OF DINOSAURS' 32¢ stamps. There were three different cachet embossed 2D/3D holograms of *Triceratops, Spinosaurus,* and *Tyrannosaurus,* produced by Light Impressions, Inc., on the FDCs (Fig. 3-10.4). A very unusual holographic cachet decoration was four small *photopolymer reflection* holograms of dinosaurs. In Fig. 3-10.5 these cachet holograms are reproduced and the FDC with these holograms. (Note that the polymer hologram images are not at all visible in the scanned FDC envelope). More of the issued stamps featuring dinosaurs were attached to two other Uncovers 'THE AGE OF DINOSAURS' FDCs. Here, with the *Diplodocus* and *Hylaeosaurus* Light Impressions, Inc. cachet holograms, shown in Figs. 3-10.6 through 3-10.7 next to the FDCs. US stamps featuring dinosaurs were also issued in 1989. The same cachet holograms were used on the 1989 FDCs (See Fig. 3-2.2.)

Fig. 3-10.6. The FDC with the *Diplodocus* cachet hologram.

 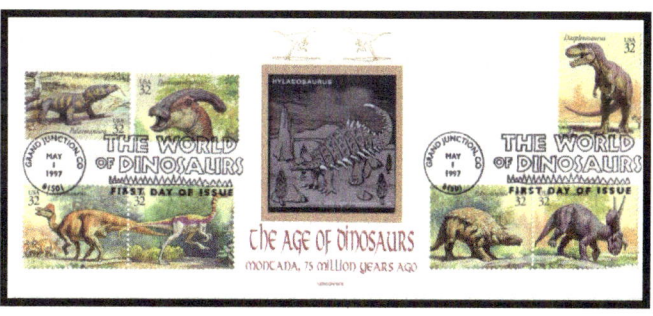

Fig. 3-10.7. The FDC with the *Hylaeosaurus* cachet hologram.

Fig. 3-10.8. Stamp with hologram showing the *ship*.

Fig. 3-10.9. Stamp with hologram showing *75 ÅR*.

Fig. 3-10.10. The souvenir sheet with the two-image hologram.

Fig. 3-10.11. The Åland souvenir sheet FDC.

The Scandinavian country **Åland** issued a souvenir sheet on **June 9**, **1997**, to celebrate the 75-year-anniversary of the island Åland's autonomy. [18] The two-channel hologram is switching between a *three-masted ship on a wavy sea* (Fig. 3-10.8) and '*75 ÅR*' (years) (Fig. 3-10.9) surrounded by *fireworks* (**No. 55**). The stamp is part of a souvenir sheet (Fig. 3-10.10) showing waves crashing against the rocks in the background of a statue 'Havets Folk' (the People of the Sea). The statue by Matti Haupt shows a man and a woman. The woman represents a figure head and the man steers a vessel. On the stamp, the man glances at the hologram. The man's and the woman's heads are tied together by the roaring waves of the sea. The FDC is shown in Fig. 3-10.11. This stamp won 'The most beautiful stamp of Europe in 1997' at the IBRA International Stamp Show. Pirkko Vahtero designed this stamp. Hologram Industries SA in France produced the holograms and the Finnish company Setec Oy printed the sheets. Issued was also a special limited-edition sheet 'Jubileumstavla' framed and signed by the artist.

For the return of Hong Kong to China (July 1, 1997) eleven territories issued on **June 20**, **1997**, similar souvenir sheets with different stamps but all with the following text: *BEST WISHES & GOOD FORTUNE* in holographic foil. 'To mark the return of Hong Kong to China, 1st July, 1997' is printed on a red area at the bottom of the sheet with the number of the country which issued the sheets. The eleven souvenir sheets (**No. 56** to **66**) were issued in **Ascension Island** (1-11), **British Indian Ocean Territory** (2-11), **Samoa** (3-11), **Tristan Da Chuna** (4-11), **Falkland Islands** (5-11), **British Antarctic Territory** (6-11), **South Georgia & South Sandwich Islands** (7-11), **St Helena** (8-11), **Bahamas** (9-11), **Tuvalu** (10-11) and **Isle of Man** (11-11), The holographic text which appears the same on all sheets is shown in Fig. 3-10.12 and some of souvenir sheets in Figs. 3-10.13 through 3-10.18.

Fig. 3-10.12. The holographic text.

Fig. 3-10.13 Samoa.

Fig. 3-10.14 Tristan Da Chuna.

Fig. 3-10.15 British Indian Ocean Territory.

Fig. 3-10.16. St Helena.

Fig. 3-10.17. Tavulu.

Fig. 3-10.18. Isle of Man.

USA issued on **July 25, 1997**, several FDCs for the 'Legendary Football Coaches' 32¢ stamps. Several different FDCs were issued with a Light Impressions, Inc. cachet hologram shown in Fig. 3-10.19. One limited-edition (40) FDC honoring George Halas and Vince Lombardi is shown in Fig. 3-10.20. This FDC on the old prepaid envelop with the 25¢ hologram stamp was first issued in September 9, 1990.

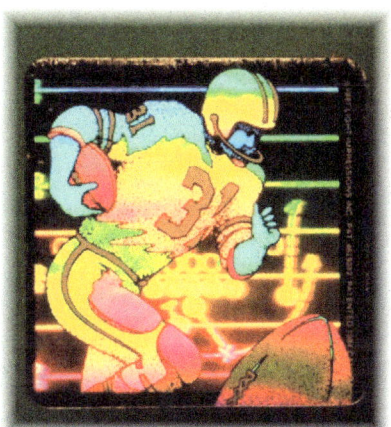
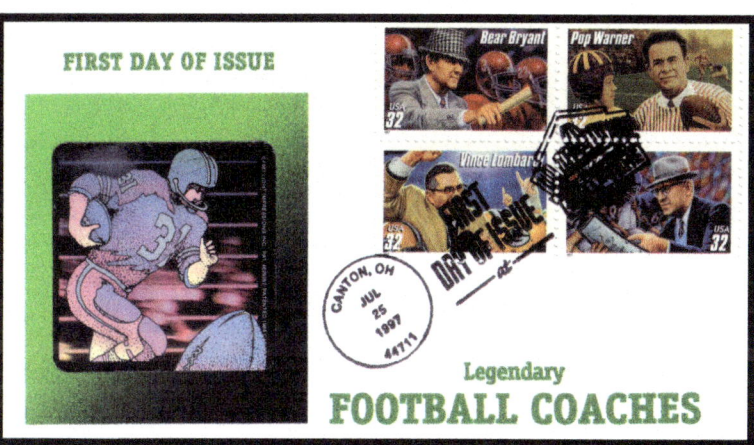

Fig. 3-10.19. FDC 'Legendary Football Coaches' FDC.

Fig. 3-10.20. The limited-edition FDC (27/40) 'Legendary Football Coaches' issued on July 25, 1997.

Fig. 3-10.19. The two holograms and the Chinese National Games 1997 FDC.

China issued a FDC on **October 12, 1997**, for 'The Opening Ceremony of 'The 8th National Games' which was held in Shanghai.' There are two small 2D/3D cachet holograms on the envelope which has two National Games 97 stamps, one 0.50-yuan and one 1.50-yuan stamp. The two holograms and the envelope, designed by Zhu Jinde, are shown in Fig. 3-10.19.

3-11. Holographic stamps and souvenir sheets issued in 1998

1998 was the year when several very special hologram stamps were issued. The largest definitive self-adhesive hologram stamp was the Grenada-Grenadines tiger stamp, where the entire stamp is a hologram. Equally large hologram stamps included the four Lady Diana memorial hologram stamps issued in four countries. An animated hologram was attached to the solar eclipse souvenir sheet from Netherlands-Antilles, in which the hologram shows the solar eclipse. Indonesia issued five definitive hologram stamps and Lithuania issued a souvenir stamp with a hologram. China continued issuing the traditional New Year stamp folder with a hologram.

Fig. 3-11.1. The *tiger* hologram and the Chinese card issued in 1998.

The New Year Presentation Folder in **P. R. China** was issued on **January 5, 1998**, by China National Philatelic Corporation. The folder has a circular 2D/3D *tiger* hologram attached to the left inside page, produced by Qingdao Qimei Picture Co. Ltd. Four ordinary Chinese stamps are attached to the opposite side as the hologram. More information about the folder is provided in **Table 1**. Chen Jingyi was responsible for the design of both the hologram and folder, shown in Fig. 3-11.1.

On **February 10, 1998**, **Grenada-Grenadines** issued large holographic stamps for Grenada-Grenadines Lunar New Year. The holographic self-adhesive stamp features a photograph of a *walking tiger* in front of the Chinese character '*Year of the Tiger*'. There are two versions: one four-stamp block (each $1.50) of a tiger (Fig. 3-11.2, **No. 67**) and one $3.00 large stamp with the same image enlarged in size (Fig. 3-11.3, **No. 68**). The country name, denomination, and the theme are all printed on the surface of the hologram. The $3 stamp is the largest size hologram stamp issued so far. These stamps were produced by Thomas Cvetkovich, Chromagem Inc. in the USA.

Fig. 3-11.2. The four *tiger* stamp sheet.   **Fig. 3-11.3.** Large *tiger* hologram stamp.

Fig. 3-11.4. Photographs recorded from five different phases of the solar eclipse hologram on the stamp.

Fig. 3-11.5. Solar eclipse souvenir sheet.

Fig. 3-11.6. Solar eclipse FDC.

Netherlands-Antilles issued on **February 26, 1998**, stamps and a souvenir sheet with a hologram stamp for the total solar eclipse observed from Curaçao on that date. [19] The SAROS 130 souvenir sheet which has a perforated 750-ct stamp on it depicts a map of the Caribbean Sea and Curaçao. The circular hologram, attached to the stamp of a dark black sky, shows a *continuous animated solar eclipse* when the hologram is moved during observation (**No. 69**). The effect is shown in Fig. 3-11.4 where five different photographs from different viewing positions have been recorded from the same hologram on the stamp. The sheet is shown in Fig. 3-11.5 and the FDC in Fig. 3-11.6. Three ordinary stamps in the same set (85, 110, 225 ct) were also issued. The stamps were designed by Robert Willems. The hologram was produced by OpSec (UK) and printed by Joh. Enschedé in the Netherlands.

On **October 8, 1998**, a large limited-edition (10,000) ten-stamp hologram souvenir sheet was issued in **Germany** 'Für die Wohlfartspflege.' It was included in the Deutsche Post Phil Selection Album. The stamps on the sheet depict two birds, aquatic warblers (*Acrocephalus paludicola*) [in German: Seggenrohrsänger]. The sheet size is 210 mm by 105 mm and the stamp size is 35 mm by 35 mm. *Two aquatic warblers in the reed* appear in hologram image with the surrounding German text: 'Seggenrohrsänger', 'DEUTSCHLAND' and 'FÜR DIE WOHLFAHRTSPFLEGE' (**No. 70**). The stamp denomination is 110+50 pF. The sheet is based on the German stamp which is shown next to the hologram sheet in Fig. 3-11.7. The master hologram sheet was produced by Irina Menz at Holographic Systems München GmbH. More information about this hologram sheet and the PostPhil Selection Album, in which it was included, are found in Chapter 5, Section 5-3.

Fig. 3-11.7. The German stamp and the ten-stamp 'Seggenrohrsänger' hologram souvenir sheet.

Fig. 3-11.8. Souvenir sheet.   **Fig. 3-11.9**. Lithuanian FDC issued on October 9, 1998.

Fig. 3-11.10. The special Lithuanian folder with the hologram stamp.

On **October 9, 1998, Lithuania** issued a souvenir sheet to commemorate the 1918 founding of Lithuania's postal administration office. [20] At the top of the sheet is a stamp with a circular hologram in the centre, showing the *post horn emblem of Lithuania's postal service in front of Africa with the Eurasian continent in the background* (Fig. 3-11.8, **No. 71**). The selvage includes an inscription marking the 80th anniversary and a symbolic dove carrying a letter. H. Ratkevičius designed the souvenir sheet, Hologram Kft (Miklós Varga) in Hungary was responsible for the hologram and Budapest's Security Printing House printed the stamp. Figure 3-11.9 shows the FDC and in Fig. 3-11.10 a special presentation folder.

During the same month, on **October 19, 1998, Indonesia** issued hologram stamps with five stamps of ducks and geese: 4,000 rupial Magpie Goose (**No. 72**), 5,000 rupial Spotted Whistling Duck (**No. 73**), 10,000 rupial Salvador's Teal (**No. 74**), 15,000 rupial Radjah Shelduck (**No. 75**), 20,000 rupial White-winged Wood Duck [21] (**No. 76**). Each stamp has a small circular embossed hologram attached to it featuring *flying ducks and the bird-and-globe emblem* of the Indonesian Post Office with '*POSINDONESIA*' in the background. Each stamp also includes micro-printing hidden on the portrayed ducks. A souvenir sheet (54,000 rupial) was also issued with all five stamps (**No. 77**). Pradhika Studio designed the stamps and Perum Peruri in Indonesia printed the stamps. The hologram producer was Applied Holographics Plc. The five different stamps are shown in Fig. 3-11.11 and the souvenir sheet with the five stamps in Fig. 3-11.12.

Fig. 3-11.11. Five stamps from Indonesia with small circular holograms attached.

Fig. 3-11.12. The souvenir sheet with five stamps from Indonesia.

Four countries: **Grenada (No. 78)**, **Grenada/Grenadines (No. 79)**, **Guyana (No. 80)**, and **St.Vincent/Grenadines (No. 81)** issued on **November 5, 1998**, four large and slightly different Lady Diana, Princess of Wales, Memorial Stamps, 1961-1997. The holographic self-adhesive stamps feature photographs of *Princess Diana in front of famous London city scenes or buildings*. The stamps are as large as the Grenada stamps of the tiger, mentioned above. These holograms were produced by Thomas Cvetkovich, Chromagem Inc. in the USA. The four Diana stamps are shown in Fig. 3-11.13.

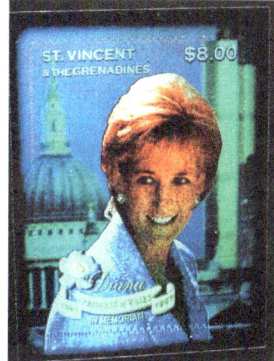

Fig. 3-11.13. *Lady Diana* Memorial hologram stamps.

Fig. 3-11.14. French 1998 CNEP Cinderella sheet with hologram.

A Cinderella sheet was issued in **November 1998** by **France** honoring France's first postage stamp. The hologram stamp shows *Cérès*, a goddess of agriculture, and the *years 1849 and 1999*. It is the 20-centime black Cérès stamp issued January 1, 1849. The CNEP (Chambre Syndicale Française des Négociants et Experts en Philatélie) souvenir sheet shows the old Cérès stamps (**No. 82**). Part of the stamp contains a perforated stamp of the CNEP logo. The stamp was issued for the 52nd Fall Salon Philatelique 98 in November 1998 and has no postal value (Fig. 3-11.14). Cartor Security Printing printed the sheets. The hologram of Cérès was produced by Hologram Industries S.A. in France.

3-12. Holographic stamps and souvenir sheets issued in 1999

The approaching new millennium brought about an increased number of hologram stamps and souvenir sheets being issued. One can mention here the definitive hologram stamps from Canada, France (including six African countries, all with the same hologram), Germany, The Netherlands, Malaysia, Australia and Namibia. Malaysia issued the Petronas Twin Towers hologram stamp which is very beautiful. The animated hologram images on the stamps issued in Canada, Germany and Australia are all worth mentioning. The dove stamp, the comet collision on Jupiter stamp and the millennium stamp issued in these three countries are unique and, so far, represent the most advanced holographic images used on stamps. China continued issuing the traditional New Year stamp folder with a hologram.

Fig. 3-12.1. The first Czech Republic official postcard with hologram and micro text (first address line).

Fig. 3-12.2. Two-channel security hologram.   **Fig. 3-12.3.** Railway postcard.   **Fig. 3-12.4.** Postfila postcard.

The year 1999 saw an explosion in the amount of holographic stamps and souvenir sheets being issued. It started with a series of prepaid postcards from the **Czech Republic**. [22] The first postcard was issued on **January 4, 1999** (Figure 3-12.1). A small hologram (Fig. 3-12.2) was attached as a security measure, which is a rare postal application of holograms (**No. 83**). It is a two-channel hologram, switching between the *post horn emblem of Czech post office* [left] *and a flying pigeon* [right]. The holograms were produced by Czech Holography s. r. o. in Prague. The Post Printing House (Postovni Tiskarna Cenin Praha a. s., PTC) in the Czech Republic printed the cards.

The first address line contains micro text, an additional security feature in addition to the hologram (See Fig. 3-12.1). All postcards have the micro text imprint. The prepaid 4–Koruna postcard was the domestic postage, postcards with a 7-Koruna imprinted stamp was for international destinations at surface rate. Later during the year, four different types of postcards were issued with the same security hologram. The four types of postcards issued:

- Official postcards with or without cachet imprint,
- Official postcards with topical cachet imprint for Postfila with ![postfila] mark (in different colors),
- Official postcards with topical cachet imprint for private customers with ![postfila] mark followed by *PP*,
- Postcards with topical cachet imprint by private customers but without consent of the Czech postal service (not regarded as a philatelic collectable item).

The postcard in Fig. 3-12.1 is an example of an officially issued card of the first type and another of this type with a cachet imprint is shown in Fig. 3-12.3 (Termination of Railway Mail Transport, issued on May 12, 1999). The second type of card, with the Postfila mark added, shown in Fig. 3-12.4, (officially issued on July 2, 1999 for PHILEXFRANCE 99 stamp exhibition in Paris). The Postfila postcards were officially issued by postal service for national or international events where the Czech Republic philatelic service participated. Eleven official postcards, twelve Postfila cards and about one hundred private cards were issued in 1999. The Czech security hologram has also appeared on block of stamps and booklets. When issued, some of them are reported in the following Chapters.

Fig. 3-12.5. The *rabbit* hologram and the Chinese card issued in 1999.

The New Year Presentation Folder in **P. R. China** was issued on **January 5, 1999**, by China National Philatelic Corporation. The folder has a circular 2D/3D *rabbit* hologram attached to the left inside page, produced by Qingdao Qimei Picture Co. Ltd. Four ordinary Chinese stamps are attached to the opposite side as the hologram. More information about the folder is provided in **Table 1**. The hologram was designed by Chen Jingyi and the folder by Yang Ying, both shown in Fig. 3-12.5.

Hungary issued a holographic souvenir sheet on **February 11, 1999**, for the August 11 total solar eclipse. A narrow holographic foil, attached to the stamp, covers the path through central Europe, which marks *the area covered by the total eclipse* (**No. 84**). The souvenir sheet shows a map with parts of Hungary, Slovakia, Austria, and Croatia (Fig. 3-12.6). A total of 200,000 sheets were issued and each sheet is serially numbered in **red**. The numbering shows up in yellow when illuminated under UV light. Under UV illumination one can also see two different versions of folkloric sun representations, alternating, each version is shown six times within one block. Károly Vagyóczky designed the stamp which was printed by Pénzjegynyomda Co. (Hungarian Bank Note Company) in Budapest. The FDC is shown in Fig. 3-12-7.

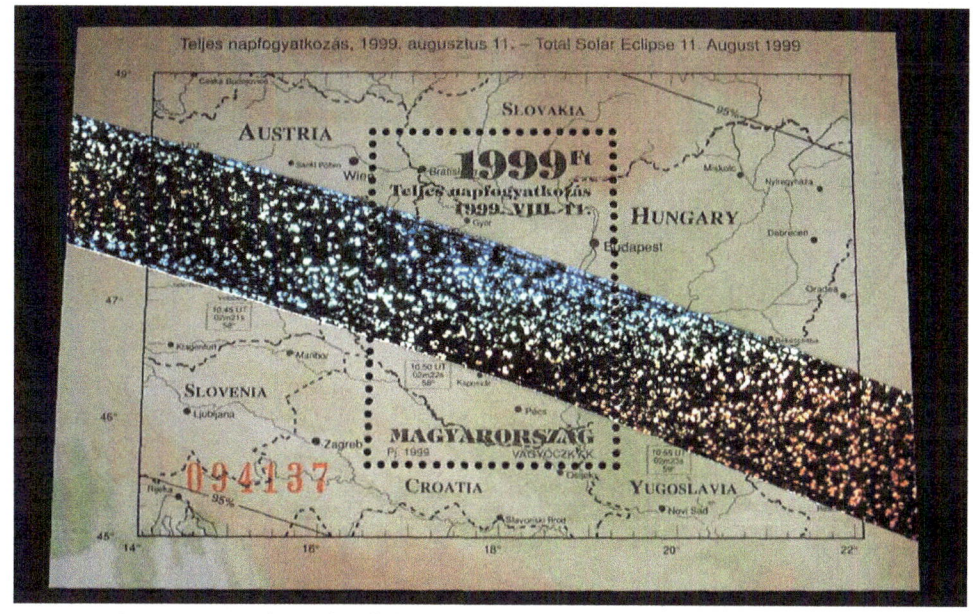

Fig. 3-12.6. Holographic foil showing the *covered area of the total solar eclipse*.

Fig. 3-12.7. Hungarian FDC with the 1999 solar eclipse souvenir sheet.

The next country to issue a holographic item in 1999 was **Kyrgyzstan** which issued on **April 27, 1999**, a souvenir sheet supporting WWF, World Wide Fund for Nature. The holograms of *Corsac foxes* (*Vulpex fox*) are unevenly cut and attached to the four se-tenant stamps. The sheet contains two sets of two 10c stamps (**No. 85** and **86**), one 30c stamp (**No. 87**) and one 50c stamp (**No. 88**). In addition to the eight-stamp-sheets (**No. 89**) four postcards with photographs of foxes were issued, each of them with one of the stamps attached on the front of the card. These items were issued for the International Stamp Exhibition in Nuremberg, Germany, which took place between April 27 and May 4, 1999. The holograms were produced by 3D AG in Switzerland. The sheets were printed by GOSZNAK in Moscow. The 10c hologram stamp is shown in Fig. 3-12.8 and the full eight-stamp sheet in Fig. 3-12.9.

Fig. 3-12.8. *Fox* hologram on a stamp from Kyrgyzstan.

Fig. 3-12.9. Souvenir sheet with eight *fox* hologram stamps.

On **May 6**, **1999**, **The Netherlands** issued a booklet (Fig. 3-12.10) of holographic stamps with two different stamps: 'I LOVE STAMPS' and 'STAMPS LOVE ME' (**No. 90** and **91**). [23] The hologram (Fig. 3-12.11) contains the word '*LOVE*' where '*O*' has the shape of a *heart* and is repeated across the hologram. The stamps were issued in booklets of five stamps (**No. 92**). The holograms were produced by Hologram Industries SA in France. Experimental Jetset designed the stamps and they were printed by Walsall Security Printers in England. The two different stamps are shown in Fig. 3-12.12 and the FDC in Fig. 3-12.13.

Fig. 3-12.10. Booklet with hologram stamps.

Fig. 3-12.11. *LOVE* hologram.

Fig. 3-12.12. Four hologram stamps.

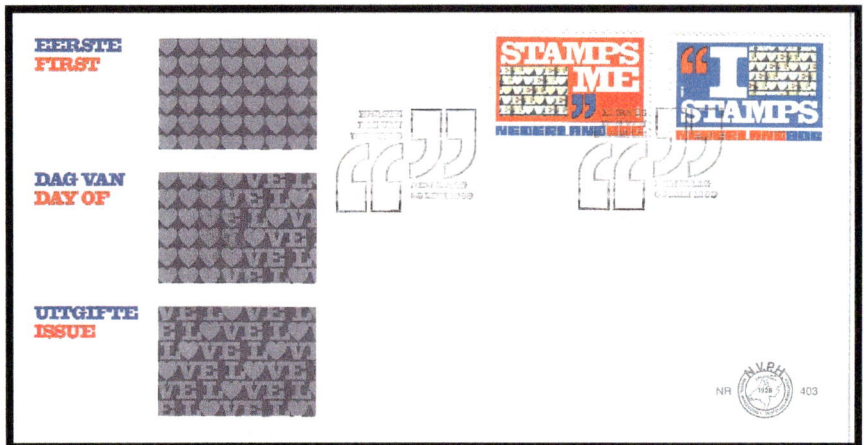
Fig. 3-12.13. FDC with the two hologram stamps.

On **May 17**, **1999**, **Macau** issued a souvenir sheet with a hologram stamp honoring tele-communications in Macau (**No. 93**). The circular hologram on the stamp (Fig. 3-12.14) shows the *Earth with an arrow pointing at Macau*. In the background behind the globe there are ten repeated lines with the following text: *MACAU CTT*. On both the sheet and the stamp are drawings of TV sets, PCs, and a communication satellite dish (Fig. 3-12.15). Macau, like Hong Kong in 1998, returned to China on December 20, 1999. Ng Wai Kin designed the sheet and Imprensa Nacional-Casa da Moeda printed the souvenir sheet. The FDC with the souvenir sheet is shown in Fig. 3-12.16. A gold overprinted version was issued for the July MACAU 1999 in China –Shanghai stamp exhibition (See Fig. 3-12.61).

Fig. 3-12.14. The circular hologram.

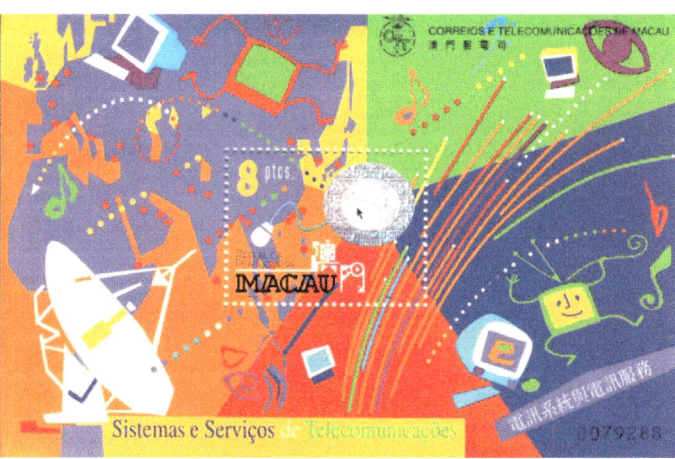
Fig. 3-12.15. Macau souvenir sheet.

Fig. 3-12.16. Macau FDC.

France issued its first definitive hologram stamp on **July 2, 1999**. [24] The stamp was issued for the 150-year anniversary of France's first postage stamp (Fig. 3-12.17). The first French stamp was engraved in 1849 by Jacques-Jean Barre. The circular hologram shows *The Head of Cérès*, a goddess of agriculture, and the years *1849* and *1999* (Fig. 3-12.18). The small round hologram is different from the 1998 CNEP hologram. The stamp (40.5 mm x 52 mm) was printed with a se-tenant label (6.5 mm x 52 mm) which reads: Philexfrance 99 - Paris (**No. 94**) and was issued for the PHILEXFRANCE'99 - Paris Expo, July 2 - 11, 1999. Aurelie Baras designed the stamp and French Government Printing Office printed the stamps. This round Cérès hologram was produced by Applied Holographics Plc in England. Figure 3-12.19 shows the FILEXFRANCE'99 FDC. A Cérès anniversary card with the stamp (Fig. 3-12.20) was issued as well as a limited-edition FDC with both the hologram stamp and a MONNAIE DE PARIS silver coin (Fig. 3-12.21). The Cérès commemorative 1-Franc coin celebrates the 125-year-anniversary of the world-wide agreement of Postal Services, which laid the foundations of the Universal Postal Union (U.P.U.).

Fig. 3-12.17. French stamp with a hologram.

Fig. 3-12.18. *Cérès* hologram.

Fig. 3-12.19. FDC with the French Cérès stamp.

Fig. 3-12.20. Cérès card.

Fig. 3-12.21. FDC with the Cérès stamp and a coin.

In addition to the Cérès stamp, **France** issued also a CNEP Cinderella stamp (Fig. 3-12.22). The hologram stamp shows *Cérès* and the years *1849* and *1999*. It features the 20-centime black Cérès stamp issued January 1, 1849. The 1999 CNEP stamp features a postman on a motorbike, a TGV train, an air balloon, airplanes and stamps flying in the sky (**No. 95**). This stamp sheet which shows all means of transporting mail was issued for the PHILEXFRANCE 99 - Paris Expo on **July 3**, **1999**. The sheet has no postal value. For this CNEP sheet the same rectangular Hologram Industries' hologram of *Cérès* was attached as appeared on the 1998 CNEP sheet. Cartor Security Printing in France printed the sheet.

Fig. 3-12.22. The French second CNEP Cinderella sheet with a *Cérès* hologram stamp.

Fig. 3-12.23. New Caledonia hologram stamp.

Fig. 3-12.24. The PHILEXFRANCE 99 New Caledonia souvenir sheet.

For the PHILEXFRANCE 99 - Paris Expo **New Caledonia** issued on **July 2, 1999**, a very special souvenir sheet honoring New Caledonia's first postage stamp, issued in 1859. [25] The stamp with the hologram (Fig. 3-12.23) located in center of the sheet, shows the *effigy of Emperor Napoleon III*, *cagou birds*, the years *1859* and *1999*, and country's French name: *Nouvelle-Calédonie*. In addition to embossed holography, the souvenir sheet in Fig. 3-12.24 contains stamps which demonstrate four printing processes: intaglio, offset, thermography, offset with frequency-modulation screening (stochastic screen), and 22-carat gold-foil embossing (**No. 96**). All stamps feature stamp-on-stamp designs of New Caledonia's first stamp. The designer of this beautiful souvenir sheet was Claude Andréotto. The French company Hologram Industries S.A. produced the holograms and Cartor Security Printing in France printed the souvenir sheets.

Fig. 3-12.25. *Cérès* hologram.

Fig. 3-12.26. The stamps from Congo, Gabon, Guinea, Ivory Coast, Niger, and Senegal, all with the same hologram.

Six of the former French colonies in Africa issued also holographic stamps on **July 3, 1999**. These stamps from **Congo (No. 97)**, **Gabon (No. 98)**, **Guinea (No. 99)**, **Ivory Coast (No. 100)**, **Niger (No. 101)** and **Senegal (No. 102)** are all different but with same Hologram Industries' *Cérès* hologram (Fig. 3-13.25) which was used on the French 1998 and 1999 CNEP sheets. The rectangular holograms are attached at an angle of 15° on all these stamps which were all issued for the PHILEXFRANCE 99 - Paris Expo. Claude Andréotto designed the stamps and Cartor Security Printing in France printed all these stamps. The stamps No. 97 through 102 are featured in Fig. 3-12.26. The different 10-stamp sheets are shown in Figs. 3-12.27 through 3.12.32. Note: The Ivory Coast stamps may have been issued later, on September 10, 1999.

Fig. 3-12.27. The ten-*Cérès* hologram Congo sheet.

Fig. 3-12.28. The ten-*Cérès* hologram Gabon sheet.

Fig. 3-12.29. The ten-*Cérès* hologram Guinea sheet.

Fig. 3-12.30. The ten-*Cérès* hologram Ivory Coast sheet.

Fig. 3-12.31. The ten-*Cérès* hologram Niger sheet.

Fig. 3-12.32. The ten-*Cérès* hologram Senegal sheet.

On **August 20, 1999, Brazil** issued its second souvenir sheet. The fish of Pantanal sheet with eight se-tenant stamps of Brazilian fish: 22c dourado, 31c pirapulanga, 36c dourado-cachorro, 51c mato-grosso, 80c cascudo-chicote, 90c piauçu, 1.05r abramites sp and 1.20r ancistrus sp (stamp **No. 103** and sheet **No.104**). The stamps were issued for the Stamp Exhibition CHINA'99 in China and to promote a large complex of aquariums to be built in Mato Grosso do Sul. One hologram (Fig. 3-12.33) is attached to one of the stamps, which features the '*Year of the Rabbit*' and the *logo* for the China exhibition. Another identical hologram is attached to the top selvage. The eight-stamp souvenir sheet is shown in Fig. 3-12.34. The designer of the sheet was Maristela Colucci and the fish photos by Paula Robson De Souza. OpSec (UK) produced the master and Holografica Producoes Ltda in Brazil the holograms. The Brazilian State Mint printed the stamps.

Fig. 3-12.33. Hologram.

Fig. 3-12.34. The souvenir sheet from Brazil with two holograms.

On **August 21, 1999**, **Switzerland** issued jointly with **China** a souvenir sheet which has a small circular two-channel 2D/3D hologram attached at the selvage (Fig. 3-12.35, **No. 105**). The original China-Switzerland sheet was issued on November 25, 1998. The same sheet, now with a hologram, was reissued one year later to commemorate the World Philatelic Exhibition in China which took place between August 21 and 30, 1999 (Fig. 3-12.36). The hologram depicts *'SWISS POST' in front of a set of radial lines*. The block shows Chillon Castle and its reflection in Lake Geneva. On the right side of the sheet there is a pagoda reflected in Slender West Lake, Yangzhou, China. The legendary Bridge 24 (24 m long, 24 dm wide, 24 jade balusters, 24 steps on each side) serves as a link between two sides of the sheet. This sheet exists only on a silk-lined Chinese-size (230x120 mm) envelope (Fig. 3-12.37). Hansjörg Anderegg designed the sheet and Hélio Courvoisier S.A. printed the stamp.

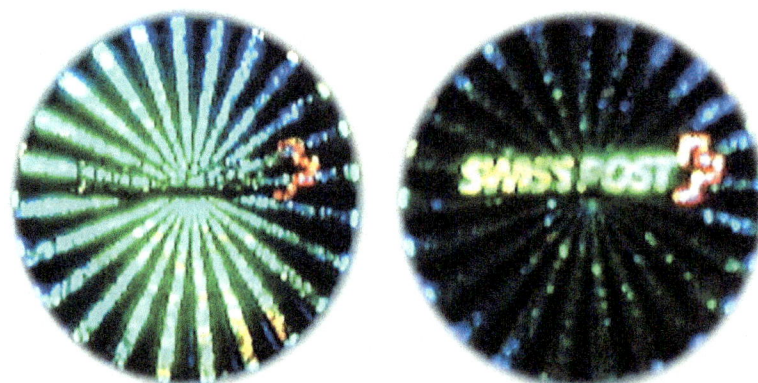

Fig. 3-12.35. The circular hologram on the stamp.

Fig. 3-12.36. The Chinese-Swiss souvenir sheet.

Fig. 3-12.37. The souvenir sheet on the silk-lined envelope.

Malaysia issued on **August 30, 1999**, a souvenir sheet with a RM5 stamp of the 452 m high *Petronas Twin Towers* as a beautiful hologram (Fig. 3-12.38, **No. 106**). The sheet features the Malaysian flag 'Stripes of Glory' above a night scene of the Kuala Lumpur skyline (Fig. 3-12.39). They were issued in limited edition and individually numbered sheets. In addition three other stamps were issued; a 30-sen stamp which features the twin Towers on a clear day; a 50-sen stamp which shows wire frame drawings of the architectural structures of the Twin Towers; and a 1RM stamp which features the Towers lit up at night. The 88-storey PETRONAS TWIN TOWERS building was designed by the architect Cesar Pelli. The stainless steel cladding of the towers' exterior gives the appearance of silver ribbons and glass which reflects the sunlight and sparkles like a multi-faceted diamond. A 58.4 meter sky bridge at levels 41 and 42 links the towers at 170 meter above street level. Each tower is served by 29 double-decker high speed lifts that can carry passengers to the top floors in less than two minutes. Tower 1 houses the corporate headquarters of Petroleum Nasional Berhad (PETRONAS), the national oil corporation of Malaysia and the owner of the Twin Towers. CBN Worldwide Sdn designed the souvenir sheet. De La Rue Holographics in England produced the holograms. Crown Agents Stamp Bureau and Walsall Security Printers, UK, printed the sheets. An imperforated variation of the souvenir sheet is shown in Fig. 3-12.40. Two FDCs are shown in Fig. 3-12.41, one very special limited-edition (10000) FDC with a PEWTER cachet stamp. Another FDC with an imperforated souvenir sheet on a plastic foil envelope covered with holographic *stars*. This FDC has a thin Wooden Petronas Twin Towers relief cachet decoration, as shown in Fig. 3-12.42.

Fig. 3-12.38. *Petronas Twin Towers* hologram stamp.

Fig. 3-12.39. Souvenir sheet from Malaysia.

Fig. 3-12.40. The souvenir sheet with the imperforated hologram stamp.

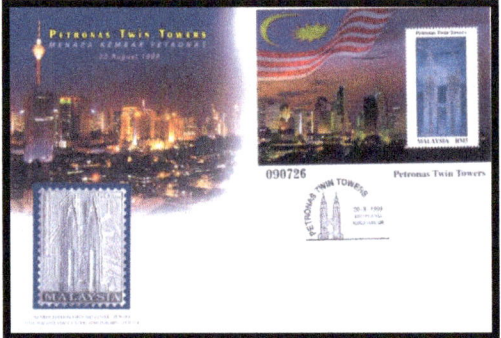

Fig. 3-12.41. Two *Petronas Twin Towers* hologram souvenir sheet FDCs.

Fig. 3-12.42. The Petronas Twin Towers FDC with *stars* and Wooden Petronas Twin Towers cachet decoration.

During the Stamp Collecting Month in **Australia** a miniature sheet was issued on **October 1, 1999**. It was the 'Small Pond' with six stamps featuring the following creatures: Javelin Frog, Roth's Tree Frog, Northern Dwarf Tree Frog, Magnificent Tree Frog, Sacred Kingfisher and a Dragonfly (*Rhyothemis graphiptera,* Rambur). The *Dragonfly's wings* are created with pieces of shimmering foil (**No.107**). This spectacular insect has brightly colored wings and is very fast-flying (up to about 60 km/h). The souvenir sheet shows a little pond from the Kimberley region of northern Australia. The sheet was designed by Cathleen Cram and Kevin Stead made the animal illustrations for the small pond stamps. His paintings are so lifelike that they are often mistaken for photographs. Stead used real frogs and photos of frogs as his inspiration for this sheet, which took him six months and 250 pages of sketches to complete. The souvenir sheet is shown in Fig. 3-12.43.

Fig. 3-12.43. 'Small pond' souvenir sheet with the *dragonfly's wings* hologram stamp.

 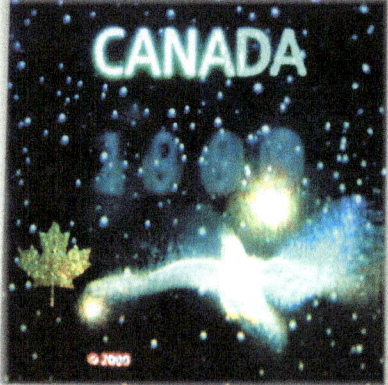 

Fig. 3-12.44. Photographs recorded from three different directions of the animated hologram stamp.

Fig. 3-12.45. The four hologram stamp sheet.   **Fig. 3-12.46.** Keepsake hologram stamp.

In 1999 **Canada** issued its second definitive hologram stamp on **October 12, 1999**. These self-adhesive hologram stamps are very interesting and were issued with two other stamps to celebrate the new Millennium. [26- 28] These stamps were part of the Official Millennium Keepsake by Canada Post. The animated 3D hologram pictures a *dove in flight*, marking the momentous passage from 1999 to 2000 (Fig. 3-12.44). The hologram depicts the graceful motion of the dove's brilliant wings which was captured in 60 photographic frames. It also shows a *star field*, the years *1999-2000*, '*Canada*' and the *Canadian Maple Leaf*. The hologram is based on 60 computer-generated images of the dove in flight. The self-adhesive stamp was issued in miniature sheets of four stamps (Fig. 3-12.45, **No. 108**). There was also the 'Keepsake edition' with the special hologram (Fig. 3-12.46, **No. 109**). The keepsake package is shown in Fig. 3-12.47. The FDC with a hologram stamp is shown in Fig.3-12.48. Uncut press sheets were also issued, each featuring nine souvenir sheets, and signed by Canada Post's Chairman of the Board, André Ovellett (Fig. 3-12.49). Georges de Passillé from Canada Post and Pierre-Yves Pelletier designed the holographic stamps. George Sivy, Image Engine, Utah, made the computer-generated animation for the holographic stereogram using Nichimen and Lightwave software programs. Thomas Cvetkovich of Chromagem Inc. (USA) made the shims for the hologram embossing. Crown Roll Leaf (USA) produced the embossed holograms. Patrick Choquet of Gravure Choquet and Crown Canada attached the hologram to the stamps. Ashton-Potter in Canada printed the stamps.

Fig. 3-12.47. 'The Official Keepsake' from Canada Post.

Fig. 3-12.48. FDC with hologram stamp from Canada.

Fig. 3-12.49. Limited-edition uncut press sheet signed by Canada Post's Chairman of the Board, André Ovellett.

On **October 14, 1999, Germany** issued its first definitive stamps with a hologram in a series titled 'Cosmos'. Two of the semipostal stamps have a hologram. [29] The stamps were issued to support the German Federal Association of Free Welfare Work (Sozialwerk Wohlfahrtsmarken der Bundesarbeitsgemeinschaft der Freien Wohlfahrtpflege e.V.). In 1999, this charity organization celebrated its 50th year. The support in 1999 was for the victims of the Turkish earthquake. The 110-Pf hologram stamp (**No. 110**) shows a *comet collision with Jupiter* (Fig. 3-12.50). Comet Shoemaker-Levy 9 collided with Jupiter in 1994. After one orbit the comet was ripped apart and plunged into Jupiter's atmosphere. From July 16 until July 22, 1994, fragments of the comet collided with the planet, with dramatic effect. The hologram is produced from the actual infrared images recorded in the evening of July 16, 1994, through the Calar Alto 3.5-m telescope in Spain using the Max-Planck-Institute Infrared (2.3 μm) Camera. The images were recorded by Douglas Hamilton, University of Maryland. The hologram shows the first fragments of the comet colliding with Jupiter and later a bright cloud over the impact area is visible (lower left of the planet). The bright object to the right of the planet is the Galilean satellite Io. Pawel Stepien of Holografia Polska, Poland, made a 3D computer-generated hologram based on 100 recorded images of the collision. Irina Menz at Holographic Systems München GmbH recorded the master plate for this hologram as well as for the other COSMOS stamp. The 300-Pf stamp (**No. 111**) shows a satellite above the Earth and *our Milky Way in gamma light radiation* as observed from the Earth (Fig. 3-12.51). This image was recorded by the Gamma telescope COMPTEL onboard the NASA Compton Observatory (CGRO, Compton Gamma-Ray Observatory). The two holographic stamps were included in a set of five space-related stamps. One of them features an x-ray image of an exploding star, another the Andromeda galaxy and the third the Swan constellation. An extra 50 Pf for charity is added to the 110-Pf holographic stamp and 100 Pf value to the 300-Pf holographic stamp. The COSMOS stamps were designed by Benjamin Blasé and Applied Holographics

Plc in England embossed the two different holograms. The Bundesdrukerei GmbH in Berlin applied the holograms and printed the stamps in sheets of ten. In Fig. 3-12.52 four photographs of the animated hologram show the approaching comet and the impact on the surface of Jupiter. The two ten-stamp sheets are shown in Fig. 3-12.53. The FDC with all five COSMOS stamps is shown in Fig. 3-12.54 and in Fig. 3-12.55 part of the presentation folder with the two hologram stamps are reproduced.

Fig. 3-12.50. German stamp with *Jupiter* hologram.

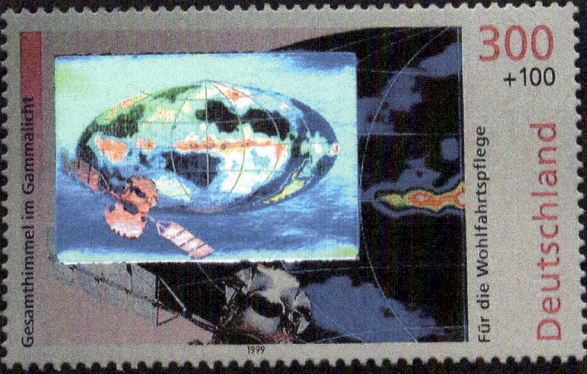

Fig. 3-12.51. German stamp with *Gamma telescope* image.

Impact

Fig. 3-12.52. Four photographs of the animated hologram showing the approaching comet and the impact on the surface of Jupiter. The approaching comet is visible in the lower left side of the planet and in the third photo the impact is clearly visible. The white object on the right side of the planet is its moon Io.

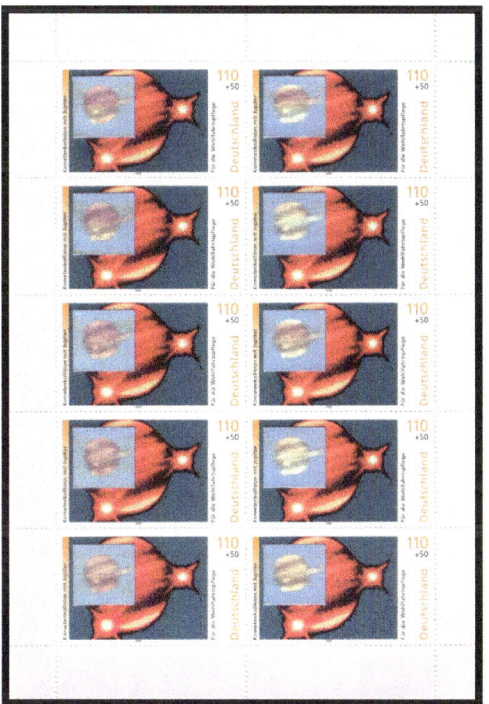

Fig. 3-12.53. The two ten-hologram stamp sheets.

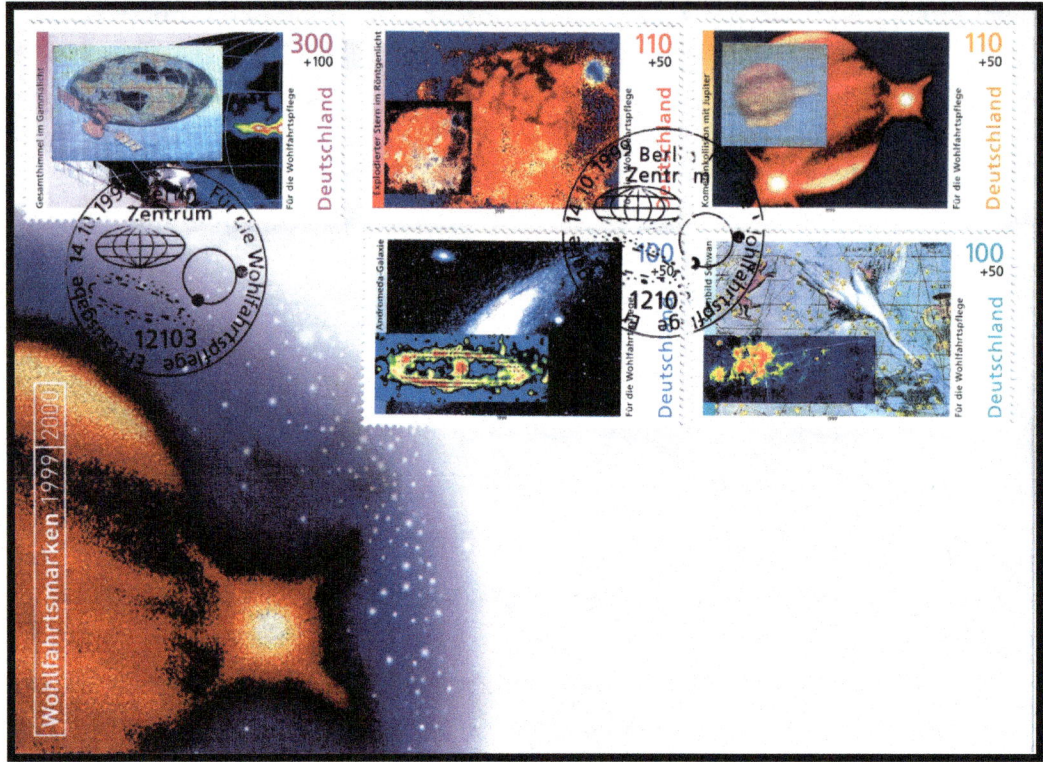

Fig. 3-12.54. The German FDC with all five Cosmos stamps.

Fig. 3-12.55. Part of the presentation folder with the two hologram stamps.

Fig. 3-13.56. The two-channel hologram switching between *1999* and *2000*.   **Fig. 3-13.57.** The author on the stamp.

Fig. 3-12.58. One of the 'Celebrate 2000' FDCs issued.

Fig. 3-12.59. A prepaid postcard with a stamp on the front.

Australia issued a definitive two-channel hologram (dot-matrix) stamp. The stamps were issued on **November 1, 1999**. Australia issued this stamp to celebrate the Millennium shift and the year 2000. The two-channel hologram shifts between *1999* and *2000* (Fig. 3-12.55) with *fireworks* in the background. The stamp itself features colorful fireworks (**No. 112**). Fig. 3-12.58 depicts one of several issued FDCs. This special FDC was issued on January 1, 2000 by GPO Sydney with two stamps, one with a December 31, 1999 cancellation and one with a January 1, 2000 cancellation. A prepaid postcard with a stamp on the front of the card is shown in Fig. 3-12.59. 'Celebrate 2000' sheets of ten stamps as well as sheets of twenty stamps were printed. This stamp was also available as a personalized stamp.[30] For example, a digital photo could be printed on the tab of the stamp (here the author, Fig. 3-12.57). This photo on the tab was recorded during 'The Stamp Show 2000' in London which took place between May 23 and 28, 2000. This new service and technology came from Sprintpak, Australia Post's stamp production division and Excel Digital. The digital photo is printed on the tab with Fuji Xerox Docucolor. The author's personalized stamps were printed in sheets of twenty (Fig. 3-12.60). The Australian stamp was designed by Chris Shurey. The stamps were produced by Applied Holographics Plc in cooperation with Avon Graphics. The stamps were printed by SNP Ausprint.

Fig. 3-12.60. The World's first personalized 'Celebrate 2000' twenty-stamp sheet.

Fig. 3-12.61. The 'Small Pond' STAMPEX overprinted sheets.

On **November 5, 1999**, **Australia** issued several overprinted versions of the 'Small Pond' souvenir sheet for the STAMPEX exhibition in Adelaide, which took place between November 5 and 7, 1999, at the Ridley Centre, Wayville Showgrounds, Adelaide. One souvenir sheet was with gold overprint (**No.113**). The other one (**No. 114**) was a souvenir sheet with black overprint and the STAMPEX logo. The two overprinted sheets are shown in Fig. 3-12.61. The Victorian Philatelic Council (VPC) issued on October 24, 1999, a very limited edition (250-300) overprinted 'Small Pond' sheet for the 46th Annual Congress at the ANDA Show.

Fig. 3-12.62. The overprinted Macau souvenir sheet.

On **December 19, 1999**, **Macau** issued an overprinted version of the Macau telecommunications souvenir sheet (**No. 115**). Both black and gold overprinted versions were issued for the MACAU 1999 in China – Shanghai stamp exhibition. The gold lettering in both Portuguese and Chinese appears in the upper left corner of the sheet (Fig. 3-12.62).

The last country to issue a souvenir sheet with a 3D hologram stamp in 1999 was **Namibia**. The N$9 stamp was issued on **December 31, 1999**, to celebrate the new millennium (**No. 116**). A circular hologram of the *Earth* is located in the center of the stamp (Fig. 3-12.63). This TURN OF THE MILLENNIUM sheet shown in Fig. 3-12.64 was designed by J. J. Koos van Ellinckhuijzen. The hologram was produced by OpSec (UK) and printed by Joh. Enschedé Security Printers, The Netherlands. The FDC is shown in Fig. 3-12.65.

Fig. 3-12.63. The Earth hologram.

Fig. 3-12.64. The Namibia souvenir sheet.

Fig. 3-12.65. The souvenir sheet on the FDC envelope.

3-13. Holographic stamps and souvenir sheets issued in 2000

As was the case in the preceding year, 2000 was also a year when many definitive stamps and souvenir sheets were issued. As it was the first year of the new Millennium, Post Authorities around the world wanted to do something special which in many cases resulted in adding holograms to stamps. Finland, a country that had already issued many hologram stamps, issued also new hologram stamps that year. Hungary, another country with several previously issued hologram stamps, issued a special Gabor souvenir sheet with a two-channel hologram and other interesting features. An important event in the USA was the issue of several hologram stamps, including a round hologram stamp and other space-related hologram stamps. At the end of the year innovative hologram stamps were issued in Hong Kong.

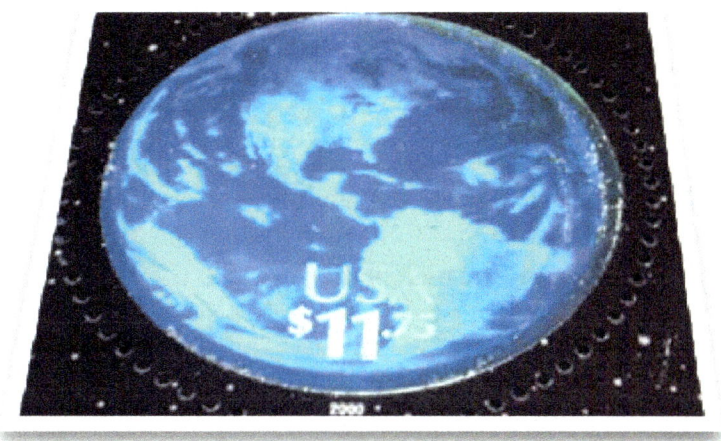

Fig. 3-13.1. Millennium envelope from South Africa.

South Africa issued a millennium 2000 envelope on **January 1**, **2000**. There is a 'standard postage millennium stamp' on the envelope with Johannesburg cancellation. *2000 millennium* is printed on the lower left side of envelope using holographic foil (Fig. 3-13.1). The envelope is marked 6.112.

In **Singapore** on **January 1**, **2000**, a set of four se-tenant stamps and a miniature sheet were issued (Fig. 3-13.2, **No. 117**). The 'Stamping the new Millennium' stamps and souvenir sheet depict information technology, arts and culture, heritage and globalization, captured on stamps: Singapore's aspiration and progress in the new millennium. At the top margin of the sheet, *SINGAPORE 2000* appears in holographic foil letters. Sylvia S. H. Tan designed the sheet and Hélio Courvoisier S.A., Switzerland, printed them. The FDC is shown in Fig. 3-13.3.

Fig. 3-13.2. Souvenir sheet from Singapore.

Fig. 3-13.3. Souvenir sheet FDC from Singapore.

Fig. 3-13.4. Czech Republic year 2000 official postcard. **Fig. 3-13.5**. Postfila postcard 'THE STAMP SHOW 2000' in London.

Czech Republic continued to issue prepaid postcards with holograms (**No.83**), for example, a postcard 'Prague – European Cultural Capital for the Year 2000' which was issued on **January 3**, **2000** (Fig. 3-13.4). Like the postcards issued in 1999, the first address line contains micro text, an additional security feature in addition to the hologram. An example of a postcard of the Postfila type is shown in Fig. 3-13.5. This card was issued on May 22, 2000, for THE STAMP SHOW 2000 in London. The Postfila postcards were officially issued by postal service for national or international events where the Czech Republic philatelic service participated. Eight official postcards, eleven Postfila cards and over one hundred private cards were issued this year in the Czech Republic.

The 1999 Australian Millenium hologram stamps (**No. 112**) have been promoted at many stamps shows during 2000. This was the stamp which could be personalized by having a photo printed on the stamp tab. This was probably that reason why it was available at the shows since it was possible to have photos taken and personalized sheets printed at the shows. An example of one of the many stamp shows around the world was the CANBERRA STAMP SHOW 2000 for which **Australia** issued a ten-stamp sheet on **March 18**, **2000**, shown in Fig. 3-13.6. The Canberra show took place between March18 and 20, 2000. At THE STAMP SHOW 2000 in London, which took place between May 23 and 28, 2000, the author had his personalized stamp sheets printed (see Figs. 3-12.57 and 3-12.60).

Fig. 3-13.6. The 'CANBERRA STAMP SHOW' sheet.

Fig. 3.13.7. Reissued 'Small Pond' souvenir sheet overprinted for BANGKOK 2000.

For BANGKOK 2000, **Australia** reissued on **March 25**, **2000**, the 'Small Pond' souvenir sheet (**No. 118**). The BANGKOK 2000 exhibition took place between March 25 and April 3 for which this new overprinted mini-sheet was issued (Fig. 3-13.7). Compare this overprinted one with the souvenir sheet in Fig. 3-12.43. Another reissue of the Small Pond souvenir sheet was for the Canberra Stamp Show 2000 - Supporters Club. This issue was limited to only 100 sheets and issued on **March 18**, **2000**.

For the fifth time hologram stamps were issued in **Finland**. This time it was a three-stamp miniature sheet, each stamp denominated FIM 3.50. It happened on **May 30**, **2000**, when the 'Mathematical Thinking Science Sheet' was released (**No. 119**). [31] The stamps of the sheet form the Tangram Puzzle - an ancient Chinese puzzle. The purpose is to form two smaller squares of equivalent sizes by reorganizing the pieces of the puzzle. The stamps are basic geometrical units: a triangle stamp features girls in a laboratory with molecular structure models in the background, representing science education. A parallelogram has DNA research as its topic, and a square with four-color pattern over eyes symbolizing digital communication, part of Sierpinski triangle aerial. The triangular shaped hologram label, which is not one of the stamps, is shown in Fig. 3-13.8 and features a set of *triangles of different sizes*. The sheet shows the Heureka Science Center in Finland (Fig. 3-13.9). The sheet was designed by Susanna Rumpu and Ari Lakaniemi with photographs by Matti Lehto, Kirill Lorech, and Harri Hietala. The hologram was produced by OpSec (UK) and the sheet printed by Joh. Enschedé Security Printers, the Netherlands. The FDC is shown in Fig. 3-13.10.

Fig. 3-13.8. Hologram.

Fig. 3-13.9. Heureka Science Center souvenir sheet.

Fig. 3-13.10. The new FDC, the fifth time Finland issued holographic stamps.

On **June 13**, **2000**, **Hungary** reissued the 1994 PHILKOREA Cinderella sheet to commemorate the Korean summit which took place between June 13 and 15 in Korea (Fig. 3-13.11, **No. 120**). The stamp issued by Kft Budapest, is overprinted with the following Hungarian inscription: 'Koreai csucstalalkozo Phenjan 2000.VI.13-15' which means 'Korean summit'. Compare this one with the sheet issued in 1994, shown in Fig. 3-7.23.

Fig. 3-13.11. Reissued Hungarian Cinderella sheet for the Korean Summit in 2000.

Fig. 3-13.12. Monaco Sydney 2000 Olympic stamps with holographic foil.

Monaco issued a set of two stamps (**No. 121** and **122**) for the Sydney 2000 Olympics on **June 23**, **2000**. The *Olympic Rings* and *SYDNEY* are of holographic foil. The fencing and rowing stamps were designed by Prat and are shown in Fig. 3-13.12.

Hungary issued an innovative 2000-ft holographic Millennium miniature sheet on **June 30, 2000**, to celebrate Dennis Gabor's (1900-1979) 100-year-birthday (**No. 123**). [32] The round hologram at the lower left corner of the sheet is a two-channel hologram. One image is a *portrait of Gabor* (visible when illuminated from the top of the stamp) and the other is a *drawing of the holographic principle* (when illuminated from the left side of the stamp) as shown in Fig. 3-13.13. This miniature sheet is a real philatelic curiosity. It was made with offset, UV and screen-printing using OEI inks, which was used for the first time in Hungarian stamp printing. Some of the motifs on the sheet can be seen only under UV light. On the miniature sheet everything takes place under the 'aegis of numbers'. The main motif is the number 2000 depicted as a part of the universe and in it there is the blue planet. The Earth is surrounded by elliptical orbits which are built up of Roman numerals and year numbers described with the application of different number systems (Fig. 3-13.14). Moving the miniature sheet, on the upper right and left sides, the Roman numerals 'XX' and 'XXI' can be seen in fields changing from blue to green, symbolizing the turn of the millennium. Each sheet is serially numbered in black. Under UV light the black serial numbers turn into green by fluorescence. Along the stamp perforation: 'Jeles magyar matematikusok' [outstanding Hungarian mathematicians] can be read, as can the names of 57 famous Hungarian mathematicians. Károly Vagyóczky designed the stamp which was printed by the State Printing House, Budapest. Hologram Kft (Miklós Varga) was responsible for the hologram. The FDC is shown in Fig. 3-13.15.

Fig. 3-13.13. Two-channel *Gabor* hologram.

Fig. 3-13.14. Gabor souvenir sheet from Hungary.

Fig. 3-13.15. Gabor FDC with Hungarian souvenir sheet.

On **July 6**, **2000**, the 'Legends of Baseball' 33¢ stamps were issued in the **USA**. The US Postal Service honored 20 nominees for the 'Major League Baseball All-Century Team' with a 20-stamp sheet. The following baseball legends are depicted: George Sisler, Ty Cobb, Christy Mathewson, Eddie Collins, Jackie Robinson, Roberto Clemente, Walter Johnson, Babe Ruth, Mickey Cochrane, Rogers Hornsby, Pie Traynor, Jimmie Foxx, Cy Young, Tris Speaker, Lefty Grove, Lou Gehrig, Dizzy Dean, Josh Gibson, Honus Wagner, and Satchel Paige. Fig. 3-13.16 shows the Ty Cobb FDC with a cachet 2D/3D *baseball player* hologram produced by Light Impressions Inc. in 1987.

Fig. 3-13.16. FDC with the Ty Cobb stamp and a cachet 2D/3D baseball hologram.

Fig. 3-13.17. Private overprinted limited-edition (2771/4000) butterfly sheet.

An overprinted **private** version of the 1991 *butterfly* souvenir sheet was issued during the WORLD STAMP EXPO 2000, July 7-16, 2000, in Anaheim, California. This limited edition of 4000 sheets was issued on **July 7, 2000** (**No. 124**). The se-tenant stamps were first issued in **Poland** in 1991 (See Fig. 3-4.21). The Phila Nippon'91 logotype is overprinted with EXPO 2000 and on the top of the sheet is printed in black: Anaheim, CA July 7-16, 2000. In addition, these sheets are numbered at the lower right corner (Fig. 3-13.17). Please note that on January 15, 1994, this block was withdrawn by the Polish Post by the administrative order #96, dated November 30, 1993. [11]

Mongolia issued a WWF (World Wide Fund for Nature) souvenir sheet at 'Anaheim EXPO 2000' on **July 7, 2000**. The sheet consists of two sets of four different 2D/3D hologram stamps, denomination 50, 100, 200, 250 Tugrik. The four stamps depict *Przewalski's Wild Horses (Equus przewalskii)* shown in Fig. 3-13.18, (**No. 125** through **128**). The WWF panda logo is printed at the four corners of the sheet. The sheet was designed by Owen Bell. Figure 3-13.17 shows the four hologram stamps on the sheet. The eight-stamp sheet is shown in Fig. 3-13.19 (**No. 129**). One of the four FDC envelopes and one of the four FDC cards are shown in Figs. 3-13.20 and 3-13.21.

Fig. 3-13.19. The four hologram stamps of *Przewalski's Wild Horses*.

Fig. 3-13.19. Souvenir sheet from Mongolia.

Fig. 3-13.20. FDC envelope.

Fig. 3-13.21. FDC postcard.

The first American definitive stamps with holograms were issued in the **USA** at the Anaheim EXPO 2000. [33,34] These stamps were the main attractions at the stamp show. The stamps are in a series of stamps issued for SPACE ACHIEVEMENT AND EXPLORATION. The first round stamp ever issued in the USA is also a hologram stamp. The round souvenir sheet was issued on **July 7, 2000** (**No. 130**). The round stamp depicts a *view of Earth from space, with the North American continent centered in the upper part of the globe. $11.75*, the denomination, is also part of the holographic image (Fig. 3-13.22). This hologram contains microtext, only visible through a magnifying lens (Fig. 3-13.23). It is located east of the top of Brazil over the ocean, just above one of the cloud formations and consists of the letters *USPS*. The round souvenir sheet, shown in Fig. 3-13.24, includes the circular hologram stamp in the middle, surrounded by perforations and a wide dark ring, which changes into a green outer ring bearing two lines of text: 'SPACE ACHIEVEMENT AND EXPLORATION' around the top, and 'WORLD STAMP EXPO 2000' around the bottom. Two samples of FDCs with this hologram are shown in Fig. 3-13.25. There was also one FDC issued with an ASDA cachet *Earth* hologram by Colorano, which is shown in Fig. 3-13.26. This hologram was previously used on the 1992 'Space Accomplishments' FDC, shown in Fig. 3-5.16.

Fig. 3-13.22. The circular hologram on the round US stamp

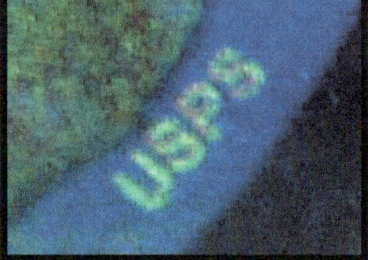

Fig. 3-13.23. Microprint: USPS.

Fig. 3-13.24. USA's first round stamp with the hologram in the center.

Fig. 3-13.25. Two different FDCs with the round hologram stamps.

Fig. 3-13.26. A cachet *Earth* hologram on one of the FDCs.

Fig. 3-13.27. *Landing on the Moon* hologram stamp.

Fig. 3-13.28. Microprint: USPS.

The next day, on **July 8, 2000**, the LANDING ON THE MOON stamp was issued. This sheet, with a hologram of the *Lunar Excursion Module (LEM), a few feet above the Moon surface against the symbolic backdrop of an immense moon rising over the horizon* is shown in Fig. 3-13.27. When the stamp is moved up and down, the flame seems to burst out of the lander's rocket nozzle and change color, from a bright red-orange to a deep blue-violet. This hologram also contains micro-printing, only visible through a magnifying lens (Fig. 3-13.28). It is located on the door near the center of the lunar lander and consists of the letters *USPS* arranged vertically. This holographic stamp is rectangular and the holographic image includes also the denomination *$11.75*. (**No.131**). The sheet shows an April 1972 photograph of Apollo 16 lunar module pilot Charles M. Duke Jr. on the Moon collecting lunar samples at the rim of Plum crater near Descartes landing site (Fig. 3-13.29). The photo was taken by mission commander John W. Young. Lettering on the sheet to the left of Duke reads: 'LANDING ON THE MOON'. One example of a FDC with this stamp is shown in Fig. 3-13.33 together with two 'ESCAPING THE GRAVITY OF EARTH' FDCs.

Fig. 3-13.29. Landing on the Moon sheet with hologram stamp.

Fig. 3-13.30. *Space Shuttle docking* hologram.

Fig. 3-13.31. *Astronauts outside Space Station* hologram.

Fig. 3-13.32. Escaping the Gravity of Earth souvenir sheet with two hologram stamps.

On **July 9**, **2000**, the 'ESCAPING THE GRAVITY OF EARTH' souvenir sheet was issued. It has two adjacent rectangular stamps with holograms. The design on the stamp at left, based on a computer generated NASA image, depicts the *Space Shuttle docking with the orbiting International Space Station (ISS) above Earth with Mexico's Yucatan peninsula visible in the foreground and partly concealed by the station is the peninsula of Florida* (Fig. 3-13.30). This hologram also has the micro-printed *USPS* letters included in the image, only visible through magnification, which is located on the top right-hand corner of the Earth, close to the tip of the rightmost solar panel of the space station. The stamp at right, based on a NASA artist's conception of the station, shows a closer view of *two astronauts at work outside the space station's cabin module* (Fig. 3-13.31). Both holographic images contain also the denomination *$3.20*. (**No. 132**). The portrait-format souvenir sheet shows astronauts David Leestma and Dr. Kathryn D. Sullivan in space, working in the open cargo bay outside the shuttle Challenger during mission STS 41-G in October 1984. A view of Earth fills the upper half of the scene (Fig. 3-13.32). Two of the FDCs together with one 'LANDING ON THE MOON' FDC are shown in Fig. 3-13.33.

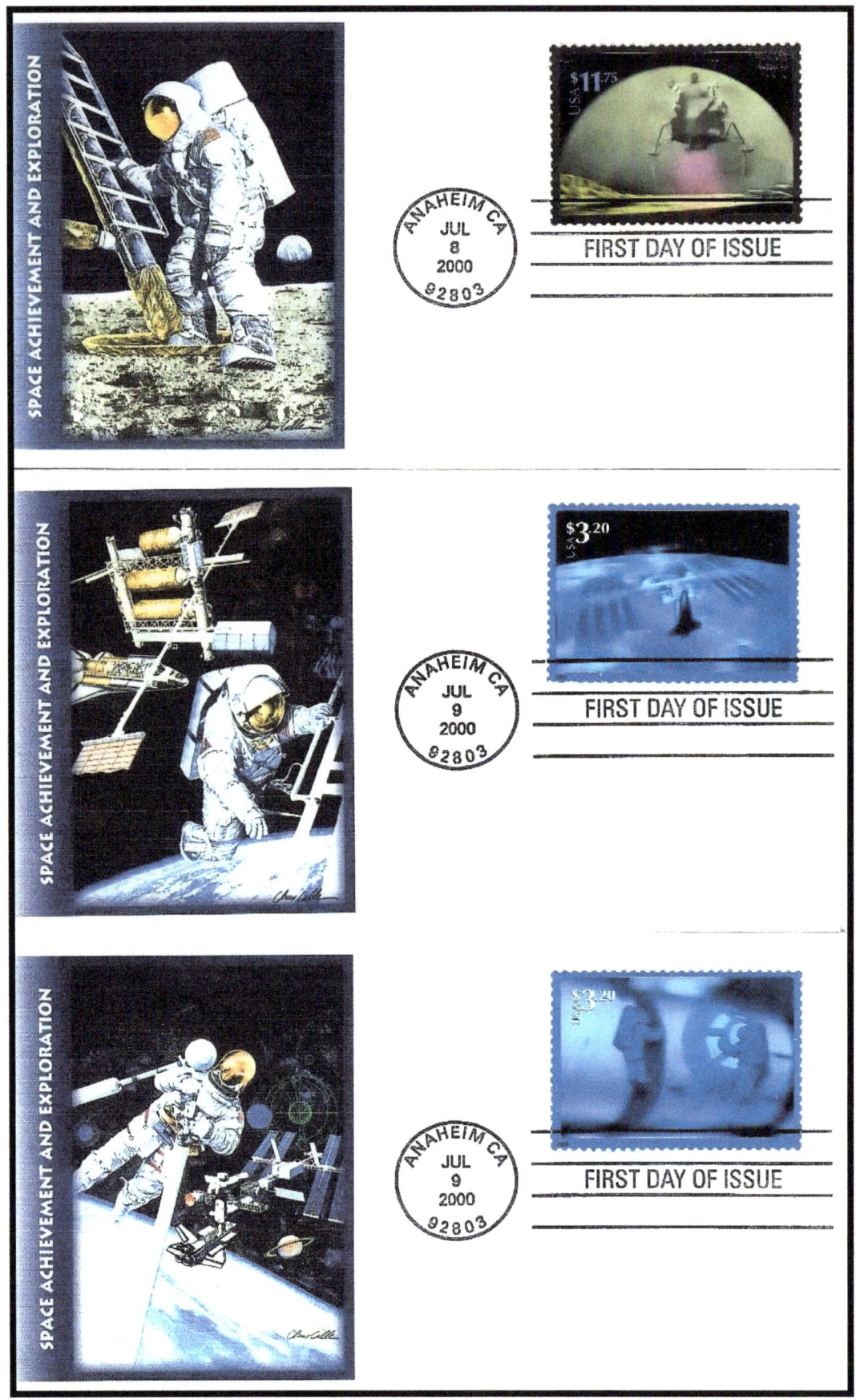

Fig. 3-13.33. Three FDCs with the space hologram stamps.

Fig. 3-13.34. 'SPACE ACHIEVEMENT AND EXPLORATION' uncut press sheet with all 15 stamps.

A large, 40 cm by 50 cm, uncut press sheet was released on **July 13, 2000 (No. 133)**. The sheet contains the five souvenir sheets with a total of 15 stamps, including the three sheets with the four holograms (Fig. 3-13.34). A total of two million of each of the five sheets were manufactured, split into 1.695 million individual souvenir sheets and 305 thousand to be included in the uncut press sheet.

The non-holographic stamps on the other two souvenir sheets in this series are related to 'PROBING THE VASTNESS OF SPACE' and 'EXPLORING THE SOLAR SYSTEM.' The first one (issued July 10) has six stamps of different telescopes and observatories against a backdrop of Eagle nebula. The second one (issued July 11) contains five pentagonal postage stamps depicting various views of the sun against a backdrop of the Moon, Saturn and an array of stars.

The four US holographic stamps were created by a team of people and companies to realize the vision of Dick Sennett, founder and retired CEO of Sennett Security Products. The designer of the stamps, Richard Sheaff, Dana Sheaff & Co., Scottsdale, AZ, worked with holographer Fernando Catta-Preta, Trace Holographic Art & Design, Inc., Charlottesville, VA, to design the holographic images. Catta-Preta coordinated the activities involving input from USPS, NASA and the rest of the holographic companies involved. NASA digital images from space were used by Marco Zambetti to create the ISS model and used for some of the holographic images. The LEM hologram, for example, was recreated as a model from a NASA image and shot as an achromatic 3D image against a background with a color chasing flame burst to slow down its descent. Allen Suffield of Aztec Model Makers Ltd in England was responsible for the lunar lander model used to record the hologram. The Earth hologram and the Space Station holograms were based on digital images converted into holographic images. Thomas Cvetkovich, Chromagem Inc, Youngstown, OH, worked with Blue Ridge Holographics, Charlottesville, VA, to create the masters for the holograms. Wavefront Technology, Paramount, CA, recombined the images and Foilmark, through its Holopak OVD Security Solutions Division, located in

East Brunswick, NJ, embossed all the holograms. Engraver was Southern Gravure, Franklin, TN. The printing contractor, Sennett Security Products, Chantilly, VA, converted and finished the final product. The stamps were printed by American Packaging Corp., Columbus, WI, and processed at Unique Binders, Fredericksburg, VA. The intention to include micro printing in the holograms was not really to deter counterfeiting, but to show the increased level of security possible with holograms. The hologram itself is a very good security device. According to the USPS, the space stamp edition marks the most significant scientific achievement, so far, undertaken by the US Postal Service.

Fig. 3-13.35. Australian space-themed stamps with holographic foil.

Fig. 3-13.36. Two space sheets overprinted in gold and silver.

Space-themed stamps and a miniature sheet were issued in **Australia** on **October 3**, **2000**. The 45c stamps present a view of life on Mars in the not-too-distant future. These six stamps on the sheet were issued for 'Stamp Collecting Month'. Two large stamps are entitled 'Launch site and Spacecraft', two commemorative sized stamps are entitled 'Astronaut and Terrain', and two small stamps are entitled 'Flight Crew and Robots'. The miniature sheet, which combines these stamps into a single view of 'Space Settlement' features translucent diffractive foil on the spacecraft and the astronaut's visors (Fig. 3-13.35, **No. 134**). One FDC for the miniature sheet was issued. Two overprinted versions (one in gold and one in silver, **No. 135**) of this sheet were issued on **October 22**, **2000**, for the ANDA show in Melbourne, the '47th Annual Victorian Philatelic Congress' (Fig. 3-13.36).

In **October 27**, **2000**, a red sheet of self-adhesive Christmas Seals with holograms were issued by **Åland** Post Office (**No. 136**). The self-adhesive stamps were designed by Pirkko Vahtero. The four holograms are cut in the shape of a *bell*, a *candle*, a *ball*, and a *bird* (Fig. 3-13.37). Printed on the stamps is: 'God Jul ÅLAND' which means 'Merry Christmas ÅLAND'. The sheet contains 20 stamps. The profit deriving from the sale is used for charity and in 2000 it supported The First Heart Association in Åland 'Vårt Hjärta r.f.' Cartor Security Printers printed the stamp sheets (Fig. 3-13.38).

Fig. 3-13.37. The four 2000 Christmas Seals with holographic foil.

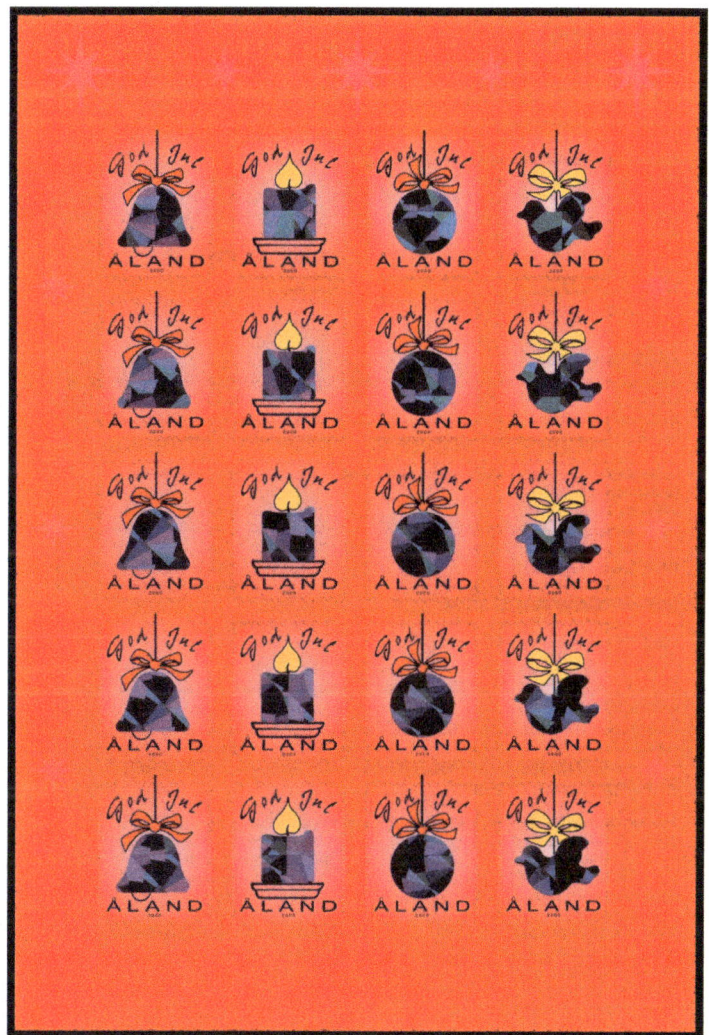

Fig. 3-13.38. The 20-stamp Christmas Seal sheet.

France issued a definitive stamp on **December 9, 2000 (No. 137)**. The 4.50 Fr (0.96€) stamp is marked MÉTALLURGIE 1999-2000. An image of the *Eiffel tower* is created using holographic foil and shown in Fig. 3-13.39. There is also a rocket next to the Eiffel tower. The stamp was designed by Jean-Paul Cousin. The FDC is shown in Fig. 3-13.40 and an A4 presentation sheet in Fig. 3-13.41.

Fig. 3-13.39. Métallurgie stamp.　　　　**Fig. 3-13.40.** Métallurgie FDC.

Fig. 3-13.41. French Métallurgie A4 presentation sheet.

On **December 31**, **2000**, **Hong Kong** issued a postage sheet with two hologram stamps to celebrate the advent of 21st Century (Fig. 3-13.42, **No. 138** and Fig. 3-13.43, **No. 139**). [35] The innovative hologram stamp sheetlet contains two different complex 2D/3D hologram stamps. One hologram is a definitive stamp in a new rendition of the Landmarks definitive HK$20. It depicts the *Hong Kong Convention Center and Exhibition Center* (Fig. 3-13.44) when illuminated from above. When illuminated from the left side, the following text is visible along the bottom right side: *HONG KONG CONNVENTION AND EXHIBITION CENTER* (Fig. 3-13.45). The long vertical hologram on the shetlet depicts the transformation of Hong Kong from the 20th century to the 21st century. It incorporates colorful 3D effects *showing changes in landscape and major buildings* during different times of the century, together with special effects showing *fireworks* (Fig. 3-13.46). This multi-channel hologram contains *airport runway lighting* and animation of the *landing of an airplane* at the Hong Kong International Airport at Chek Lap Kok, illustrated in Fig. 3-13.46. This hologram stamp was the largest one (size: 135mm x 40 mm) used on a stamp sheetlet up until 2000. Colin Tillyer designed the definite stamp and the sheetlet was designed by Liliane Tsui. Cantor Security Printing in France printed the sheet.

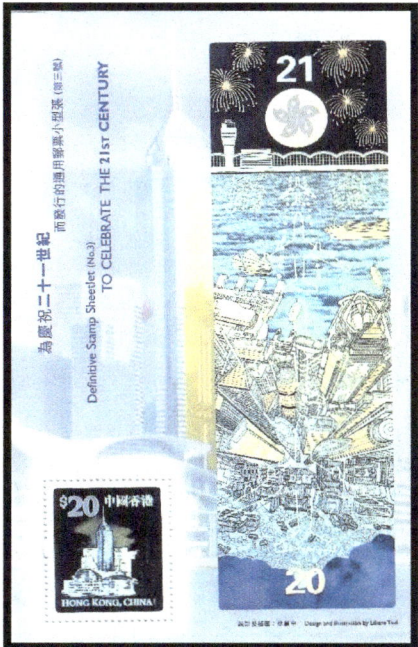
Fig. 3-13.42. Hong Kong souvenir sheet.

Fig. 3-13.43. Large hologram stamp.

Fig. 3-13.44. Hong Kong hologram stamp when illuminated from above.

Fig. 3-13.45. Hong Kong hologram stamp when illuminated from the left side.

Fig. 3-13.46. Animation of an airplane landing.

3-14. Holographic stamps and souvenir sheets issued in 2001

The number of hologram stamps and souvenir sheets issued just before and after the millennium shift reached a peak. During 2001 rather few hologram stamps were issued. However, three new countries issued definitive hologram stamps for the first time: Belarus, Libya and Great Britain. Australia also issued a hologram stamp that year, and postcards with a security hologram were issued in Greece.

 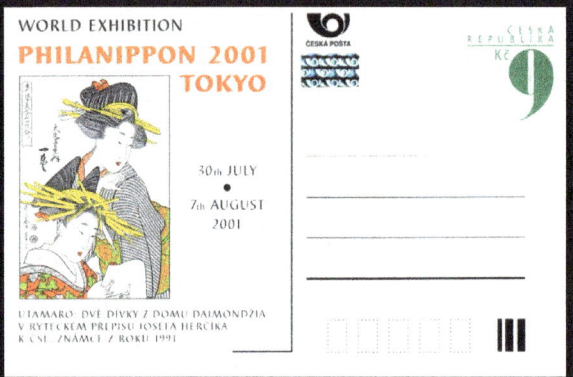

Fig. 3-14.1. Czech Republic European Union official postcard. **Fig. 3-14.2.** Postfila postcard 'PHILANIPPON 2001' in Tokyo.

Czech Republic continued to issue prepaid postcards with holograms, for example, the 5.40-kc postcard 'European Union' which was issued on **January 2, 2001**. Like previously issued postcards, the first address line contains microtext, an additional security feature in addition to the hologram. An example of a Postfila postcard is shown in Fig. 3-14.2. This postcard was issued on July 30, 2001, for 'PHILANIPPON 2001' in Tokyo. The Postfila postcards were officially issued by postal service for national or international events where the Czech Republic philatelic service participated. Ten official postcards, thirteen Postfila cards and about eighty private cards were issued in 2001.

Australia issued on **January 8, 2001**, two Christmas Island stamps and a mini-sheet commemorating the lunar New Year: Year of the Snake 2001, shown in Fig. 3-14.3. The *snake* on the $1.35 stamp is formed using holographic foil (**No. 140** through **142**). The upper part of the *Year of the Snake 2001* sheet is printed using holographic foil as well as the Chinese version of it. The stamps were designed by Luis Chiang, Philatelic Group, Australia Post Headquarters in Melbourne.

Fig. 3-14.3. Christmas Island souvenir sheet with holographic foil printing.

Fig. 3-14.4. Overprinted Space miniature sheet issued for 'Hong Kong 2001.'

Once again, on **February 1, 2001, Australia** issued an overprinted version (with the conference logo using gold foil located in the lower left corner, **No. 143**) of the Space miniature sheet first issued in **Australia** on October 3, 2000 (See Fig. 3-13.34). This version was for stamp exhibition 'Hong Kong 2001' Stamp Exhibition, shown in Fig. 3-14.4.

On **April 24, 2001, Australia** issued a series of five 'Colour My Day' stamps with tabs. The four normal stamps issued: Let's Party, Smile, Leaps and Bounds, and Bayulu Banner. One of them, named 'Celebrate 2001', has a holographic foil attached (Fig. 3-14.5, **No. 144**). This 45c-stamp celebrates the 'real' millennium with some reference to celebrating nationhood on the centenary of Federation. The hologram features *abstract streamers*. The stamp was designed by Janet Boschen of the Australia Post Design Studio. There are two versions of these stamps, one with a tab which can be personalized with a photo, and one with a tab with a continuation of the same design as the stamp itself. The other stamps were designed by Jimmy Chan, Chris Shurey and Doug Pitt. The FDC with all five stamps is shown in Fig. 3-14.6.

Fig. 3-14.5. The 'Celebrate 2000' stamp with holographic foil.

Fig. 3-14.6. 'Colour My Day' FDC.

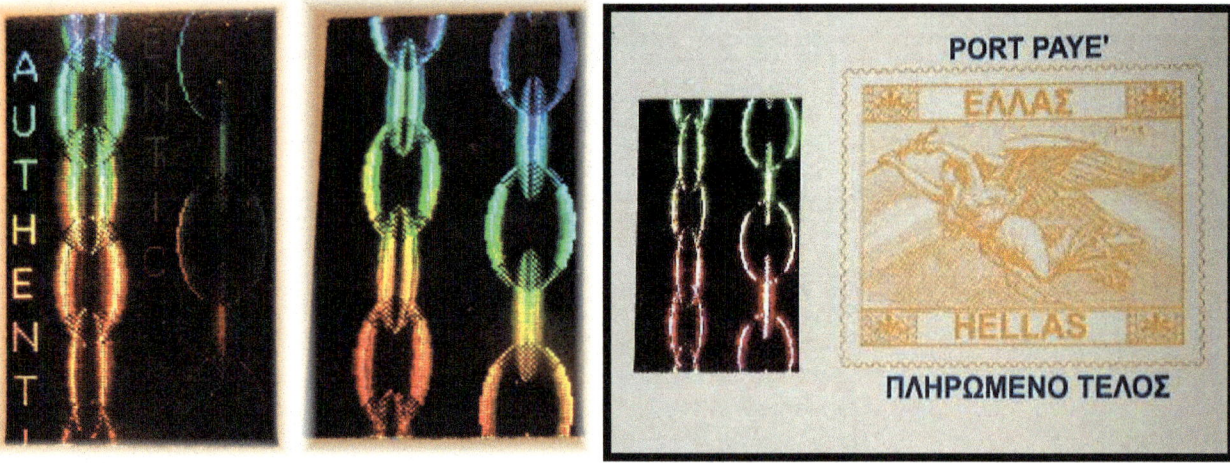

Fig. 3-14.7. Holographic label observed from the left side and the right side located next to the printed stamp.

Fig. 3-14.8. Some of the postcards issued in Greece.

The Hellenic Post in **Greece** issued in **June 2001** three different sets of prepaid glossy postcards with a holographic label next to a printed stamp on the address side. The holographic label depicts *vertical chains* when observed from the right side. When viewed from the left side, *AUTHENTIC* is visible next to the chains (Fig. 3-14.7). The position of text in the holograms varies from card to card, which means that often only part of *AUTHENTIC* is visible. The postcard photos were provided by Studio Kontos and printed by Alex Matsoukis S.A. The postcards were designed by Hellenic Post's Advertising and Sales Promotion Division. The following postcards were produced: Acropolis (4) and Sounio (1) Vergina (2) and Epidavros, a set of 4. Two of the Acropolis postcards, one of the Vergina and the Sounio one are shown in Fig. 3-14.8. The holograms were produced by Applied Holographics Plc and printed by Matsoukis Graphic Arts Printing Company in Greece.

Fig. 3-14.9. Belarus hologram stamp.

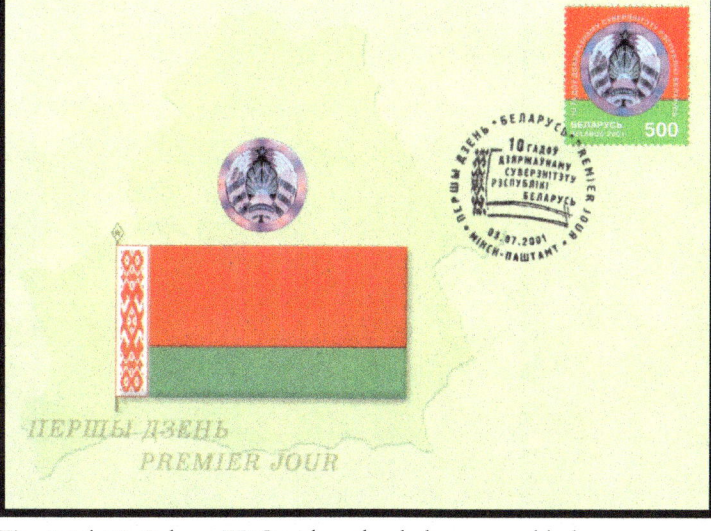

Fig. 3-14.10. Belarus FDC with cachet hologram and hologram stamp.

Fig. 3-14.11. Belarus 30-stamp sheet.

On **July 3**, **2001**, **Belarus** issued a 500-br holographic stamp to celebrate its 10th anniversary (Fig. 3-14.9, **No. 145**). The hologram features the *Belarus coat-of-arms*. The stamp was designed by O. Gaico. There were two FDC versions: one with a cachet hologram and one without a hologram. The hologram on the stamp was also used as the cachet hologram. The FDC with the cachet hologram is shown in Fig. 3-14.10 and a 30-stamp sheet in Fig. 3-14.11.

Fig. 3-14.12. 2001 '32nd Anniversary of September Revolution' sheet with 16 stamps.

On **September 1**, **2001**, **Libya**, officially the Great Socialist People's Libyan Arab Jamahiriya, issued a large sheet with 16 stamps for the '32nd Anniversary of September Revolution' shown in Fig. 3-14.12 (**No. 146**). The stamp nomination on the souvenir sheet is 100 dirhams each. Colonel Muhammar Gaddafi is featured on some of these stamps. Figure 3-14.13 shows the holographic diffractive effect. In addition, two small souvenir-sheets, 300 dirhams each were also issued, one with a gold foil stamp and one with a silver foil stamp (**No. 147** and **148**). In the lower left corner of these stamps is a hologram with *20 small circles* (Ø2 mm). The nomination '300' is printed in the middle of the hologram. One such Colonel Muhammar Gaddafi stamp is shown in Fig. 3-14.14 and the silver version souvenir sheet is shown in Fig. 3-14.15. The stamps and sheets were designed by M.A. Siala. The FDC with the silver and gold stamps are shown in Fig. 3-14.16. There is also another hologram on the FDC, which is a cachet hologram. This diffractive foil hologram stamp, size 40 mm x 40 mm, has simulated perforation and a 'MAP OF LIBYA' in the middle and under it LIBYA, both printed in green. This cachet hologram has appeared on several FDCs issued during 1995 – 2000. All the FDCs with this cachet hologram were not officially issued by the Libyan Post authority and should not be regarded as an item of philatelic value. However, the hologram may have been attached to an official FDC and placed on top of the printed logo. [36]

Fig. 3-14.13. The holographic diffractive effect.　　**Fig. 3-14.14.** The minisheet holographic diffractive effect.

Fig. 3-14.15. 2001 '32nd Anniversary of September Revolution' minisheet.

Fig. 3-14.16. 2001 '32nd Anniversary of September Revolution' FDC.

Fig. 3-14.17. Reissued overprinted Kyrgyzstan souvenir sheet.

On **September 11, 2001, Kyrgyzstan** re-issued the 1999 Corsac souvenir sheet supporting WWF, World Wide Fund for Nature (**No. 149**). The holograms of *foxes* are unevenly cut and attached to the four se-tenant stamps. The sheet is overprinted in gold: '40th Anniversary 1961 – 2001' at the top of the sheet as well as at the bottom of each stamp. The four 10 som stamps are overprinted with the new denomination 25.00 som. The two 30 som and the two 50 som stamps are not overprinted. This sheet was issued for the 'International Stamp Exhibition in 2001'. The holograms were produced by 3D AG in Switzerland and the sheets printed by GOSZNAK in Moscow. The overprinted sheet is shown in Fig. 3-14.17 to be compared with the original 1999 sheet in Fig. 3-12.9.

On **September 20, 2001**, two prepaid postcards (size: 148 mm x 105 mm) were issued in **Switzerland** to honor Marcus Pfister the author of successful children's books, for example, The Rainbow Fish. His books have been published in several languages and distributed in many countries. In the books the rainbow fish has beautiful shimmering scales made of diffractive holographic foil. The rainbow fish with the *holographic gills* is feature on the two postcards. One card is the CHF 0.70 'Rainbow fish swimming alone' and the other card is the CHF 0.90 'Rainbow fish with starfish'. On the address side is the imprinted stamp, each stamp with corresponding image as is on the picture side. They are also marked with the nomination and HELVETIA. The cards were designed by Markus Pfister, Spiegel bei Bern, and printed by Nord-Süd Verlag AG, Gossau. The two 'Rainbow Fish' postcards are shown in Fig. 3-14.18.

Fig. 3-14.18. The two 'Rainbow Fish' postcards.

Fig. 3-14.19. The *boron molecule* hologram stamp.

Royal Mail in **Great Britain** issued a definitive hologram stamp as part of a series of six stamps to recognize the great work done by British Nobel Prize laureates over the last hundred years. [37] The stamps were issued on **October 2, 2001**. The following five non-holographic stamps were included: 2nd Class NVI (19p) – Chemistry, A carbon 60 molecule, Sir Howard Kroto was awarded a Nobel Prize for discovery of this class of molecule; 1st Class NVI (27p) - Economic Sciences, A world view in Intaglio; E Rate NVI (37p) - Peace. The Peace Nobel Prize is represented by a white dove; 40p - Physiology or Medicine. This is the first scented stamp issued by Royal Mail. It emits the unique medicinal smell of eucalyptus; 45p - Literature. The Nobel Laureate for 1948, T.S. Eliot, has his entire poem, 'The Ad-dressing of Cats' micro-printed on this stamp. The stamp with a hologram is a 65p - Physics stamp. This stamp was issued to honor Dennis Gabor* who was awarded the Physics Nobel Prize for holography in 1971. An animated hologram of a *boron molecule* is attached to the stamp (Fig. 3-14.19, **No. 150**). 'PHYSICS - Nobel Prize 100th Anniversary' is printed at the bottom of the stamp. When the hologram stamp is tilted, the electrons in the boron molecule are spinning. One half of the issued 50-stamp sheets is shown in Fig. 3-14.20 and the presentation pack with all five stamps in Fig. 3-14.21. The stamps were designed by HGV and printed by Joh. Enschedé Security Printers, The Netherlands. The hologram, produced by OVD Kinegram of Switzerland, was added to the printed stamp by Enschedé. Two FDCs are shown in Fig. 3-14.22. Special FDCs were issued in Great Britain. One of them was with a cachet reproduction of the Hungarian 1988 Gabor stamp (see Fig. 3-1.7) shown in Fig. 3-14.23. Another FDC was the limited-edition (5000) 'Nobel Prize Centenary 1901-2001' cover produced by Tony Buckingham. In addition to the six stamps there is a £2 coin included in this FDC. This FDC is shown in Fig. 3-14.24. There was also the Benham limited-edition (5000) FDC, shown in Fig. 3-14.25, with the stamps attached to a photo of the Concert Hall in Stockholm, Sweden, and a photo of Alfred Nobel on the cover.

---

* Dennis Gabor was born in Budapest, Hungary, on June 5, 1900. In 1933 Gabor was invited to Britain to work at the British Thomson-Houston company in Rugby, Warwickshire. He became a British citizen in 1946, and it was while working at British Thomson-Houston that he invented holography in 1947. He died in London on February 2, 1979.

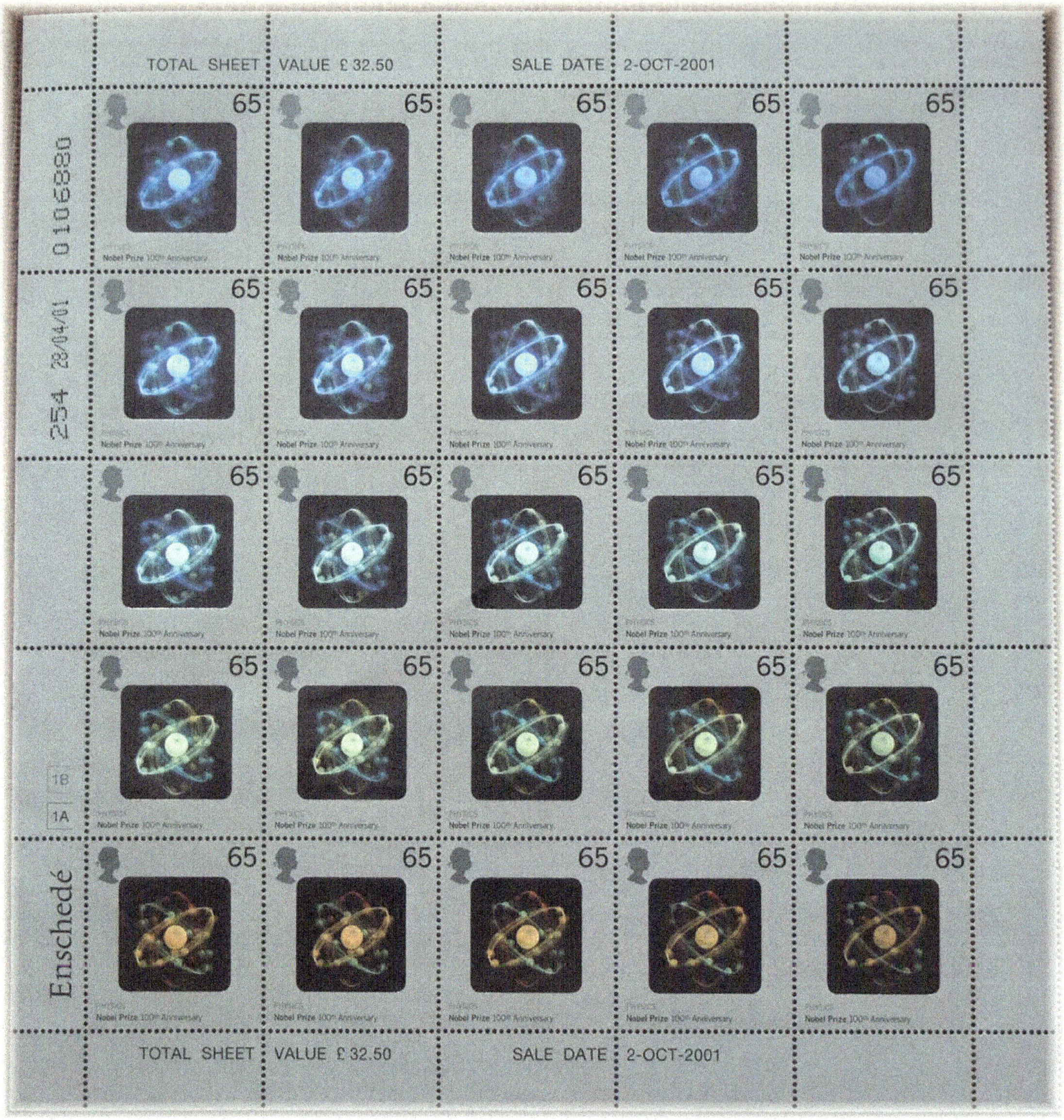

Fig. 3-14.20. The *boron molecule* 25-stamp sheet.

Fig. 3-14.21. The Nobel Prize six-stamp presentation pack.

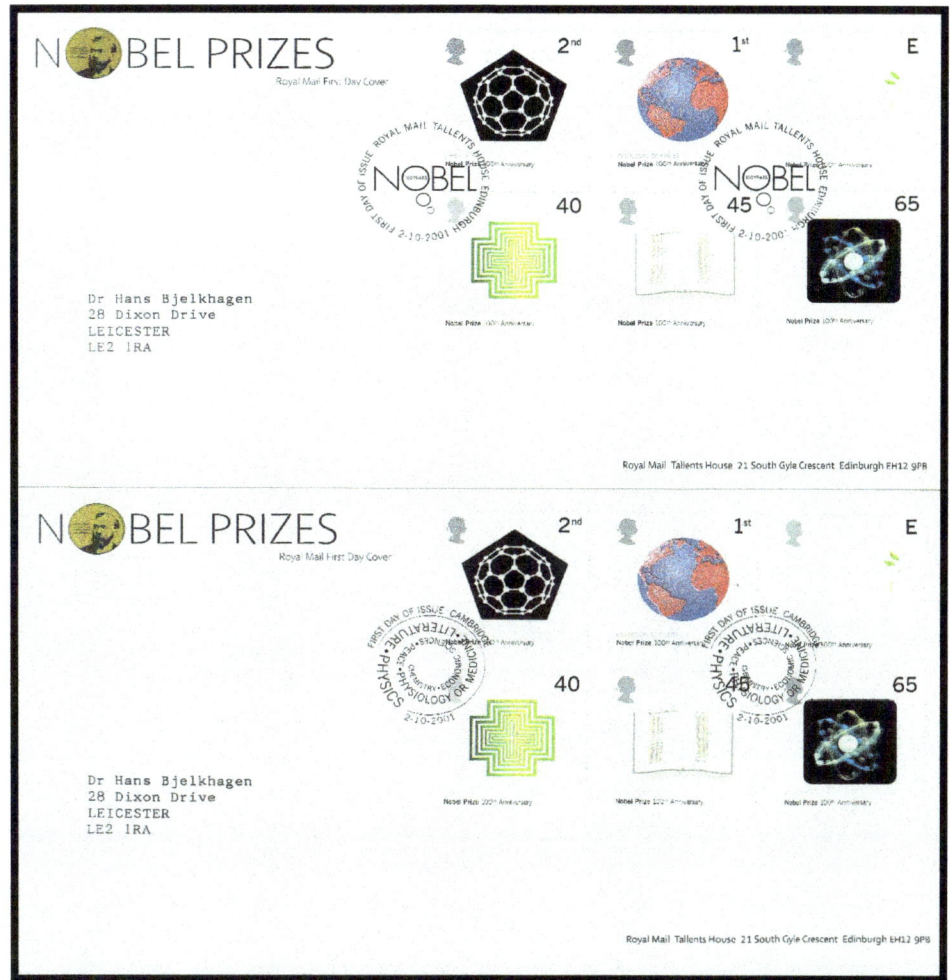

Fig. 3-14.22. Two UK Nobel Prize FDCs with the five issued stamps and different cancellations.

Fig. 3-14.23. The Gabor Nobel Prize Centenary FDC with the hologram stamp.

Fig. 3-14.24. The limited-edition (1093/5000) Tony Buckingham Nobel Prize Centenary FDC.

Fig. 3-14.25. The Bentham limited-edition (1358/5000) Nobel Prize Centenary FDC.

Fig. 3-14.26. The four Christmas Seals with holographic foil.

Fig. 3-14.27. The 20-stamp Christmas Seals sheet.

On **October 16**, **2001**, a green sheet of self-adhesive Christmas Seals with holograms were issued by **Åland** Post Office (Fig. 3-14.26, **No. 151**). The self-adhesive green stamps designed by Pirkko Vahtero depict four Christmas tree decorations. The holograms are cut in the shape of a *heart*, an *angel*, a *cracker*, and a *gingerbread cookie*. Printed on the stamps is: 'God Jul ÅLAND' which means 'Merry Christmas ÅLAND'. The 20-stamp sheet is shown in Fig. 3-14.27. The profit deriving from the sale is used for charity and in 2001 it supported the Åland children's foundation, 'Ålands barnfond r.f., Östersjöfonden.'

3-15. Holographic stamps and souvenir sheets issued in 2002

Switzerland issued definitive hologram stamps for the first time in 2002. Romania issued a limited-edition souvenir sheets with holograms when Romania was invited to join NATO. Libya issued another set of holographic foil stamps that year. Åland continued to issue Christmas seals, and both Singapore and Hong Kong issued Christmas stamps with holographic foil decoration.

Fig. 3-15.1. Hologram on the Swiss stamp.   **Fig. 3-15.2**. Ten-stamp sheet.

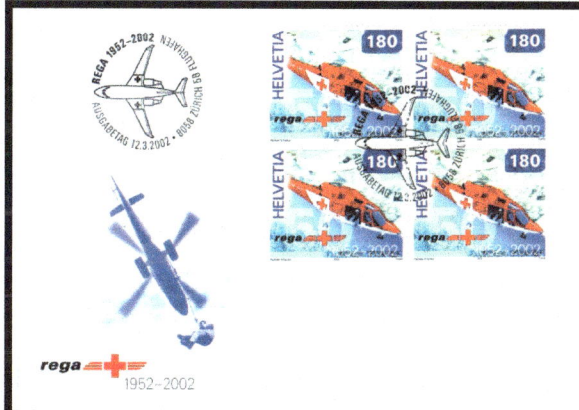

Fig. 3-15.3. The FDC with four of the Swiss hologram stamps.   **Fig. 3-15.4**. The FDC card with the Swiss hologram stamp.

Switzerland issued its first definitive hologram stamp on **March 12, 2002, (No. 152)**. [38] The stamp was issued to celebrate the 50-year anniversary of the Red Cross and Swiss Air Rescue Service (REGA). The stamp shows a helicopter in the sky. The *rotor* of an Augusta A-109-K2 helicopter on the stamp is holographic. The triangular hologram attached at the upper right part of the stamp depicts an *ambulance aircraft (Hawker 800 B) above mountain landscape* (Fig. 3-15.1). The stamps were designed by Rapaël Schenker and printed by the French company Cartor Security Printing in La Loupe near Paris. The hologram was produced by Hologram.Industries S.A., Marne-la-Vallée, in cooperation with Cartor Security Printing in France. This type of hologram is called a *gyrogram* which is based on an interference micro lithography technique. A ten-stamp sheet is shown in Fig. 3-15.2, a FDC with four stamps in Fig. 3-15.3 and a presentation card in Fig. 3-15.4.

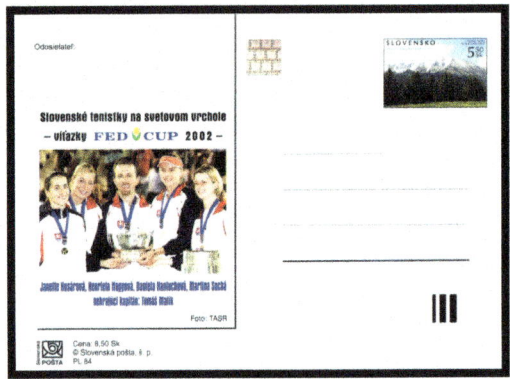
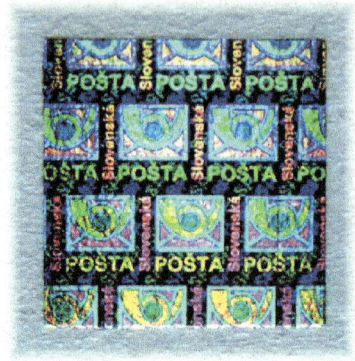

Fig. 3-15.5. A Slovakian 2002 postcard with hologram.   Fig. 3-15.6. Security hologram.

Slovakia started to issue prepaid postcards with a security hologram label. One example of a **2002** card issued (**November 29**) with the *POŠTA Slovenská LOGO* hologram attached is shown in Fig. 3-15.5. The card depicts four Slovak woman top tennis players, Janette Husárová, Henrieta Nagyová, Daniela Hantuchová and Martina Suchá with their captain Tomáš Malík. The newly produced security hologram is shown in Fig. 3-15.6. The card carries also a 5.50-Sk printed stamp. Starting in 2002 and every year thereafter, different cards were issued with the security hologram.

Czech Republic continued to issue prepaid postcards with hologram security labels, for example, sixteen different 5.40 kc postcards 'Architectural monuments in the Czech Republic 2002' on **May 22**, **2002**. Like previously issued postcards, the first address line contains microtext, an additional security feature in addition to the hologram. In addition to the architectural postcards another eight official postcards were issued. Nine Postfila cards and about seventy private cards were also issued in 2002.

The Hellenic Post in **Greece** issued in **June 2002** different prepaid (domestic and international) stationary envelopes with hologram labels next to a printed stamp on the envelope, an example is shown in Fig. 3-15.7. The hologram label in Fig. 3-15.8 depicts *elliptical and square geometric patterns* and is attached under the printed stamp. ITW provided the holographic labels and Matsoukis Graphic Arts Printing Company in Greece was responsible for the printing.

In **September 2002** airmail Christmas envelopes were issued. This time the vertical hologram label was attached on the left side of the printed stamp on the envelope, an example is shown in Fig. 3-15.9. The hologram label in Fig. 3-15.10 shows *Hellenic Post, prepaid product and EΛTA*.

Fig. 3-15.7. Envelope issued in June with an attached hologram label.   Fig. 3-15.8. Hologram label.

Fig. 3-15.9. Christmas envelope with an attached hologram label.   Fig. 3-15.10. Hologram label.

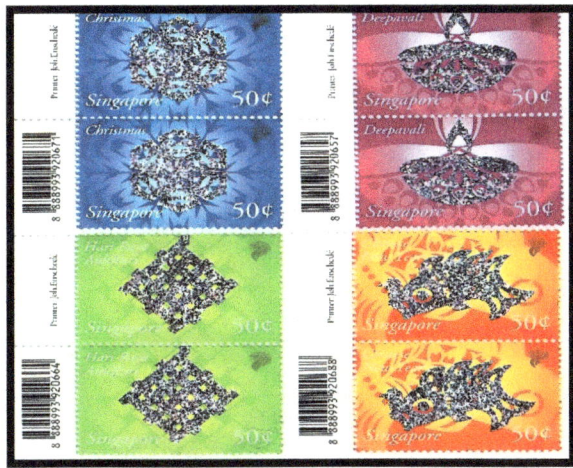

Fig. 3-15.11. Four definitive 50¢ stamps.

Fig. 3-15.12. Four self-adhesive NVI stamps.

Fig. 3-15.13. Singapore Festivals FDC.

On **August 21**, **2002**, **Singapore** issued two different sets of four 'Festivals' stamps for Deepavali (The Festival of Light), Hari Raya Aidilfittri (marks the end of the Muslim fasting month of Ramadan), Christmas and the Chinese New Year (**No. 153** through **160**). One issued set of the four stamps were normal the 50¢ definitive stamps. The other stamps were self-adhesive stamps of two types: 'For Local Addresses Only' (FLAO) and 'No-Value Indicator' (NVI). These stamps have *different shaped icons* made of holographic foil. The figures are icons commonly associated with each festival. Wong Wui Kong designed the stamps which were printed by Joh. Enschedé Security Printers. The two sets of the four stamps are shown in Figs. 3-15.11 and 3-15.12 and the FDC in Fig. 3-15.13.

Fig. 3-15.14. '33rd Anniversary of September Revolution' mini-sheet with 16 stamps.

On **September 1, 2002, Libya** issued like previous year a 16-stamp sheet. This sheet, size 148 mm x 208 mm, was issued for the '33rd Anniversary of 1st September Revolution' and is shown in Fig. 3-15.14 (**No. 161**). The stamp nomination on the souvenir sheet is 100 dirhams each. Colonel Muhammar Gaddafi is featured on some of these stamps. In addition, two small souvenir-sheets, 300 dirhams each were also issued, one with a gold foil stamp and one with a silver foil stamp (**No. 162** and **163**). This time the hologram is attached at the lower right corner. The hologram with *20 small circles* (Ø2 mm) is the same as was used in 2001. The nomination '300' is printed in the middle of the hologram. Figure 3-15.13 shows the gold stamp. The stamps and sheets were designed by M.A. Siala. The FDC with both the silver and gold stamps are shown in Fig. 3-15.16. On the FDC is also the Libyan map cachet hologram which was, as already mentioned, not used on the officially issued FDCs. This cachet hologram has appeared on several FDCs issued during 1995 – 2000. All the FDCs with this cachet hologram should not be regarded as an item of philatelic value.

Fig. 3-15.15. The minisheet with the gold stamp.

Fig. 3-15.16. The FDC with the silver and gold stamps.

For the third year, on **October 9**, 2002, self-adhesive Christmas Seals with holograms were issued by **Åland** Post. (**No. 164**). The four seals depict: a *Christmas tree*; *a Lantern*; *Christmas porridge*, and a *Snowman*. Some areas of them are covered with *holographic foil*. (Fig. 3-15.17). Printed on the stamps is: 'God Jul ÅLAND' which means 'Merry Christmas ÅLAND'. The blue sheet this year contains 20 stamps. The self-adhesive stamps were designed by Pirkko Vahtero and were printed by Cartor Security Printers. One the sheet is shown in Fig. 3-15.18. The profit deriving from the sale is used for charity and in 2002 it supported: 'Ålands Lungskadeförening r.f.,' which will use the contribution for an adaption and recreational camp for families with children suffering from asthma and allergies.

Fig. 3-15.17. The four Åland Christmas seals issued in 2002.

Fig. 3-15.18. The 20-stamp Åland Christmas Seal sheet.

Fig. 3-15.19. The hologram on the stamp.

Fig. 3-15.20. Souvenir sheet No. 2597 from Romania.

Fig. 3-15.21. Souvenir sheet No. 3321 on the limited-edition (166/1000) FDC.

Romania issued a stamp sheet on **November 22, 2002**, which has two identical 131000L stamps with a triangular-shaped hologram attached in the top right corner. The hologram on the stamp depicts *ribbon bands above a star with a leaf underneath* (Fig. 3-15-19). The souvenir sheet was for the 'Romania invited to join NATO' (Fig. 3-15.20, **No. 165**). All stamp sheets are numbered in the left bottom corner. The total edition of souvenir sheets was 49,000 of which 1000 were used for 1000 official FDC covers, one (No. 21) shown in Fig. 3-15.21. The covers are numbered on the back. Octavian Penda designed the stamp sheets and Cartor Security Printing in France printed them.

HOLOGRAPHY AND PHILATELY

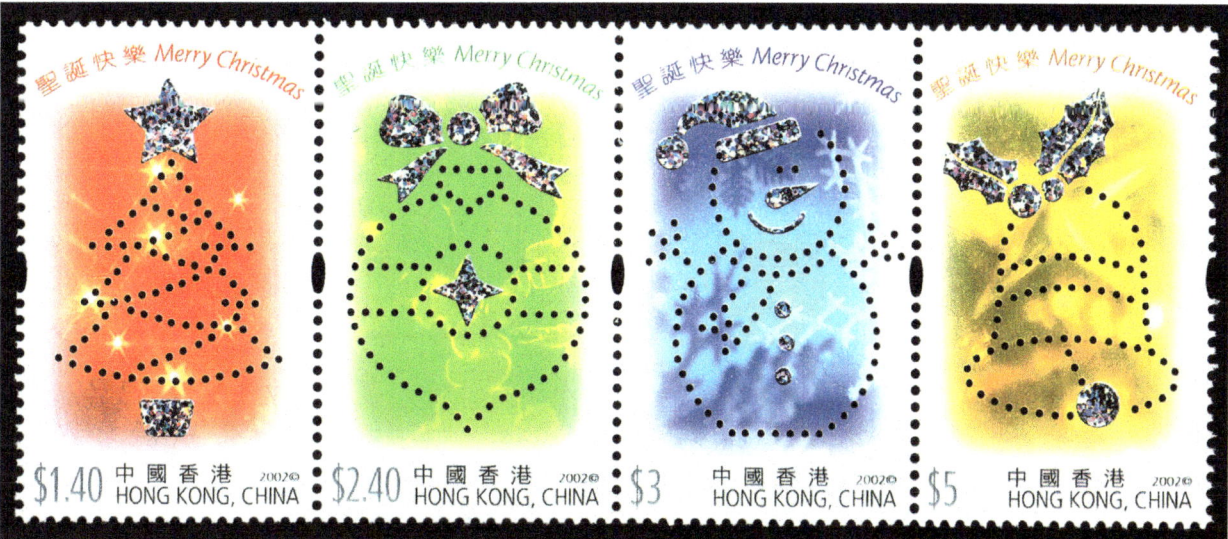

Fig. 3-15.22. Hong Kong Christmas stamps.

Fig. 3-15.23. Hong Kong Christmas stamp sheet.

Hong Kong issued Christmas four stamps on **November 24, 2002** (**No. 166** through **169**). The stamps have the following perforated figures and objects: a *Christmas tree*, a *Christmas tree ornament*, a *bell*, and a *snowman*. Parts of the figures are made out of holographic foil. The nominations are $1.40, $2.40, $3 and $5. 'Merry Christmas' is also printed at the top of each one of them. Four of the stamps are shown in Fig. 3-15.22 and the 16-stamp sheet in Fig. 3-15.23.

3-16. Holographic stamps and souvenir sheets issued in 2003

During 2003 there was an increase in the number of hologram stamps and souvenir sheets. Libya continued issuing stamps covered with colorful holographic foil. Both the United Nation Postal Administration and Slovenia issued definitive hologram stamps for the first time. Portugal issued its first hologram souvenir sheet. Australia, Brazil, Canada and Macau, countries which had issued a number of hologram stamps over many years, all issued new hologram souvenir sheets that year.

Fig. 3-16.1. Examples of two Slovakian 2003 postcards. **Fig. 3-16.2.** Security hologram.

Slovakia continued to issue prepaid postcards with the security hologram label in **2003**. Examples of two cards, the Slovak Nitre Agricultural Museum (issued April 30) and the NITRAFILA Dostnavnikova card (issued June 13), both with the *POŠTA Slovenská LOGO* hologram attached are shown in Fig. 3-16.1. The security hologram is shown in Fig. 3-16.2. There is also a Sk 7 printed stamp on the cards.

Czech Republic continued to issue prepaid postcards with hologram security labels during **2003**. Like previously issued postcards, the first address line contains microtext, an additional security feature in addition to the hologram. Twenty-eight official postcards were issued. Twelve Postfila cards and about fifty private cards were also issued in 2003.

On **March 2**, **2003**, **Libya** issued for the third time holographic stamps, this year it was a mini-sheet with six stamps, 200 dirhams each, size 187 mm x118 mm (**No. 171**). This sheet was issued for the 'People's Authority Declaration' shown in Fig. 3-16.3. Colonel Muhammar Gaddafi is featured on the upper left stamp. The FDC is shown in Fig. 3-16.4.

Fig. 3-16.3. Libya minisheet.

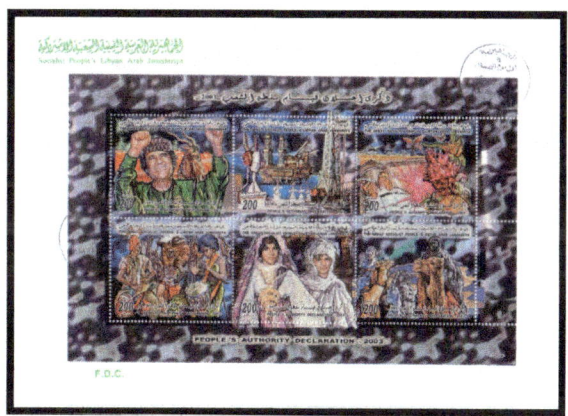

Fig. 3-16.4. The minisheet FDC.

Fig. 3-16.5. UN hologram stamp.

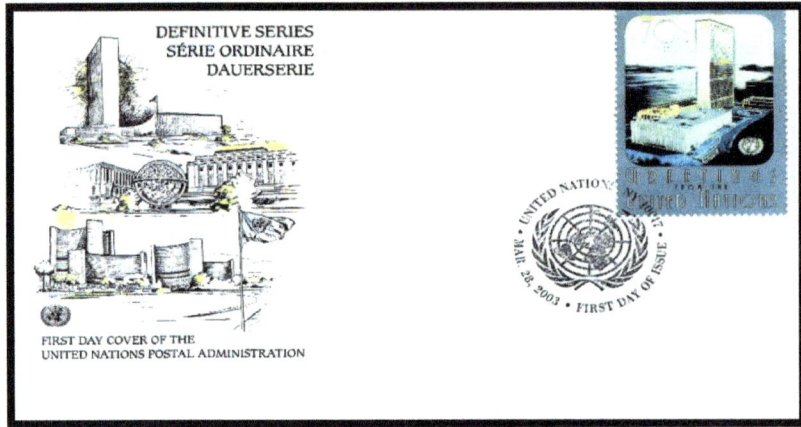

Fig. 3-16.6. FDC with the UN hologram stamp.

Fig. 3-16.7. The *UN New York building* hologram.

United Nations Postal Administration (UNPA) issued a definitive hologram stamp on **March 28, 2003** (Fig. 3-16.5, **No. 172**). The stamp is UNPA's first hologram stamp and was a special New York – UN issue. The hologram on the $0.70 stamp shows the *UN building in New York*. Under the hologram on the stamp is written 'Greetings from the United Nations'. The FDC is shown in Fig. 3-16.6, the attached hologram in Fig. 3-16.7 and in Fig. 3.16.8, the 20-stamp sheet. The stamp was designed by Robert Stein and Rorie Katz at UNPA in New York. The hologram was produced by Walsall Security Printers Ltd in Great Britain.

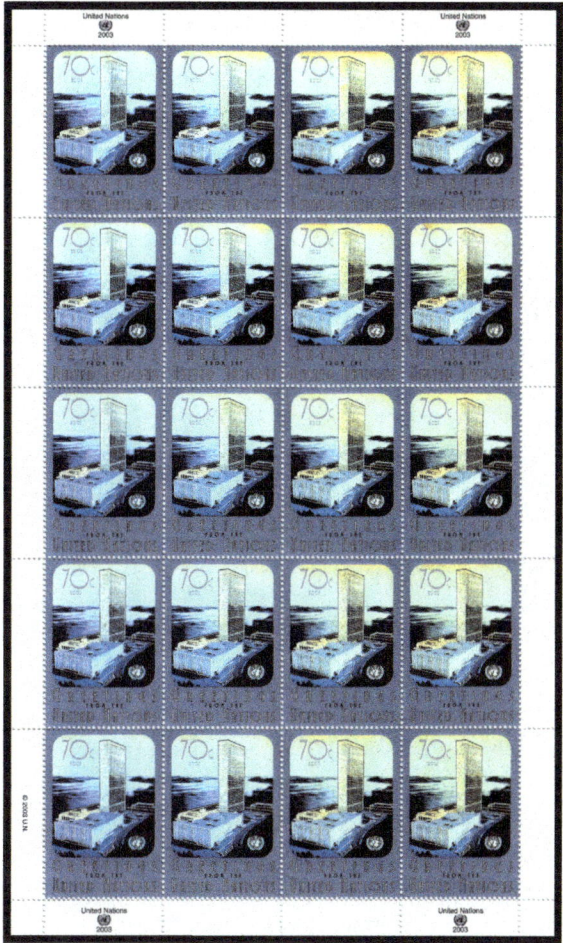

Fig. 3-16.8. UN 20-stamp sheet.

Guernsey issued on **July 3, 2003**, a £5 definitive stamp 'Letters on Stamps' with the letters of the alphabet inside a blue frame (**No.173**). The stamp shown in Fig. 3-16.9 has the *Queen's head*, country name *Guernsey* and the £5 nomination printed in holographic foil giving a 'wave' effect. The alphabet letters are printed in thermochromic ink which fades from pale orange to white when exposed to heat. 'Heat sensitive: please touch' vertically printed on the right side of the stamp. The FDC is shown in Fig. 3-16.10. The stamp was issued in blocks of four stamps, designed by Andrew Fothergill and printed by Joh. Enschedé Security Printers, The Netherlands.

Fig. 3-16.9. The Guernsey stamp.

Fig. 3-16.10. The Guernsey 'Letters on Stamps' FDC.

 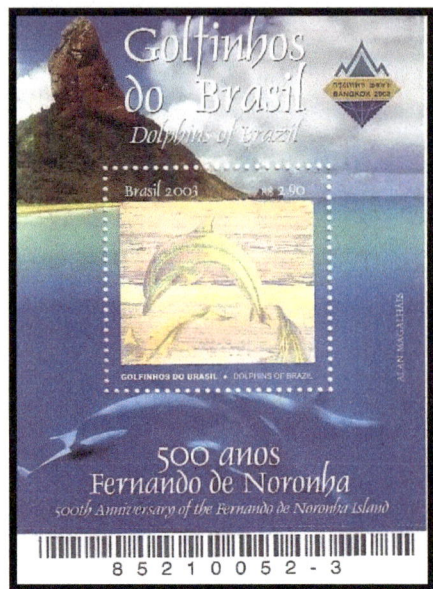

Fig. 3-16.11. *Dolphins* hologram. **Fig. 3-16.12.** Brazil souvenir sheet.

On **August 10**, **2003**, a souvenir sheet was issued in **Brazil**. In the middle of the sheet is a stamp with a hologram of *dolphins* (Fig. 3-16.11, **No. 174**). The Dolphins of Brazil sheet celebrates the 500th anniversary of the Fernando de Noronha Island. This souvenir sheet shown in Fig. 3-16.12 was produced for the Bangkok 2003 stamp exhibition. The island in South Atlantic Ocean, 360 km northeast of Cape São Roque; with its adjacent islets it constitutes part of the Pernambuco state in Brazil. The main island, rising to 332 m, has an area of 26 square km and is of volcanic origin. Given in 1504 to its Portuguese discoverer, Fernando de Noronha, the island later became a dependency of Pernambuco, Brazil. The hologram of the *spinner dolphin* (*Stenella longirostris*) was produced by the Brazilian company Holografica in Cambuci. The stamp was designed by Alan Magahaes and printed by Casa de Moede do Brasil.

To celebrate the 150th Anniversary of the first Portuguese stamp, **Portugal** issued a souvenir sheet on **September 23**, **2003** (**No. 175**) and also to commemorate Francisco de Borja Freire (1790-1869), the designer and engraver of the first Portuguese stamp issued in 1853. Four different souvenir sheets were issued of which one is a stamp with a hologram. The long stamp with the hologram on the souvenir sheet depicts Queen D. Maria II with the Portuguese Mint building in the background. Both Francisco de Borja Freire's signature and the master tool (a 25 reis coin with the Queen's profile) for embossing the first stamp are also featured on the sheet. The hologram stripe across the stamp within the souvenir sheet has *six CTT Portuguese Post Authority Emblems*, with the one on the left side being the first one used and the one on the right side the current symbol. The hologram on the stamp is shown in Fig. 3-16.13 and the souvenir sheet in Fig. 3-16.14. The hologram was produced by INETI in Portugal in cooperation with IMPRENSA NACIONAL CASA DAMOEDA (INCM) – the Portuguese National Press and Mint which printed all four souvenir sheets.

Fig. 3-16.13. *Portuguese Post Authority Emblems* featured in the hologram image on the stamp.

Fig. 3-16.14. Souvenir sheet from Portugal with hologram stamp.

Australia issued on **September 24, 2003**, a 'Bugs and Butterflies' souvenir sheet with translucent foil (**No. 176**). In the olden days (back in the 1970s) Australia Post and collectors used to celebrate Stamp Week. In the early 90s it was decided to take National Stamp Week to new heights and turn it into National Stamp Collecting Month planned to commence in October 1993. And so began Stamp Collecting Month. Now in its 17th year, Stamp Collecting Month has been a cool annual event for kids generally between the ages of six and thirteen. Each year Australia Post celebrates Stamp Collecting Month by bringing out a new stamp issue that has a theme that kids can enjoy and have some fun with. This miniature sheet depicts six different insects; the brilliant blue Ulysses Butterfly (*Papilio Ulysses joesa*); the nymph Leichhardt's Grasshopper (*Petasida ephippigera*); the Vedalia Ladybird (*Rodolia cardinalis*); the Green Mantid (*Orthodera ministralis*) shown with a captive damselfly; the spectacular Emperor Gum Moth Caterpillar (*Opodiphthera eucalypti*); and the beautifully patterned Fiddler Beetle (*Eupoecila australasiae*). The Birdwing Butterfly (*Ornithoptera priamus*), found in Queensland, is featured on the miniature sheet blended into the background picture. The *Birdwing butterfly's wing* has holographic foil pattern attached to it. Also to be found, although perhaps not immediately, are a stick insect, ant, slater, weevil, moth, scorpion, cicada, lacewing, cranefly, centipede, mosquito and dragonfly. These creatures are hidden within the design. This design technique is one of the hallmarks of the work of Graeme Base, Melbourne, who designed the stamps and souvenir sheet. Pack design: Symone Lambert, Australia Post design Studio. The holographic effect on the *butterfly wing* is shown in Fig. 3-16.15 and the souvenir sheet in 3-16.16.

Fig. 3-16.15. Holographic effect.   **Fig. 3-16.16**. Australian 'Bugs and Butterflies' souvenir sheet.

Fig 3-16.17. Canadian space achievements stamps. **Fig. 3-16.18.** Holographic *star*.

Canada issued a sheetlet with eight circular stamps on **October 1, 2003**, shown in Fig. 3-16.17. These 48¢ self-adhesive stamps were issued to celebrate the Canadian Space Program and decades of Canadian achievements and presence in space (**No. 177**). For over 40 years, this country's space program has developed pioneering technologies that have advanced the science of space and helped to improve our world. In the past two decades, eight Canadian astronauts have flown into space aboard NASA's space shuttles, more than any other country except the United States. Garneau was the first among them; he now serves as president of the Canadian Space Agency. To honor the achievements of Canadian astronauts and the space program that has made their work possible, Canada Post issued eight domestic rate (48¢) self-adhesive stamps as a unique stamp pane, each depicting one of our astronauts that have flown in space. With the launch of the satellite Alouette-1 in 1962, Canada entered the space age. Alouette was the first satellite designed and built by a country other than the United States or Russia, and its success established the reputation of Canadian space program. The Canadian Space Agency was formed in 1989 to coordinate space research, technology and the astronaut program. They illustrate how space, technology and education can deliver a better future for all humanity. On each stamp there are photos of the following eight astronauts: Marc Garneau, Roberta Bondar, Steve McLean, Chris Hadfield, Robert Thirsk, Bjarni Tryggvason, Dave Williams, and Julie Payette. In the center of the stamp is a micro-embossed *holographic star* (Fig. 3-16.18). The bottom of the pane illustrates the 'Canadian space handshake' of 2001, when the 'Canadarm2' on the International Space Station transferred its launching cradle to the Canadarm on the shuttle Endeavour, with astronaut Chris Hadfield at the controls. [The Mobile Servicing System (MSS), better known by its primary component Canadarm2, is a robotic system and associated equipment on the International Space Station (ISS)]. The eight stamps were designed by Pierre-Yves Pelletier in spherical shapes that call to mind the path of an orbit. They were based on a photograph provided by Canadian Space Agency. The twinkling star is an image found on the Canadian Space Agency's logo; it represents a productive, energy-producing star, believed to have influence over human destiny. Its twinkling appearance is the result of holographic hot stamping and micro-embossing. Gravure Choquet Inc. was responsible for the embossing and hot-stamping. Lowe Martin Company Inc. printed the stamps.

Fig. 3-16.19. Australian *Bugs and Butterflies* overprinted souvenir sheets.

During 2003 **Australia** issued three overprinted versions of the 'Bugs and Butterflies' minisheet, shown in Fig. 3-16.19 (first issued on September 24, 2003, see Fig. 3-16.3), at the following shows:

October 4, 2003: 2003 World Philatelic Exhibition in Bangkok, October, 4 to 13, **No. 178**,

October 10, 2003: ANDA & APTA Coin, Banknote & Stamp Show in Melbourne, October 10 to 12, **No. 179**,

November 21, 2003: ANDA & APTA Coin, Banknote & Stamp Show in Sydney, November 21 to 23, **No. 182**.

Macau issued on **October 29, 2003**, a souvenir sheet with a circular stamp on which a circular hologram is attached. There is Grand Prix in Macau every year since 1954. To Celebration of the 50th Anniversary of Macao Grand Prix, Macau issued a numbered limited edition of commemorative souvenir sheets (**No. 180**). The sheet was designed by Stephen Chung Kui Sing. The sheet is shown in Fig. 3-16.20, the hologram in Fig. 3-16.21, and the FDC in Fig. 3-16.22.

Fig. 3-16.20. The Macau Grand Prix sheet.

Fig. 3-16.21. Stamp with hologram.

Fig. 3-16.22. The Grand Prix FDC.

Fig. 3-16.23. Color shift in hologram on stamp.

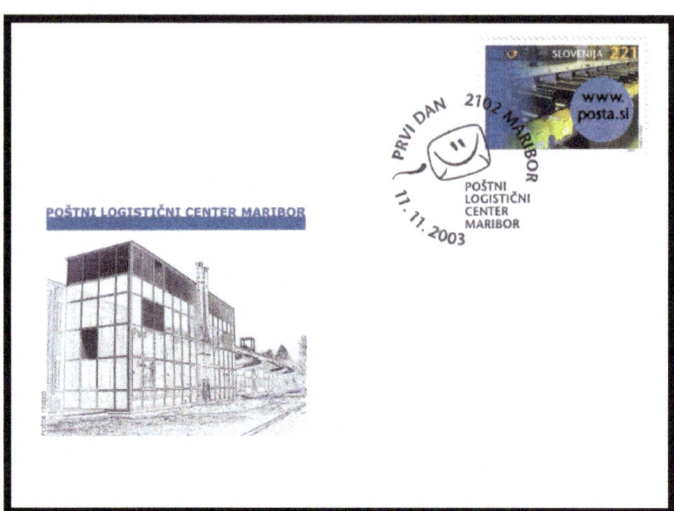

Fig. 3-16.24. FDC from Slovenia.

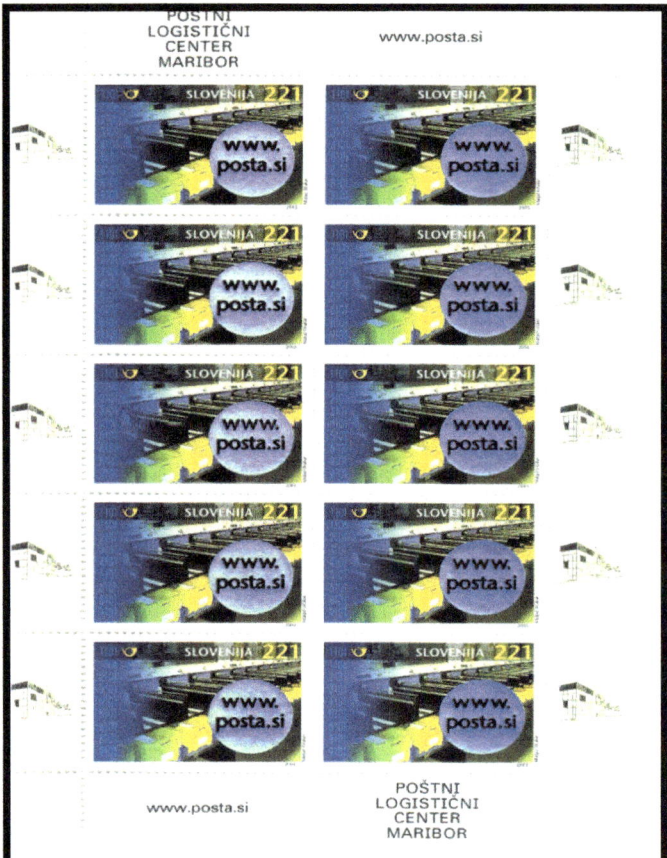

Fig. 3-16.25. Stamp sheet from Slovenia.

Slovenia issued its first definitive stamp with a hologram on **November 11, 2003 (No. 181)** for the opening of the new leading-edge Post of Slovenia's sorting facility in Maribor. The stamp depicts an automatic letter sorting machine and has a circular hologram attached in the lower right corner of the stamp. The hologram has Slovenia's postal website address: **www.posta.si** printed on it against a *colorful background* of diffractive holographic foil (Fig. 3-16.23). The stamp was designed by Matjaž Učakar and printed by Joh. Enschedé Security Printers, The Netherlands. The Maribor sorting facility is featured on the FDC shown in Fig. 3-16.24 and a ten-stamp sheet in Fig. 3-16.25.

3.17 Holographic stamps and souvenir sheets issued in 2004

At the beginning of 2004 Canada issued a stamp with holographic foil in the traditional Lunar New Year stamp series, and at the end of the year Christmas stamps were issued. Czech Republic started issuing sheets of stamps with the hologram security label attached, previously used on their postcards. Two such sheets were issued. Postal stationary with hologram labels was issued in Greece for the Summer Olympics. Libya continued issuing holographic foil stamps, and South Africa issued for the first time a hologram souvenir sheet.

Fig. 3-17.1. The 49¢ and $1.40 stamps.   **Fig. 3-17.2**. Mini-sheet with the $1.40 stamp.

Fig. 3-17.3. Overprinted mini-sheet.

Canada issued on **January 8**, **2004**, a 49¢ stamp (**No. 183**) and a $1.40 stamp (**No. 184**) for the Chinese Year of the Monkey, 'King on Cloud' stamp. Canada Post's very popular Lunar New Year stamp series celebrates its eighth year with a difference. This year's stamps illustrate a narrative - two scenes from the classic Chinese tale Journey to the West. Journey to the West is the fabulous and funny 16th century tale of Sun Wu-k'ung, the Monkey King a troublemaking trickster who relentlessly defies authority but is redeemed in the end. Canada Post has chosen this clever character to represent the Year of the Monkey in 2004. In this year's spirit of simian mischief, one stamp design at the domestic rate (49¢) and one stamp design in a souvenir sheet at the international rate ($1.40) honor the mythical monkey whose antics define the term 'monkey business' (**No. 185**). The stamps tell the Monkey King's story through their design as well as their imagery. The two stamps with the holographic *Monkey King* are shown in Fig. 3-17.1 and the mini-sheet with the $1.40 stamp is illustrated in Fig. 3-17.2. There's a direct relationship between the printing processes and the story told. For example, clear holographic foil is applied to the *monkey's image*, because the shifting color represents so well the monkey's transforming character. Being the attention-seeker he is; Monkey also appears in the foreground of both images, embossed to ensure he stands out. Gold foil was also applied to the stamps to highlight typographic elements and Chinese characters, attracting the eye in a way that gold ink would not. On the domestic rate stamp, Monkey is shown in confrontation with the Jade Emperor, whose throne he has tried to usurp. On **January 30, 2004**, an overprinted version of the mini-sheet was issued for the Hong Kong 2004 Stamp Expo – 17th Asian International Philatelic Exhibition which took place between January 30 and February 3, 2004. This version is shown in Fig. 3-17.3 (**No. 186**). The stamps designed by Louis Fishauf were based on illustrations by Anita Kunz. Canadian Bank Note Company, Ltd. and Gravure Choquet Inc. printed the stamps and souvenir sheets.

Czech Republic continued to issue prepaid postcards with hologram security labels during **2004**. Like previously issued postcards, the first address line contains microtext, an additional security feature in addition to the hologram. Twenty-four official, thirteen Postfila cards and about sixty private cards were issued in 2004.

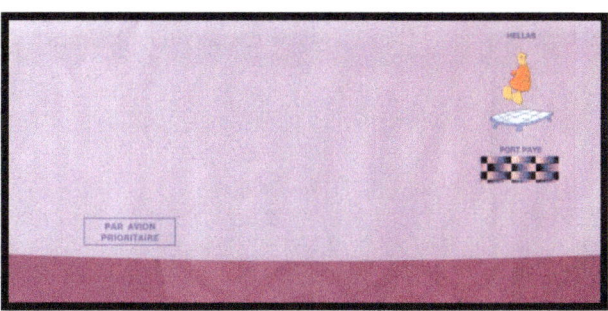

Fig. 3-17.4. Front and back of the prepaid trampoline envelope with the hologram label.

Greece issued in **April 2004** postal stationary, this time for the 2004 Summer Olympic Games, officially known as the 'Games of the XXVIII Olympiad' held in Athens from August 13 to 29, 2004 with the motto: 'Welcome Home'. Athens 2004 marked the first time since the 1996 Summer Olympics that all countries with a National Olympic Committee were in attendance. It was also the first time since 1896 that the Olympics were held in Greece. As in 2002 many different prepaid envelopes (domestic and international) envelopes were issued. The security hologram label used in 2002, shown in Fig. 3-15.8, was used again in 2004. An example of one of the envelopes for abroad issue is the 'Trampoline' envelope. The front and back of the envelope is shown in Fig. 3-17.4.

On **May 1**, **2004**, **Czech Republic** issued a sheet of ten 9.00 CZK stamps shown in Fig. 3-17.5 (**No. 187**). The topic was *Politics & Government* and, in particular, to celebrate the ten new member countries of the European Union. The joint postage stamp of the nine of the ten countries acceding to the European Union (Czech Republic, Estonia, Cyprus, Lithuania, Latvia, Hungary, Malta, Slovakia, Slovenia) is based on a design provided by the Maltese Post and are issued with slight modifications in arranged sheets of ten stamps and coupons. The stamp shows a part of plastic map of Europe, Czech flag in the left lower corner of the stamp and flags of the other nine countries acceding to the European Union in the center of the stamp with twelve golden stars. Side margins contain the names of acceding countries in English, on the upper margin there are the following printed texts: Spojená Evropa, United Europe. On the lower margin the two-channel *security hologram label* is attached (previously used on postcards, see Fig. 3.12.2), shown here in Fig. 3-17.6. There is one FDC including commemorative cancellation the cachet of which is a three-colored map of a part of Europe, where the member countries of the EU are marked in a blue color, the admittance countries in yellow and some states outside the EU in grey. The names of the admitted states are in Czech. Graphic Artist: JP Advertising Agency Limited for the Post of Malta (FDC-Jan Solpera) The cover was printed by Varius Praha, a.s. The Czech Post Printing House in Prague printed the stamps.

Fig. 3-17.5. Czech Europa sheet.

Fig. 3-17.6. Hologram security label.

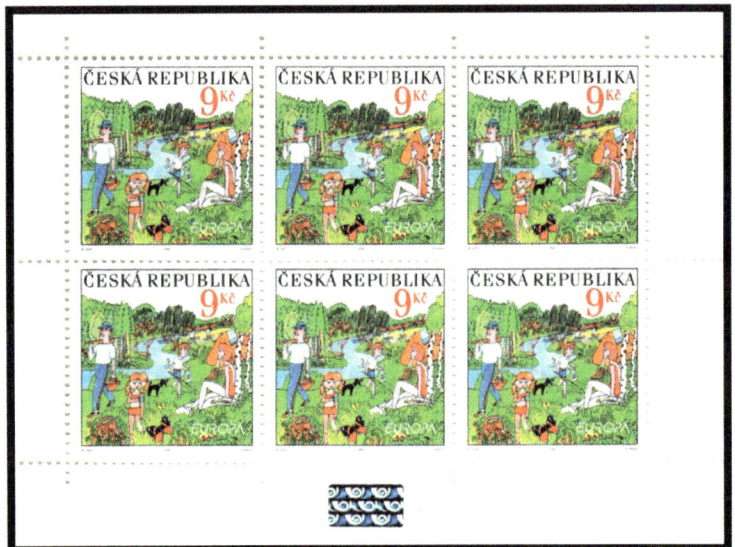

Fig. 3-17. 7. Czech six-stamp Holiday sheet.

Fig. 3-17.8. Hologram security label.

Four days after the Europe sheetlet was issued in **Czech Republic** another sheetlet was issued on **May 5, 2004**. Now it was a sheet of six 9.00 CZK stamps with the topic 'European Tourism', shown in Fig. 3-17.7 (**No. 188**). Featured on the stamp is a picture of the summer holiday published in the children book 'Spectacular Views' written by F. Nepil and illustrated by the academic painter Miloslav Jágr (1927-1997). M. Jágr was a teacher of film and television graphic design at the Institute of Applied Arts. He was one of the leading authors of illustrations for children as well as adults and the author of theatre costumes, posters and graphic design. In the center of the lower part of the sheet there is the two-channel *security hologram label* (Fig.3-17.8). The artist Pavel Hrach designed the stamp and was engraved by Bohumil Sneider. The Post Printing House in Prague printed the stamps.

On **May 29, 2004**, a Miss Universe USD 0.75 stamp was issued in **Ecuador**. The 53rd Miss Universe pageant was held in Centro de Convenciones CEMEXPO, Quito, Ecuador, on June 1, 2004. It was won by Jennifer Hawkins of Australia. The FDC, shown in Fig. 3-17.9, has a holographic cachet decoration *Miss Universe from the Center of the World*, as also featured on the stamp itself.

Fig. 3-17.9. The holographic cachet and the Miss Universe FDC.

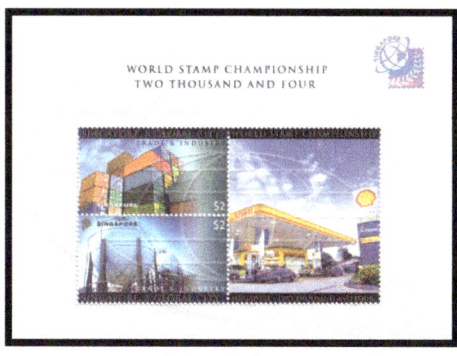 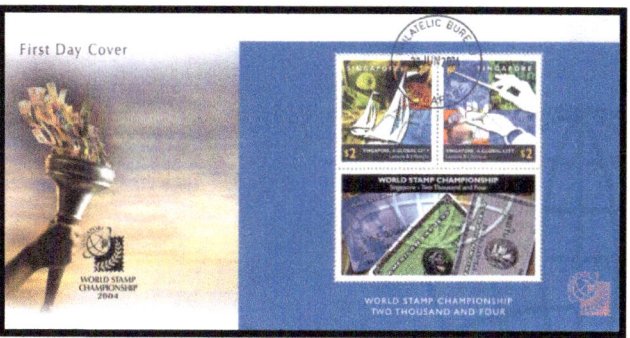

Fig. 3-17.10. The Shell souvenir sheet.   **Fig. 3-17.11.** The American Express FDC.

Fig. 3-17.12 The *SINGAPORE 2004* logo.

several souvenir sheets were issued by the Singapore Philatelic Bureau on **June 23**, **2004**, in **Singapore**, for the 'World Stamp Championship 2004' or 'SINGAPORE 2004'. All these sheets have an overprinted holographic *event logo*. The stamp event took place at SUNTEC International Convention and Exhibition Centre (SICEC) from August 28 to September 1, 2004. For the World Stamp Championship 2004 three sets of fifteen souvenir sheets were issued, some of the stamps had been issued in previous years. All of them are now with the overprinted holographic *event logo*. One of the sets of souvenir sheets, issued 2004, was 'Singapore, A Global City - Trade & Industry'. The year 2004 marked the 150th anniversary of the first use of stamps in Singapore, when the East India Company first introduced postage here. The stamps were for the Straits Settlements, which Singapore was then a part of. AIA, Glaxo Smithkline, HSBC, Shell, and Sony were the companies featured in this set. American Express, Coca Cola, McDonald's, Reader's Digest, and Swatch were featured in 'Leisure & Lifestyle 2002' stamp set and the 2003 'Communications & Technology' set - CNN, Creative Technology, Microsoft, Siemens, and Singapore Airlines. A sample of the 2004 souvenir sheets, the SHELL sheet is shown in Fig. 3.17.10 and the AMERICAN EXPRESS FDC in Fig. 3-17.11. The holographic *event logo* is shown in Fig. 3-17.12.

In addition to all the overprinted souvenir sheets, a special printer's sample sheet with six stamps without denomination was also issued. Two sample versions were produced, one imperforated and one perforated. One of the stamps has an embossed hologram cut in the shape of a *ship* which contains the text *VALID* and a *bird*. The sheet was designed and printed by Bacon & Bacon. The sheet is shown in Fig. 3-17.13 and the hologram stamp in Fig. 3-17.14.

Fig. 3-17.13. 'World Stamp Championship 2004' Cinderella sheet.   **Fig. 3-17.14.** The *ship* hologram.

Fig. 3-17.15. The souvenier sheet with *bird* hologram stamp.

Fig. 3-17.16. The FDC with the *bird* hologram stamp.

On **October 9**, **2004**, **South Africa** issued the one-stamp miniature sheet to celebrate '75 years of Airmail Services' (**No. 189**). World Post Day is celebrated every year around the world to mark the founding of the Universal Postal Union in 1874 in the Swiss Capital, Bern. It was declared World Post Day by the UPU congress held in Tokyo, Japan in 1969. The miniature sheet, shown in Fig. 3-17.15, features the first aircraft that was used to transport mail when the Airmail service was established in South Africa 75 years ago. The *bird* on the R12.05 stamp is covered with a holographic foil. Designed by Hein Botha, the stamp area of the miniature sheet features a bird in hologram foil, with a DH60 Gipsy Moth aircraft in the background. This aircraft is similar to the one used on the first Airmail stamp issued in South Africa. The foiled bird symbolises our modern times and the DH60 Gipsy Moth reflects on the history of airmail in South Africa. The FDC is shown in Fig. 3-17.16. The sheet was printed by Joh. Enschedé Security Printers, The Netherlands.

A special souvenir sheet with ten personalized stamps and ten different tabs was issued in **Australia** on **October 12, 2004**, when the Disney PIXAR 'Monsters, Inc' movie was released (**No. 190**). The Let's Party (Balloons) 50¢ stamp was previously issued on January 7, 2003. The sheet was designed by Hannah Mattner, Cozzolino Ellet Design Division Pty. Ltd., and printed by SNP Ausprint. Another sheet with ten personalized stamps and tabs was issued in October for the Disney PIXAR movie 'Finding Nemo' (**No. 191**). The 50¢ stamp was previously issued on March 16, 2004. This sheet was designed by Brian Sadgrove and printed by SNP Sprint. Transparent diffractive foil is attached to the upper part of the sheets. The Monster Inc. sheet is shown in Fig. 3-17.17 and the Finding Nemo sheet in Fig. 3-17.18.

Fig. 3-17.17. The 'Monnsters, Inc.' sheet.

Fig. 3-17.18. The 'Finding Nemo' sheet.

Fig. 3-17.19. Fashion City sheet.

Fig. 3-17.20. Fashion city FDC.

Fig. 3-17.21. Logo.

Thailand issued a souvenir sheet with holographic foil on **December 5, 2004**, for the Bangkok Fashion City initiative to illustrate the colorful graphic design of male and female models. Three 3-Baht stamps and one 15-Baht stamp (**No. 192** through **195**) were issued and a souvenir sheet (**No. 196**). There is diffractive effect on the Bangkok fashion City logo on the sheet and the stamps. The stamps were designed by Charlin Yamapai and printed by the British Security Printing Public Company Limited, Thailand. The souvenir sheet is shown in Fig. 3-17.19, the FDC in Fig. 3-17.20 and the logo diffractive effect in Fig. 3-17.21.

On **December 20, 2004**, **Libya** continued to issue stamps with holographic foil. This year they issued the 'Khairi Nuri Khaled' stamp, denomination 500 dirhams in blocks of four stamps (**No. 197**). The stamps were designed by M.A. Siala. The block is shown in Fig. 3-17.22, the stamp in Fig. 3-17.23 and the FDC in Fig. 3-17.24. On the FDC is also the Libyan map cachet hologram which was, as already mentioned, not used on the officially issued FDCs. The FDCs with this cachet hologram should not be regarded as an item of philatelic value.

Fig. 3-17.22. The Khairi Nuri Khaled sheet.

Fig. 3-17.23. The Khairi Nuri Khaled stamp.

Fig. 3-17.24. The Khairi Nuri Khaled FDC.

3-18. Holographic stamps and souvenir sheets issued in 2005

The United Nations Postal Administration issued its second hologram stamp. The Czech Republic continued issuing sheets of stamps with the security hologram label, a new one was issued in May. Italy, a newcomer, issued its first definitive space-related hologram stamp. Jersey issued a lovely H. C. Andersen souvenir sheet. Thailand issued a new type of holographic diffraction pattern on its Insect stamps. Åland issued Christmas-related hologram stamps.

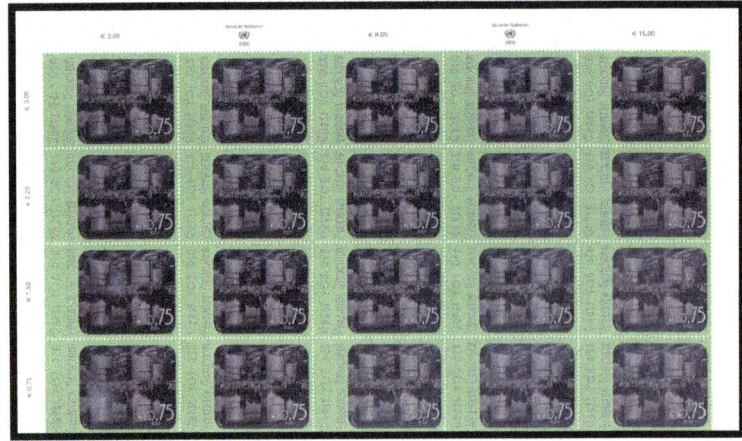
Fig. 3-18.1. Vienna International Center UN 20-stamp sheet.

Fig. 3-18.2. UN hologram stamp.

Fig. 3-18.3. *Vienna International Center* hologram.

Fig. 3-18.4. Vienna International Center FDC.

On **February 4**, **2005**, **United Nations Postal Administration** (UNPA) issued its second definitive hologram stamp, the Vienna definitive stamp, in the denomination of €0.75 (Fig. 3-18.1 and 3-18.2, **No. 198**). The hologram stamp depicts the *Vienna International Center* shown in Fig. 3-18.3. On the left side of the hologram is printed 'GRUSS VON DEN VEREINTEN NATIONEN' [Greetings from United Nations]. The horizontal sheets of 20 stamps have two marginal inscriptions, two in the top margin and two in the bottom margin. The marginal inscription consists of the United Nations emblem with the text 'Vereinte Nationen' [United Nations] above the emblem and the year 2005 below the emblem. In addition the copyright symbol appears in the lower left margin. The stamps were printed by Cartor Security Printing, France. The first UN hologram stamp was issued in 2003 of the United Nations Headquarters complex in New York (See Fig. 3-16.5). The 2005 FDC is shown in Fig. 3-18.4.

Czech Republic continued to issue prepaid postcards with hologram security labels during **2005**. Like previously issued postcards, the first address line contains microtext, an additional security feature in addition to the hologram. Twenty-four official postcards were issued. Fourteen Postfila cards and thirty-seven private cards were also issued in 2005.

Fig. 3-18.5. H C Andersen 'The Ugly Duckling' minisheet.   **Fig. 3-18.6.** Holographic *fairy*.

Fig. 3-18.7. The H C Andersen FDC with 'The Ugly Duckling' sheet.

Jersey issued miniature sheets on **April 2, 2005**, to highlight the bicentenary of the birth of the famous Danish story teller Hans Christian Andersen and his Fairy Tales. He was born in Odense, Denmark, on April 2, 1805. His talent for writing enchanting fairy tales has established him as one of the great children's writers. The miniature sheet with a hologram is the 'The Ugly Duckling' sheet (Fig. 3-18.5, **No. 199**) which is decorated with a holographic foil *fairy* on the upper left corner of the sheet, shown in Fig. 3-18.6. The FDC envelope illustration shows H C Andersen with a scene from his story Thumbelina in the background, reproduced in Fig. 3-18.7. The other stamps in the H C Andersen series were: the 33p Little Red Riding Hood, the 34p The Little Mermaid, the 41p Beauty and the Beast, the 50p Rumpelstiltskin and the 73p The Goose that Laid the Golden Eggs. The artist Michael Pollard was responsible for the stamps, miniature sheet and the FDC. The sheets were printed by Cartor Security Printing, France.

Fig. 3-18.8. Czech Republic Gastronomi sheet.

Fig. 3-18.9. Hologram security label.

Czech Republic issued its third sheetlet with the security hologram label on **May 4, 2005**, (**No. 200**). This year it was the 'Agriculture and Gastronomy' sheet of six 9.00 CZK stamps (Fig. 3-18.8). The stamp depicts a typical Czech menu. Like the previous 2004 Czech stamps the same two-channel *security hologram label* (Fig. 3-18.9) is attached at the middle of the lower margin. The Czech Post Printing House in Prague printed the stamps.

On **May 26, 2005**, **Jersey** issued the H C Andersen miniature sheet with the 'Jersey at Nordia 2005' overprint to mark the opening of the International Stamp Exhibition 'Nordia 2005' which took place in Gothenburg, Sweden, May 26 through 29, 2005. The sheet (**No. 201**) with the overprint is shown in Fig. 3-18.10 and the FDC in Fig. 3-18.11.

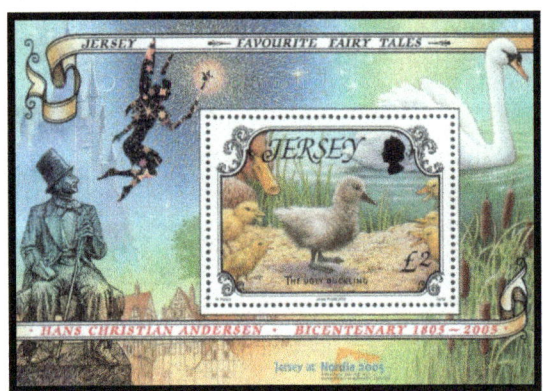

Fig. 3-18.10. The H C Andersen sheet with 'Jersey at Nordia 2005' overprint.

Fig. 3-18.11. The FDC with the Nordia 2005 overprinted The Ugly Duckling stamp.

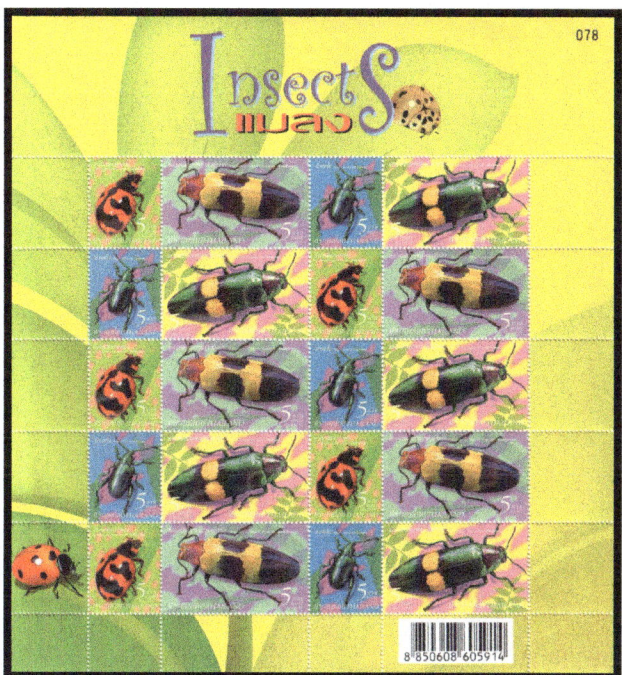

Fig. 3-18.12. The Thailand Insect sheet.

Fig. 3-18.13. Holographic *pattern*.

Fig. 3-18.14. Thailand Insect FDC.

On **May 31**, **2005**, **Thailand** issued the Insects postage stamps, a set of four insects with *transparent holographic foil*. (**No. 202** through **205**) and a souvenir sheet (**No. 206**). The purpose was to promote stamp collecting activities and to publicize insects found in Thailand. The 5.00 Baht stamps pictured the following insects: Fabricius (*Coccinella transversalis*), Saunders (*Chrysochroa buqueti rugicollis*), Drury (*Sagra femorata*), and Akiyama (*Chrysochroa maruyamai*). The sheet with the Insect stamps is shown in Fig. 3-18.12 and the iridescent effect in Fig. 3-18.13. In Fig. 3-18.14 the FDC with four Insect stamps is shown. The stamps were designed by Udorn Niyomthum, Thailand Post Company Ltd and printed by Thai British Security Printing Public Company Ltd in Thailand.

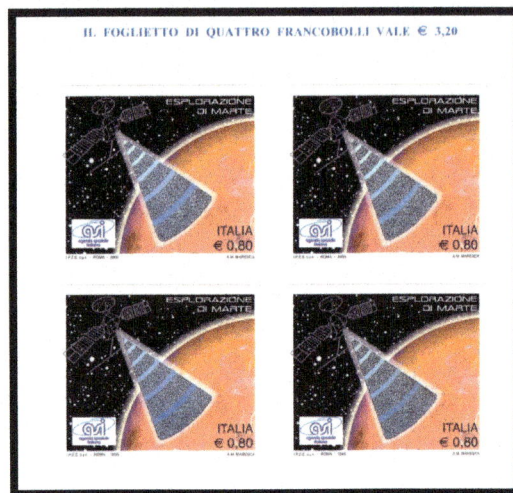

Fig. 3-18.15. Italian four-stamp sheet.

Fig. 3-18.16. The stamp with the *radar beam* hologram.

Italy issued on **September 21, 2005**, a self-adhesive definitive stamp for the program of exploration of Mars, which features a radar satellite orbiting a planet. The four-stamp sheet is shown in Fig. 3-18.15 (**No. 207**). The issue represents Italy's involvement in the Mars Exploration Program. At the bottom left of the stamp, the logo of the Italian Space Agency (ASI) is located, which is in charge of coordinating Italy's involvement. A figure-shaped hologram is applied in the middle of the stamp representing the propagation of *the radar's electromagnetic rays* on which the acronym 'ASI' features repeatedly (Fig. 3-18.16). The words 'ESPLORAZIONE DI MARTE' [MARS EXPLORATION], 'ITALIA' and the denomination €0,80 complete the stamp. It was design by Anna Maria Maresca and printed by the Stamped Paper Department at the Istituto Poligrafico e Zecca dello Stato S.p.A. The hologram was designed by the Holography Workshop, New Security Products Division, Stamped Paper Department.

Åland issued on **October 10, 2005**, a €0.45 Christmas stamp featuring two brownies below a hologram of *twinkling stars* in the sky (Fig. 3-18.17, **No. 208**). The FDC is shown in Fig. 3-18.18 and the *twinkling stars* in the hologram in Fig. 3-18.19. The stamp was designed by Pirkko Vahtero. Cartor Security Printing printed the stamps.

Fig. 3-18.17. Christmas stamp.

Fig. 3-18.18. Åland Christmas stamp FDC.

Fig. 3-18.19. The *twinkling stars* in the hologram.

Fig. 3-18.20. The Snowman Christmas booklet from Canada.   **Fig. 3-18.21.** Holographic *snowflakes*.

Fig. 3-18.22. The Snowman stamp FDC.

On **November 2, 2005, Canada** issued the 'Christmas – Snowman' self-adhesive stamp booklet shown in Fig. 3-18.20, (**No. 209**). The 2005 holiday season marked the first time Canada Post issued both secular- and religious-themed stamps. The secular stamp, injected with a child's magical sense of the season, features the Snowman, an icon of the winter season in North America. He is portrayed among holographic *shimmering snowflakes* and northern lights by designer and illustrator Hélène L'Heureux (Fig. 3-18.21). Like a finely wrapped gift, the booklet of twelve domestic rate (50¢) stamps opens to reveal a dozen festive Snowman stamps set against a wintery blue and green background that's embedded with cheery bonus envelope seals. The Snowman stamp with its simple geometric lines and cheerful colors, the stamp begs a longer look with its glistening snowflakes, created through the use of clear holographic hot stamping. Both the whiteness of the snow and the refractory colors that one experiences as a sparkling effect when the sun shines against the snow on a bright day is captured in this stamp. The FDC is shown in Fig. 3-18.22. The stamps were produced by Lowe-Martin Company Inc.

3-19. Holographic stamps and souvenir sheets issued in 2006

The United Nation Postal Administration issued its third hologram stamp. The Czech Republic continued issuing sheets of stamps with the security hologram label. One such sheetlet was issued this year. USA issued two interesting stamps, the X-Plane stamps. Jersey, Malaysia and Thailand issued fish and sea shell hologram sheets. Åland issued again Christmas-related hologram stamps.

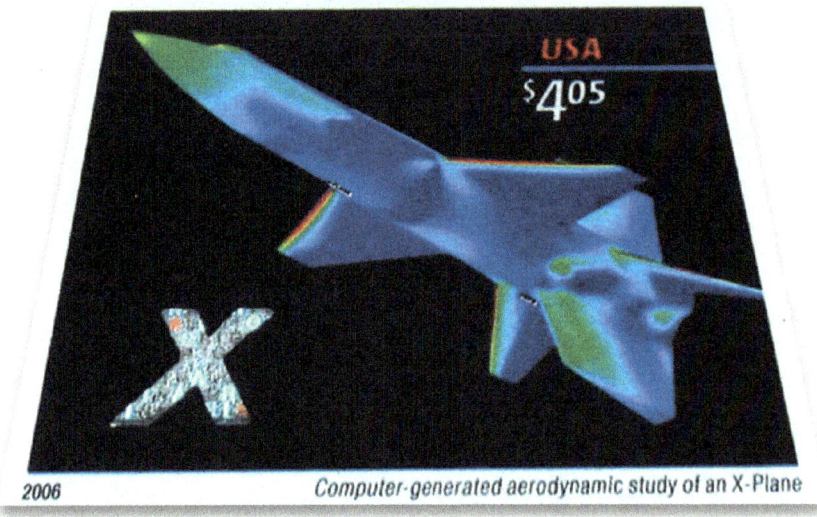

Fig. 3-19.1. The UN hologram stamp. **Fig. 3-19.2**. *Armillary Sphere* hologram. **Fig. 3-19.3.** Geneva UN stamp.

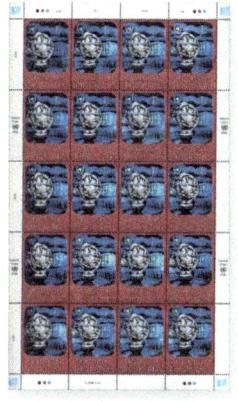 

Fig. 3-19.4. The 20-stamp sheet. **Fig. 3-19.5.** The UN 2006 FDC.

On **February 3**, **2006**, **United Nations Postal Administration** (UNPA) issued the Geneva definite CHF 1.30 stamp (**No. 210**). Previously UNPA released a 70-cent hologram definitive in 2003 and a €0.75 hologram definitive in 2005, making this the third hologram stamp of the series. The 2006 stamp depicts the Armillary Sphere (Cycle of Life) by Paul Manship. The sculpture is located at the UN Office in Geneva. The Geneva hologram stamp is shown in Fig. 3-19.1 and the *Armillary Sphere* hologram in Fig. 3-19.2. Printed under the hologram is: 'SALUTATIONS DES NATIONS UNIES' [Greetings from United Nations]. Previously, a normal UN CHF 1.40 stamp was issued on January 30, 1987 with the same picture as featured in the hologram stamp. It was adapted as a stamp by Rocco J. Callari at United Nations in New York from a UN photograph. The 20-stamp sheet is shown in Fig. 3-19.4 and the FDC in 3-19.5. The stamp was designed by Rorie Katz and printed by Joh. Enschedé Stamps Security Printers. Fig. 3-19.6 shows a special limited-edition, triple-cancelled silk cover with all three UN hologram stamps. This envelope has the following cancellations: The 2003 hologram stamp - cancelled on March 28, 2003, the 2004 hologram stamp - cancelled on February 4, 2004, and the 2006 hologram stamp - cancelled on February 3, 2006.

Fig. 3-19.6. The limited-edition, triple-cancelled silk cover with all three UN hologram stamps.

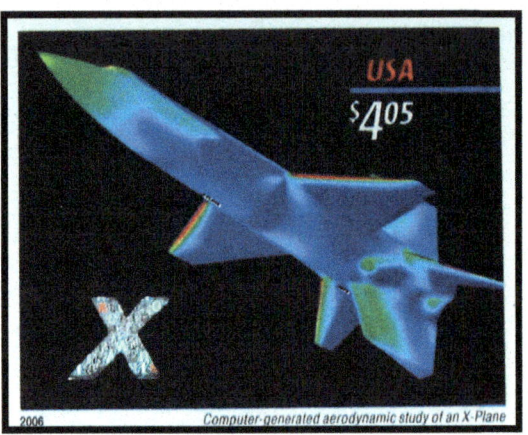 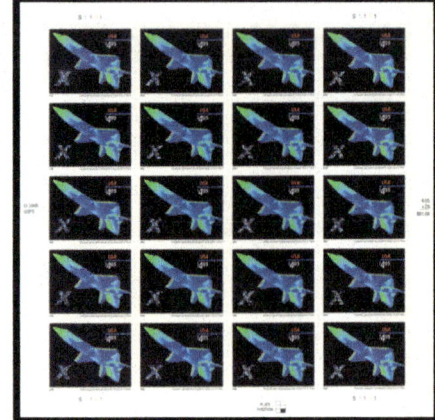

Fig. 3-19.7. The X-Plane $4.05 stamp and the 20-stamp sheet.

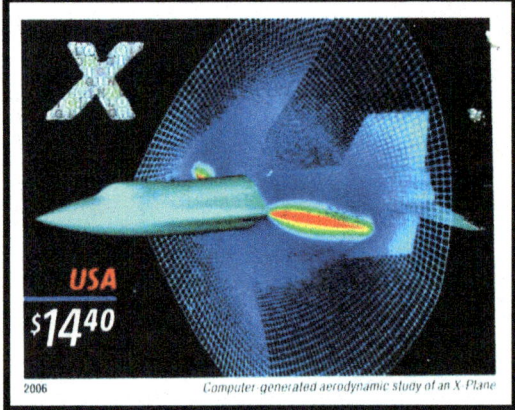 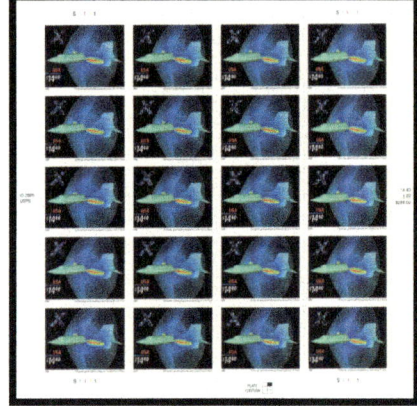

Fig. 3-19.8. The X-Plane $14.40 stamp and the 20-stamp sheet.

On **March 17, 2006, USA** issued two X-Plane stamps; the $4.05 Priority Mail (**No. 211**) and the $14.40 Express Mail (**No. 212**) stamps. The new stamps commemorate the X-Planes, a series of experimental vehicles involving the U.S. military, NASA and companies such as Bell Aircraft, Boeing, Northrop and Lockheed Martin. From the first X-Plane flight in 1946 to the present, a variety of vehicles — manned and unmanned aircraft, cruise missiles, gliders and spacecraft — has helped extend the nation's reach into space. One of the best known — and the fastest and highest-flying, winged vehicle — was the X-15. The X-15 program was a joint effort by NASA, the Air Force, and the Navy. Thus the X-15 was air launched from a B-52 aircraft at about 45,000 ft and speeds upward of 500 mph. The airplane first set speed records in the Mach 4-6 range and later Mach 5.27 on June 23, 1961; It also set an altitude record of 354,200 feet (67 miles) on August 22, 1963. The highly successful program contributed to the development of the Mercury, Gemini, and Apollo piloted spaceflight programs as well as the Space Shuttle program. The program's final flight was performed on October 24, 1968. Art Director and stamp designer Phil Jordan, of Falls Church, VA, really went to the source for this look at the X-Plane. Jordan selected a computer-generated image of the X-15 from NASA studies. The colors show various scales of pressures and temperatures - blue is the lowest and red is the highest. The $4.05stamp shows the X-15 rotated upward to reveal the most surface area. The $14.40 stamp shows the colors against a meshed grid to illustrate how air is forced around and behind the plane. The two designs have text under the image reading, 'Computer-generated aerodynamic study of an X-Plane.' The design includes a '*X*' hologram on the lower left side of the $4.05stamp (Fig. 3-19.7) and on the upper left side of the $14.40 stamp (Fig. 3.19.8). The large holographic foil with alphabetic *letters* was used for the cut-out X-shaped holograms. The stamps were issued in panes of 20. The US space hologram stamps, issued in 2000, had microtext (USPS) included in the holograms (see Fig. 3-13.22). Microtext printing appears on these two new stamps as well. However, this time the microtext is directly printed on the paper and not in the holographic foil on the stamps. Each stamp has both **X-PLANE** and **USPS** printed on the planes (Fig. 3-19-9). Several different FDCs were issued. Two FDCs are shown in Fig. 3-19.109. Two X-PLANE AMERICAN COMMEMORATIVE CANCELLATIONS information sheets are shown in Fig. 3-19.11. The stamps were printed by Sennett Security Products (SSP) / Banknote Corporation of America, Inc. (BCA).

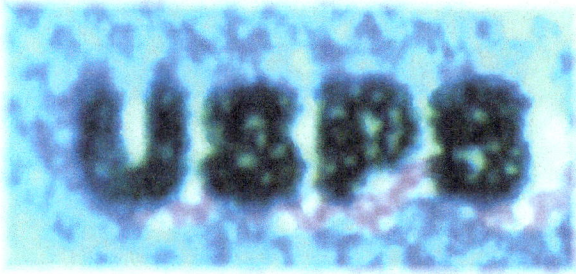

Fig. 3-19.9. The microtext in both X-Plane stamps.

Fig. 3-19.10. Two X-Plane FDCs with the $4.05 and $14.40 stamps.

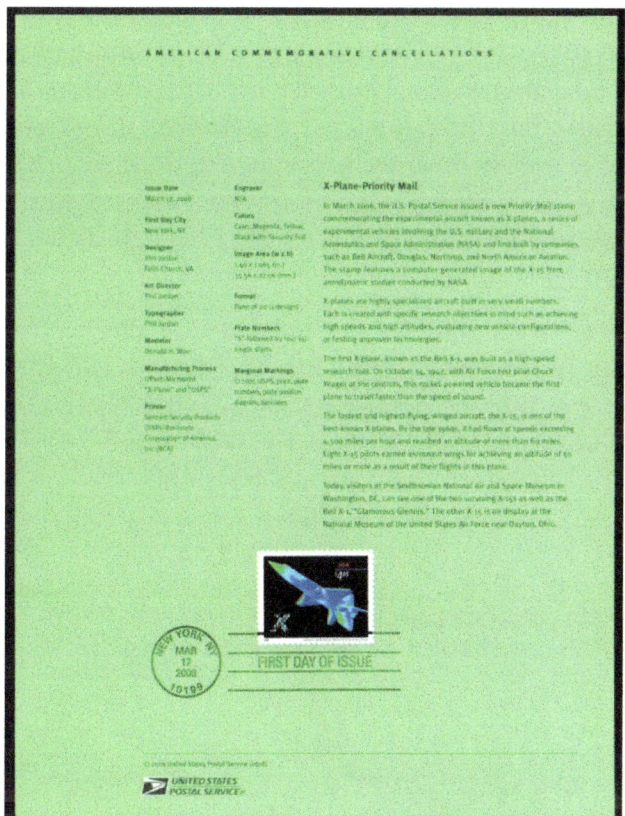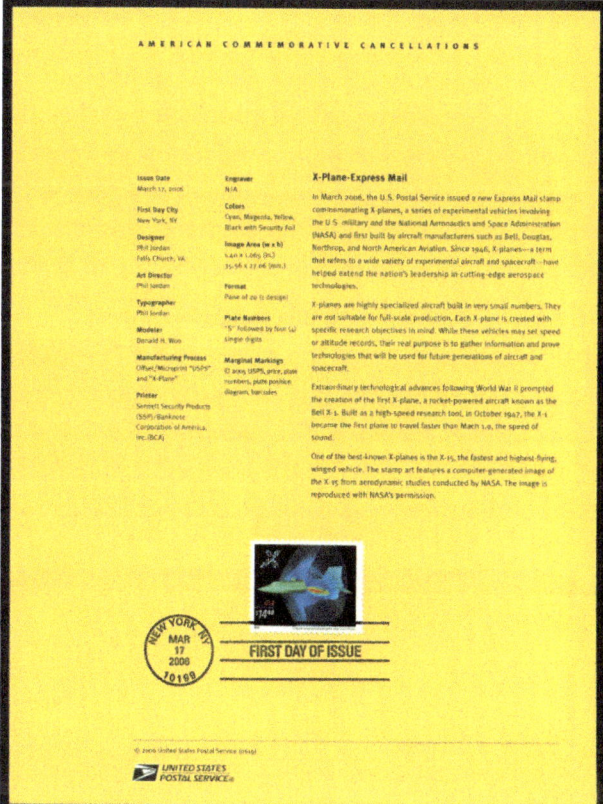

Fig. 3-19.11. The AMERICAN COMMEMORATIVE CANCELLATIONS sheets.

Fig. 3-19.12. Jersey's oval-shaped stamp in the miniature sheet. **Fig. 3-19.13**. The *Ormer* hologram.

On **April 4, 2006**, the 'Marine Life VI - Sea Shells' stamps and miniature sheet (**No. 213**) were issued in **Jersey**. The sea around Jersey is rich with all kinds of sea life and Jersey Post's sixth set of stamps in the Marine Life series depicts some of the beautiful 'Sea Shells' that may be found under the sea and washed up on the Island's many beaches. The six sea shell stamps images have been enhanced with the use of a printing technique called *thermography* which helps to give an almost 3D appearance. The areas of thermography create a slightly raised and shiny texture which intensifies the already vibrant colors of the shells. Thermography produces raised printing similar in appearance to engraving but using a completely different process. In thermography, a special powder is added to the document with it adhering to the ink printed on the paper. After removing the excess powder the printed piece is heated and the powder and ink mixture dries to form a raised effect on the paper. The following sea shells were depicted on the six stamps: 34p Flat periwinkle (*Littorina littoralis*), 37p Painted top shell (*Callistoma zizyphinum*), 42p Dog cockle (*Glycymeris glycymeris*), 51p Variegated scallop (*Clamys varia*), 57p Blue rayed limpet (*Helcion pellucidum*), and 74p European cowrie (*Trivia monacha*). The miniature sheet contains different techniques featuring an *Ormer* shell (*Haliotis tuberculata*). The shell is depicted within an oval £2 stamp. The inside of the shell has been embellished with a translucid, iridescent, hot stamped holographic foil which recreates the same mother of pearl effect found in actual Ormer shells. Responsible for these special techniques incorporated in creating the Sea Shell stamps was Cartor Security Printers in France. The stamps and miniature sheet were based on paintings by the wildlife artist as Nick Parlett. The miniature sheet is shown in Fig. 3-19.12 with the *Sea Shell* hologram on it, in Fig. 3-19.13.

On **May 25, 2006, Malaysia** issued the 'Fresh Water Fish Series III' with four stamps and a souvenir sheet (**No. 214**). The four normal stamps are: the 30-sen Jelawat carp fish, the 50-sen Patin fish, the 50-sen Sebarau fish and the RM1 Temoleh fish. The RM5 souvenir features two fish: the Keli Kaya (*Clarias batrachus*) and the Baung (*Mystus nemurus*). The *Baung fish* is covered with holographic foil, shown in Fig. 3-19.14 and 3-19.15. A FDC (shown in Fig. 3-19.16), a presentation pack and a special folder were also made available. The stamps and souvenir sheet were designed by Hazel Design and printed by Percetakan Keselamatan Nasional Sdn Bhd.

Fig. 3-19.14. The 'Fresh Water Fish Series III' **s**ouvenir sheet. **Fig. 3-19.15**. The *Baung fish* hologram.

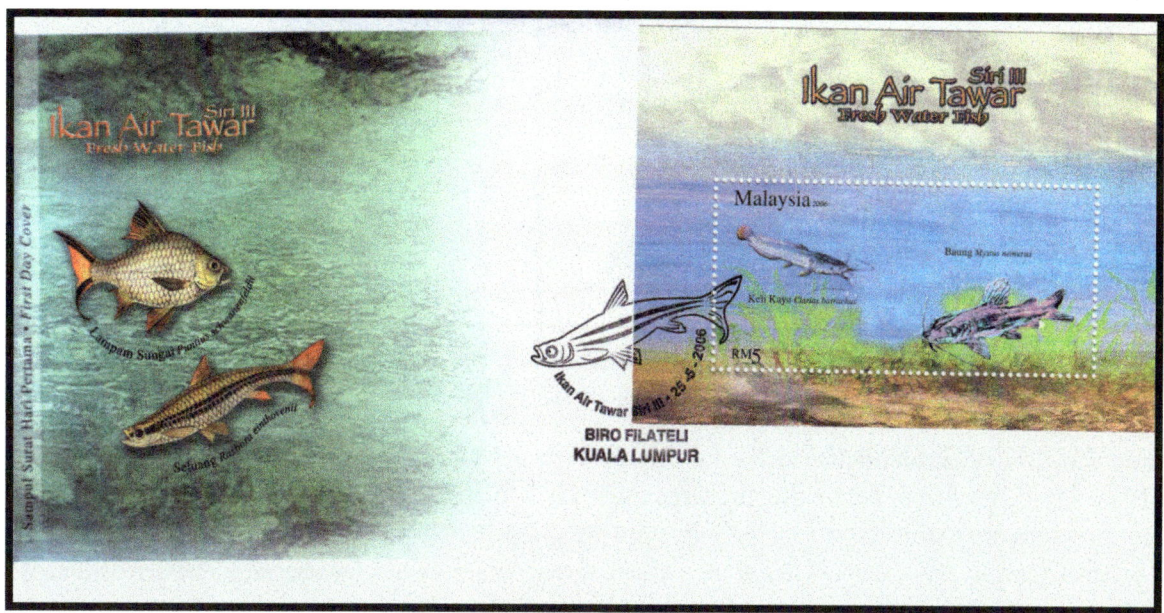

Fig. 3-19.16. The 'Fresh Water Fish Series III' souvenir sheet FDC.

On **May 27, 2006, Thailand** issued the overprinted Insects souvenir sheet for the Washington 2006 Stamp show (**No. 215**). This sheet has only eight stamps (Fig. 3-19.17). The first Insect sheet issued on May 31, 2005, was larger with 16 stamps (See Fig. 3-18.12).

Fig. 3-19.17. The overprinted Insects sheet.

Fig. 3-19.18. The anemonefish souvenir sheet. **Fig. 13-9.19.** The *sea* hologram foil on the sheet.

On **June 24**, **2006**, **Thailand** issued the 'Anemone Fish – Marine Life' series of stamps and a souvenir sheet (**No. 216**). Anemone Fish, with their spectacular, colorful appearance in orange, red, black, yellow and white stripes are featured on four 3-Baht stamps. The following anemone fish were depicted: Clark's Anemonefish (*Amphiprion clarkii Bennett*), False Clown Anemofish (*Amphiprion ocellaris Cuvier*), Pink Skunk Crownfish (*Amphiprion perideration Bleeker*), and Saddleback Anemonefish (*Amphiprion polymnus Linnaeus*). The 20.00-Baht souvenir sheet, shown in Fig. 3-19.18, includes the four stamps and the *sea* on the upper part of the sheet is covered with transparent diffractive holographic foil (Fig. 13-19.19). There are also larger sheets where the souvenir sheet above is in the middle of it. The stamps were designed by Mayuree Narknisorn, Thailand Post Company Ltd and printed by Thai British Security Printing Public Company Ltd, Thailand.

Between **June 9** and **July 9**, **2006**, during the FIFA Football (soccer) World Cup in **Germany**, a set of twelve prepaid City-Postcards (45c + 20c) were issued. Fig. 3-19.20 shows the front and the address side of the Hamburg card, one of the issued postcards. All cards have a *FIFA WORLD CUP 2006 emblem* hologram (Fig. 3-19.21) on the address side. The hologram has holographic microtext (Fig. 3-19.22) and each hologram is individually marked with laser-written numbers. The holograms were also used for officially licensed FIFA products. The following cities were included in the set of postcards: Berlin, Cologne, Dortmund, Frankfurt, Gelsenkirchen, Hannover, Kaiserslautern, Leipzig, Munich, Nuremburg and Stuttgart. In addition to the postcards, this hologram security label was also attached to several FIFA World Cup envelopes (Fig. 3-19.23) and to presentation folders.

Fig. 3-19.20. Example of one of the postcards (picture and address side). **Fig. 13-9.21.** *FIFA emblem* hologram logo.

Fig. 13-9.22. The *FIFA emblem* microtext.

Fig. 3-19.23. *FIFA World Cup logo* hologram on one of the envelopes.

On **September 22, 2006, Iran** issued two different self-adhesive hologram stamps. Both rectangular stamps, denomination 4400 Rial (Fig. 3-19.24, **No. 217**), and circular stamps, denomination 5500 Rial (Fig. 3-19.25, **No. 218**) were issued. The 4400 Rial-stamps were issued in panes of 48 stamps and the 5500 Rial-stamps in panes of 25 stamps. The self-adehesive stamps which depict the *Iranian post emblem* came attached to both white and brown paper. The hologram stamps were produced by the Boad Negar Iranian Company.

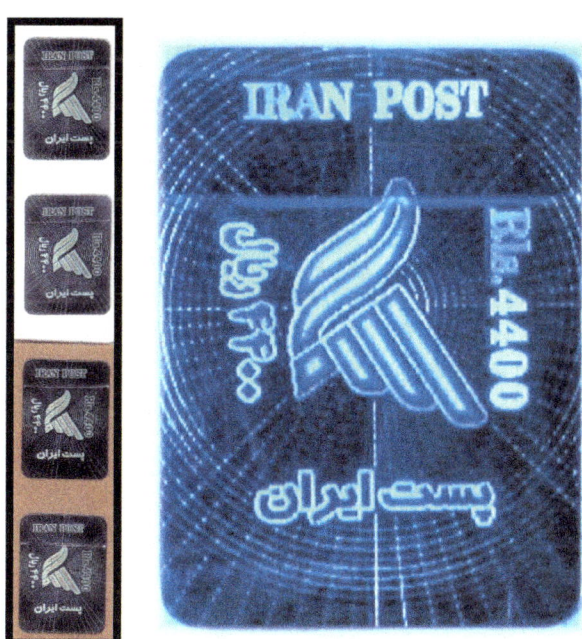

Fig. 3-19.24 The Rial 4400 hologram stamp.　　　　**Fig. 3-19.25.** The Rial 5500 hologram stamp.

Fig. 3-19.26. The Åland Christmas stamp. **Fig. 3-19.27.** The Åland Christmas FDC.

On **October 9, 2006**, **Åland** issued Christmas stamps. The 2006 Christmas stamp is reminiscent of the Åland Christmas traditions of past times, when people used to ride by horse and sleigh to the early service on Christmas Day below the sparkling starry sky. The stamp, designed by the Finnish artist Päivi Mansikka-Aho, shows a family returning home by horse and sleigh from the early Christmas service at the church of Finström (Fig. 3-19.26, **No. 219**). The sky on the stamp is covered with glittering hologram *stars*. The denomination is 'Christmas Postage 06', and this is the first Åland stamp of this denomination, which could be used as postage for Christmas greetings within Åland as well as to Finland and Sweden. The FDC, shown in Fig. 3-19.27, which was issued in connection with the Christmas stamps, is decorated by a lantern. The stamps were printed by Cartor Security Printing.

On **November 16, 2006**, both **Jersey** and **Thailand** issued overprinted versions of the Marine Life VI Sea Shells (**No. 220**) and Anemonefish sheets (**No. 221**), respectively. These sheets were for the international BELGICA'06 Stamp Show in Brussels, which took place between November 16 and 20, 2006. The two overprinted sheets are shown in Fig. 3-19.28.

Fig. 3-19.28. The two BELGICA'06 overprinted sheets from Jersey and Thailand.

Fig. 3-19.29. The four Philippine Colonial Churches Christmas stamps.

Fig. 3-19.30. Hologram *stars*.

Philippines issued four 'Philippine Colonial Churches' Christmas stamps on **November 24, 2006**. The hundreds of churches that were built throughout the Philippines were a product of the missionary enterprise of the Spanish regime that began in 1521. In 1899, when the last of the Spanish fleet left the Philippines, they left behind, among many irrevocable influences, hundreds of brick and stone churches throughout the archipelago, among which are:

- Manila Cathedral also known as the minor basilica of the Immaculate Conception (**No. 222**),

- St. Augustine Church also known as Paoay Church which was built in 1694 , (**No. 223**),

- Miagao Church in the town of Miagao, Iloilo, built between 1787 and 1797 (**No. 224**),

- Barasoain Church is the site of the Constitutional Convention of the first Philippine Republic (**No. 225**).

The four stamps are shown in Fig. 3-19.29. The *stars* (Fig. 3-19.30) in sky on all stamps are holographic as well as *PASKO 2006* printed at the bottom of each stamp. The stamps were designed by Jesus Alfredo D. Delos Santos and printed by Amstars Company, Inc.

Czech Republic continued to issue prepaid postcards with hologram security labels during **2006**. Like previously issued postcards, the first address line contains microtext, an additional security feature in addition to the hologram. Twenty-five official postcards were issued. Fifteen Postfila cards and thirty-one private cards were also issued in 2006.

3-20. Holographic stamps and souvenir sheets issued in 2007

Finland continued issuing hologram stamps; two new stamps were issued and one souvenir sheet. Peru issued several stamps with holograms. Hong Kong issued a very large beautiful souvenir hologram sheet honoring the 10th anniversary of the establishment of the Hong Kong Special Administrative Region and return to China. Thailand issued a series of stamps for the celebrations of His Majesty the King's eightieth Birthday Anniversary. One of them was a nice 2D hologram portrait of the H. M. King Bhumibol Adulyadej. Chile issued its first hologram stamps, and Canada continued to issue Christmas hologram stamps.

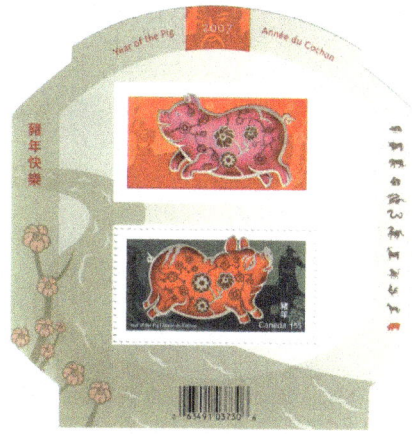

Fig. 3-20.1 The 52¢ pig stamp.　　　　　　Fig. 3-20.2 The pig souvenir sheet.

To mark the arrival of the Year of the Pig - Chinese New Year - **Canada** issued a 52¢ stamp (**No. 226**) and a special souvenir sheet on **January 5**, **2007**, (**No. 227**). The year of the Pig stamp was the eleventh issue within a twelve-year series. An element that the stamp's design reflects is that of cloisonné, a unique art form that is thought to have originated in Beijing during the Yuan Dynasty (1271-1368). This sophisticated enameling technique integrates gold or bronze metal strips and is an extremely popular technique. The stamp's pig mimics this art form with foil-stamped flowers covering his body. The single stamp reflects the new domestic rate of 52¢, and the stamp on the souvenir sheet, the new international rate of $1.55. The Pig issue included a domestic stamp, an international stamp, a souvenir sheet, an official FDC and an uncut press sheet. The *contour line* of the pig is holographic, shown in Fig. 3-20.1. The souvenir sheet is shown in Fig. 3-20.2. John Belisle of Signals Design and Alain Leduc, Manager of Stamp Design and Production at Canada Post, were responsible for the stamps. Lowe-Martin Company Inc. printed the stamps. An uncut press sheet of twelve souvenir sheets (quantity: 12,000) was also issued.

On two occasions in January definitive stamps with holograms were issued in **Peru**. On **January 5, 2007**, 'The Pirates of Callao' a two-stamp set was issued for the first 3D animated movie in Peru and Latin America (**No. 228** and **229**). On the upper left corner of the stamps is a hologram of a *clapper board* attached. The two stamps are shown in Fig. 3-20.3 and the FDC in Fig. 3-20.4.

Fig. 3-20.3 The two 'Pirates of Callao' stamps.

Fig. 3-20.4 'The Pirates of Callao' FDC.

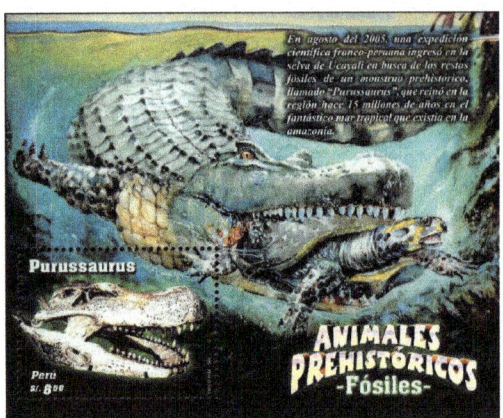 

Fig. 3-20.5. The 'Prehistoric Animals' souvenir sheet. **Fig. 3-20.6.** 'Prehistoric Animals' FDC.

The second issue in **Peru** was the 'Prehistoric Animals – Purussaurus' souvenir sheet which was issued on **January 16**, **2007**, (**No. 230**). The *ANIMALES PREHISTÓRICOS – Fósiles –* is printed with holographic foil on the souvenir sheet. The stamp is shown in Fig. 3-20.5 and the FDC in Fig. 3-20.6.

Finland, the country with many issued hologram stamps, issued two stamps with holograms on the same day in January. One of them issued on **January 24**, **2007**, was a stamp to celebrate 50 years of TV broadcasting in Finland (**No. 231**). The denomination €0.70 corresponded to the postage for a domestic first class letter in 2007. The stamp depicts an old RCA TV camera with a holographic *blue-violet* background covering the entire stamp. There is also a butterfly antenna on the stamp. (Fig. 3-20.7). The FDC is shown in Fig. 3-20.8.

Fig. 3-20.7. The *TV camera* hologram stamp.

Fig. 3-20.8. The 50-year TV broadcasting FDC.

Fig. 3-20.9. 'International Polar Year' miniature sheet.

Fig. 3-20.10. *Snow flake* hologram.

Fig. 3-20.11. 'International Polar Year' miniature sheet FDC.

Another issue, also on **January 24, 2007** in **Finland** was a miniature sheet, the 'International Polar Year' miniature sheet with two 70c stamps (**No. 232**). Two stamps partly overlap each other on the sheet, and the part shared by both stamps has a glittering *snowflake* hologram attached. The International Polar Year (IPY) was a multidisciplinary research campaign and joint project by tens of countries and scientific organizations with the aim to increase research into the Polar Regions and to expand awareness of these regions' importance globally. The participants in the project from Finland were universities and research institutions. One of the subjects for the research in Finland was the aurora borealis, and the northern lights also star in one of the stamps of the International Polar Year miniature sheet. The other stamp depicts a snowflake, which points to the high standards of research performed in Finland into snow and ice. In the lower left-hand corner of the miniature sheet there is a close-up of icy blueberry twigs to refer to research into adaptations by plants to changes in the climate and environment. The lower right-hand corner of the sheet includes a map showing the Finnish research stations taking part in research projects for IPY. The sheet is shown in Fig. 3-20.9, the *Snow flake* hologram in Fig. 3-20.10 and the FDC in Fig. 3-20.11. Susanna Rumpu and Ari Lakaniemi designed the miniature sheet. Pekka Honkakoski, Pekka Luukkola and Heikki Nikki took the photos used in the illustrations for the stamp sheet which was printed by Cartor Security Printers, France.

Fig. 3-20.12. The stamps with the *clapper board* hologram.

Fig. 3-20.13. The 'Dragones Destino de Fuego' FDC.

For the third time in 2007 stamps were issued in **Peru**. The Peruvian Film 'Dragones Destino de Fuego' [National Contemporary Cinema - Dragons – fates] stamps were issued on **February 5, 2007**, (**No. 233** and **234**). Like the stamps issued in January, these stamps have the same *clapper board* hologram attached in the upper left corner. The two stamps are shown in Fig. 3-20.12 and the FDC in Fig 3-20.13.

On **July 1**, **2007**, **Hong Kong** issued stamps honoring the 10th anniversary of the establishment of the Hong Kong Special Administrative Region and return to China in 1997. To celebrate this event a set of six commemorative stamps on were issued. In addition a very large sheetlet was issued with three $10-stamps depicting 'A Symphony of Lights' (**No. 235**). The use of *semi-translucent holographic technology* was used to make the sheetlet which is shown in Fig. 3-20.14. The hologram sheet showcases a highly reflective visual image, capturing the moment when dazzling fireworks display lights up the sky over the Victoria Harbor. With 'A Symphony of Lights' being recognized by the Guinness World Records as the largest light and sound show in the world, this hologram sheetlet is also one of the largest issued and of high collection value. The sheet was designed by Benny Lau and printed by Cartor Security Printing. The FDC is shown in Fig. 3-20.15 and the special commemorative present pack in Fig. 3-20.16.

Fig. 3-20.14. Holographic stamp sheetlet containing a set of three $10 stamps.

Fig. 3-20.15. The Hong Kong holographic stamp sheetlet FDC.

Fig. 3-20.16. Special present folder with the souvenir sheet and the six conventional stamps.

201

Fig. 3-20.17. The Miniature Sheet, the one issued on July 7 and the Bangkok 2007 overprinted version issued August 3.

Fig. 20-3.18. *Emperor Moth* Stamp covered with holographic foil, under direct and diffuse illumination.

On **July 7, 2007, Malaysia** issued a series of four stamps: the '**Insects - Series III**' including a souvenir sheet (**No. 236**). One notable fact about insects is that they are the most diverse groups of animals on earth with the number of species ranging from two million to possibly four million, outnumbering the amount of all other animal species on earth. In Malaysia alone, thousands of insect species exist and the diversity of the insect species in this country is made possible due to the range of habitats and climate in Malaysia. The special insect stamps featured the images of some of the most well-known and unique insects in Malaysia. On the definitive stamps the following insects are featured: Lantern flies (*Fulgora pyrorhyncha*) or lantern bugs which are very colourful, with yellow, black, red, blue and green markings on their bodies; the bright colors of the Fruit Bug (*Dysdercus cingulatus*) is usually a warning sign that the bug is distasteful; the Short-horned Valanga Grasshopper (*Valanga nigricornis*). Generally, the hind legs of grasshoppers are large and muscular and are specially developed for jumping; and the Longhorn Beetle (*Rhaphipodus hopei*).which is amongst the biggest longhorn beetles in Malaysia. A distinctive feature in the new stamp collection is the Miniature Sheet, where the image of the Emperor Moth (*Antheraea helfer*) is depicted. Interestingly, Malaysia has the largest and most beautiful moths in the world. The *Emperor moth* is highlighted with diffractive transparent holographic foil. The brightly orange-yellow colored Emperor Moth has a huge wingspan and is one of the most spectacular moth species in the world. The wings are very hairy and marked with 'eye-spots' and the antennae are short and feathered. The caterpillars of this species are colorful, fat and hairy. In Fig. 3-20.17 two versions of the souvenir sheets are shown. The one issued on July 7 and the overprinted one, the 'Bangkok 2007' version which was issued on **August 3, 2007, (No. 237)**. The 20th Asian International Stamp Exhibition was the third Asian international philatelic exhibition. This event was held between August 3 and 12, 2007 at Siam Paragon, the largest shopping complex in Thailand. In Fig. 3-20.18 the holographic effect is visualized by illumination using a spotlight (left photo) and an extended light source (right photo). The FDC is shown in Fig. 3-20.19. The stamps and souvenir sheet were design by Hazel Design and printed by Percetakan Keselamatan Nasional Sdn Bhd.

Fig. 3-20.19. Emperor Moth Miniature Sheet FDC.

The 'BLAST OFF! – 50 YEARS IN SPACE' stamps and souvenir sheet were issued in **Australia** on **October 2, 2007, (No. 238)**. The five issued 50c stamps were: the 1957 Sputnik 1, the 1965 Voskhod 2, the 1969 Apollo 11, the 1977 Voyager at Saturn, and the 1998 Space Shuttle / International Space Station. The souvenir sheet included a strip of these five stamps plus the $1 Hubble Space Telescope / Spiral Galaxy stamp. The *space* above the Earth on the upper left part of the souvenir sheet is covered by diffractive holographic foil. The sheet is shown in Fig. 3-20.20. A Prestige Booklet was issued with the front and back covers graced with holographic *stars* (Fig. 3-20.21).

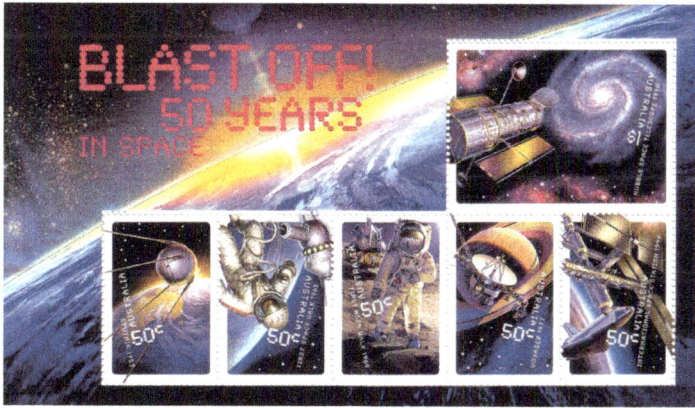

Fig. 3-20.20. The 'BLAST OFF!–50 YEARS IN SPACE' sheet.

Fig. 3-20.21. The 'BLAST OFF prestige booklet, front and back covers.

Fig. 3-20.22. The reindeer Christmas *snowflakes* stamps.

Fig. 3-20.23. The reindeer Christmas FDC.

On **November 1, 2007, Canada** issued the Christmas domestic rate (52¢) PERMANENT™ stamp which depicts a single leaping reindeer in a booklet of twelve stamps (**No. 239**). A stylized reindeer in mid-leap appears to take flight, bursting out of the stamp frame. The effect is achieved through careful positioning of the silhouetted form, antlers and hind hoof just outside the frame. Over a background of shifting color, scattered *snowflakes* printed in clear holographic foil give the scene a shimmer that recalls the festive spirit of the season. Designer Hélène L'Heureux, who also created the Snowman stamp for Christmas 2005 (see Fig. 3-18.20), designed the reindeer stamp as a companion piece. The two share many design elements, including the snowy background landscape of rolling hills. The holographic *snowflakes* are another common element-in fact, they were printed from the original plate created for the Snowman stamp, but used in reverse so the snowflakes would be positioned differently. The stamps, printed by Lowe Martin Company Inc., are shown in Fig. 3-20.22 and the FDC in Fig. 3-20.23.

On November 15, 2007, a set of four 250 CLP$ Christmas stamps were issued in Chile. The stamps were issued in sheets of 80 of the four designs (No. 240 through 243). On the stamps there are diffractive *stars* in the sky made of holographic foil. The four stamps are shown in Fig. 3-20.24 and the *stars* on one of the stamps in Fig. 3-20.25. The stamps were printed by Casa de Moneda de Chile.

Fig. 3-20.24. The Peru set of four Christmas stamps.

Fig. 3-20.25. The stars on one of the stamps.

Fig. 3-20.26. The King of Thailand sheet.

Fig. 3-20.27. The *King of Thailand* hologram stamp.

Fig. 3-20.28. The FDC with *King of Thailand* hologram stamp.

On **December 5, 2007, Thailand** issued the 2nd series of stamps for the celebrations of His Majesty the King's 80th Birthday Anniversary. Bhumibol Adulyadej (Phumiphon Adunyadet) was born December 5, 1927, and is the current King of Thailand. Having reigned since June 9, 1946, he is the world's longest-serving current head of state and the longest-serving monarch in Thai history. Although Bhumibol is a constitutional monarch, he has several times made decisive interventions in Thai politics, including the 2005-2006 Thai political crises. He was credited with facilitating Thailand's transition to democracy in the 1990s, although in earlier periods of his reign he supported military regimes. He is one of the wealthiest men in the world. Thailand Post Company was responsible for issuing commemorative stamps, which are produced in three sets. The first set shows a portrait of His Majesty the King in the grand public audience at the open balcony of the Ananta Samakhom Throne Hall, Dusit Palace, on June 9, 2006, when Thailand celebrated the 60th anniversary of His Majesty's accession to the throne. The second set comprises nine types, and each type consists of one million stamps (**No. 244**). It depicts His Majesty the King during various periods of his life, from his childhood up to the present (Fig. 3-20.26). A numbered imperforated limited-edition (1000) souvenir sheet was also issued together with a perforated sheet, both with the same number printed at the right margin of the two sheets. The 80-baht stamp has a hologram portrait of *H.M. the King Bhumibol Adulyadej*, which is shown Fig. 3-20.27 and in Fig. 3-20.28 the FDC with this stamp together with two of the other stamps on the sheet. The stamps, designed by Veena Chantanatat, were printed by Cartor Security Printing.

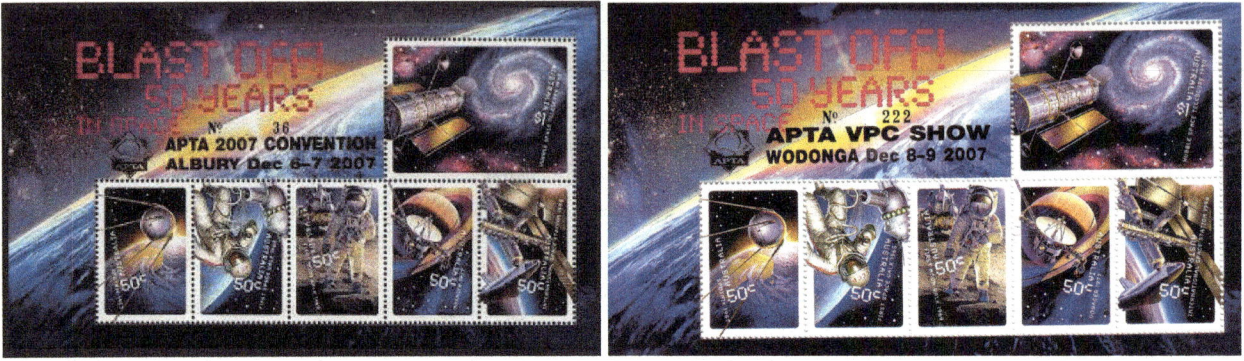

Fig. 3-20.29. The overprinted APTA 2007 ALBURY sheet. **Fig. 3-20.30.** The overprinted APTA VPC WODONGA sheet.

Two overprinted versions of the 'Blast off in Space' sheet were issued in **Australia** for two stamp exhibitions. The first one was issued on **December 6**, **2007**, for the APTA 2007 Convention in Albury, which took place between December 6 and 7, 2007, (**No. 245**). Only a very limited-edition (100) of this one was issued. The second one was issued on **December 8**, **2007**, for the APTA VPC Show in Wodonga, which took place between December 8 and 9, 2007, (**No. 246**). The two sheets are shown in Figs. 3-20.29 and 3-20.30.

P. R. China issued six stamps and a souvenir sheet (**No. 247**) on **December 20, 2007**, for next year's Summer Olympics in Beijing. With a total face value of 8.6 yuan, the stamps feature the National Gymnasium, the China Agricultural University Gymnasium, the Beijing University Gymnasium, the Qingdao Olympic Sailing Center, the Laoshan Velodrome and the National Swimming Center, or the Water Cube. A 6-yuan commemorative cover sheet depicting the National Stadium, or the Bird's Nest, was issued together with the stamps. The stadium design implemented steel beams in order to hide supports for the retractable roof; giving the stadium the appearance of a bird's nest. The stadium was built in the Olympic Green Village, Chaoyang District. The stadium officially opened on June 28, 2008. The souvenir sheet, shown in Fig. 3-20.31, has holographic *Chinese and English lettering* in the upper left corner. The pentagonal stamp on the sheet depicts the new stadium.

Fig. 3-20.31. The Bird's souvenir sheet with holographic lettering.

Fig. 3-20.32. The Paulet two-set rocket stamps.

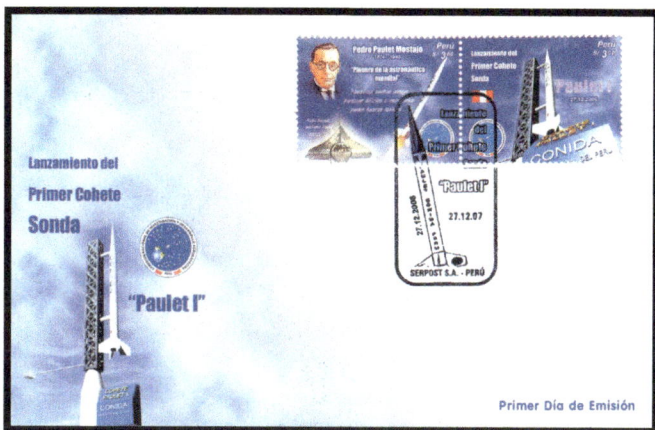

Fig. 3-20.33. The Paulet rocket stamps FDC.

Peru issued 3 PEN se-tenant stamps on **December 27, 2007**, to celebrate the anniversary of the launch of the First Peruvian Space Rocket-Probe 'Paulet 1', which took place on December 27, 2006. Pedro Paulet Mostajo (1874 – 1945) was a Peruvian scientist who allegedly in 1895 was the first person to build a liquid-fuel rocket engine and, in 1900, the first person to build a modern rocket propulsion system. One of the stamps depicts Pedro Paulet and the second stamp the rocket at the launch site with *Paulet 1* in holographic lettering (**No. 248**). The stamps are shown in Fig. 3-20.32 and the FDC in Fig. 3-20.33.

Various prepaid postal envelopes with the hologram security label were issued in **Greece** during **2007**. One example is the Business Express Post envelope as shown in Fig. 3-20.34.

Fig. 3-20.34. A Business Express Hellenic Post envelope.

3-21. Holographic stamps and souvenir sheets issued in 2008

Singapore issued a new type of hologram stamp with morphing effect for the new Lunar year, the year of the Rat. Türkmenistan issued three sets of hologram stamps: a green set, a silver set, and a gold foil set. Austria issued a special souvenir sheet with a diffractive effect and four Swarovski crystals. Thailand continued to issue hologram stamps. One was the Thai Postal Service anniversary souvenir sheet with a stamp with a 2D hologram portrait of King Chulalongkorn and the other was the Peacock series with beautiful holographic effects. China issued a souvenir sheet with hologram stamps for the XXIX Olympiad. Åland continued to issue stamps with holographic foil, this year both Christmas stamps and Christmas seals.

Fig. 3-21.1. The Zodiac Rat year sheet.

Fig. 3-21.2. The Zodiac Rat year sheet FDC.

Fig. 3-21.3. The $5 stamp morphing effect.

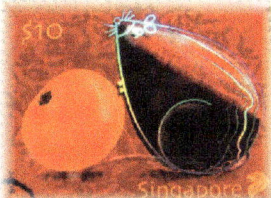 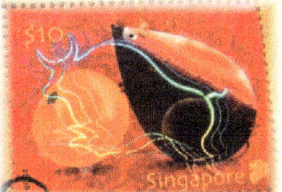
Fig. 3-21.4. The $10 stamp morphing effect.

For the new Lunar year 2008 **Singapore** issued stamps and a collectors' sheet on **January 18, 2008**. The new cycle of the Chinese calendar starts with the zodiac animal Rat which is depicted on the stamps. The denominations of the two stamps on the sheet are $5 and $10 (**No. 249 to 251**). Featuring a first-in-the-world unique printing technique, the *rats* on the stamps are covered with high reflective index transparent holographic foil with morphing effect. Morphing means an image changes (or morphs) into another through a seamless transition. Under this special effect, one can simultaneously view the Rat and the outgoing zodiac animal, the Boar on the $5 stamp. The $10 stamp features the same interesting effect with the Rat and next year's animal, the Ox. The stamps and sheet were designed by Leo Teck Chong. The collectors' sheet was printed by Cartor Security Printing. The sheet is shown in Fig. 3-21.1 and the FDC, cancelled with a special Rat postmark, in Fig. 3-21.2. The morphing effect is demonstrated in Fig. 3-21.3 and 3-21.4. Overprinted versions were issued for TAIPEI'08, OLYMPEX'08 and JAKARTA'08.

Macau issued also stamps and a souvenir sheet for the Lunar year 2008, which happened on **January 23, 2008**. The Macao's Post Office issued a set of Philatelic issues dedicated to the Lunar Cycle which was based on the 'Five Elements' - Metal, Wood, Water, Fire and Earth. The denominations of the five stamps in the series are: 1.50, 1.50, 1.50, 1.50 and 5.00 Patacas (**No. 252**). The souvenir sheet denomination is 10.00 Patacas (**No. 253**). The stamps and sheet were designed by Wilson Chi Ian Lam and printed by Sprintpak in Australia with embossing and hot stamping with gold and holographic foil. The five stamps are shown in Fig. 3-21.5 and the souvenir sheet in Fig. 3-21.6.

Fig. 3-21.5. The five Macau Rat stamps with the hologram stamp at the left end.

Fig. 3-21.6. The Macau Rat souvenir sheet.

Fig. 3-20.7. The green, the gold and silver series of the seven hologram stamps.

Fig. 3-20.8. Illustrations of the some of the hologram stamps.

Türkmenistan issued on **June 1**, 2008, three sets of seven self-adhesive definitive hologram stamps in the Fauna series. The first set was on green foil (**No. 254**), the second on gold foil (**No. 255**) and the third on silver foil (**No. 256**). The three series depict animals and birds living on open spaces of Central Asia. All three set denominations are: A, D, G, G, O, S, and T and the featured animals on the stamps are: Great white leopard, Ram, Pelican, Lynx, Grey Heron, Deer, and Partridge (yellow-necked spurfowl). The three sets of seven stamps are shown in Fig. 3-20.7. Three examples of the stamps, correctly illuminated, are shown in Fig. 3-20.8.

A special miniature sheet was issued in **Austria** on **June 5**, **2008**, (**No. 257**) for the 2008 European soccer championships (UEFA EURO 2008) hosted by Austria and Switzerland. Swarovski, the famous Austrian crystal manufacturer, produced the crystals for the stamps. The souvenir sheet was adorned with four Swarovski crystals, two on each side of the Union of European Football Associations' Henri Delaunay trophy cup named after the former UEFA Secretary General. This valuable trophy made of sterling silver weighs 8 kg and is 60 cm high, with the names of the European Champions engraved on the back. The stamp shows the Cup against a blue background, and is decorated with four particularly large original Swarovski crystals and is covered with a weak diffractive foil. The sheet is shown in Fig. 3-21.9.

Fig. 3-21.9. The EURO 2008 stamp.

  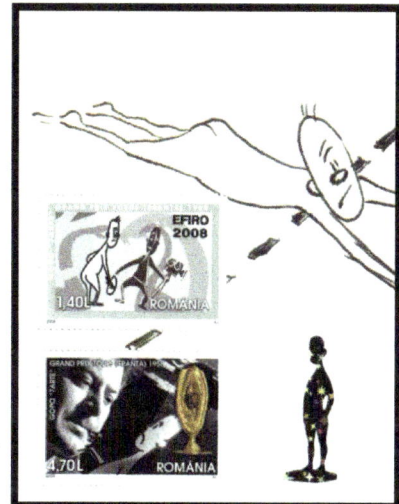

Fig. 3-21.10. The GOPO '7 ARTS' sheet with the *Little Man*.

Fig. 3-21.11. The limited-edition (500) GOPO sheet with the overprinted stamp.

The film producer Ion Popescu-Gopo created the 'Little Man' a cartoon movie which was awarded with the 1958 Grand Prize for the Best Animation Film in the Tours Film Festival (France) for his movie '7 ARTS'. Gopo's most known cartoon character is a little black and white nude character designed in simple lines. For remembering this major event for Romanian cinematography, Romfilatelia in **Romania** issued on **June 22, 2008**: GOPO: '7 ARTS' Grand Prix, Tours, France, 1958, a set of two stamps and a miniature sheet. The miniature sheet with the two stamps and the attached has the *Little Man* cut out of holographic foil, shown in Fig. 3-21.10 (**No. 258**). The stamps and sheet were designed by Alexandra Irimia. A limited-edition (500) souvenir sheet with the 'EFIRO 2008' overprint in gold on the 1.40L stamp was issued. (**No. 259**) This sheet was included in a special philatelic folder. The sheet with the overprinted stamp is shown in Fig. 3-21.11.

On **August 1, 2008**, a souvenir sheet with five stamps was issued in **Thailand** for the 125th Anniversary of Thai Postal Service (1st series). The commutative stamps were issued on the first day of an anniversary exhibition at Queen Sirkit National Convention Center. One of the stamps on the sheet was a hologram stamp (**No. 260**). The sheet illustrates a series of stamps on stamps issuances. The 5-Baht stamp on the sheet illustrates stamp printing by using 100 dpi screening technique. The 25.00-Baht stamp illustrates the *one Solot postage stamp* as a hologram and using 600 dpi screening technique in the background. This Thai Postage Stamp First Issue, the one Solot was issued on August 4, 1883. The stamp which depicts *King Chulalongkorn* in profile was designed by William Ridgeway at Waterlow & Sons Ltd. in London where the stamps were printed. This stamp is also depicted on the 5-Baht stamp on the upper left corner on the sheet. The other two 5 Baht stamps illustrate stamp printing by using 300 dpi screening technique. The 10

Baht stamp illustrates stamp printing by using mixed 100 dpi, 300 dpi and 600 dpi screening technique. The name of this first set, the 'Solot set' is derived from the lowest value in the set, which is the one Solot. The 2008 stamps and the sheet were designed by Udorn Niyomthum of Thailand Post Co. Ltd. Cartor Security Printing Company in France printed the stamps. The sheet is shown in Fig. 3-21.12 with the hologram stamp next to it. The FDC with the hologram stamp and two of the other stamps is shown in Fig. 3-21.13.

Fig. 3-21.12. The Thai sheet with the *One Solot* hologram stamp.

Fig. 3-21.13. The FDC with the *One Solot* hologram stamp.

August 1	Red sheet
August 2	Light yellow sheet
August 3	Pink sheet
August 4	Light green sheet (Fig. 3-21.14)
August 5	Orange sheet
August 6	Light blue sheet
August 7	Purple sheet
August 8	Dark blue sheet
August 9	Yellow sheet
August 10	Dark green

Table 3-21.1. The ten colored sheets.

Fig. 3-21.14. Light green sheet.

In addition to the five-stamp souvenir sheet ten souvenir sheets with the hologram stamp were issued each day between **August 1** and **10, 2008**, (**No. 261** to **270**). The issued colored sheets are shown in Table 3-21.1 on the next page and one of the issued sheets are shown in Fig. 3-21.14.

Argentina issued a souvenir sheet on **August 2**, **2008** for the 'China World Philatelic Expo' in Beijing (**No. 271**). The $4 (ARS) stamp issued for the 2008 Olympic Games (Summer Olympics) in Beijing is part of the sheet. The sheet, printed by Letra Viva SA, Buenos Aires, is shown in Fig. 3-21.15.

Fig. 3-21.15. The Argentina sheet.

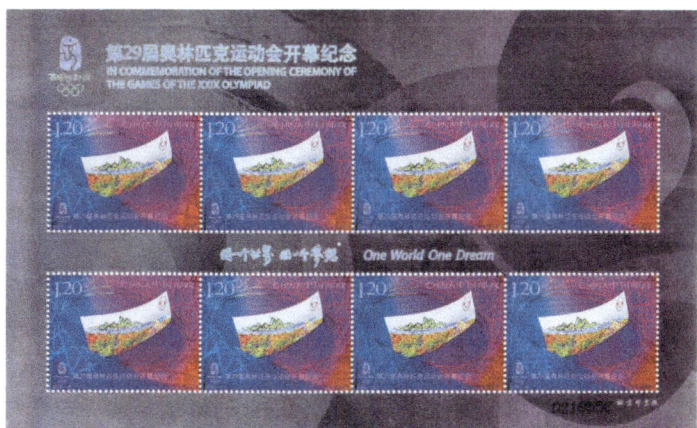

Fig. 3-21.16. The holographic *Bird Nest* Sheetlet II.

Fig. 3-21.17. The *Bird Nest* hologram stamp.

On **August 8, 2008, P. R. China** issued stamps and several souvenir sheets for the Opening Memorial of the Games of the XXIX Olympiad which took place between August 8 and 24, 2008. One of the sheets (Sheetlet II) was an eight-stamp tinfoil sheet with hologram stamps (**No. 272**). The 1.20-Yuan hologram stamp depicts the *bird nest stadium* with the Chinese and English holographic lettering at the upper left corner and in the middle of the sheet. The Stadium looks like a bird's nest (See the souvenir sheet in Fig. 3-20.31). The 2008 Summer Olympics Opening Ceremony was held at the Beijing National Stadium. It took place on August 8, 2008. The number 8 is associated with prosperity and confidence in Chinese culture. The ceremony was directed by Chinese filmmaker Zhang Yimou and featured a cast of over 15,000 performers, and was dubbed beforehand as the most spectacular Olympics Opening Ceremony ever produced. A rich assembly of ancient Chinese art and culture dominated the ceremony. China National Philatelic Corporation (CNPC) was responsible for the stamps and souvenir sheets. They were designed by Zhang Yimou, Chen Mingjie at CNPC Information & Technology Department and printed by the Beijing Postage Stamp Printing Works. The Sheetlet II is shown in Fig. 3-21.16 and a stamp on it in Fig. 3-21.17.

On **August 9, 2008, Thailand** issued two 10-Baht Peacock stamps (**No. 273** and **274**) and a souvenir sheet (**No. 275**). Among animals, peacocks are unique in their sounds and colorful plumage, some of which displays exquisite designs. Peacocks belong to the same family as pheasant. There are two species; one found in Africa, for example the Congo peacock, and the other found in Asia and are divided into two kinds; Indian or blue peacocks and Thai or green peacocks. Featured on the stamps is the green peafowl (*Pavo muticus*) which is found in the tropical forests of Southeast Asia. The Thai peacocks on the stamps are covered with iridescent, transparent diffractive holographic foil as well as the plumage on the sheet. The Peacock stamps demonstrating the holographic effect are shown in Fig. 3-21.18. Two souvenir sheets are shown in Fig. 3-21.19 and Fig. 3-21.20. The two-stamp peacock FDC is shown in Fig. 3-21.21 and one of the ten-stamp sheets in Fig. 3-21.22. The peacock issue was designed by Mayuree Narknisorn, Thailand Post Co. Ltd. and printed by Thai British Security Printing Public Co. Ltd., Thailand.

Fig. 3-21.18. The two different Peacock stamps showing the diffractive effect.

Fig. 3-21.19. One souvenir sheet showing the diffractive effect.

Fig. 3-21.20. Another issued souvenier sheet.

Fig. 3-21. 21. The FDC with two Peacock stamps.

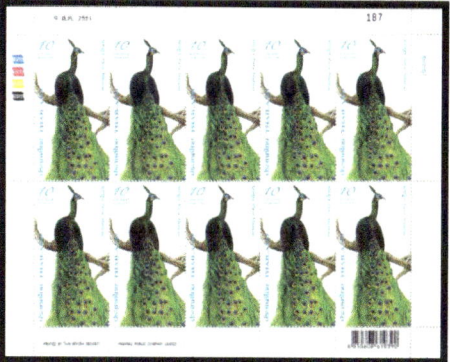

Fig. 3-21. 22. A ten-stamp Peacock sheet.

On **September 19**, **2008**, **P. R. China** issued a Cinderella sheet (**No. 276**) for the opening of the Nanchang Zhonghua Stamp Expo in China. The sheet (Fig. 3-21.23) is based on the 'Summer Palace' stamps issued on May 10, 2008. Three versions (one color, one b/w and the two superimposed to create the third stamp) of the Shiqikong Bridge stamp are included in the sheet, however, all without denomination. The upper right corner of the sheet is printed with holographic foil *text*. The stamps and the sheet were designed by Xiao Yutian. China National Philatelic Corporation was responsible for the issue and printed by Henan Provincial Posts and Telecommunications Printing House.

Fig. 3-21. 23. The Nanchang Zhonghua Stamp Expo Cinderella sheet.

Fig. 3-21.24. The Angel stamp.   **Fig. 3-21.25.** The Angel Christmas FDC.

Åland issued on **October 9**, **2008**, the Angel Christmas 2008 stamp (**No. 277**). The Christmas stamp motif is that of an angel, to many people the symbol of Christmas. The artist, Eva-Jo Hancock first created an angel from textile, paper and other materials before photographing the merry angel which now appears on the stamp. The angel holds a heart in her hand, and the *snowflakes* as well as the *Earth* beneath are covered with glittering holographic foil (Fig. 3-21.24). The denomination (€0.55) of the stamp 'Julpost 08' implies that the stamp can be used as postage for Christmas greetings to Åland, Finland and Sweden at a reduced price during a limited period of time in November and December. The FDC is shown in Fig. 3-21.25. The stamps were printed by Joh. Enschedé Security Printers.

On same day **Åland** issued also Christmas seals with holograms (**No. 278**). The artist Marianne Häggblom designed the Christmas seals. The motifs are easily associated with Christmas: *Santa Claus*, *Christmas-red tulips*, a *bullfinch* and an *angel* (Fig. 3-21.26). The 20 self-adhesive-seal sheet is shown in Fig. 3-21.27. The Post devotes its proceeds from the sale of Christmas seals to charity each year and in 2008 it supported the Joy Stables and Mariehamn Fire & Rescue Services. At the back of each sheet is a lottery number. Some of the many fine prizes are a travel voucher for €1 000, two weekend-stays at the hotel Havsvidden in Geta, Åland, and five digital cameras.

Fig. 3-21.26. The four 2008 Christmas seal stamps.

Fig. 3-21.27. The 20-seal sheet.

Fig. 3-21.28. The presentation sheet.   **Fig. 3-21.29.** The AFI Award.

To celebrate the award of 'The Castle' as being Australia's favorite film of all time, **Australia** issued on **December 8**, **2008**, a special stamp sheetlet pack in honor of this classic Australian film (**No. 279**). *The Castle* was announced as Australia's favorite film at the L'Oreal AFI (Australian Film Institute) Awards. *The Castle* is the Kerrigan family's story of their battle with the airport to keep their beloved house. In recognition of 50 years of the AFI, a public poll was conducted in late July 2008 by the AFI in association with Australia Post. This is the first time that an Australian stamp issue has been produced based on the voting preferences of the Australian public. In recognition of the public vote, five films were chosen. These appeared as five 55c stamps and were issued on November 3, 2008 as the Favorite Australian Films stamp. The special embellished stamp presentation pack which was given to all attendees and presenters at the AFI Awards Ceremony consists of self-adhesive stamps of *The Castle* as part of the sheetlet and also self-adhesive stamps of other Favorite Australian Films. In the middle of the sheetlet is the *AFI Award* covered with holographic foil. The AFI Award was presented to *The Castle* team. Noel Leahy, Group Manager of Philatelic, Australia Post. Jo Mure designed the stamps and printed by McKellar Renown. The presentation sheet with the movie stamps and the AFI Award is shown in Fig. 3-21.28 and the holographic effect in Fig. 3-21.29.

3-22. Holographic stamps and souvenir sheets issued in 2009

Singapore continued issuing the lunar year hologram stamps with morphing effect. 2009 was the year of the ox. Both Lichtenstein and Indonesia issued astronomic hologram stamps. Japan and Romania issued sheets with holograms in the 'Preserve the Polar regions and Glaciers' series. Portugal issued interesting stamps illustrating the five senses, in which the one illustrating vision depicted spectacles with hologram lenses. In Malaysia the stamp series 'Citizen of Malaysia' with a special hologram souvenir sheet was issued. Ecuador issued a souvenir sheet. Canada and Switzerland issued Christmas stamps with holograms. Multicolored minerals stamps were issued in the Ukraine with relief stamping and holographic film.

Fig. 3-22.1. The Zodiac Ox year sheet.

Fig. 3-22.2. The Zodiac Ox year sheet FDC.

Fig. 3-22.3. The $5 stamp morphing effect.

Fig. 3-22.4. The $10 stamp morphing effect.

Singapore issued stamps and a collectors' sheet on **January 9, 2009**, for the new Lunar year, the year of the Ox. It is the second year in the Zodiac Cycle. The ox is depicted on the stamps. The denominations of the two stamps (**No. 280** and **281**) on the miniature sheet (**No. 282**) are $5 and $10. The same unique printing technique which was introduced in 2008 was also used in 2009. The *ox* on the stamps is covered with high reflective index transparent holographic foil with morphing effect. Under this special effect, one can simultaneously view the Ox and the outgoing zodiac animal, the Rat on the $5 stamp. The $10 stamp features the same interesting effect with the Ox and next year's animal, the Tiger. The stamps and sheet were designed by Leo Teck Chong. The sheet was printed by Cartor Security Printing. The sheet is shown in Fig. 3-22.1 and the FDC, cancelled with a special Ox postmark, in Fig. 3-22.2. The morphing effect is demonstrated in Fig. 3-22.3 and 3-22.4. Overprinted versions were issued for TAIPEI'08, OLYMPEX'08 and JAKARTA'08.

Lichtenstein issued definitive hologram stamps for the first time on **March 2, 2009**. It was the 'Europa 2009 - Astronomy issue' with a single stamp design (face value CHF 1.30, **No. 283**). It was selected via a competition held in collaboration with the Liechtenstein School of Art. The winning design, by Leta Krähenbühl, is printed on hologram foil and depicts a *stylized supernova* (Fig. 3-22.5). An important design element within the artwork is a tiny white dot at the center of the design. It represents a White Dwarf, the culmination of the star's collapse. A Maxi Card (photo: Keystone) depicting a region of the night sky that carries a single stamp was issued as well as a FDC. The Maxi Card and the FDC are shown in Fig. 3-22.6 and Fig. 3-22.7. The 20-stamp sheet is shown in Fig. 3-22.8. The stamps were printed by Austrian State Printing Company in Vienna.

Fig. 3-22.5. The *supernova* stamp.

Fig. 3-22.6. The Maxi Card.

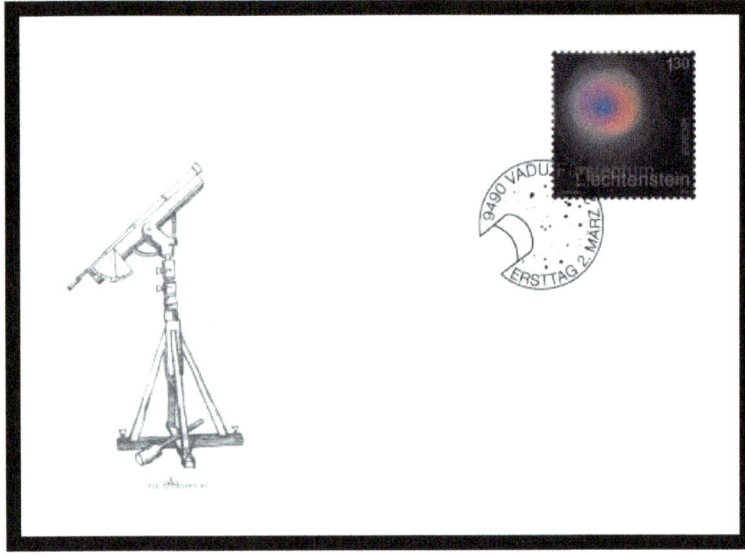
Fig. 3-22.7. The 'Europa – 2009' FDC.

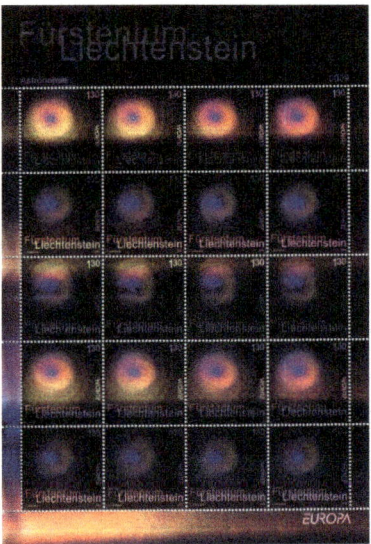
Fig. 3-22.8. The 20-stamp sheet.

On **March 21, 2009**, the 'Preserve the Polar Regions and Glaciers' souvenir sheet was issued in **Romania**. At the beginning of the 21st century, one of the major problems that mankind has to face and will have to face also in the future is represented by the global warming phenomenon affecting the Arctic ice cap which is melting fast. In 2007, the ice cap reached the lowest sizes registered in the last 30 years of satellite record. The special thematic philatelic issue follows the initiative launched in May 2007 by the presidents of Chile and Finland states. In full agreement the Postal Administrations from these two countries proposed also to other states to join the program of creating a postage stamps issue having as theme preserve the polar regions and glaciers. A series of Northern European countries, but also Australia, Canada, New Zealand, Brazil, South Africa and many other countries joined this project. Romania was one of them. The Finnish Philatelic Center's director Markku Penttinen was acting as the leader of this campaign. The 'International Polar Year 2007-2009' stamps issued by the participating countries all had the same specific sign: the graphic symbol of an ice crystal and next to it the outline of the white continent. The design – a "protected" ice crystal - was created by Saku Heinänen a Finnish graphic designer. About 42 countries announced they were committed to participate with the issue of at least one stamp during the first quarter of 2009. In addition to the 1.60L and 8.10L stamps issued in Romania, two different souvenir sheets were issued: one block with **black** numbers (edition of 23500) and one with **red** numbers with silver logo and an *ice crystal* hologram (edition of 1000, Fig. 3-22.9, **No. 284**). The Romanian stamps were designed by Mihai Vamasescu.

Fig. 3-22.9. The limited-edition (172/1000) sheet with **red** numbers with the *ice crystal* hologram.

Fig. 3-22.10. The Astronomy souvenir sheet.

Fig. 3-22.11. The stamp with holographic foil.

Fig. 3-22.12. The limited-edition (139/5000) souvenir sheet FDC.

Indonesia issued a hologram souvenir sheet for the 'International Year of Astronomy' on **May 2, 2009**, commemorating the 400th years of the telescope usage in the field of astronomy pioneered by Galileo Galileo (1564 - 1642). The sheet (**No. 285**) has three 5000-Rp stamps, one with *holographic foil*. Leftmost stamp features the 1609 Galilean telescope, rightmost stamp a portrait of Galileo and the holographic foil stamp carries the International Year of Astronomy (IYA2009) logo. The right and left stamps also carry the logo in a smaller size. As a background, the sheet shows Omega Centauri galaxy recorded through the telescope of Bosscha Observatory. Note the small image of the Bosscha Observatory in the lower right of the sheet. The stamps and sheet were designed by Tata Sugiarta and printed by Perum Peruri. The souvenir sheet is shown in Fig. 3-22.10, the holographic stamp in Fig. 3-22.11 and the limited-edition FDC (5000) with the Bosscha Observatory cachet image in Fig. 3-22.12.

Czech Republic issued sheet of six 17-CZK stamps on **May 6, 2009**, the 'EUROPA - Astronomy - 400th Anniversary of Keplers Laws' issue (**No. 286**). In addition to the Galilean telescope 400th anniversary, the Czech postage stamp commemorates instead the 400th anniversary of publication of J. Kepler's Astronomia Nova. The Association of European Public Postal Operators PostEurop declared 'Astronomy' as this year's common theme for the postage stamp issue EUROPA. At the initiative of professional astronomers associated in the International Astronomical Union the year 2009 was proclaimed by the UNESCO as the International Year of Astronomy under the auspices of the UN. The astronomer, mathematician, physicist and astrologer, Johannes Kepler (1571 - 1630), was a man of significance not only for the Czech environment. In 1600 he came to Prague already as a convinced follower of Kopernik's system. At the Emperor Rudolf II's court he became a colleague of Tycho Brahe and after the latter's death (1601) he took the position of the Emperor's mathematician and astronomer. The same security hologram label (as previously used on the 2004 and 2005 sheets) is attached at the middle of the lower margin. The Kepler six-stamp sheet is shown in Fig. 3-22.13. The stamps were designed by Jan Ungrád and engraved by Bohumil Šneider. The Czech Post Printing House in Prague printed the stamps.

Fig. 3-22.14. The Kepler six-stamp sheet with the security hologram.

Fig. 3-22.15. The Japanese sheet.   **Fig. 3-22.16**. The Japanese FDC.

On **June 30**, **2009**, **Japan** issued four die-cut, self-adhesive 80-yen stamps (**No. 287** through **290**) on a souvenir sheet (**No. 291**) in the 'Preserve the Polar regions and Glaciers' international series. These stamps are also having holograms and it is the first time Japan issues such stamps. The sheet features animals of the Arctic and Antarctic Polar Regions. The four stamps show a *Polar Bear with Cubs*, an *Arctic Fox*, a *Weddell Seal*, and an *Adelie Penguin*. The holograms create outlines of the animals in the design shown in Fig. 3-22.15 and the FDC in Fig. 3-22.16. A holographic *ice crystal* at the upper right corner on the souvenir sheet and on the stamps as well indicates that the issue is part of the 'Preserve the Polar Regions and Glaciers' project. The souvenir sheet stamps were designed by Hoshiama Ayaka and Hoshiyama Rika and printed by Toppan Printing.

An overprinted limited-edition (200) self-adhesive sheetlet of 'The Castle' favorite film award in **Australia** was issued on **July 23, 2009**. The overprinted AFI Award sheetlet (**No. 292**) was issued for the Melbourne Stampshow'09 and is shown in Fig. 3-22.17. The 09'National Philatelic Exhibition took place at the Function Room, Melbourne Park Tennis Centre, between July 23 and 26, 2009. The overprint depicts the Stampshow'09 logo.

Fig. 3-22.17. The limited-edition (112/200) overprinted AFI Award sheetlet.

Ecuador issued on **August 14**, **2009**, three stamps, one unique cork stamp and a normal, se-tenant paper stamp pair. A limited-edition (6000) miniature sheet (**No. 293**) celebrating the Bicentennial of the Independence was also issued. The se-tenant stamps are included in the miniature sheet (Fig. 3-22.18). On the top margin of the sheet is a hologram shown in Fig. 3-22.19. The left side of the sheet has printed holographic text: *EMISIÓN ESPECIAL* as shown in Fig. 3-22.20. Only 200 souvenir sheet FDCs were issued, one of them is shown in Fig. 3-22.21.

Fig. 3-22.18. The Bicentennial souvenir sheet.   Fig. 3-22.19. The hologram.

Fig. 3-22.20. The *EMISIÓN ESPECIAL* text.   Fig. 3-22.21. The limited-edition (130/200) FDC.

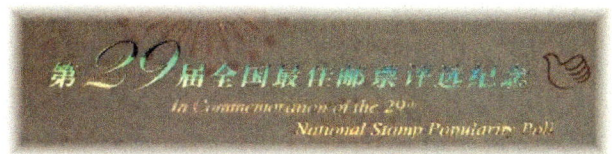

Fig. 3-22.22. The Chinese sheet with holographic *lettering*.

P. R. China issued on **August 16, 2009**, the China block 155 for the '29th National Best Stamp Popularity Poll' (**No. 294**). The souvenir sheet has holographic Chinese and English holographic *lettering* in the upper left area of the sheet. The sheet, shown in Fig. 3-22.22, was printed by Beijing Postage Stamp Printing Works.

Malaysia issued on **August 31, 2009**, issued the stamp '1Malaysia' concept which is based on the principles of 'People First, Performance Now' which was introduced by the sixth Prime Minister of Malaysia Dato' Sri Najib Tun Razak. This concept meets the needs of Malaysians and is in line with the existing Federal Constitution and the principles of the Rukun Negara (National Principles). The '1Malaysia' issue aims to strengthen the relationship and cooperation amongst the many races in Malaysia towards becoming united, able and ready to take on any challenges that might come its way. The idea is that this would bring Malaysia to greater heights in the eyes of the world. Five regular '1Malaysia' 30-sen stamps were issued: 1Malaysia (a 3D image of the '1Malaysia' logo in front of the map of Malaysia); Unity (Unity of the various races and ethnic groups in Malaysia); People First (Depicts Malaysian citizens from various sectors of society); Performance Now (the Nation's rapid development in the fields of science and technology, economy and information technology) and National Principles (The five principles of Malaysia: Belief in God, Loyalty to the King and Nation, Sovereignty of the Constitution, Rule of Law, and Good Behavior and Morality). Three of these stamps are shown on the FDC. The RM5 miniature sheet (**No. 295**) with a stamp covered with a holographic transparent foil depicts the *Citizen of Malaysia* from the various race and ethnic groups surrounding the '1Malaysia logo'. In Fig. 3-22.23 this sheet with the hologram is shown and the FDC in Fig. 3-22.24. There are two watermark versions of the hologram sheet, one with the CPM watermark and one with the inverted CPM mark, see Fig. 3-22.25 and Fig. 3-22.26. The stamps were designed by Hazel Design Sdn. Bhd and printed by Percetakan Keselamatan National Sdn. Bhd.

Fig. 3-22.23. The '1 Malaysia' sheet with the hologram. **Fig. 3-22.24**. The '1 Malaysia' FDC sheet.

Fig. 3-22.25. The SPM watermark. **Fig. 3-22.26**. The SPM inverted watermark.

On **October 2, 2009**, the 'Stamps of the Five Senses' were issued in **Portugal.** The following stamps, dedicated to each of the five senses, were issued: spectacle with hologram *lenses*, coffee cup, ice-cream, and two scented and textured stamps which allowing for experiencing real physical interaction: the touch feels the embossed ink coming out of the tube, the smell receives the aroma of the cup of coffee, the sight detects holographic images on the *spectacle lenses* that change according to the position of the stamp (Fig. 3-22.27, **No. 296**), the taste identifies the flavor of vanilla on the glue of the stamp that shows an ice-cream, the ear is sensitive to the noise made by the file when you rub its rough surface. The five stamps are shown on the FDC shown in Fig. 3-22.28. Thanks to improved technology in graphical arts, a set of elements, which is usually absent in common stamps, has been incorporated in this collection, becoming a differentiating fact in this emission and imparting an innovative character to stamps in the landscape of contemporaneous philately. The stamps were designed by João Machado. All stamps were printed by Cartor Security Printing.

Fig. 3-22.27. The *spectacle* stamp.

Fig. 3-22.28. The 'Stamps of the Five Senses' FDC.

Fig. 3-22.29. The Gandhi FDC (276/1000) with cachet hologram.

Fig. 3-22.30. The *Gandhi* cachet hologram.

Fig. 3-22.31. The Non-Violence FDC with *Gandhi* cachet hologram.

On **October 2, 2009**, **India**, issued stamps to celebrate the 140th birth anniversary of Mahatma Gandhi and also for the 'International Day of Non-Violence'. Both issued FDCs have holograms of *Gandhi* attached to the envelopes. (Figs. 3-22.29 through 3-22.31). The first FDC was limited to 1000 wase designed and issued by Eeshan Prakashan and South India Philatelists' Association, Chennai, India. Mahatma Gandhi, leader of the Indian independence movement and pioneer of the philosophy and strategy of non-violence, was born on October 2, 1869. According to UN General Assembly resolution of June 15, 2007, which established the commemoration, the International Day is an occasion to disseminate the message of non-violence, including through education and public awareness. Quoting the late leader's own words, he said: "Non-violence is the greatest force at the disposal of mankind. It is mightier than the mightiest weapon of destruction devised by the ingenuity of man." An 'INTERNATIONAL DAY OF NON-VIOLENCE' special folder with the same *Gandhi* hologram, as on the FDC, was also issued. The *Gandhi* hologram is shown in Fig. 3-22.33. Both of them have: 'Non-violence is the first article of my faith' by Gandhi printed on them. The cover and folder were approved by the Chief Postmaster General, Tamilnadu Circle, Chennai. The cachet holograms on the covers and folders are individually marked with laser written edition numbers: the covers are marked C-followed by the edition number and the folders are marked F-followed by the edition number. These markings are located at the bottom middle of the holograms. However a limited edition (200) was issued without numbers.

Fig. 3-22.32. Special Gandhi hologram folder.

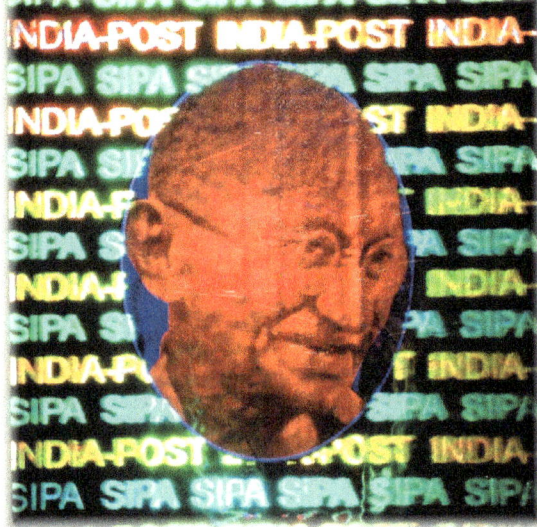

Fig. 3-22.33. *Gandhi* hologram.

Referring to 'Non-violence', it should be mentioned that the Swedish artist Carl Fredrik Reuterswärd, a pioneer in art holography, made the 'Non-Violence' gun sculpture which is located outside the United Nations building in New York. The sculpture is shown in Fig 3.22.34. The 'Non-Violence' sculpture has been featured on a Swedish stamp which was issued on August 3, 1995, shown in Fig. 3.22.35. This stamp was issued to mark the 50-year-anniversary of the United Nations. A *Non-Violence* hologram of a miniature version the sculpture is shown in Fig. 3-22.36. This hologram, produced in co-operation between the artist and HOLOMEDIA in Sweden, was on the cover of the Swedish newspaper Svenska Dagbladet on December 31, 1986.

Fig. 3-22.34. 'Non-Violence' sculpture by Carl Fredrik Reuterswärd.

Fig. 3-22.35. The 'Non-Violence' Swedish stamp.

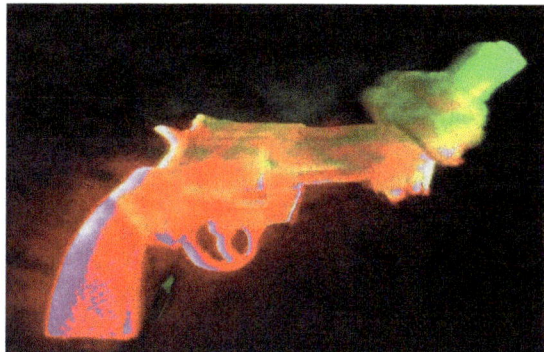

Fig. 3-22.36. *Non-Violence* hologram.

For the 'OLYMPIC & PARALYMPIC GAMES' to take place in London 2012, Royal Mail in **Great Britain** issued a set of ten Olympic stamps, 'THE JOURNEY TO 2012', on **October 22**, **2009**, (**No. 297**). On the back of the Pack (Pack number: M18) there is an individually numbered *XXX Olympic Logo* hologram. The Olympic stamp pack is shown in Fig. 3-22.37 with the hologram on the back next to it.

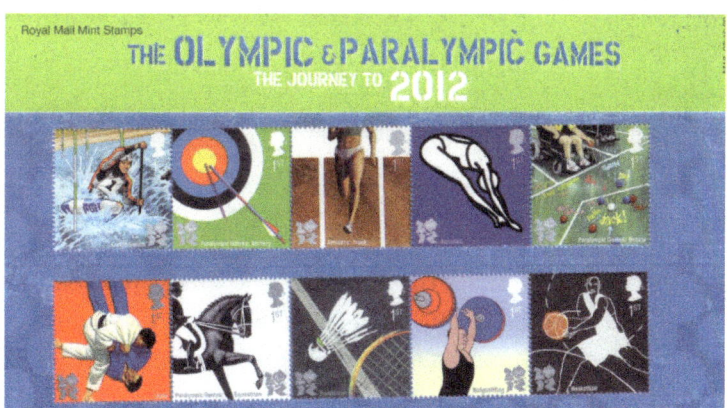

Fig. 3-22.37. THE JOURNEY TO 2012 stamps pack with the *XXX Olympic* logo hologram on the back.

Fig. 3-22.38. *Snowflakes* stamp.

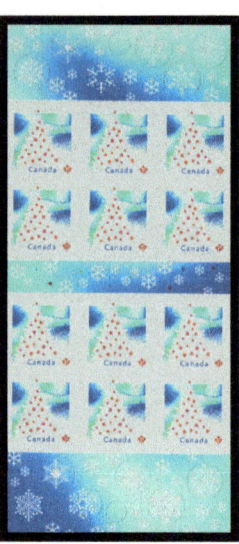

Fig. 3-22.39. Christmas stamps.

Fig. 3-22.40. The FDC with Shining Tree cancellation.

On **November 2**, **2009**, **Canada** issued the PERMANENT™ domestic-rate stamp featuring a radiant snow-covered Christmas tree (**No. 298**). The tree is pictured before a landscape of rolling hills and scattered snowflakes. The stamp was part of the holiday series that includes the 2005 snowman and the 2007 reindeer stamps. Like the two that preceded it, this stamp's festive backdrop features a landscape of rolling hills and scattered *snowflakes* printed in clear holographic foil, which glitter in the light. The stamp was designed by Hélène L'Heureux and printed by Lowe-Martin Company Inc. Alain Leduc, manager of Stamp Design and Production at Canada Post explained: "It's the mixture of holographic foil and simple, upfront imagery and design that make these stamps so interesting visually." The stamp is shown in Fig. 3-22.38, the twelve-stamp booklet in Fig. 3-22.39 and the FDC in Fig. 3-22.40.

Fig. 3-22.41. The three Christmas stamps.

Fig. 3-22.42. The Swiss Christmas stamp FDC.

Switzerland issued also Christmas stamp. The following stamps were issued on **November 20, 2009**: 'Santa Claus hat' (CHF 0.85, No. 299), 'Christmas tree' (CHF 1.00, No. 300), and 'Gift' (CHF 1.30, No. 301), all with a hologram *star*. Swiss Post wanted to create a festive atmosphere for the dispatch of letters and parcels during the Christmas season. The stamps also include season's greetings in Switzerland's four national languages. The stamps were designed by the Bernese artist Jenny Leibundgut and printed by Cator Security Printing. The three stamps are shown in Fig. 3-22.41 and the FDC in Fig. 3-22.42.

On **December 23, 2009**, the postage block (**No. 302**) of six stamps 'Minerals of Ukraine' was issued in **Ukraine**. The following minerals are featured on the stamps: Quartz (1.50 UAH), Natural Sulfur (1.90 UAH), Topaz (2.00 UAH), Beryl (2.20 UAH), Tiger's-eye (3.30 UAH), and α-kertschenite (4.85 UAH). The block is multicolored with relief stamping and embossing by film with holographic effect. The sheet contains microprint: 'Л. Мельнік'. Selvages of the block are artistically decorated with Ukrainian text and chemical formulas. The block was designed by Larissa Melnik and printed by Integrated Printing Plant Ukraine, a company involved in document security printing. The minerals block with the microtext is shown in Fig. 3-22.43, the holographic effect in Fig. 3-22.44 and the FDC in Fig. 3-22.45.

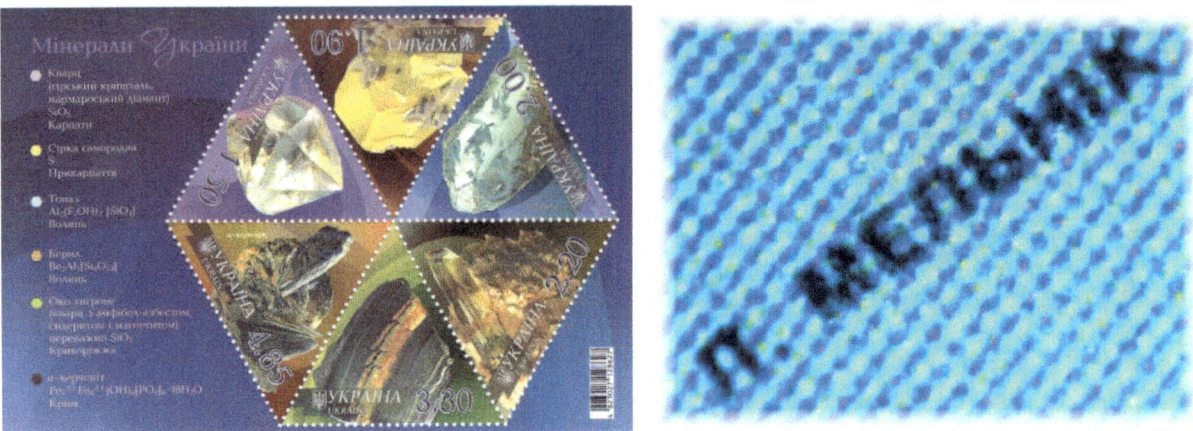

Fig. 3-22.43. The 'Minerals of Ukraine' stamps and the microtext.

Fig. 3-22.44. The hologram effect.

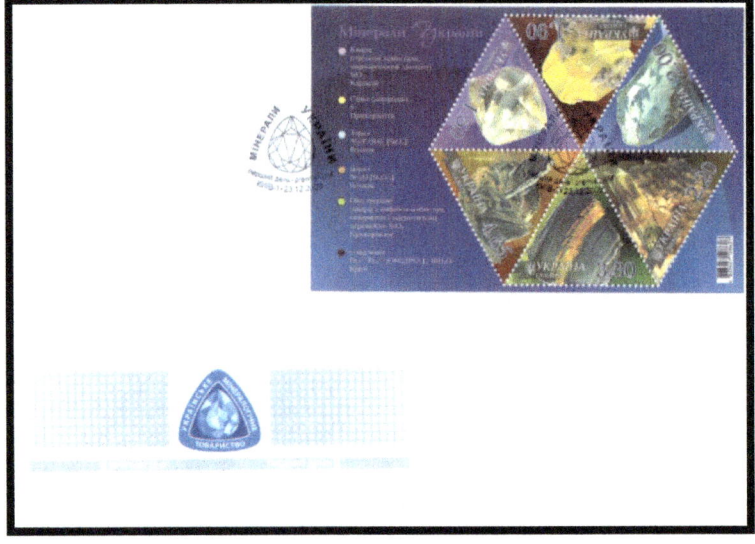

Fig. 3-22.45. The 'Minerals of Ukraine' FDC.

3-23. Holographic stamps and souvenir sheets issued in 2010

Macau issued stamps with holograms for the Lunar year of the Tiger. Like the preceding year, another Lunar year hologram stamp with the morphing effect was issued in Singapore. South Africa issued a miniature sheet with a hologram. The Czech Republic issued several stamps and booklets with the usual security hologram label. France issued a butterfly souvenir sheet with butterflies with holographic iridescent wings. For the first time stamps with holograms were issued in Nigeria. As in 2009, Switzerland issued a set of Christmas stamps with holograms. Thailand issued booklets with self-adhesive hologram stamps. Singapore issued beautiful festivals stamps, using the holographic foil printing technique. A second minerals stamp sheet was issued in the Ukraine with relief stamping and holographic film.

Fig. 3-23.1. The Macau Lunar Tiger hologram stamp and the five stamps.

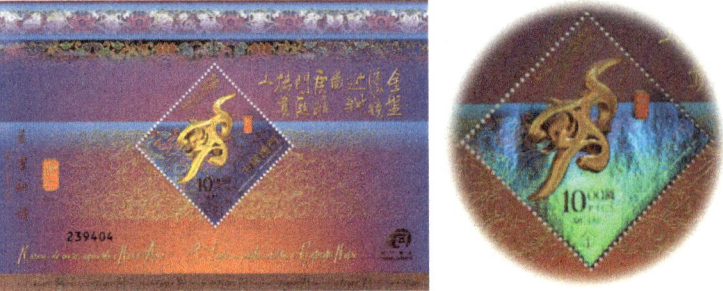

Fig. 3-23.2. The Macau Tiger souvenir sheet and the stamp on it.

Macau issued on **January 2, 2010**, stamps and a souvenir sheet for the third Chinese Zodiac series: the 'Lunar Year of the Tiger'. The stamps combine the different forms of the Tiger and the distinguishing characteristics of the Five Elements - metal, wood, water, fire and earth. The denominations of five stamps in the series are: 1.50, 1.50, 1.50, 1.50 and 5.00 Patacas, (**No. 303**). The souvenir sheet denomination is 10.00 Patacas (**No. 304**). The 'Metal Tiger' stamp is applied with emboss printing technique to highlight the image of intrepid tiger while the hot foil stamping with holographic and gold are used respectively on the cloud patterns, the face values and the characters. The stamps and sheet were designed by Wilson Chi Ian Lam and printed by Sprintpak in Australia. The stamps and souvenir sheet are shown in Figs. 3-23.1 and 3-23.2.

Singapore issued on **January 8, 2010**, two Lunar year stamps (**No. 305** and **306**) and a collectors' sheet (**No. 307**). The Tiger which is third in the Zodiac Cycle, is depicted on the stamps. The denominations of the two stamps on the sheet are $5 and $10. The *Tiger* on the stamps is covered with high reflective index transparent holographic foil with morphing effect. This technique was introduced in 2008, repeated in 2009, and once again used in 2010. Under this special effect, one can simultaneously view the Tiger and the outgoing zodiac animal, the Ox on the $5 stamp. The $10 stamp features the same interesting effect, with the Tiger and next year's animal, the Rabbit. The stamps and sheet were designed by Leo Teck Chong. The sheet was printed by Cartor Security Printing. The sheet is shown in Fig. 3-23.3 and the FDC, cancelled with a special Tiger postmark, in Fig. 3-23.4. The morphing effect is demonstrated in Fig. 3-23.5 and 3-23.6. For LONDON'10 and BANGKOK'10 overprinted versions exist.

Fig. 3-23.3. The Zodiac Tiger year sheet.

Fig. 3-23.4. The Zodiac Tiger year sheet FDC.

Fig. 3-23.5. The $5 stamp morphing effect.

Fig. 3-23.6. The $10 stamp morphing effect.

Fig. 3-23.7. The Digital Divide sheet.   **Fig. 3-23.8**. The Digital Divide FDC.

South Africa issued on **January 18, 2010**, the 'Breaking the Digital Divide' stamps (**No. 308** to **312**) and miniature sheet (**No. 313**). The gap between people with effective access to digital and information technology and those with very limited or no access at all, is referred to as the digital divide. The 7th Plenipotentiary Conference of the Pan African Postal Union (PAPU) requested PAPU member countries to issue a commemorative stamp to mark the founding of the Union on 18 January 1980. As a member of PAPU, the South African Post Office is marking this event by issuing this miniature sheet with the theme 'The post, a veritable means of bridging the digital divide'. The five stamps in a variety of shapes, which make up this miniature sheet, illustrate how people can use the resources made available by the Post Office to carry out daily activities required to function in a modern technologically driven world. An image of a post box combined with computer codes, for example, symbolizes two ways of spreading information. In South Africa, even people in deep rural areas can communicate using cell phones. Sending SMS messages, which is a low-cost and effective way of communicating, is also depicted on the miniature sheet. Rozanne Backhouse was responsible for the artwork. While the subject of bridging the digital divide is highly technical, the artist managed to illustrate the topic in such a way that anyone can understand it. As a single unit, the miniature sheet forms a rectangle, but the individual stamps contained within the miniature sheet have different shapes. Three of the stamps are triangular, one is rectangular and one has unequal sides. Diffractive holographic *foil* (e.g. in the shape of a *keyboard*) is used on the stamps and the sheet. Joh. Enschedé Stamps B.V printed the stamps and the souvenir sheet shown in Fig. 3-23.7 and the FDC in Fig. 3-23.8.

On **January 28, 2010**, **Thailand** issued two booklets with definitive self adhesive stamps (**No. 314** through **319**), both in the 'Memorable Words' series. One was with six different 3-Baht stamps and the other with the same six different 3-Bath stamps (**No. 320**), in sheets of ten stamps (**No. 321**). Part of the stamps is covered with holographic foil patterns. Shown in Figs. 3-23.9 and 3-23.10 are the two different booklets and the six stamps with the holographic pattern in Fig. 3-23.11. Thailand Post Co. Ltd issued the booklets and printed by Thai British Security Printing Public Co. Ltd.

Fig. 3-23.9. The 'Memorable Word' six-stamp sheetlet.   **Fig. 3-23.10**. The 'Memorable Word' booklet.

Fig. 3-23.11. The 'Memorable Word' stamps with the holographic pattern.

Fig. 3-23.12. The Missy dog booklet.   **Fig. 3-23.13.** The Missy Dog stamps with the hologram.

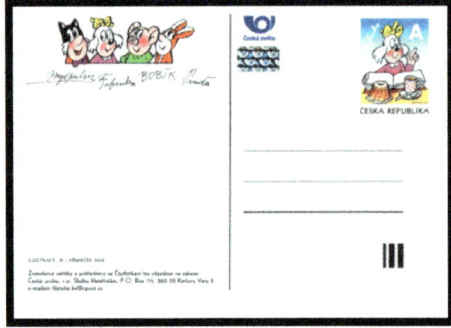

Fig. 3-23.14. The Missy dog postcard with the security hologram next to the printed stamp.

Czech Republic issued on **April 28**, **2010**, a booklet of ten self-adhesive definitive 10-CZK stamps (**No. 322**). This was a first in a series of the cult comics' Čtyřlístek [Four-Leaf Clover]. Fifinka, the Missy Dog, is the only 'girl' of the four characters designed and created by illustrator Jaroslav Němeček. The good housewife Fifinka is reading a cookbook, with a cup of white coffee and a cake on the table before her. The Čtyřlístek stories have been published for an unbelievable more than 40 years. Fifinka is the first character to appear on a stamp. Like the previous Czech stamps, the same security hologram (shown in Fig. 3-18.9) is attached at the top left corner of booklet. The front of the booklet is shown in Fig. 3-23.12 and the stamps with the security hologram in Fig. 3-23.13. The Czech Post Printing House in Prague printed the stamps. Prepaid postcards were also issued with the security hologram as shown in Fig. 3-23.14.

Czech Republic issued a sheet of six 17-CZK stamps (**No. 323**) on **May 5**, **2010**, the 'EUROPA - Children's Book – Karel Čapek – Dášeňka' issue. Karel Čapek (1890 – 1938) an author who has written many books. This children's books issue, features Čapek's book: Dášeňka, [The Life of a Puppy] published in 1933. Like the previous 2004 and 2005 Czech stamps, the same security hologram is attached at the middle of the lower margin, shown in Figs. 3-23.15). The stamps were designed by K. Kučera. The Czech Post Printing House in Prague printed the stamps.

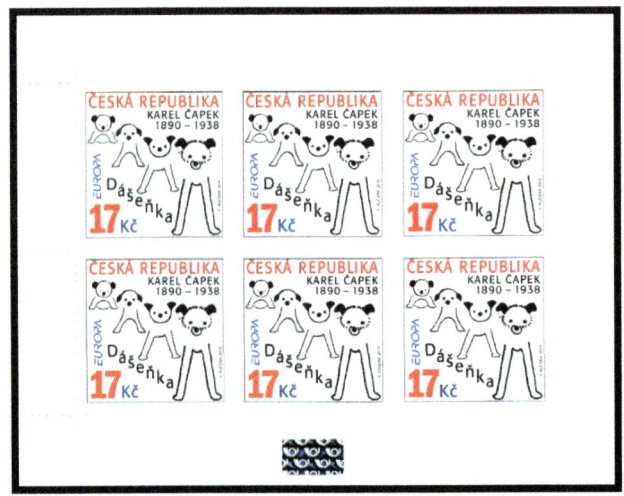

Fig. 3-23.15. The Dášeňka sheet with the security hologram.

 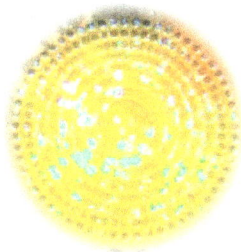 

Fig. 3-23.16. The Firefly sheet with the light effect. **Fig. 3-23.17**. The Firefly FDC.

On **May 10**, **2010**, five firefly stamps and a souvenir sheet were issue in **Malaysia**. Fireflies are beetles and are locally known as 'kelip-kelip', 'kunang-kunang' or 'api-api'. In Malaysia there are many types of fireflies, these stamps feature several species found in Malaysia. Fireflies are insects that enjoy humid environments and love moisture. Most fireflies are nocturnal insects and come out just after sunset. The main attraction in the firefly is the light it produces. The color of the light varies according to its species. The light is actually the result of a bio-chemical reaction at the light organs near the end of its abdomen. The light flashes are a communication tool for mating purposes. The congregating fireflies, (*Pteroptyx spp*.), is featured in the 30-sen stamp and the miniature sheet. There are currently eight identified species of Pteroptyx fireflies in Malaysia. *Pteroptyx valida* and *Pteroptyx bearni* are featured on the 30-sen stamps and *Lychnuris sp*. on the 50-sen stamps, whereas the firefly, *Pteroptyx tener*, is featured on the RM5.50-miniature sheet. The 5-Baht stamp (**No. 324**) and the miniature sheet (**No. 325**) is very unique as at the bottom of the firefly's abdomen where light is emitted is printed using a special transparent holographic foil to reflect a real firefly flashing at night, shown in Fig. 3-23.16. The FDC is shown in Fig. 3-23.17. The stamps were designed by World Communication Network Resources Sdn Bhd. Percetakan Keselamatan Sdn Bhd printed the stamps.

The '50-Years Alfons Mucha' booklet was issued in **Czech Republic** on **May 26**, **2010**. It contains six self-adhesive definitive 21-CZK stamps (**No. 326**). The stamps depict the famous work by the painter Alfons Mucha (1879 – 1939). One booklet with face value stamps represented by the letter 'Z', and another one with face value stamps represented by the letter 'E' were issued. Like the previous Czech stamps, the same security hologram (see Fig. 3-18.9) is attached at the back of the booklets. The cover of the 'Z'-stamp booklet is shown in Fig. 3-23.18. The hologram is attached to the back of the 'Z' and 'E' booklets, as shown in Fig. 3-23.19. The stamps, based on Alfons Mucha art, were designed by Zdeněk Ziegler. The Czech Post Printing House in Prague printed the stamps.

Fig. 3-23.18. The Mucha 'Z' stamp booklet cover.

Fig. 3-23.19. The Mucha booklets with the attached holograms.

Fig. 3-23.19. The UNPA Koblenz FDC.

United Nations Postal Administration (UNPA) in Vienna issued a card with the Vienna and Geneva UN cancelled hologram stamps on **June 1 - 4, 2010**. It was for the Stamp Exhibition in Koblenz, Germany, which took place between June 1 and 4. UNPA issues a special souvenir card when participating in a stamp exhibition or show. The Vienna series started in 1980 and became known as 'white cards'. For almost twenty years the cards were only available at the exhibition itself. Since some years the cards can be part of a standing order from UNPA. From 1980 both the Geneva and Vienna offices services their 'own' part of Europe. Vienna takes care of exhibitions in Austria, Germany and Eastern Europe like the Koblenz exhibition for which this card was issued, shown in Fig. 3-23.19. Geneva continues to participate in exhibitions in Western and Southern Europe.

For the London 2012 'OLYMPIC & PARALYMPIC GAMES' Royal Mail in **Great Britain** issued on **July 27, 2010**, a set of ten Olympic stamps, which was the 'ON TRACK FOR 2012'set (**No. 327**). On the back of the Pack (Pack number: 444) there is an individually numbered *XXX Olympic Logo* hologram. The 2010 Olympic stamp pack is shown in Fig. 3-23.20 with the hologram next to it.

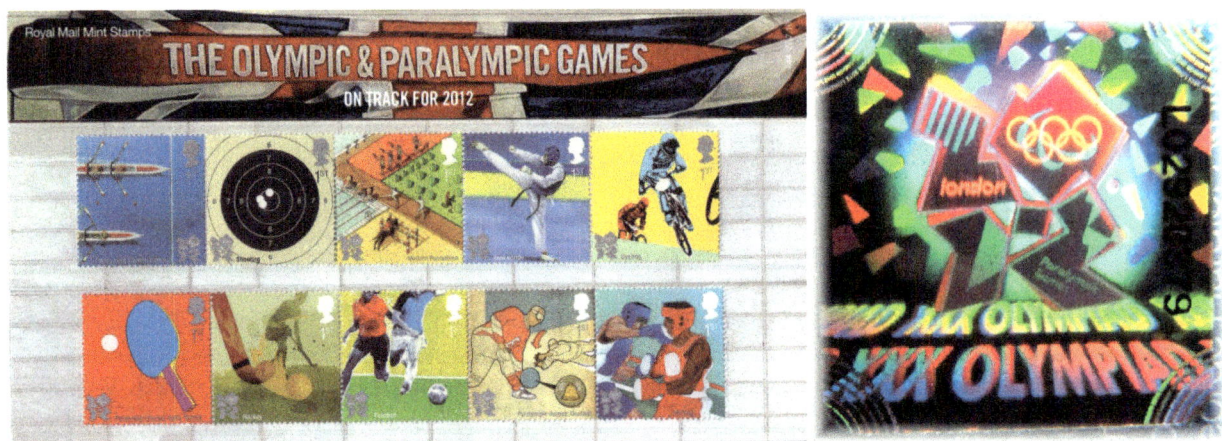

Fig. 3-23.20. ON TRACK FOR 2012 stamps pack with the *XXX Olympic* logo hologram on the back.

Fig. 3-23.21. The Papillon sheet. Fig. 3-23.22. The diffractive effect on the Papillon stamps.

France issued on **September 6**, **2010**, 'Les Papillons' [The Butterflies] stamps, in the Nature 2010 series. The stamps (**No. 328** to **331**) and a souvenir sheet (**No. 332**) featuring various butterflies. The butterfly is considered a symbol of grace and lightness. The copper marshes, the blue morpho and thecla of bramble are all included. The fourth stamp is dedicated to the caterpillar's big forked tail. The moth in the adult form is characterized by two pairs of wings covered with scales fines. The denominations of the four stamps are €0.75 x 2, €0.58 and €0.95. The €6.88 denomination souvenir sheet is shown in Fig. 3-23.21. The *wings* of the butterflies on the stamps are covered with holographic foil giving a nice iridescent effect, shown on the two stamps in Fig. 3-23.22. Christophe Drochon designed the stamps.

Nigeria issued twelve definite hologram stamps on **October 9**, **2010**. One set of stamps was the '2000 Years of Nigerian Arts' series with the following stamps: 'Terracotta Head', Ile-Ife, Osun State (₦20, **No. 333**), 'Bronze Bowl', Awka, Anambra State (₦30, **No. 334**), 'Lander Brothers Anchorage', Asaba, Delta State (₦50, **No. 335**), 'Slave Chain', Badagry, Lagos State (₦50, **No. 336**), and 'A Seated Human Figure', Tada, Niger State (₦120, **No. 337**). These five portrait-format stamps have a circular hologram attached as well as the 'Elephants at Yankari Game Reserve', Bauchi State, landscape-format stamp (₦90, **No. 338**). The other stamps have a square hologram attached: 'Igbo-Ukwu Bronze', Awaka, Anambra State (₦30, **No. 339**), 'Argungu Fishing Festival', Kebbi State (₦100, **No. 340**), 'IFE Terracotta', 14th -16th Century, Osun State (₦20, **No. 341**), 'Monkey Colony' in Lagwa-Mbaise, Imo State, (₦50, **No. 342**), 'Nok Terracotta', Kaduna, Kaduna State (₦50, **No. 343**), and 'Lander Brothers Anchorage', Asaba, Delta State (₦50, **No. 344**). The circular hologram has a pattern of *small squares* and the square hologram consists only of a piece of *diffracting foil*. John Makop designed the stamps, shown in Fig. 3-23.23. Nigerian Security Printing & Minting Co. Ltd., Victoria Island Lagos, printed the stamps with the circular holograms, which are also printed with fluorescent ink used for the country name and nomination. Superflux Int. Ltd. (SIL), Ikeja, and Lagos & Kalamazoo Security Print Ltd. printed the other hologram stamps with the additional security phosphor 'NIPOST' overprint.

Fig. 3-23.23. The twelve stamps from Nigeria with circular and square holograms.

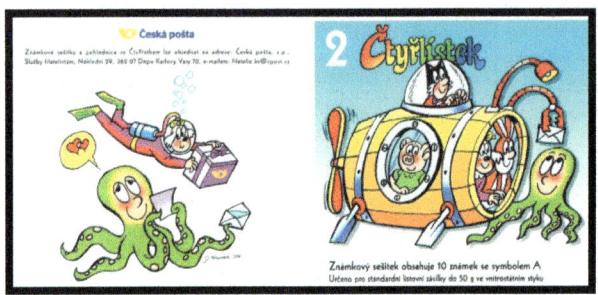 

Fig. 3-23.24. The Cat Scientist booklet. **Fig. 3-23.25**. The Cat Scientist stamps with the hologram.

Czech Republic issued another booklet of ten self-adhesive definitive 10-CZK stamps (**No. 345**), the 'Myšpulín Cat Scientist', on **October 20, 2010**. This was the second of the Čtyřlístek comics characters featured on a stamp. The cat scientist depicted on the stamp creates a chemical reaction setting off a firework of flowers coming out of the heated flask. The stamp identified with the letter 'A' corresponding to the price of domestic letters up to 50 g. Like the previous Czech booklets, the same security hologram (see Fig. 3-18.9) is attached at the top left corner of booklet. The booklet cover is shown Fig. 3-23.24 and the inside with the security hologram is shown in Fig. 3-23.25. Jaroslav Němeček designed the stamps and the Czech Post Printing House in Prague printed the stamps. Prepaid postcards were also issued with the security hologram next to the printed stamp.

Singapore issued eight Festivals stamps (**No. 346** through **353**) on **October 20, 2010**, featuring an innovative stamp design using holographic foil printing technique. Singapore's rich and vibrant multicultural heritage is best reflected in the many colorful festivals celebrated throughout the year. Beautifully illustrated with traditional motifs and symbols, this set of eight festival stamps celebrates the four most important festivals in Singapore - Chinese New Year, Hari Raya Aidilfitri, Deepavali and Christmas. The holographic foil on the stamps provides a shimmering, prismatic effect which creates a spectrum of changing colors exemplifying the diverse mix of cultures in Singapore. The Special Collectors' sheet, shown in Fig. 3-23.26, has four 55¢ and four S$1.10 stamps, all with the holographic foil (**No. 354**). Note: The 1st stamps are without holographic patterns. The same stamps on the Special Collectors sheet, denomination $1.10, have holographic patterns. The FDC is shown in Fig. 3-23.27. The stamps and souvenir sheet were designed by Tze Ngan and printed by Southern Colour Print.

Fig. 3-23.26. The Festivals souvenir sheet. **Fig. 3-23.27**. The Festivals FDC.

Fig. 3-23.28. The Christmas stamps with holographic *stars*.

Fig. 3-23.29. The Christmas stamp FDC.

Switzerland issued three Christmas stamps on **November 4**, **2010**, with the three motifs: the CHF 0.85 'candle' (**No.355**), the CHF 1.00 'snow crystal' (**No. 356**), and the CHF 1.40 'angel' (**No. 357**). Each of the three stamps includes a holographic *glittering star*. The stamps, shown in Fig. 3-23.28, were designed by Jenny Leibundgut from Berne and printed by Giesecke & Devrient GmbH, Leipzig, Germany. The FDC is shown in Fig. 3-23.29.

On **December 31**, **2010**, a second postage block (**No. 358**) of six stamps 'Minerals of Ukraine' was issued in **Ukraine**. The following minerals are featured on the stamps: Syngenite (2.00 UAH), Rhodonite (1.50 UAH), Labradorite (2.00 UAH), Agate (1.50 UAH), Amber, (2.00 UAH), and Carpathite (1.50 UAH). The block is multicolored with relief stamping and embossing by film with holographic effect. The sheet contains microprint 'Л. Мельнік'. Selvages of the block are artistically decorated with Ukrainian text and chemical formulas. The block was designed by Larissa Melnik and printed by Integrated Printing Plant Ukraine, a company involved in document security printing. The minerals block with the microtext is shown in Fig. 3-23.30, the holographic effect in Fig. 3-23.31 and the FDC in Fig. 3-23.32.

Fig. 3-23.30. The 'Minerals of Ukraine' stamps and the microtext.

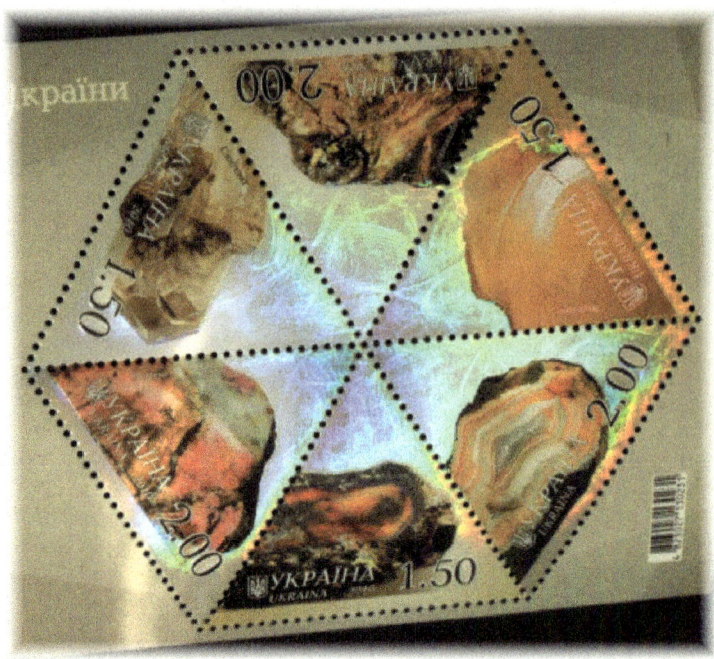

Fig. 3-23.31. The hologram effect.

Fig. 3-23.32. The 'Minerals of Ukraine' FDC.

3-24. Holographic stamps and souvenir sheets issued in 2011

To celebrate 100th anniversary of the founding of Taiwan, a souvenir sheet was issued with holographic diffraction effect. Macau issued another hologram stamp for the New Lunar Year - the year of the Rabbit - with holographic diffractive effect. Several Czech booklets and stamp sheets with a security hologram were issued. UNPA issued three different sets of colorful stamps for the International Year of Forests. Japan issued the first souvenir sheet in the Constellations Series. Christmas stamps with diffractive effect were issued in both Canada and Russia.

Fig. 3-24.1. The Fireworks sheet.

Fig. 3-24.2. The Fireworks FDC.

Fig. 3-24.3. The Optical Variable Film - Proof sheet.

To celebrate the 100th anniversary of the founding of the Republic of China, **Taiwan**, Chunghwa Post issued a souvenir sheet on **January 1, 2011**. The sheet, shown in Fig. 3-24.1 (**No. 359**), includes four stamps, each depicting a firework sight fused into a river nightscape. From left to right: the Double Tenth Day fireworks display in Taipei (NT$5), Taipei 101's New Year fireworks display (NT$5), the Lantern Festival fireworks display on Kaohsiung's Love River (NT$25), and the Dragon Boat Festival fireworks display in Taoyuan County's Longtan (NT$25). The background of the souvenir sheet features a fireworks display by the Taipei Ferris Wheel, which conveys a sense of universal celebration. The sheet is hot stamped with optical variable film to highlight the fireworks displays and the play of light and shadow on the Ferris wheel. A stamp folio was released along with this souvenir sheet. The FDC is shown in Fig. 3-24.2. A special presentation folder was issued with a transparent optical variable film sheet demonstrating the holographic effect, shown in Fig. 3-24.3. The stamps and sheet were designed by Up Creative Design & Advertising Corporation and printed by the Central Engraving and Printing Plant.

Fig. 3-24.4. The hologram stamp and the four Rabbit stamps.

Fig. 3-24.5. The Rabbit souvenir sheet.

Fig. 3-24.6. The Rabbit FDC.

Macau issued on **January 5**, **2011**, five stamps and a souvenir sheet to welcome the Lunar New Year, the year of the Rabbit. The rabbit's nature from the 'Five Elements' is 'Metal Rabbit', so it is the main character of the five stamps. The 5.00-PTC stamp has holographic foil outside the circular center with the rabbit (**No. 360**). The souvenir sheet presents a vivid scene of a metal rabbit jumping out of a magician's hat (**No. 361**). The 'Metal Rabbit' stamp is applied with emboss printing technique to highlight the image of metal rabbit on the bright full moon, while the hot foil stamping with holographic and gold are used respectively on the stamp's surface, the face values and the characters. The diamond shaped stamp has holographic foil as well as some of the figures on the sheet. The stamps were designed by Wilson Chi Ian Lam. The five stamps are shown in Fig. 3-24.4, the souvenir sheet in Fig. 3-24.5 and the FDC in Fig. 3-24.6.

Czech Republic issued on **February 9**, **2011**, another booklet of ten self-adhesive definitive 10-CZK stamps (**No. 362**), the 'Čtyřlístek Piňďa' booklet. This was the third of the Čtyřlístek comics characters featured on a stamp. The stamp features Piňďa the Rabbit as a painter with brushes in his hand and a box of water paints. The stamp identified with the letter 'A' corresponding to the price of domestic letters up to 50 g. The cover and the inside of the booklet are shown in Figs. 3-24.7 and 3-24.8. Like the previous Czech booklets, the same security hologram (see Fig. 3-18.19) is attached at the top left corner of booklet. Jaroslav Němeček designed the stamps and the Czech Post Printing House in Prague printed the stamps. Like before prepaid postcards were also issued with the security hologram.

Fig. 3-24.7. The Rabbit Painter booklet.

Fig. 3-24.8. The Rabbit Painter stamps with the hologram.

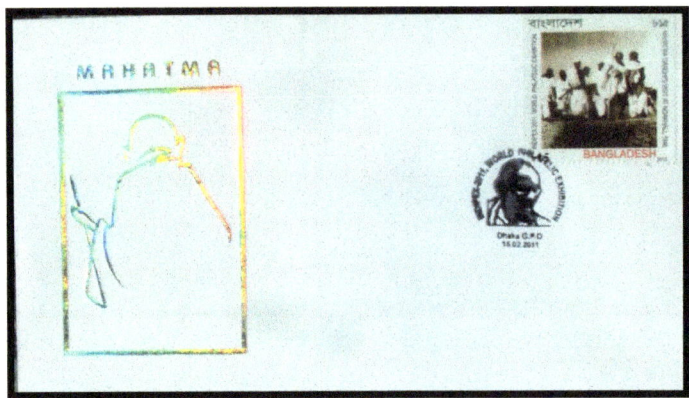

Fig. 3-24.9. The two Bangladesh FDCs with *Gandhi* cachet holograms.

On **February 10, 2011, Bangladesh** issued three Gandhi stamps for the INDIPEX 2011, World Philatelic Exhibition which took place between February 12 and 18, 2011, in New Delhi, India. One FDC has a cachet hologram of *Gandhi* attached. There is also a similar but non-holographic gold foil cachet version of this FDC. Another FDC, issued on **February 16, 2011**, has also a cachet hologram which is a holographic *Gandhi contour drawing*. Both FDCs, shown in Fig. 3-24.9, are with the 'Mahatma Gandhi visit at Noakhali 1946' stamp.

Czech Republic issued on **May 4, 2011**, another booklet of ten self-adhesive definitive 10-CZK stamps (**No. 363**), the 'Čtyřlístek Bobík' booklet. This was the fourth and final one of the Čtyřlístek comics characters featured on a stamp. Bobík the Pig, sitting on the grass, playing guitar and singing a love song. The stamp identified with the letter 'A' corresponding to the price of domestic letters up to 50 g. Like the previous Czech booklets, the same security hologram (see Fig. 3-18.19) is attached at the top left corner of booklet. The cover and inside of the booklet are shown in Fig. 3-24.10 and 3-24.11. Jaroslav Němeček designed the stamps and the Czech Post Printing House in Prague printed the stamps. Like before prepaid postcards were also issued with the security hologram.

Fig. 3-24.10. Bobík the Pig booklet.   **Fig. 3-24.11**. Bobík the Pig stamps with the hologram.

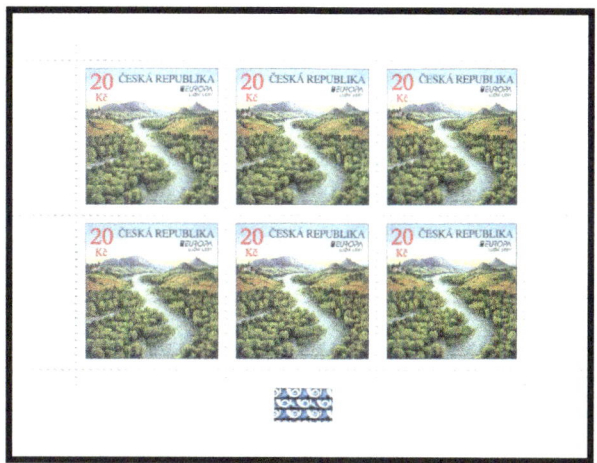

Fig. 3-24.12. The 'Alluvial Forests' sheet with the security hologram.

Czech Republic issued a sheet of six 20-CZK stamps on **May 4, 2011**, the 'EUROPA – Alluvial Forests'. The 2011 central theme for the annual EUROPA issue was 'Forests' (**No. 364**). Czech Republic issued the Alluvial Forest 20-CZ stamp. An alluvial forest is a hardwood forest found on low levees, ridges and terraces with a high level of underground water within the floodplains of streams and rivers. The largest alluvial forest in the Czech Republic grows at the confluence of the Morava and Dyje rivers. Primary trees found include poplar, oak, ash, elm, alder, willow, and lime tree. Like the previous Czech stamp sheets, the same security hologram is attached at the middle of the lower margin. The sheet is shown in Fig. 3-24.12. The stamps were designed by Adolf Absolon. The Czech Post Printing House in Prague printed the stamps.

On **June 1, 2011**, the Circus stamps were issued in **Romania**. Two stamps (the 0.50-lei stamp, clown face with big top tent for hat, and the 8.10-lei stamp, clown with bow tie and top hat) and a miniature sheet were issued (**No. 365**). The miniature sheet is shaped as a circus tent with the two se-tenant stamps in the sheet which is shown in Fig. 3-24.13. It is covered with holographic *stars*. In the glory period of the Roman Empire, the circus represented one of the most accessible and favourite forms of entertainment. In Ancient Rome, the word 'circus' meaning a circle or ring, defined the spaces having this shape where manifestations time took place. The Romanian State Circus in Bucharest, built in 1961, was one of the biggest in Europe at that time. The stamps of the Circus postage stamps issue reproduce the images illustrating the atmosphere specific to circus performances meant to entertain the audience. The stamps were designed by Mihai Vămăşescu.

Fig. 3-24.13. The Circus souvenir sheet.

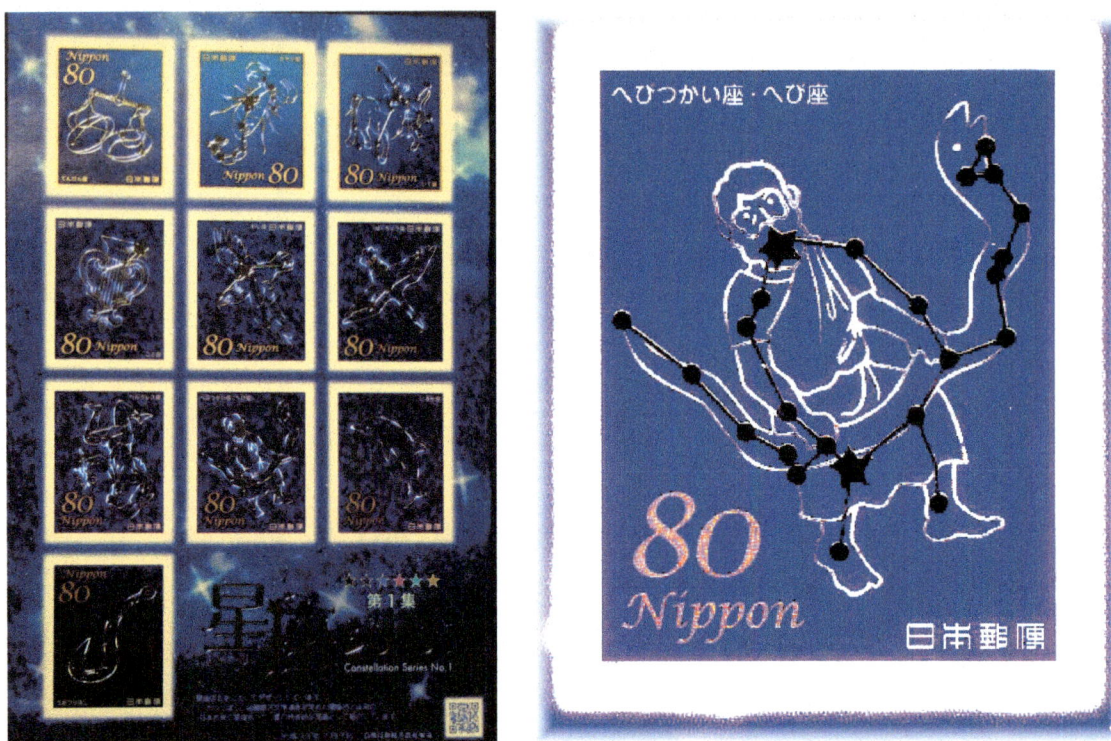

Fig. 3-24.14. The Japanese souvenir sheet and one of the stamps.

Japan issued a sheetlet of ten self-adhesive stamps on **July 7**, **2011**, the 'Constellations Series, Part 1' Japan Post, aiming to promote culture and science, issued the souvenir sheet with Zodiac stamps (**No. 366**). The stamps depict constellations of Libra, Scorpios, Sagittarius, Lyra, Aquilla, Cygnus, Hercules, Ophiuchus, Delphinius, Manai-a-Kalani (Maui's Fishhook, the Polynesian version of Scorpios). The *constellations* on the stamps are printed using the hologram foil offset print method. The sheet is shown in Fig. 3-24.14. The stamps were designed by Hoshiyama Rika and printed by Hanshiki Printing.

For the London 2012 'OLYMPIC & PARALYMPIC GAMES' Royal Mail in **Great Britain** issued on **July 27**, **2011**, a set of ten Olympic stamps, which was the 'GET READY FOR 2012' set (**No. 367**). On the back of the Pack (Pack number: 458) there is an individually numbered *XXX Olympic Logo* hologram. The 2011 Olympic stamp pack is shown in Fig. 3-24.15 with the hologram next to it.

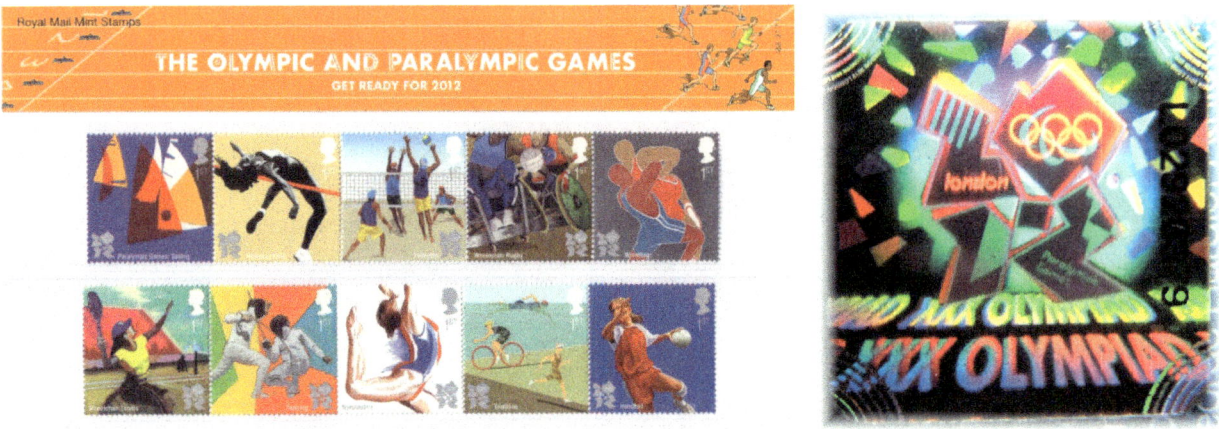

Fig. 3-24.15. GET READY FOR 2012 stamps pack with the *XXX Olympic* logo hologram on the back.

Fig. 3-24.16. The PHILANIPPON'11 Japanese souvenir sheet.

Japan issued a special commemorative 'PHILANIPPON'11' sheetlet of ten self-adhesive stamps on **July 28, 2011**. Japan organized the Japan World Stamp Exhibition which took place between July 28 and August 2, 2011, at the Pacifico Yokohama Exhibition Hall. World Stamp Exhibitions are held all over the world every year with aims to develop philately, opening world-renowned stamp collections to the public, and promote stamps of the member countries of the Federation Internationale de Philatelie (FIP). The theme of PHILANIPPON'11 is 'Stamps Link the World'. The Anime and Manga stamps on the sheet were first issued on January 21, 2011. For the stamp exhibition two commemorative sets were issued. One of them was the one with Astro Boy, Doraemon, Hello Kitty and Pikachu beaming at the stamp collectors of the world in vivid, joyous color. The denomination *80 yen, PHILANIPPON 2011* and the *Exhibition Logo* are printed with holographic foil on the sheet shown in Fig. 3-24.16 (**No. 368**). The stamps were designed by Morita Motoharu.

On **August 5, 2011**, **Kyrgyzstan** re-issued the 1999 Corsac souvenir sheet supporting WWF, World Wide Fund for Nature. The holograms of *foxes* are unevenly cut and attached to the four se-tenant stamps. The sheet is overprinted in gold: '50th Anniversary 1961 – 2011' at the top of the sheet and at the bottom of each stamp (**No. 369**). At the bottom of the sheet 'WWF 50 YEARS OF CONSERVATION 1961-2011' is printed in gold. The two 30-som and the two 50-som stamps are overprinted in red with the new denominations 60-som and 90-som, respectively. The four 10-som stamps on the sheet are not overprinted. The holograms were produced by 3D AG in Switzerland and the sheets printed by GOSZNAK in Moscow. The overprinted sheet is shown in Fig. 3-24.17 to be compared with the 2001 overprinted version, shown in Fig. 3-14.17 as well as the original 1999 sheet in Fig. 3-12.9.

Fig. 3-24.17. Reissued overprinted Kyrgyzstan souvenir sheet.

Fig. 3-24.18. The Mozart booklet with the security hologram.

Czech Republic issued on **August 31, 2011**, the 'Wolfgang Amadeus Mozart' booklet of six self-adhesive definitive 20-CZK stamps (**No. 370**). The booklet theme is an expressively conducting Wolfgang Amadeus Mozart with the Don Giovanni score and the Prague's Estates Theatre in the background. The stamp identified with the letter 'E' corresponding to the price of international priority letters up to 20 g. Like the previous Czech booklets, the security hologram is attached at the back of booklet (see Fig. 3-18.19). The booklet front and back are shown in Fig. 3-24.18. The stamps were designed by Marina Richterová. The Czech Post Printing House in Prague printed the stamps.

Czech Republic issued on **October 5, 2011**, another booklet of ten stamps, the 'Pat & Mat' booklet (**No. 371**). The definitive vertical picture stamp, identified with the letter 'A', depicts figures from a popular TV series of bedtime stories for children. The stamp portrays the tinkers Pat and Mat in their brotherly embrace. The stamp was designed by Jan Chvojka who also wrote scripts for popular Pat & Mat film series. The stamp identified with the letter 'A' corresponding to the price of domestic letters up to 50 g. Like the previous Czech booklets, the same security hologram (see Fig. 3-18.19) is attached at the top left corner of booklet. The booklet is shown in Fig. 3-24.19. Czech Post Printing House in Prague printed the stamps.

Fig. 3-24.19. The Pat & Mat stamps with the security hologram.

Fig. 3-24.20. The two-channel *SIPA* hologram.

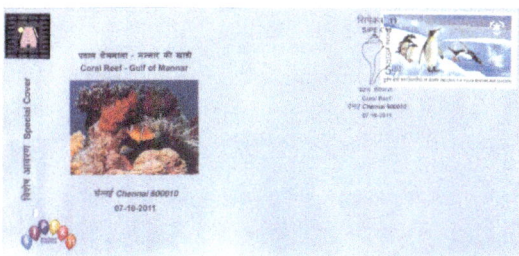

Fig. 3-24.21. The 'Coral Reef' cover.

Fig. 3-24.22. The 'Grizzled Squirrel' cover.

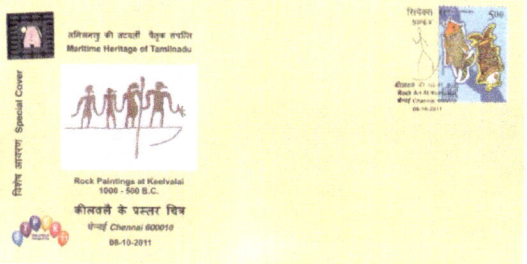

Fig. 3-24.23. The 'Rock Paintings' cover.

Special covers were issued in **India** during the Philatelic Exhibition, SIPEX'11, which took place between October 7 and 9, 2011 at Chennai. On **October 7, 2011**, the 'Coral Reef - Gulf of Mannar' was issued. It has a South India Philatelists' Association (SIPA) two-channel hologram in the upper left corner of the envelope. The stamp is one of the Preserve the Polar Regions and Glacier 2009 5.00-INR stamp, issued in India. The cover is marked TN/5/2011. The two hologram images are shown in Fig. 3-24.20 and the cover in Fig. 3-24.21. Two other covers were issued the next day on **October 8, 2011**, the 'Endangered Grizzled Squirrel' and 'Maritime Heritage of Tamilnadu - Rock Paintings of Keelvalai' envelopes, marked TN/06/2011 and TN/07/2011 respectively, shown in Fig. 4-24.22 and 4-24.23. The stamp on the first one is The Silent Valley 2009 5.00-INR stamp and the second one is the 2010 5.00-INR Pisces stamp (Astrological Signs Issue). Both envelopes have the SIPA hologram attached. The covers were designed by South India Philatelists' Association.

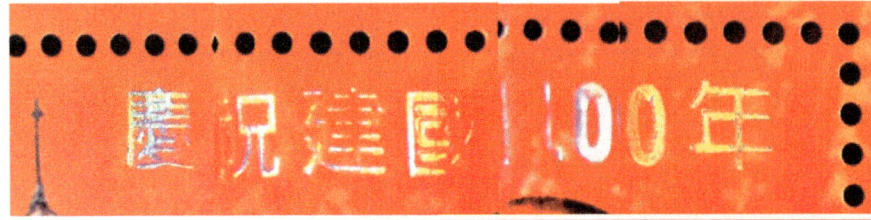

Fig. 3-24.24. Founding of the Republic of China sheet with the holographic *Chinese text*.

To celebrate the 100th anniversary of the founding of the Republic of China, (Taiwan), Chunghwa Post (**Taiwan** Post) issued a second souvenir sheet, in addition to the January one, on **October 10, 2011**. Four stamps were issued and a NT$25 souvenir sheet, shown in Fig. 3-24.24 (**No. 372**). The stamp on the sheet has holographic *Chinese text* in the upper right corner. The color scheme of the souvenir sheet reflects the blue sky, white sun and red earth of the national flag. The design features the national flag, the Presidential Office Building and a portrait of Dr. Sun Yat-Sen with the ROC constitution as the background. The Chinese wordings, located above Yat-Sen's head, 'Celebrating the 100th Anniversary of the Founding of the Republic of China' is hot stamped with optical diffractive variable film. Sheets with Specimen printed on them were also issued. The stamps and sheet were designed by Up Creative Design and Advertising Corporation and printed by Cardon Enterprise Co., Ltd. (To photograph the entire holographic text it is necessary to record part of it with its correct illumination and then add the individual photographs).

On **October 13, 2011**, the **United Nations Postal Administration** (UNPA) issued three mini-sheets of eight stamps to commemorate the International Year of Forests 2011. These stamps were the last in a series issued during the 60th Anniversary year of UNPA. Designed by artist, Sergio Baradat, these vibrant stamps remind everyone that trees and forests provide a vital link to life on earth. Baradat's colorful designs remind us all that one third of the Earth's land surface is covered by trees. The director Jan McAlpine of the UN Forum on Forests Secretariat within DESA mentioned when the stamps were issued: "Just as the rings within trees hold the history of life on earth; stamps mark historic milestones." A German (€ denomination, **No. 373**), a Swiss (CHF denomination, **No. 374**) and an American (US$ denomination, **No. 375**) set of stamps were issued, all three with different stamps. The stamps are covered with very small diffractive spots. The three UN Forest year sheets are shown in Figs. 3-24.25 through 3.24.27 with close-up photos of the diffractive spots.

Fig. 3-24.25. The Vienna UN 'WÄLDER' eight-stamp sheet with the tiny diffractive spots.

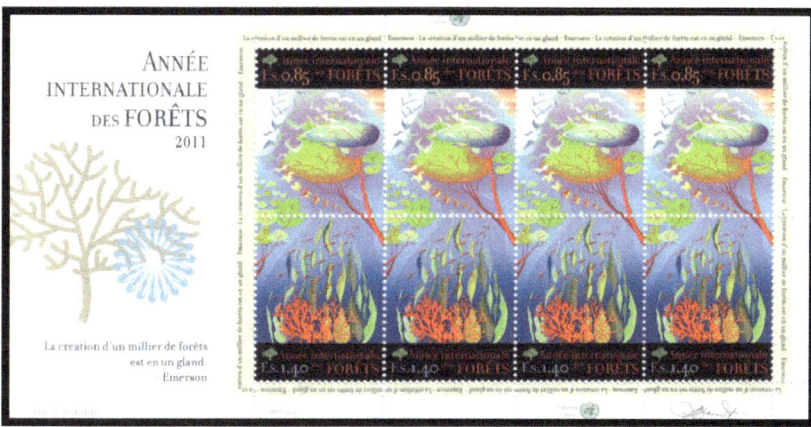 

Fig. 3-24.26. The Geneva UN 'FORÊTS' eight-stamp sheet with the tiny diffractive spots.

Fig. 3-24.27. The New York UN 'FORESTS' eight-stamp sheet with the tiny diffractive spots.

Fig. 3-24.28. The *livyatan melvillei* souvenir sheet with holographic *text*.

Peru issued on **October 17, 2011**, a souvenir sheet in the series of 'Prehistoric Animals'. It was the 'Livyatan melvillei' souvenir sheet (**No. 376**). The *ANIMALES PREHISTÓRICOS – Fósiles –* is printed with holographic foil on the souvenir sheet. In November 2008, fossil remains of livyatan melvillei were discovered in the sediments of Pisco formation at Cerro Colorado, 35 km south-southwest of Ica, Peru. The remains include a partially preserved skull with teeth and mandible of a sea monster three times the size of a modern day killer whale. The Leviathan sea creature existed around 12 million to 13 million years ago, in the middle of the Miocene Age. It is not known why they became extinct. The remains of the Leviathan Melvillei are kept at the Natural History Museum in Lima. The sheets were printed by Thomas Greg and Sons in Peru. The souvenir sheet is shown in Fig. 3-24.28.

Canada issued Christmas stamps on **November 1, 2011**. A festive sprig of holly is featured on the Christmas stamp (**No. 377**). Designer Hélène L'Heureux scattered *snowflakes* in clear holographic foil throughout the design of this stamp. The stamp has a contemporary feel, and shares many of the other bold design elements common to the earlier stamps in the series, including strong graphic shapes and the snowy background landscape of rolling hills. For centuries, people all over the world have used holly with vibrant red berries and shiny green leaves to decorate their houses during the holiday season. This issue was the fourth in the continuing holiday series with holographic effects. The booklet is shown in Fig. 3-24.29, one of the stamps in Fig. 3-34.30 and the FDC in Fig. 3-24.31.

Fig. 3-24.29. The Holly stamp booklet.   Fig. 3-24.30. The stamp.

Fig. 3-24.31. The Holly stamp FDC.

Fig. 3-24.32. Four of the twelve Lunar Year Sheets.

Fig. 3-24.33. The Granada Lunar Year sheet and the Ox stamp on it.

On **November 15, 2011** similar LUNAR NEW YEAR twelve-hologram stamp sheets were issued in the following countries: **Antigua & Barbuda (No. 378)**, **Liberia (No. 379)**, **Guyana (No. 380)**, **Grenada (No. 381)**, and **Grenada Carriacou & Petite Martinique (No. 382)**. The twelve stamps on the sheets depict the twelve Lunar year animals. Each stamp is surrounded by a diffractive holographic foil *frame*. Four of the twelve-stamp sheets are shown in Fig. 3-24.32 and in Fig. 3-24.33, the Grenada sheet and one of the stamps on it, the Grenada Ox stamps with holographic foil.

Fig. 3-24.34. The '100 years of Girl Guide Movement in India' cover with the SIPA hologram.

The South India Philatelists' Association (SIPA) two-channel hologram (see Fig. 3-2420) was used on the '100 years of Girl Guide Movement in India' cover. The limited-edition (200) cover marked TN/10/2011 was issued in **India** on **November 11, 2011**. The hologram is attached in the lower left corner of the envelope. The Special Cover shown in Fig. 3-24.34 was sponsored by South India Philatelists' Association, Chennai, for the Southern Railway State Bharat Scouts and Guides. It was designed by Gora Bhuvan Babu.

Traditionally thematic New Year stamps are issued in **Russia**. In 2011 a 20-rubel stamp was issued which depicts a red Christmas ball with snowflakes on a gray background (**No. 383**). The stamps were issued on **December 1, 2011**. The Russian New Year message and the snowflakes are printed with holographic foil. The Russian stamp and nine stamp sheet are shown in Fig. 3-24.35 and the FDC in Fig. 3-24.36.

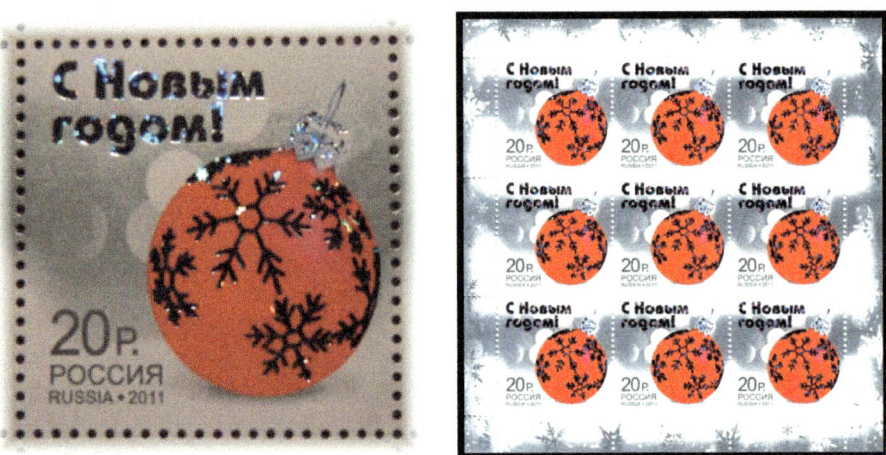

Fig. 3-24.35. Russian Christmas stamp and nine-stamp sheet.

Fig. 3-24.36. The Russian FDC with the hologram stamp.

Fig. 3-24.37. The Czech 'Une femme douce' with the hologram stripe.

During **2011 Czech Republic** issued thirteen numbered commemorative sheets with a security hologram stripe at the bottom of the card. One example is the film poster card for the 1970 French movie 'Une femme douce' (directed by Robert Bresson) one in the Czech Film Poster series. The card, with the 10-Kč stamp was issued on **October 5, 2011**, is shown in Fig. 3-24.37. Olga Poláčková-Vyleťalová's design of this poster became an icon of the Czechoslovak film poster art.

3-25. Holographic stamps and souvenir sheets issued in 2012

Macau continued to issue hologram stamps for the Lunar New Year, the year of the Dragon, with holographic diffractive effect. A souvenir sheet was issued in Malaysia and a stamp was issued in Brazil, with a beautiful stained-glass window hologram. A unique 3D hologram stamp portrait was issued in Jersey for Queen Elisabeth II's Diamond Jubilee. Also Australia and Kiribati issued sheets with holograms or holographic text for the Diamond Jubilee. Japan issued a second souvenir sheet in the Constellations Series. A variety of stamps were issued in China. Thailand issued commemorative stamps for Queen Sirikit's 80th Birthday anniversary, of which one had holographic text. Christmas stamps with diffractive effect were issued Luxembourg.

Fig. 3-25.1. The hologram stamp and the five Dragon stamps with the hologram stamp in the middle.

Macau issued on **January 5, 2012**, five stamps to welcome the Lunar New Year, the year of the Dragon. One of the five stamps, the 5.00-PTC stamp, is covered with a dragon-shaped holographic foil. The hologram stamp (**No. 384**) and the other four holograms are shown in Fig. 3-25.1. The conceptual design of the stamp is combined with the different forms of the Dragon and the distinguishing characteristics of Metal, Wood, Water, Fire and Earth. This year, the dragon's nature from the Five Elements is water, so the dragon portrays by the Chinese traditional ink painting becomes the main character of the five stamps. The lifelike ink painting dragon of the stamp applied with holographic hot-stamping foil together with an embossed image of a dragon boat. This year, only the stamp in the series of five stamps is covered by holographic foil. The diamond-shaped stamp on the souvenir sheet is not having holographic foil this year. Like last year, the stamps were designed by Wilson Chi Ian Lam.

On **January 12, 2012**, postage stamps, entitled 'Legacy of the Loom', were issued in **Malaysia** to celebrate the Year of Dragon. The stamps contain a strip of five stamps displaying the art of weaving traditional textiles in Malaysia. Malaysia Post also released a set of limited-edition miniature sheets in the form of Ming Empress robe. The robe is embroidered with a mighty *dragon* available in gold and holographic hot-stamping foil on the RM-5.00 stamp (**No. 385**) which is part of the sheet. There is also another robe-shaped sheet with a RM-3.00 stamp with only a gold foil dragon. The stamps and sheets were designed by Peter Chuah of Orient Communications and printed by Percetakan Keselamatan Nasional Sdn Bhd.

Fig. 3-25.2. The *dragon* hologram stamp on the sheet.

Fig. 3-25.3. The 'Legacy of the Loom' miniature sheet.

Fig. 3-25.4. The Cathedral stamp.

Fig. 3-25.5. The stained glass window hologram on the stamp.

Another stamp was issued on **January 12, 2012**. This stamp was issued in **Brazil** commemorating the 150th anniversary of the Presbyterian Cathedral of Rio de Janeiro. The First Presbyterian Church of Rio de Janeiro, known now as the Presbyterian Cathedral of Rio de Janeiro, was built in January 1862. The R$1.60 stamp depicts the current Cathedral, a beautiful architectural ensemble consisting of towers, sculptures, turrets and lavish stained glass windows. Although restored, it presents traces of its original neo-Gothic structure, with multiple lines, internal and external decoration, with lots of stained glass windows. The stamp, shown in Fig. 3-25.4 (**No. 386**) depicts the architectural beauty of the Cathedral with the colored stained glass windows above the cathedral on the stamp. The beautiful round *stained glass window* hologram is shown in Fig. 3-25.5. The stamp was designed by Juliana Souza. Brazilian Mint printed the stamps.

On **April 3, 2012, Australia** issued a souvenir sheet for Queen Elisabeth II Diamond Jubilee (**No. 387**). Two se-tenant stamps with photographs of the Queen (the 60c-stamp, 'Her Majesty at her Accession', and the $2.35-stamp, 'Her Majesty Today') are included in the sheet. '*QUEEN ELISABETH II Diamond Jubilee*' is printed above the stamps using diffractive holographic foil. This stamp, shown in Fig. 3-25.6 issue was released to coincide with the birthday of the Queen. The stamps were designed by Jo Muré, Australia Post Design Studio, and printed by McKellar Renown. The Royal Philatelic Society of Victoria inc. – 6th Annual Bourse 21 April 2012.

Fig. 3-25.6. The Diamond Jubilee sheet with the holographic *text* and the overprinted limited edition (200) sheet.

Fig. 3-25.7. The Titanic sheet No.1 (1654/7000).

Fig. 3-25.8. The (354/700) FDC with Titanic sheet No.1.

Fig. 3-25.9. The Titanic sheet No. 2 (1889/7000).

Fig. 3-25.10. The (328/700) FDC with Titanic sheet No. 2.

The 100-year anniversary of the R.M.S. Titanic disaster was featured on several stamps. **Ecuador** issued two miniature sheets on **April 20, 2012**. Both sheets (an edition of 7000 each) include a different US$4.00 stamp of Titanic. The sheets are printed with *R.M.S. TITANIC 1912 – 2012* using embossed diffractive holographic foil. The sheets were designed by David Romero and Dennis Calero. The first sheet is shown in Fig. 3-25.7 (**No. 388**) and the FDC (edition 700) in Fig. 3-25.8. The second sheet is shown in Fig. 3-25.9 (**No. 389**) and the FDC (edition 700) in Fig. 3-25.10.

On **April 27, 2012**, **P. R. China** issued a set of four CNY1.20 stamps which feature Fu Lu Shou Xi: Good luck, Richness, Longevity and Happiness (**No. 390** through **393**) as well as an eight-stamp souvenir sheet (**No. 394**). The stamps have been printed with holographic foil on security paper with fluorescence coding. The stamps were designed by Wang Huming and printed by Henan Province Posts and Telecommunications Printing.

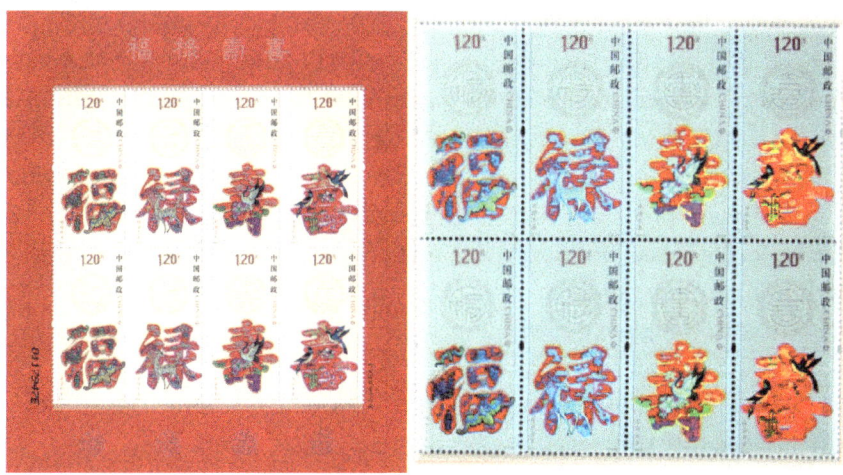
Fig. 3-25.11. The Fu Lu Shou Xi sheet with the hologram stamps.

Fig. 3-25.13. The *Queen* hologram stamp.

Fig. 3-25.14. The four-stamp sheetlet.

Fig. 3-25.15. The *Queen* hologram stamp FDC.

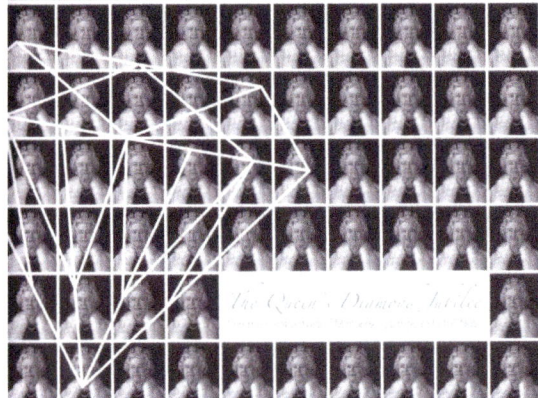

Fig. 3-25.16. The Commutative Diamond Jubilee folder.

To celebrate Queen Elisabeth II's Diamond Jubilee a £10 holographic definitive hologram stamp with a portrait of *The Queen* was issued in **Jersey** on **June 1, 2012 (No. 395)**. The holographic stereogram portrait used for the stamp was the 'Equanimity' portrait (meaning 'the quality of being calm and even-tempered') recorded in 2004 by the artist Chris Levine and holographer Rob Munday. [39] The holographic portrait of *Her Majesty - The Queen* was commissioned by Jersey Heritage Trust as part of the island's celebrations which took place 2004, marking 800 years of Jersey's heritage of continuous loyalty to the Crown. For the portrait The Queen wore a string of white pearls and the Diamond Diadem, created for King George IV and worn by Her Majesty for the procession to her Coronation. The £10 postage stamp, shown in Fig. 3-25.13, features a unique 3D achromatic b/w digital embossed stereogram hologram portrait. The value and lettering on the stamp has been produced in flat simili silver foiling. This is the first time a 3D holographic portrait has been used on a stamp. (Earlier hologram portrait stamps have been produced with 2D images only). The hologram for the stamp was created especially for Jersey Post by Rob Munday. The stamps were printed by Cartor Security Printing in France in sheetlets of four (2 across x 2 down), shown in Fig. 3-25.14 and the FDC in Fig.3-25.15. A limited-edition (1000) Commemorative Folder with mint Jersey Queen stamps which also included a Diamond Jubilee £100 banknote with a hologram security stripe were issued, shown in Fig.3-25.16.

Fig. 3-25.17. The four Kiribati Diamond Jubilee hologram stamps.

To celebrate Queen Elisabeth II's Diamond Jubilee **Kiribati** issued on **June 4**, **2012**, a set of four overprinted definitive stamps with different photographs of the Queen (**No. 396** through **399**). '*1952 ◊ DIAMOND JUBILEE ◊ 2012*' is printed at the bottom of the stamps using diffractive holographic foil. A dimond-shaped hologram with a *diamond* pattern is attached at the upper right corner of the stamps. The stamps were overprinted by The Malvern Press in Harlow, Essex, UK, in a limited edition of 3000 stamps. The four stamps with the *diamond* hologram and the *text* are shown in Fig. 3-25.17.

On **June 18**, **2012**, an overprinted 'Year of the Dragon' souvenir sheet was issued in **Malaysia** for the INDONESIA'12 stamp exhibition (**No. 400**). The World Stamp Championship and Exhibition in Jakarta took place between June 18 and 24, 2012. Both the RM3.00 dragon sheet in gold and the RM5.00 holographic *dragon* sheet were issued with the overprint 'INDONESIA 2012' logo. The overprinted holographic sheet is shown in Fig. 3-25.18.

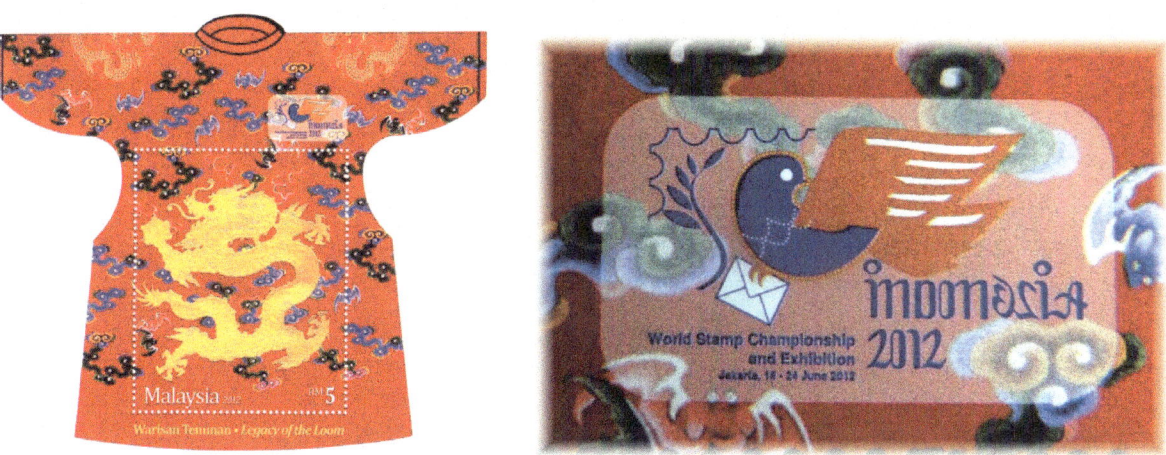

Fig. 3-25.18. The overprinted 'Year of the Dragon' souvenir sheet with the INDONESIA 2012 logo.

Fig. 3-25.19. The three 'My Own Stamp' sheets with the larger security hologram and microtext.

Czech Republic issued on **June 20, 2012**, three 25-stamp sheets of self-adhesive definitive stamps in the 'My Own Stamp' series (Fig. 3-25.19, **No. 401** through **403**). Both vertical and horizontal definitive stamps, identified with the letter 'A', 'E' and 'Z', were issued. Stamps identified with the letter 'A' correspond to the price of domestic letters up to 50 g. Two of the stamps on the three sheets are shown in Fig. 3-25.19. A larger security hologram (13x13 mm) is attached at the bottom margin of the sheets as was previously used on booklets and stamp sheets (compare Fig. 3-18.9). Additional security is provided by the microtext line under CESKÁ REPUBLIKA. Czech Post Printing House in Prague printed the stamps. Sheets marked SPECIMENT exist as well.

Ukraine issued on **June 25, 2012**, a beautiful souvenir sheet 'Ukraine welcomes EURO 2012™' with three 13.80-UAH stamps (**No. 404**). The image of the flower on the block luminesces under UV-light. On the back side of the sheet there is an individually numbered *UEFA logo* hologram. The sheet with the hologram on the back is shown in Fig. 3-25.20. Another security measure is the microprint located at the lower left corner of the block: Ю. Правдохіна, shown in Fig. 3-25.21. The block selvages are artistically decorated by Yulika Pravdokhina who also created the postmark. The selvages bear the text: 'Україна вітає EURO 2012™' [Ukraine welcomes EURO 2012™]. The block was printed by the security printer Integrated Printing Plant Ukraine.

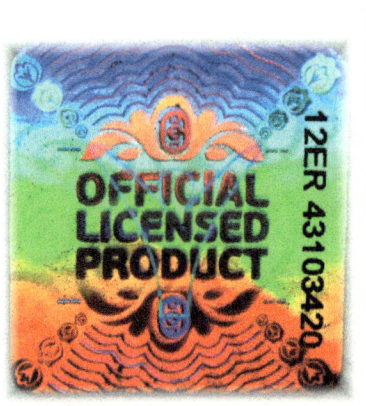

Fig. 3-25.20. The EURO 2012 sheet with the security hologram on the back of it.　　**Fig. 3-25.21.** Microtext.

Fig. 3-25.22. The 'Constellations Series, Part 2' sheet with one of the stamps.

Japan issued a sheetlet of ten self-adhesive stamps on **July 6, 2012**, the 'Constellations Series, Part 2'. Japan Post, aiming to promote culture and science by the issue of this souvenir sheet with Zodiac stamps (**No. 405**). The stamps depict constellations of Capricornus, Aquarius, Pisces, Cassiopeia, Pegasus, Andromeda, Perseus, Cepheus, Cetus Ikariboshi (Anchor, the Japanese version of Cassiopeia). The *constellations* on the stamps are printed using the hologram foil offset printing method. The sheet with ten stamps is shown in Fig. 3-25.22. The stamps were designed by Hoshiyama Rika and printed by Hanshiki Printing.

Ecuador issued three souvenir sheets on **August 1, 2012**. The individually numbered sheets were issued for the First Philatelic Exhibition of South Pacific Stamp Exhibition in Quito. It was organized by the Ecuadorian Philatelic Association (AFE) as the international part of the EXPOAFE 2012, which was held at the Cultural Center of the Pontifical Catholic University of Ecuador. EXPOAFE 2012 took place between September 17 and 22, 2012. The difference between the three sheets is that one sheet has *the stamp exhibition information text* printed using gold diffractive holographic foil (**No. 406**); the second sheet is with silver diffractive holographic foil (**No. 407**) and the third sheet with non-diffractive red foil (**No. 408**). The three sheets are shown in Fig. 3-25.23. The sheets (an edition of 3000 each) include two US$3.00 stamp of the steamship ECAUDOR Paquebot. The sheets were designed by David Romero and Dennis Calero. Two postcards were also issued with holographic printing next to the printed stamp on the cards. The two postcards (edition 700 each) are shown in Fig. 3-25.24.

Fig. 3-25.23. The two ECAUDOR Paquebot sheets (2139/3000) with holographic text.

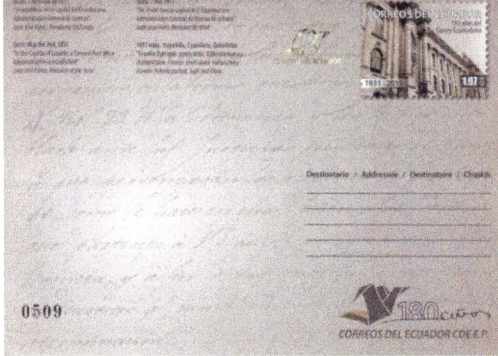

Fig. 3-25.24. The front and back of the two postcards (256/700, 509/700).

On **August 12**, **2012**, **Thailand** issued the H.M. Queen Sirikit's 80th Birthday Anniversary Commemorative Stamps. The nine stamps on the sheet feature Queen Sirikit portraits, in each decade. The sheet is shown in Fig. 3-25.25 with holographic *text* at the bottom. The special stamp in the middle of the sheet is shown in Fig. 3-25.26 (**No. 409**). This stamp was printed with an embossed, pearl ink process and with holographic gold type. The design is the same design used to commemorate the King's 80th birthday in 2007 (see Fig. 3-20.26). The FDC with three of the stamps including the special stamp is shown in Fig. 3-25.27. The colors of the stamp sheets reflect the birth days of the King and the Queen. According to Buddhist/Hindu tradition, yellow is associated with Monday, which is the birthday of the King and blue is associated with Friday, which is birthday of the Queen. The stamps and sheet were designed by Veena Chantanatat and printed by Thai British Security Printing Public Co Ltd in Thailand.

Fig. 3-25.25. The H.M. Queen Sirikit sheet. **Fig. 3-25.26**. The special stamp with holographic foil.

Fig. 3-25.27. The FDC with the special stamp.

Royal Mail in **Great Britain** issued a set of ten Olympic stamps, 'WELCOME TO THE LONDON 2012 PARALYMPIC GAMES', on **August 29**, **2012**. The set was for the 'PARALYMPIC GAMES' which took place in London in 2012. On the back of the Pack (Pack number: 475) there is an individually numbered *XXX Olympic Logo* hologram (**No. 410**). The Olympic stamp pack is shown in Fig. 3-25.26 with the hologram on the back next to it.

Fig. 3-25.28. THE LONDON 2012 PARALYMPIC GAMES stamps pack with the *XXX Olympic* logo hologram on the back.

Fig. 3-25.29. 'World Cars' booklet with the hologram on the back.

Czech Republic issued on **September 5, 2012**, the 'SVĚTOVÁ AUTA' [World Cars] booklet of six self-adhesive definitive E-stamps (**No. 411**). The booklet stamps features the following cars: 1933 Duesenberg SJ, 1931 Wikov 70, 1936 Mercedes Benz 540, 1938 Rolls Royce Phantom III, 1934 Bugatti Royale 41, and 1929 Isotta Fraschini 8A. On the front of the booklet three old Czech cars are depicted: 1928 Škoda Hispano–Suiza, 1932 Minerva Al, and 1930 Praga Grand. The stamp identified with the letter 'E' corresponding to the price of international priority letters up to 20 g. Like the previous Czech booklets, the same security hologram is attached at the back of booklet. The booklet is shown in Fig. 3-25.29. The stamps were designed by Václav Zapadlík. The Czech Post Printing House in Prague printed the stamps.

On **September 18, 2012**, a special limited-edition (500) miniature sheet was issued in **Australia**. The sheet shows a light-hearted approach to travelling through Australia's landscapes and calling at some landmark attractions: the outback town of Alice Springs, home to not only the annual Camel Cup but a notable centre for Aboriginal art and culture; Phillip Island, where Little Penguins (Eudyptula minor) parade from beach to sand dunes at sunset; Port Arthur, a reminder of Australia's grim past; the Great Barrier Reef, the world's largest coral reef system which covers 2,000 km of coastline; and Margaret River, known not only for its wines but for its barreling surf. There are five imperforated stamps on the sheet, three 69¢ stamps, one $1.65 stamp and one $2.35 stamp (**No. 412**). The stamps depict vehicles covered with diffractive foil. The presentation folder contains two numbered stamp sheets, one with and one without diffractive foil, both with the same number, which means that 500 sheets of both types were issued. The stamp and pack illustration were by Gavin Ryan and the folder designed by Sharon Rodziewicz, Australian Post Design Studio. The sheet is shown in Fig. 3-25.30.

Fig. 3-25.30. The 'Road Trip Australia' sheet (92/500) with diffractive vehicles.

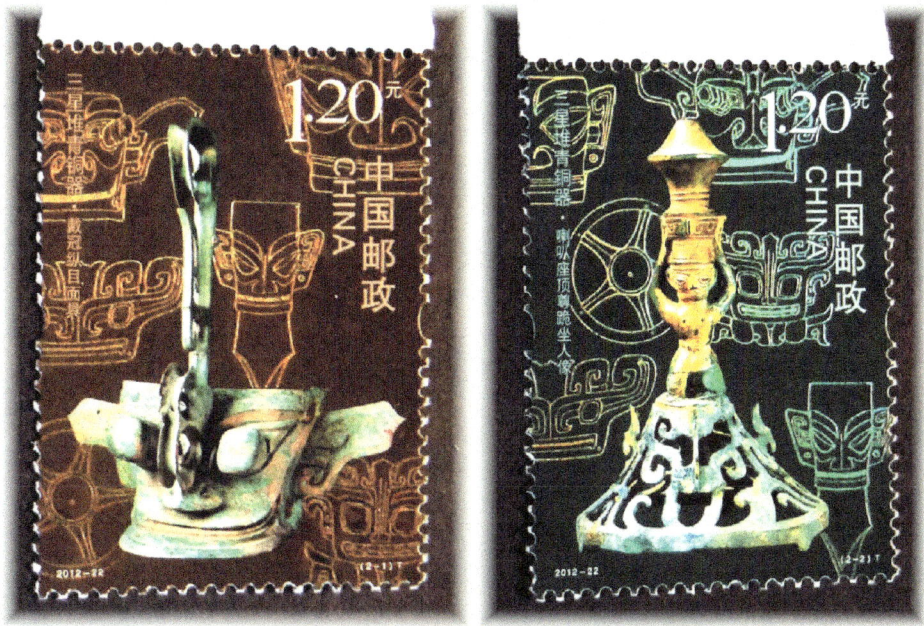

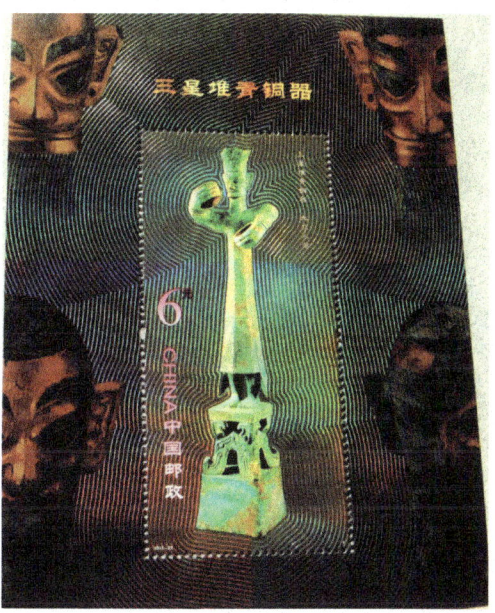

Fig. 3-25.31. The 'Sanxingdui Bronze' stamps with holographic effect.

On **September 26, 2012**, a set of two special stamps and a souvenir sheet titled 'Sanxingdui Bronze' were issued in **P. R. China** by China National Philatelic Corporation. Located in the city of Guanghan in northern Chengdu Plain, Sichuan Province, Sanxingdui is the ruins of a prehistoric culture dating back 4,800-2,600 years. Myriad artifacts have been excavated from Sanxingdui, most of which are bronze. The life-size standing figure unearthed from Sanxingdui's No.2 sacrificial pit, measuring 262 centimeters with its pedestal, is larger than any other contemporaneous bronze figure found so far in the world. Dressed in a dragon robe, the enigmatic character stands on a high base in an awe-inspiring manner. Some archaeologists have asserted the figure's identity as a combination of god, wizard, and king, or the most authoritative leader, symbolizing the highest religious and political authority. The two 1.20-Yuan stamps depict the Crowned Mask with Protruding Eyes and A Kneeling Person Bearing a Zun (**No. 413** and **414**). These two stamps need to be illuminated from the side to see the holographic *line drawings*. The 6-Yuan souvenir sheet (**No. 415**) depicts the life-size standing figure. The three stamps are covered with diffractive foil and are shown in Fig. 3-25.31. The stamps were designed by Qian Zhe and printed by Shenyang Posts and Telecommunications Printing House, Liaoning Province.

Fig. 3-25.32. MEMORY OF LONDON 2012 stamps pack with the *XXX Olympic* logo hologram on the back.

On **September 27**, **2012**, **Great Britain** issued the 'MEMORIES OF LONDON 2012' to remember the Olympic Games in London 2012. Like all the previous Olympic stamp sets, there is the individually numbered *XXX Olympic Logo* hologram on the back of the Pack (Pack number: 476). The Olympic stamp pack is shown in Fig. 3-25.32 (**No. 416**) with the hologram on the back next to it.

On **September 27**, **2012**, the 'Malaysian Festivals - Series II', a five-stamp set, was issued in **Malaysia** to commemorate the various festivities celebrated by Malaysians. The five 60-sen stamps feature five festivities: Hari Raya Haji, Mid-Autumn Festival, Thaipusam, Kaul Festival and Regatta Lepa (**No. 417** through **421**). The first three are celebrated nationwide while the Kaul Festival and Regatta Lepa are celebrated only in Sarawak and Sabah, respectively. The stamps were designed by World Communications Network Resources Sdn Bhd and printed by Joh. Enschedé Security Print in The Netherlands with special diffractive holographic foil. The five stamps are shown in Fig. 3-25.33 and the FDC in Fig. 3-25.34.

Fig. 3-25.33. The five 'Malaysian Festivals - Series II' stamps.

Fig. 3-25.34. The 'Malaysian Festivals - Series II' FDC.

Czech Republic issued on **October 5, 2012**, another booklet of ten self-adhesive definitive stamps, the 'Čtyřlístek in the King's Service' booklet (**No. 422**). Five of the definitive horizontal picture stamps, identified with the letter 'A', depict figures from the four *Čtyřlístek* friends flying a Griffin (a legendary creature with the body, tail, and back legs of a lion; the head and wings of an eagle; and an eagle's talons as its front feet). The other set of five stamps depict Myšpulín the Cat taking a photo of Bobík the Pig, Fifinka the Missy Dog, Pinďa the Rabbit, and the King. The stamp was designed by Jaroslav Němeček. Stamps identified with the letter 'A' correspond to the price of domestic letters up to 50 g. Like the previous Czech booklets, the same security hologram (see Fig. 3-18.9) is attached at the top left corner of the stamps in the booklet. The booklet is shown in Fig. 3-25.35. Czech Post Printing House in Prague printed the stamps.

Fig. 3-25.35. The King's Service booklet.

Fig. 3-25.36. The two Luxembourg Christmas stamp sheets.

For the celebrations of the end of the year, **Luxembourg** issued, on **November 5, 2012**, two Christmas stamps. The first stamp, with a face value of 0.60 + 0.05 CHF (**No. 423**), is for national mail whereas the second stamp, with a face value of 0.85 + 0.10 CHF (**No. 424**), is for franking mail sent to other European countries. The stamps, shown in Fig. 3-25.36, of a graphic design, were created by the artist Michel Olmic. The *stars* on the stamps and on the boarders of the twelve-stamp sheets are covered by holographic foil. Cartor Security Printers, in France printed the stamps.

On **November 19, 2012**, the 'Children's Hobbies' stamps and miniature sheet were issued in **Malaysia**. The six stamps feature children's hobbies: Playing Football, Fishing, Playing Music, Photography, Baking Cookies, and Collecting Stamps. The Children's Hobbies stamp collection designs featuring the characters of Boboi Boy, all in 60- sen denomination and were for the first time issued using unique security ink on the stamps. The *children* on the RM 5.00 miniature sheet, shown in Fig. 3-25.37 (**No. 425**), are covered with transparent holographic diffractive foil. The FDC is shown in Fig. 3-25.38. The stamps and sheets were designed by Animonsta Studios Sdn Bhd and printed by Joh. Enschedé Security Printing, The Netherlands. The stamps were issued in conjunction with the Stamp Week event in Setiawangsa, Kuala Lumpur, which took place between November 19 and 25, 2012. A special overprinted miniature sheet (OMG! – STAMP WEEK 2012) was issued for the Stamp Week. The overprinted sheet is shown in Fig. 3-25.39 (**No. 430**) demonstrating the diffractive effect.

Fig. 3-25.37. 'Children's Hobbies' sheet.

Fig. 3-25.38. 'Children's Hobbies' FDC.

Fig. 3-25.39. The OMG overprinted sheet with the holographic effect.

For a second time definitive hologram stamps were issued in **Nigeria**. Four stamps were issued on **November 24, 2012**, in the 'Ahmadu Bello University (ABU) Golden Anniversary' series. The fifty-year-old university is located in Zaria, Nigeria. These four stamps with a square hologram depict: 'Senate Building' (₦50, **No. 426**), 'Premier Sardauna of Sokomoto of Northern Nigeria' (₦50, **No. 427**), 'ABU Crest' (₦90, **No. 428**), and 'Shika Brown Layer' (₦120, **No. 429**). The square hologram consists only of a piece of *diffracting foil*. The stamps shown in Fig. 3-25.40 were designed by Adeniyi Taiwo Adedoja and Oshodi Abdulhafis of the ABU 50th Anniversary Committee and printed by Takoms International Ltd. The FDC is shown in Fig. 3-25.41.

Fig. 3-25.40. The four stamps from Nigeria with square holograms.

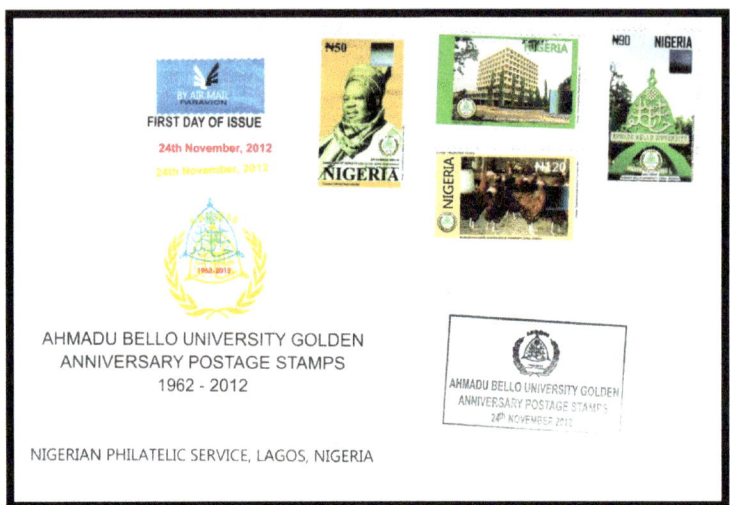

Fig. 3-25.41. The FDC with the four Nigerian stamps.

Chunghwa Post (**Taiwan**) issued the 'Deep-Sea Creatures' on **December 12, 2012**. Two souvenir sheets were issued featuring animals that live in the mesopelagic zone of waters near Taiwan. One of the sheets, shown in Fig. 3-25.42, includes four stamps: *1. Eurypharynx pelecanoides* (NT$10). This mesopelagic and bathyalpelagic fish lives at depths of 500-3,000 m. *2. Argyropelecus aculeatus* (NT$12). Commonly known as the Atlantic silver hatchetfish, it lives at depths of 200-1,000 m. Its flat silver body resembles a mirror, reflecting the colors of its surroundings to camouflage itself. The light organs along its belly also help it conceal itself by producing light that hides its own shadow. To illustrate the color of the *silver hatchetfish* on this stamp, shown in Fig. 3-25.43, the fish is covered with hot-stamped holographic foil (**No. 431**). *3. Bufoceratias shaoi* (NT$10). This species lives at depths of 500-1,200 meters. Its body is globular in shape but slightly flatter on the sides. The tip of its first dorsal fin has evolved to become a light organ called the illicium or esca, which contains many symbiotic bioluminescent bacteria. The esca can emit light to lure curious prey. *4. Regalecus glesne* (NT$12). This mesopelagic fish is found at depths ranging from the surface to 1,000 m. The world's longest bony fish, it can grow up to 11 m. The marginal inscription features *leptocephalus* (upper left corner), *ctenophora* (lower right corner) and *bobtail squid* (lower left corner). The other smaller (non-holographic) souvenir sheet with a NT$25 stamp features the *histioteuthis celetaria pacifica* fish which lives at depths of 300-500 m (Fig. 3-25.44). Densely covered with light organs, its body can emit just the right amount of light to camouflage itself. One of its eyes has evolved to be larger than the other so as to help it search for prey. To highlight the bioluminescent characteristics of these deep sea creatures, the luminescent parts of these animals are printed in luminous ink, giving the stamps a charming effect under darkness. The four-stamp sheet FDC is show in Fig. 4-25.45. The stamps and sheets were designed by Delta Designed Corporation and printed by Joh. Enschedé Security Printers, the Netherlands.

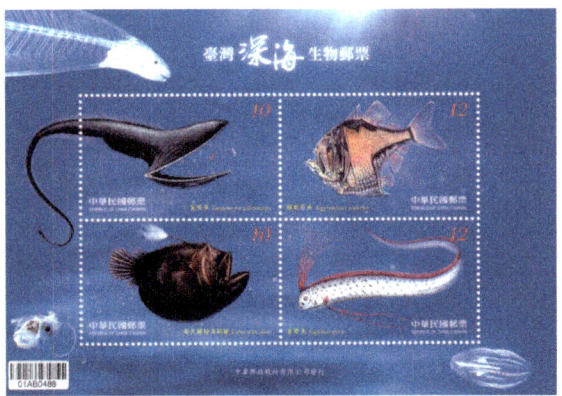

Fig. 3-25.42. The 'Deep Sea Creature' 4-stamp souvenir sheet.   **Fig. 3-25.43**. The holographic *fish* stamp.

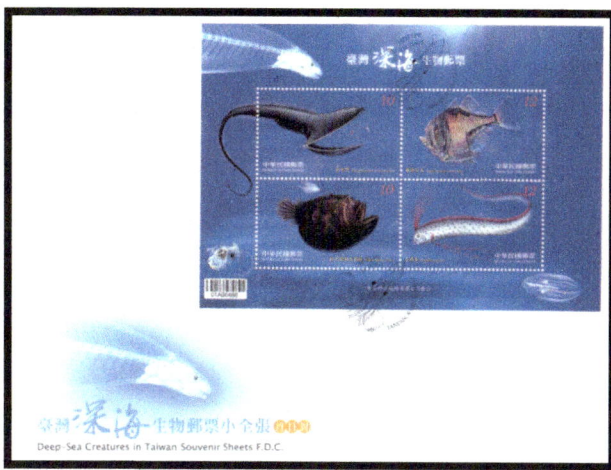

Fig. 3-25.44. The single-stamp sheet. **Fig. 3-25.45.** The four-stamp FDC with the hologram stamp.

During **2012 Czech Republic** issued fifteen numbered commemorative sheets with a security hologram stripe at the bottom of the card. One example is the František Bílek (1872-1941) card (PLZ 26) issued on November 6, 2012, for the 140-year-anniversary of Bílek's birthday. The 12-Kč stamp on the card features the drawing 'The prophets came out of the desert' which was issued on November 12, 1997. Bílek's book illustration depicted on the stamp is a typical example of his characteristic kind of expression in connecting figures of different sizes in one composition. The commemorative sheet with the stamp is shown in Fig. 3-25.46 with the security hologram stripe at the bottom.

Fig. 3-25.46. The Czech Bílek card.

Fig. 3-25.47. The Guayaguil City card GYE 002, Las Peñas Quarter.

Fig. 3-25.47. The Guayaguil City card GYE 009, Martin Aviles Building.

Ecuador has issued well over one hundred postcards since 2008. The address side of the cards has the holographic *Ecudorian Post Logo* as shown on the cards in Fig. 3-25.24. Many of the cards were issued in limited editions. Two examples of the ten Guayaquil City postcards, issued **November 26, 2012**, are described here. Only 500 of each card in this series were issued. The first card is the card marked GYE 002 (344/500) shown in Fig. 3-25.47. It depicts the Numa Pompilio Llona Street in Las Peñas Quarter. The other card, shown in Fig. 3-25.48, is the card marked GYE 009 (350/500) which has the Martin Aviles Building on the picture side.

3-26. Holographic stamps and souvenir sheets issued in 2013

Macau continued to issue hologram stamps for the Lunar New Year, the year of the Snake, with holographic diffractive effect. A souvenir sheet was issued in Malaysia and Curaçau issued a souvenir sheet for the Dutch throne succession. To honor Mother's Day, stamps and a souvenir were issued in China. Japan issued the third and fourth souvenir sheets in the Constellations Series. Israel issued its first hologram stamps with the large Children's Songs sheet. A beautiful limited-edition Collector's sheet was issued in Hungary. Another limited-edition Collector's sheet was issued in Singapore. Many stamp sheets and booklets were issued by Czech Post. The book manuscript was completed in October 2013, which means that stamps issued towards the end of 2013 are not included here.

Fig. 3-26.1. The hologram stamp and the four Snake stamps.

Fig. 3-26.2. The diamond-shaped stamp on the sheet.

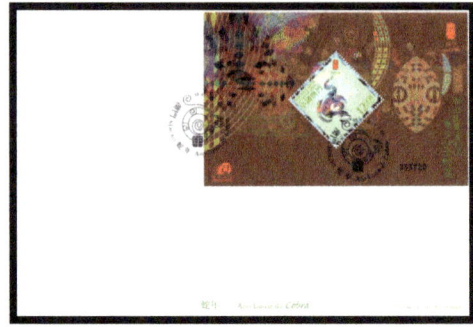

Fig. 3-26.3. The Snake sheet FDC.

Macau issued on **January 3**, **2013**, five stamps and a souvenir sheet to welcome the 'Lunar New Year of the Snake'. The conceptual design of the stamp is combined with the different forms of the snake and the distinguishing characteristics of Metal, Wood, Water, Fire and Earth. The year of snake, the snake's nature from the Five Elements is 'Water Snake', so it becomes the main character of the five stamps. The colourful 'Water Snake' is applied with emboss printing technique to highlight its scales, together with the hot foil stamping with symphony holographic on the stamp border, giving the festive spirit of Lunar New Year. The RM5.00 stamp (**No. 432**) with the holographic foil is shown in Fig. 3-26.1 together with the other four stamps. The diamond shaped stamp on the souvenir sheet (**No. 433**) is shown in Fig. 3-26.2 and the FDC in Fig. 3-26.3. The stamps were designed by Wilson Chi Ian Lam and printed by Sprintpak, Australia.

On **February 5, 2013**, the 'Exotic Pets' stamps and miniature sheets were issued in **Malaysia**. The three stamps depict the Green Iguana, the Pygmy Hedgehog and the Sugar Glider. The Royal Pyton (*Python regius*) is depicted on the RM5.00 miniature sheet which is covered with transparent holographic foil (**No. 434**). The Royal Pyton also known as Ball Python is the smallest of the African pythons and is popular in the pet trade, largely due to its typically docile temperament. The name ball python refers to the animal's tendency to curl into a ball when stressed or frightened. The color pattern is typically black or dark brown with light brown or gold sides and dorsal blotches. The belly is a white or cream that may include scattered black markings. There is also another similar miniature sheet with a RM3.00 stamp, but without holographic foil. The miniature sheet is shown in Fig. 3-26.4 and the FDC in Fig. 3-26.5. The stamps and sheets were designed by Reign Associates Sdn. Bhd. and printed by Percetakan Keselamatan Nasional Sdn. Bhd.

Fig. 3-26.4. The Royal Pytton sheet.

Fig. 3-26.5. The Royal Pyton FDC.

Fig. 3-26.6. part of the 25-stamp 'Run-Tours 2013' sheet with the large security hologram and microtext line.

Czech Republic issued on **April 10, 2013**, the self-adhesive definitive 25-A-stamp sheets in the 'Mizumo Run-Tours 2013' stamp series (**No. 435**). Stamps identified with the letter 'A' corresponds to the price of domestic letters up to 50 g. Part of the 25-stamp sheet with the security hologram label is shown in Fig. 3-26.6. The larger security hologram (13x13 mm) is attached at the bottom margin of the sheets which was introduced in 2012. Additional security is provided by the microtext line printed under ČESKÁ REPUBLIKA (see 3-25.19). Czech Post Printing House in Prague printed the stamps.

Curaçau issued on **April 30, 2013**, the 'Dutch Throne Succession' two-1000c-stamp sheet (**No. 436**). On January 28, 2013, Her Majesty the Queen Beatrix, Queen of the Netherlands, announced that she will abdicate the throne to her eldest son, Prince Willem Alexander, Prince of Orange. The Throne Succession took place on April 30, 2013. The two stamps on the Curaçao sheet feature His Majesty King Willem Alexander and Her Royal Highness Princess Beatrix. The Dutch Royal Lion is also shown (mainly on selvedge, but with parts of the paws running onto the stamps themselves). The sheet with the *crown* holograms is shown in Fig. 3-26.7. The stamps and sheets were designed by Richmond Gijsbertha and printed by Joh. Enschedé Security Printers, The Netherlands.

Fig. 3-26.7. The 'Dutch Throne Succession Sheet' with the hologram *crowns*.

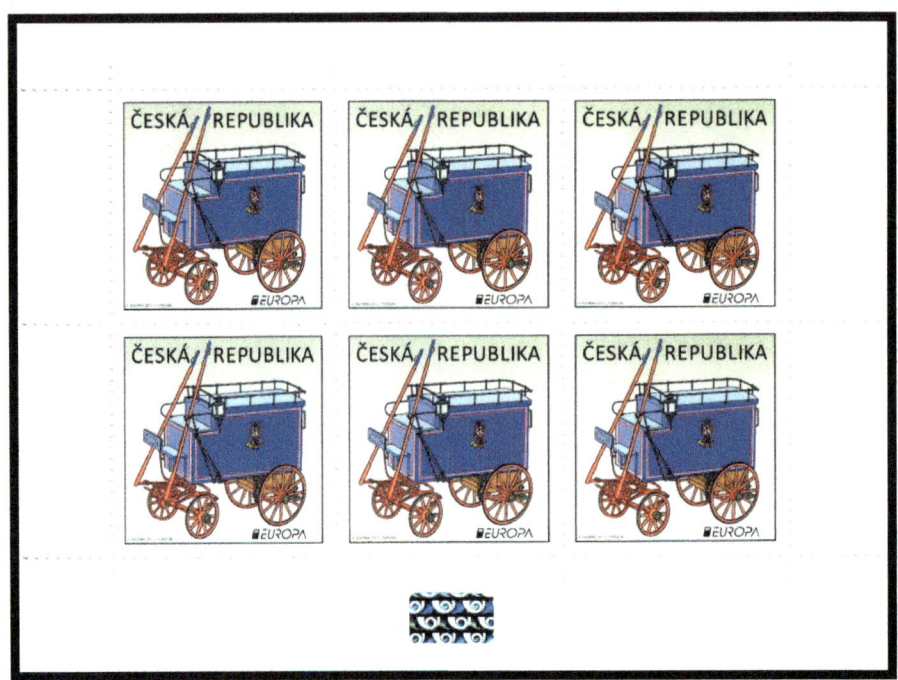

Fig. 3-26.8. The 'Postal Means of Transportation' sheet with the hologram security label.

For the celebrating 'PostEurop's 20th Anniversary – 1993-2013', the 'EUROPA – Postal Means of Transportation' a sheet of six 25-CZK definitive stamps was issued on **May 2, 2013**, in **Czech Republic** (**No. 437**). The Czech stamp depicts a symbol of Czechoslovak Post's history - horse-drawn parcel mail coach. Model IV of this coach was based on a one-horse cargo coach used by Austrian Post. Like its Austrian counterpart, it was usually drawn by a single horse. Czechoslovak Post used it for delivering parcels addressed to businesses or private recipients. Like the previous Czech stamp sheets, the small security hologram is attached at the middle of the lower margin. The sheet is shown in Fig. 3-26.8. The stamp was designed by Karel Dvořák and Jaroslav Tvrdoň. Czech Post Printing House in Prague printed the stamps.

P. R. China issued the 'Thanks Mom' stamps (**No. 438**) and souvenir sheets (**No. 439**) on **May 11, 2013**. With a denomination of 1.20 Yuan the stamp depicts a rose and foil banner with holographic *stars*. The stamps were issued in sheets of 16. A souvenir sheet with eight of the stamps inside a heart was also issued. The stamp is shown in Fig. 3-26.9 and the souvenir sheet in Fig. 3-26.10. Note that the hologram banner *star* patterns on the eight stamps are all different depending on how they were cut out of the large foil sheet. The stamps were designed by Sheng Jiahong and Jiang Wei. Beijing postage Stamp Printing Works printed the stamps.

Fig. 3-26.9. The 'Thanks Mom' stamp.

Fig. 3-26.10. The 'Thanks Mom' eight-stamp souvenir sheet.

Fig. 3-26.11. The 'For Children' booklet.

Czech Republic issued on **May 29, 2013**, the 'For Children' booklet of ten definitive self-adhesive A-stamps (**No. 440**). It was the 'Mole flying on the Rocket' stamps to commemorate Zdeněk Miler (1921-2011), Czech director and author of children's cartoons, who created the popular Krtek or Krteček [The Mole or The Little Mole] character. Stamps identified with the letter 'A' corresponds to the price of domestic letters up to 50 g. Like the previous Czech stamp booklets, the small security hologram is attached at the back of the booklet. The booklet is shown in Fig. 3-26.11. The stamp was designed by Zdeněk Miler and Otakar Karlas. Czech Post Printing House in Prague printed the stamps.

Czech Republic issued on **June 10, 2013**, the '100th Prague Mayors Eights of ČSOB Pojišťovna Rowing Competition' self-adhesive 25-A-stamp sheets, which took place between June 7 and 9, 2013 (**No. 441**). Stamps identified with the letter 'A' corresponds to the price of domestic letters up to 50 g. Part of the 25-stamp sheet with the security hologram label is shown in Fig. 3-26.12. The larger security hologram (13x13 mm) is attached at the bottom margin of the sheets. Additional security is provided by the microtext line under ČESKÁ REPUBLIKA. Czech Post Printing House in Prague printed the stamps. This sheet was an official issue of the new type of Czech Post Personal Stamps. However, such private issues ordered by companies or societies, printed by the Czech Post, could only be bought from the ordering party.

 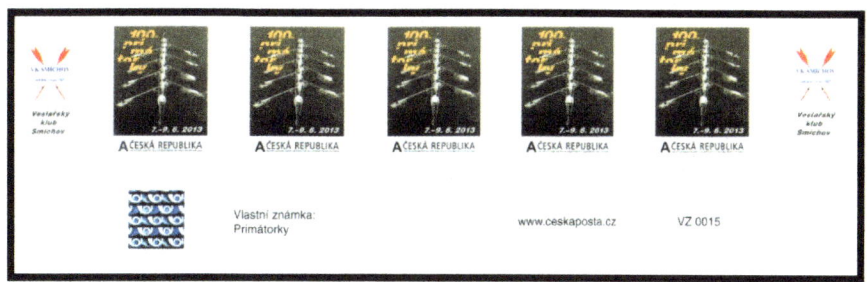

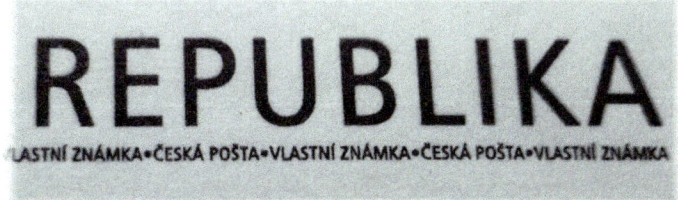

Fig. 3-26.12. Part of the 25-stamp 'Rowing Competition' sheet with the large security hologram and microtext line.

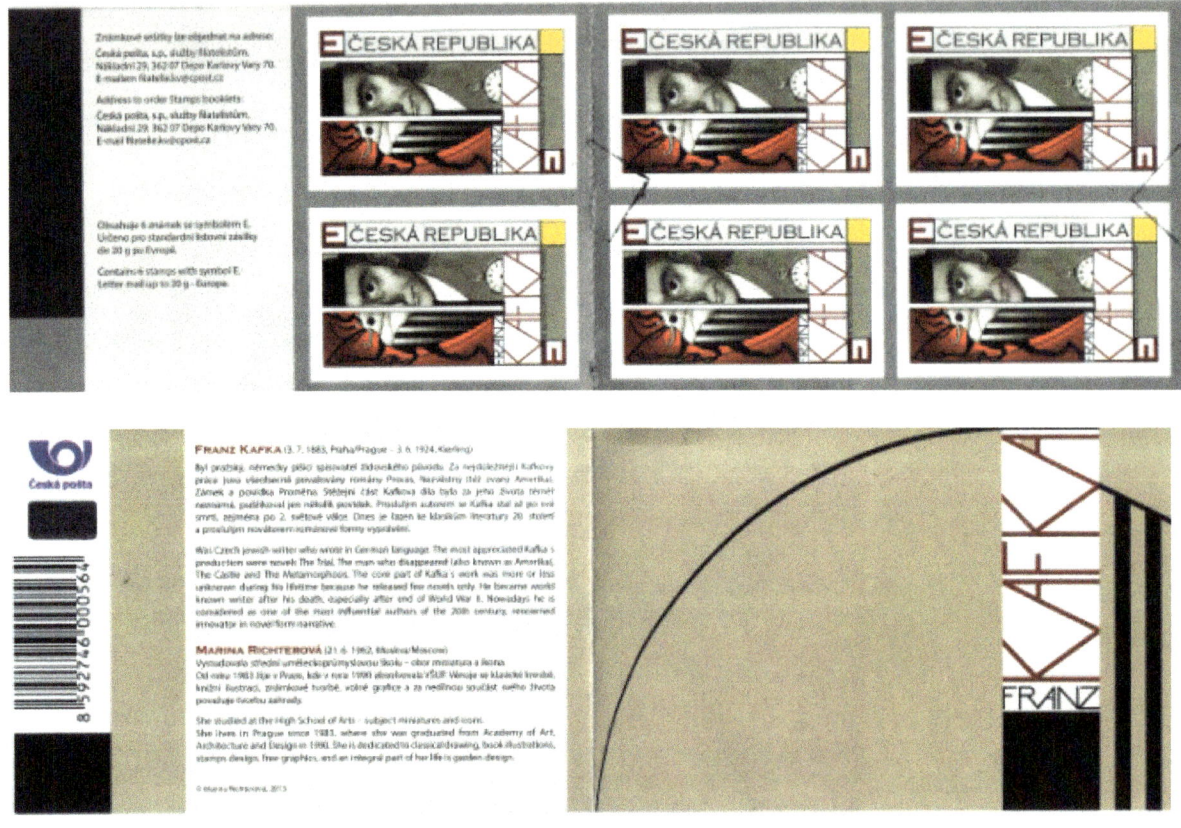

Fig. 3-26.13. The 'Franz Kafka' booklet with the hologram security label on the back.

Czech Republic issued on **June 26, 2013**, a booklet of six definitive E-stamps. It was the 'Franz Kafka' booklet (**No. 442**). The stamp's motto is LAWLESSNES - TIMELESSNESS - METAMORPHOSIS. The composition of the stamp is based on an austere geometric module which is also reflected in the booklet. The stamp portrays a realistic-looking beetle. As a symbol of relentless metamorphosis, not always for the better, the beetle is set in austere, even unsympathetic modules. Franz Kafka is best known for his novels *The Trial, The Man Who Disappeared, The Castle*, and short story *The Metamorphosis*. The key part of his work was almost unknown and only a few short stories were published during his lifetime. Kafka became famous posthumously, mostly after World War II. Today, he is considered one of the 20th century classics and a renowned innovator of the prose narrative form. The stamp identified with the letter 'E' corresponding to the price of Ordinary Item up to 50 g - European countries in international priority service. Like the previous Czech stamp booklets, the small security hologram is attached at the back of the booklet. The booklet is shown in Fig. 3-26.13. The stamp was designed by Marina Richterová and printed by Czech Post Printing House in Prague.

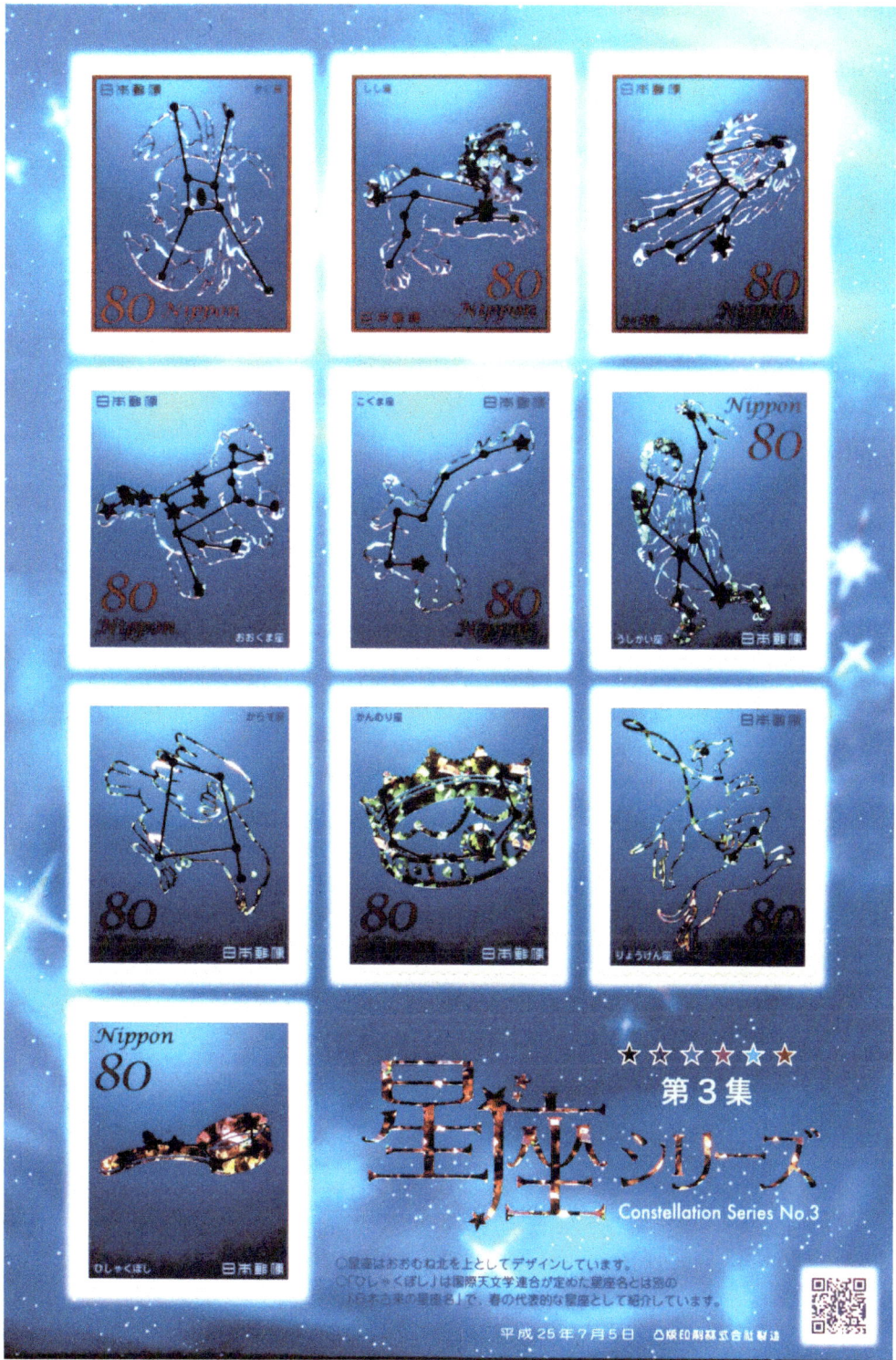

Fig. 3-26.14. The 3rd Constellation ten-stamp-sheetlet.

Japan issued the third series of Constellation stamps on **July 5, 2012, (No. 443)**. The Constellation stamps collection is issued for the purpose of promotion of natural science and culture of letter writing. The third issue is dedicated to the typical spring constellations and depicts the following constellations: Cancer, Leo, Virgo, Ursa Major, Little Bear, Bootes, Corvus, Corona, Canes Venatici and Ladle Mother and Child. The *constellations* on the stamps are printed using the hologram foil offset printing method. The sheet with ten stamps is shown in Fig. 3-26.14. The stamps were designed by Hoshiyama Rika and printed by Hanshiki Printing.

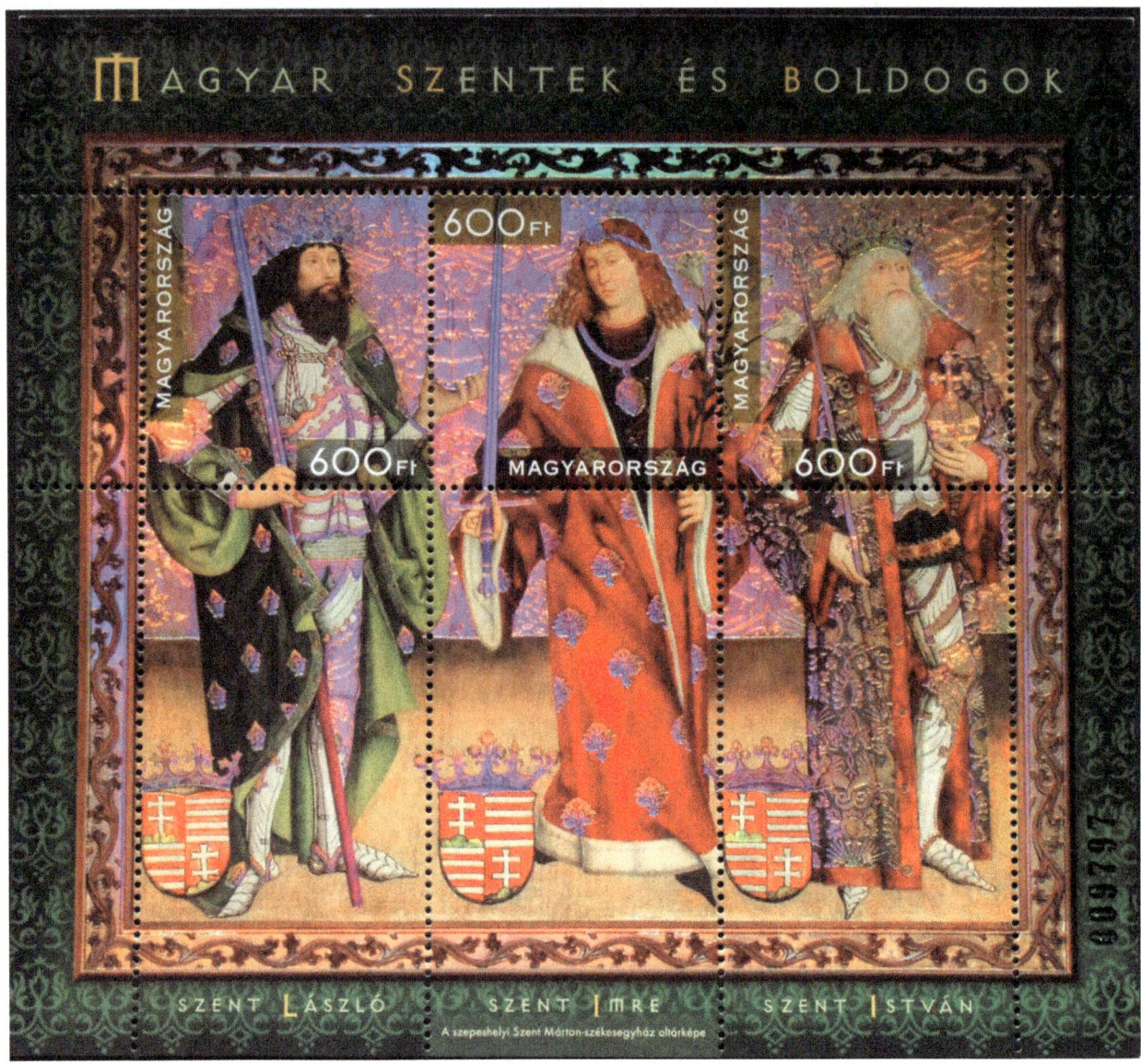

Fig. 3-26.15. The 'HUNGARIAN SAINTS AND BLESSEDS I' three-stamp souvenir sheet.

Hungary issued the 'HUNGARIAN SAINTS AND BLESSEDS I' souvenir sheet on **August 14, 2013**. The three stamps of the first miniature sheet (**No. 444**) feature the panel of the main altar of the Cathedral of Saint Martin in Spišskà Kapitula, Slovakia, which used to be part of historic Hungary. On the heraldic left on the sheet stands the middle-aged Saint Ladislas wearing a fleur-de-lys crown. In the middle is the serene-looking, youthful Prince Emeric. Next to him on the right is the elderly Saint King Stephen, who commands respect. His armour evokes the period of Sigismund of Luxemburg. He holds a golden sceptre with a long rod in his right hand and a huge orb in his left hand. The offset printed special edition has gilded motifs which are enhanced by diffraction film and embossing, lending the miniature sheet a shiny surface. Number of copies: 20,000 (standard edition); 10,000 (special edition) (Fig. 3-26.15); 5,000 (monochrome edition). 5,000 copies were made of the set, which contains a special edition numbered from 1 to 5,000 and a similarly numbered philatelic monochrome edition. The latter is sold only as part of the set. The monochrome edition may not be used to pay for postage. The miniature sheet was designed by György Kara and printed by Pénzjegynyomda Co. (Hungarian Bank Note Company) in Budapest.

Fig. 3-26.16. The 'World Stamp Exhibition 2015' **two-stamp souvenir** sheet.

Fig. 3-26.17. The 'World Stamp Exhibition 2015' **two-stamp** souvenir sheet.

In **Singapore** on **August 23, 2013**, a limited-edition (2000) collectror's sheet with two $5 stamps was issued (**No. 445**). It was the 'World Stamp Exhibition 2015, Series 2'. The stamps were issued for the stamp exhibition to take place in 2015; an exhibition Singapore successfully bidded for and was awarded the hosting rights. Two designs from the "1970: Osaka Expo" were chosen, featuring the Guppy (*Poecilia reticulate*) which is a small colorful species of freshwater tropical fish which makes it popular as an aquarium fish. Guppies often display elaborated patterns on their tail fin, with the male being generally more brightly colored; female guppies however are larger in size and have a shorter tail as compared to the males. The other stamp features the **Seashell**, also known as shell. The seashell has a hard, protective outer layer created by an animal that lives in the sea. The shells are empty because the animal has died and the soft parts have been eaten by another animal or have rotted out. The two stamps are covered with diffractive foil and are also the stamp images embossed. The Collector's sheet is shown in Fig. 3-26.16. There was also a sheet with two $2 stamps without diffractive foil, which is shown in Fig. 3-26.17. Chan Willie at Will Marketing Design designed the sheets and stamps and Thai British Security Printing printed them.

Fig. 3-26.18. The 'Children's Songs' **twelve-stamp** souvenir sheet from Israel with *CD disc* hologram in the middle.

Israel issued on **August 26**, 2013, twelve stamps on a large souvenir sheet about children's songs (**No. 446**). This stamp series includes a dozen well-known children's songs that are sung by all and passed from one generation to the next. Songs about nature and animals, time and space, family, pain and hope. These songs have been published in books, numerous versions have been recorded by Israel's finest artists and to this day they continue to be played on radio and television and in the theater. But most of all, these songs have been preserved thanks to preschool and kindergarten teachers. The twelve stamps feature the following songs: Merry Choir, I Am Always Me, A Brave Clock, What Do the Does Do?, I Wanted You to Know, Buba Zehava (Doll), Why Does the Zebra Wear Pajamas?, The Prettiest Girl in Kindergarten, The Post Van, My Dad, Horse Rider, and Brave Danny. In the middle of the sheet there is a hologram of a CD disk on four perforated no-value Israeli Music stamps (Fig. 3-26.18). The sheets were printed by Joh. Enschedé Security Printers, The Netherlands.

Fig. 3-26.19. The 'Czech Cars - Škoda I' booklet with the hologram security label at the back.

Czech Republic issued on **September 4, 2013**, the 'Czech Cars - Škoda I' booklet of eight self-adhesive definitive A-stamps with two different cars (**No. 447**). The two different booklet stamps features the Škoda 860, r. v. 1930 cars. The front page of the booklet features three cars: Škoda Laurin & Klement B 1907, Škoda Laurin & Klement 110 1925 – 1928 and Škoda 6R 1930. Stamps identified with the letter 'A' corresponds to the price of domestic letters up to 50 g. Like the previous Czech booklets, the same small security hologram is attached at the back of booklet. The booklet is shown in Fig. 3-26.19. The stamps were designed by Václav Zapadlík. The Czech Post Printing House in Prague printed the stamps.

Czech Republic issued on **September 4, 2013**, the '20 Years of Czech Post' eight self-adhesive definitive E-stamp booklet (**No. 448**). It has a field for eight My Own Stamps on the inside and two information fields according to the customer's artwork (front and back) and a Czech Post's field for standard identification of the booklet on the outside. In the case of the initial issue of My Own Stamps of Czech Post, the customized information field on the outside in the front of the booklet portrays a Czech Post's logo and the text '20 Years of Česká pošta, s.p.', the information field in the back contains an information text on Czech Post's history and barcode. In the case of customised orders, the entire (front and back) fields on the outside of the booklet will be available to the customer. Theme of the stamps is information text on Czech Post's history, wavy stamp cancel lines and Czech Post's logo. The initial issue contains four stamps in the horizontal orientation and four stamps in the vertical orientation, with identical, but differently positioned features in the picture part of the stamps; customised orders may contain stamps with up to eight different motifs in one booklet. Like the previous Czech booklets, the same small security hologram is attached at the back of booklet. Obligatory field contains the name of the country, the letter identifying the stamp value, and a microline with the text: "CZECH POST • MY OWN STAMP". Each stamp is divided by a special perforation, which is accompanied on each edge of the stamp by a unique atypical modification used as a security feature. Individual stamps on a booklet are not separated by a diecut between the perforation lines.). A stamp identified with the letter 'E' corresponding to the price of Ordinary Item up to 50 g - European countries in international priority service. The booklet is shown in Fig. 3-26.20. The stamps were designed by Ivana Havránková and Petr Foltera. The Czech Post Printing House in Prague printed the stamps.

Fig. 3-26.20. The 'Czech Post' booklet. **Fig. 3-26.21**. The 'Fill Your Tank' booklet.

Another booklet with eight self-adhesive A-stamps was also issued on **September 4, 2013**, in **Czech Republic**. It was the 'Fill Your Fuel Tank in a Cheaper Way' booklet (**No. 449**). The booklet was a joint project of Czech Post and the Ministry of Industry and Trade offered the users an interactive map with current prices of petrol and diesel at petrol stations all over the country. The initial issue contains four stamps in the horizontal orientation and four stamps in the vertical orientation, with identical, but differently positioned features in the picture part of the stamps; customised orders may contain stamps with max. eight different motifs in one booklet. In the case of the initial issue of My Own Stamps of Czech Post, the customized information field on the outside in the front of the booklet portrays a 'Fill Your Fuel Tank in a Cheaper Way' stamp with the text 'We know where you can fill your fuel tank in a cheaper way'. In the case of customised orders, the entire (front and back) fields on the outside of the booklet will be available to the customer. Stamps identified with the letter 'A' corresponds to the price of domestic letters up to 50 g. The booklet is shown in Fig. 3-26.21. Like the previous Czech booklets, the same small security hologram is attached at the back of booklet. The stamps were designed by Jan Hykel, Petr Foltera and Ivana Havránková. The Czech Post Printing House in Prague printed the stamps. Like all 'My Own Stamp' issues these two Czech stamp booklets issued on September 4, 2013, have the microtext line printed under ČESKÁ REPUBLIKA as shown in Fig. 3-26.22.

Fig. 3-26.22. The microtext on the stamps in the 'My Own stamp' booklets.

Fig. 3-26.23. The '*Inkayacu paracasensis*' and the '*Canaanimys Maquiensis*' souvenir sheets.

Peru issued on **October 22, 2013**, two souvenir sheets in the series of 'Prehistoric Animals'. It was the '*Inkayacu paracasensis*' $10.00 souvenir sheet (**No. 450**) and the $10.00 '*Canaanimys Maquiensis*' souvenir sheet (**No. 451**). *ANIMALES PREHISTÓRICOS – Fósiles –* is printed with holographic foil on the souvenir sheets. Inkayacu is an extinct genus of penguin. It lived in Peru during the Late Eocene, around 36 million years ago. Canaanimys was a tiny rodent dating to the latest Lutetian stage of the late Middle Eocene, about 41 million years ago. The sheets were designed by Christian Alvarez Mendoza, SERPOST S.A. and printed by Thomas Greg and Sons in Peru. The two souvenir sheets are shown in Fig. 3-26.23.

Czech Republic issued on **October 24, 2013**, the '40th Anniversary of the Magazine Zpravodaj' self-adhesive personalized 25-A-stamp sheets. Stamps identified with the letter 'A' corresponds to the price of domestic letters up to 50 g. The 25-stamp sheet (horizontal orientation) has the security hologram label on the right margin. There were several private issues ordered by companies or societies, printed by the Czech Post, which could only be bought from the ordering party. This issue was limited to 600 sheets only.

In early **December 2013** two other personalized 25-A-stamp sheets were issued in **Czech Republic**. The 'Bohumin City (Oderberg)' sheet of self-adhesive A-stamp sheets (horizontal orientation) has the security hologram label on the right margin. The other personalized 25-A-stamp sheet was the '120 years of Czech Tennis' (vertical orientation) with the security hologram on the bottom margin.

Japan issued 'Constellation Series IV' on **December 4, 2013**, (**No. 452**). The ten self-adhesive stamps collection was issued for the purpose of promotion of natural science and culture of letter writing. The fourth issue depicts ten representative signs of constellation often seen in winter. The following stamps were issued: Aries, Taurus, Gemini, Orion, Auriga, Sirius, Procyon, Lepus, Monoceros, and Tsuzumiboshi (Aka : Orion). The *constellations* on the stamps are printed using the hologram foil offset printing method. The sheet with ten stamps is shown in Fig. 3-26.24. The stamps were designed by Hoshiyama Ayaka and printed by Hanshiki Printing.

Fig. 3-26.24. The 4th Constellation ten-stamp sheetlet.

Definitive hologram stamps were issued for the third time in **Nigeria** on **December 20, 2013.** They refer to the '50th Year of Diplomatic Relations with Philippines' - a two-stamp joint release with the Philippines. Nigeria and the Philippines established there bilateral, diplomatic and trade relation in August 1962. The two stamps have the previously used square hologram which consists of a piece of *diffracting foil* only. The ₦50 stamp depicts a Daisy (*Mesembryanthemum*) which is the National Flower of Nigeria (**No. 453**). The Mesembryanthemum plants have large, daisy-like flowers with glistening petals. The flowers have dark centers and can be pink, white, purple, lavender, crimson, or orange. The ₦120 stamp depicts the Sampaguita (*Jasminum sambac*) which is the Philippine National Flower (**No. 454**). The Sampaguita flower became popular among the Filipinos because of its simplicity and lovely scent. Filipinos string the flowers into leis, corsages and crowns and distill their oils, sellling them in stores, streets, and outside churches. The stamps, shown in Fig. 3-26.25, were printed by Superflux International Limited (SIL), and once again feature the 'NIPOST' overprint, visible only under UV-light, shown in Fig. 3-26.26.

 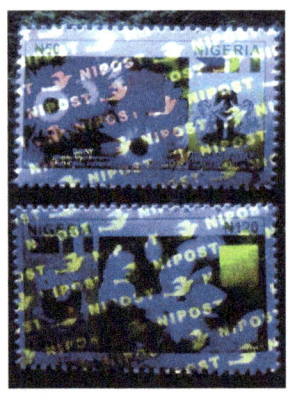

Fig. 3-26.25. The two Nigerian stamps.   **Fig. 3-26.26.** 'NIPOST' overprint.

CHAPTER 4
HOLOGRAM STAMPS IN GERMAN YEAR BOOK OF STAMPS

The German Year Book of Postage Stamps is published every Year. It describes the stamps issued in Germany during the year. Beginning in 1993, the Year Book included both a hologram stamp and a black print of one of the issued stamps. The two reproductions are depicted on an inserted sheet in the book. All these hologram stamps between 1993 and 2012 are described in this Chapter.

Hologram stamps in German Year Books between 1993 and 2012

Since 1993 hologram stamps have appeared in the annual **German Year Book of Postage Stamps** [Die Postwertzeichen der Bundesrepublik Deutschland]. The book (edition about 120,000 every year) is published at the end of the year, normally in November. In **1993**, the year book included for the first time a holographic version of one of the German stamps issued during that year. The cover of the 1993 Year Book is shown in Fig. 4.1. Later the cover looked slightly different, more like the 2001 Year Book, with only one of the issued stamps featured on the cover. The 2001 Year Book cover, shown in Fig. 4.2, has the cable-railway in Wuppertal stamp on the cover. This stamp was the one included as a hologram stamp in the book that year. These hologram stamps in the books are not valid for postage.

Fig. 4.1. German Year Book of Postage Stamps 1993.   **Fig. 4.2**. German Year Book of Postage Stamps 2001.

The first hologram was of a stamp (100 pf, size: 25x43 mm) of Sir Isaac Newton to celebrate his 350-year-birthday (January 14, 1643). The hologram shows a 3D image of *Newton in front of a drawing of a prism and a color spectrum*. This hologram was produced by Thomas Cvetkovich, Chromagem Inc. in the USA and Holopress GmbH in Germany. This stamp is shown in Fig. 4.3 together with the other hologram stamps included in every Year Book until 2012.

The **1994** holographic postage stamp (80 pf, size: 25x43 mm) was issued to celebrate the 1200-year-anniversary of Frankfurt am Main. The definitive stamp was issued on February 10, 1994. The hologram image is a recording of a drawing of *Frankfurt am Main*.

In the **1995** year book a holographic postage stamp (100 pf, size: 32x28 mm) was issued for the First International Climate Protection Convention in Berlin. The definitive stamp was issued on March 9, 1995. The hologram shows a 2D achromatic image of a *sphere (the Earth) and a rainbow in front of it*. This holographic stamp and the following ones, except the 1999 one, have been produced by Irina Menz at HSM GmbH. Holographic Dimensions Inc., Florida, produced the embossed 1995 holograms.

In **1996** a holographic stamp (100 pf, size: 35x35 mm) was produced to commemorate Martin Luther's day of death (February 8, 1546) 450 years ago. The hologram shows a *portrait of Martin Luther* by Lucas Cranach.

The year book of **1997** included a holographic stamp (100 pf, size: 28x33 mm) to celebrate the 175-year-anniversary of the carnival in Cologne. The definitive stamp was issued on February 4, 1997. The hologram shows a picture of *two dancing men in carnival costumes*.

Fig. 4.3. Hologram stamps in the German Year Book of Stamps between 1993 and 2012.

In **1998** the holographic stamp (110pf, size: 35x35 mm) was issued to celebrate the 1000-year-anniversary of Bad Frankenhausen. The definitive stamp was issued on March 12, 1998. The hologram image is a drawing of *Bad Frankenhausen*.

The **1999** year book included a holographic stamp: 'EUROPA - Marke 1999' from Berchtesgaden national park (110pf, size: 30x54 mm). The hologram depicts a *landscape with mountains*. The definitive stamp was issued on May 4, 1999.

The holographic stamp (110pf, size: 33x55 mm) in the **2000** year book was a stamp of the city Passau in the series: 'Pictures from Germany'. The hologram depicts a *view of Passau*. The definitive stamp was issued on March 16, 2000.

In **2001** the holographic stamp (110pf, size: 33x55 mm) was issued to celebrate the 100-year-anniversary of the cable-railway in Wuppertal. The definitive stamp was issued on March 8, 2001. The hologram shows a reproduction of a postcard from about 1903 with a *cable car* from that time (Fig. 4.2).

In the year book with the **2002** stamps, a holographic stamp (153c, size: 33x55 mm) of the *Museum for Communications Building in Berlin* is depicted on the stamp. The definitive stamp was issued on August 8, 2002.

The **2003** year book included a holographic stamp (55c, size: 33x55 mm) to celebrate the 150-year-anniversary of the *Bietigheim viaduct*. The definitive stamp was issued on September 11, 2003. The *viaduct above the river* is featured on the stamp.

The **2004** year book included a holographic stamp (45c, size: 35x35 mm) of the Greifswalder Oie Lighthouse. The definitive stamp together with another lighthouse stamp was issued on July 8, 2004. The *lighthouse* is featured on the stamp.

The **2005** year book included a holographic stamp (45c+20c, size: 33x55 mm) of the schooner brig Greif. The definitive stamp together with another stamp of a ship was issued on June 2, 2005. The stamps were issued 'Für die Jugend' with the additional 20c for the 'Stiftung Deutsche Jugendmarke e.V.' The *Schooner Brig Greif* is featured on the stamp.

The **2006** year book included a holographic stamp (145c, size: 35x35 mm) of the Brooklyn Bridge over the East River in New York, which was completed 1883. The bridge was designed by the German immigrant Johann August Röbling (1806-1869) and is one of the oldest suspension bridges in the United States. The definitive stamp was issued on June 8, 2006, for the 200-year-anniversary of Röbling's birthday. *Brooklyn Bridge* is featured on the stamp.

The **2007** year book included a holographic stamp (55c, size: 27x46 mm) which was issued for the 50-year-anniversary of the Deutsch Bundesbank. The definitive stamp was issued on August 9, 2007. *D-Mark as well as Euro coins and banknotes* are featured on the stamp.

The **2008** year book included a holographic stamp (45c, size: 27x46 mm) which was issued for the 125-year-anniversary of the German cog railway to the 220 m top of Drachenfels. The definitive stamp was issued on July 3, 2008. The first *steam-powered cog train* is featured on the stamp.

The **2009** year book included a holographic stamp (145c, size: 33x55 mm) which was issued for the 100-year-anniversary of the Train Ferry between Sassnitz and Trelleborg in Sweden. The definitive stamp was issued on July 2, 2009. *The 1920s Sassnitz Habor* is featured on the stamp.

The **2010** year book included a holographic stamp (55c, size: 35x35 mm) of a stamp of a historic postal sign. During the 'Tag der Briefmarke' [postage stamp day] a special postage stamp selected this year was the one of a historic poster 'Imperial German Post to Helgoland-Norderney Sylt' from 1890. The poster was printed by Ballin Steamboat Shipping Company. The definitive stamp was issued on September 9, 2010. The stamp features *the poster for the postal route Hamburg-Helgoland-Norderney Sylt*.

The **2011** year book included a holographic stamp (55c, size: 26x44 mm) which was issued for the 125-year-anniversary of the German automobile. The definitive stamp was issued on May 5, 2011. The first *Benz & Co. automobile in front of the patent drawings* is featured on the stamp.

The **2012** year book included a holographic stamp (90c - 3zł, size: 26x44 mm) a stamp in the series 'World Heritage Site' which was the 'Muskauer Park - Park Mużakowski', a joint German-Polish issue. After the end of World War II, Muskauer Park along the Neisse was divided into a German and Polish area. Pücklers Garden Paradise belongs since 2004 to the UNESCO World Heritage Site. The definitive stamp was issued in Germany and Poland on July 12, 2012. The *Muskauer Park* is featured on the stamp.

CHAPTER 5
ADDITIONAL POSTAL AND PHILATELIC ITEMS WITH HOLOGRAMS

Different prepaid postal cards, parcel forms, coupons and souvenir sheets with holograms are described here, as well as special cancellations at international laser and holography conferences. Special stamps or limited-edition items of philatelic interest are also included, such as German and Chinese unique limited-edition albums of hologram stamps and souvenir sheets, all of high philatelic value.

5-1. Prepaid cards, parcel labels and international reply coupons

Germany started in **August 1995** to issue the limited-edition (2000) PortoCard® with holograms. The first issue was three ASTRA satellite stamps with a postal value of DM 3 (Fig. 5-1.1). Among other issued PortoCards were the following: '100th Anniversary of the Radio', 'Pictures of Germany' and '100th Anniversary of Emperor-William-Memorial Church'. In **1996** and **1997** three booklets were issued, which were the 'World of the Third Dimension' PortoCards. The three topics were '50th Anniversary of the German Philatelic Society', Heinrich von Stephan' and 'Living without Drugs'.

On **October 1, 1998**, **Germany** started issuing prepaid parcel forms with a small hologram as a security measure (one of the few philatelic applications where the security aspect plays a role). [40] Different prepaid forms for domestic, European and international destinations were issued. Two of the hologram security labels are shown in Fig. 5-1.2. One of the holograms (size: 10x10mm) shows the *treble clef, bass clef* and *music note* against the background of several rows of the word *VALID*. The other one shows the *postal service logo* against the background of words *Deutsche Post* placed at a 40-degree angle. Two examples of domestic parcel forms with holograms are shown in Fig. 5-1.3. The first one with a selling price DM 8.90 intended for small packages with domestic destinations, and a maximum weight of 20 kg, one of several forms, issued on October 1, 1998. The other form was intended for European destinations for parcels with a maximum weight of 2 kg (The FELIX European form). This one was issued on **March 8**, **1999**. During the following years Germany continued issuing many such prepaid parcel forms with hologram security labels.

Fig. 5-1.1. ASTRA PortoCard.

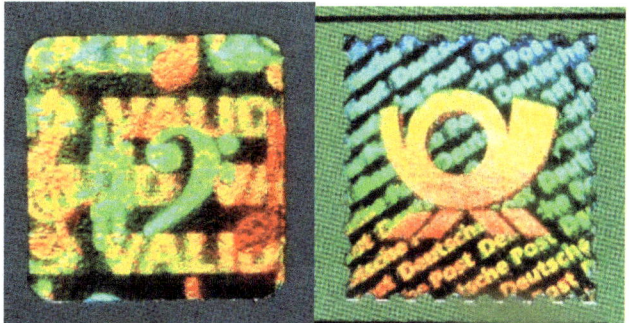

Fig. 5-1.2. Two parcel label hologram security labels.

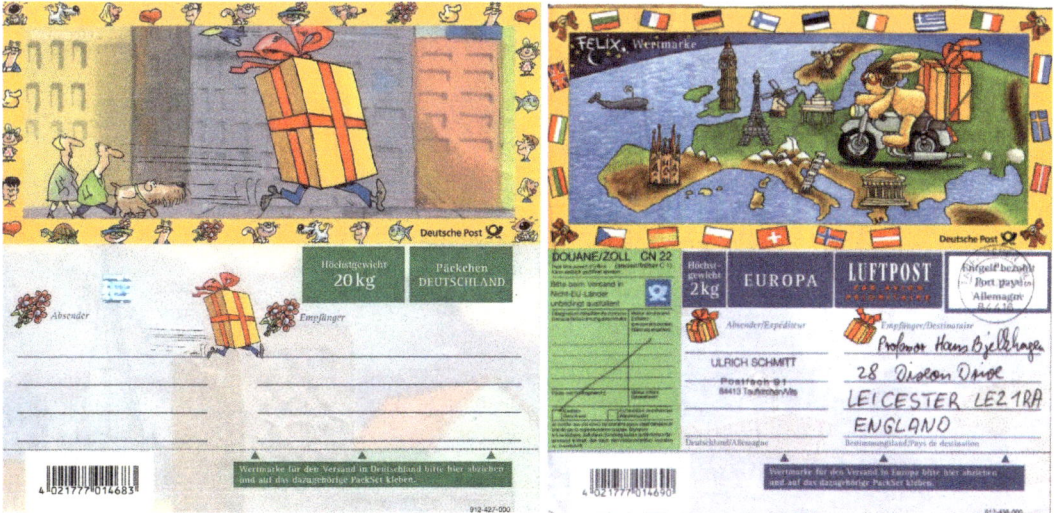

Fig. 5-1.3. German prepaid parcel forms with the two different hologram security labels.

Fig. 5-1.4. The Liberty Cash™ USPS debit card with hologram.

Prepaid **USPS** debit cards with holograms came out upon the introduction of the Liberty Cash™ program in **September 1996**, with initial trials in California, Colorado and Mall of America in Minnesota. The first card had a hologram on the reverse side, but later cards used a hologram on the front side. Prepaid cards were issued for the values of $5, $10, $20 and $50. The hologram on the card has the *US Post logo* and *UNITED STATES POSTAL SERVICE* repeatedly printed at an angle across the entire hologram surface. The hologram, the front - and reverse sides of one of the 1997 'LIBERTY CASH™ Cards' are shown in Fig. 5-1.4. It is a disposable $10 Card (#92102) with a hologram on the front side of the card.

An International Reply Coupon (IRC) is a voucher that can be redeemed for postage in any of the member countries of the Universal Postal Union (UPU). The purpose of the IRC is to allow the sender to pay postage charges for the recipient's response without having to obtain foreign stamps or send currency by mail. All IRCs issued in the member countries have the two-channel *UPU logo* security hologram shown in Fig. 5-1.5. Two examples of IRCs issued in Albania and Canada can be seen in Fig. 5-1.6.

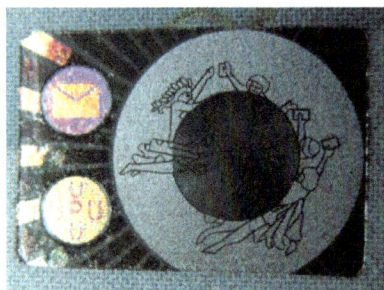

Fig. 5-1.5. The two-channel IRC hologram.

Fig. 5-1.6. Examples of two IRC forms, issued in Albania and Canada.

5-2. Holography conferences

As early as **1970**, in connection with a conference on *Optique et Holographie* in **France**, a special cancellation for postage stamps was issued. On **September 11, 1982**, six stationary postal cards (without holograms) were issued in **Romania** in connection with the International Conference and School on Lasers and Applications (LAICS'82), which took place in Bucharest between August 30 and September 11, 1989. The cards illustrate different laser applications.

Between **October 11** and **December 7, 1986**, tens of thousands of visitors were fascinated by examples of holograms on display at the exhibition HOLOMEDIA'86, in the Städtischen Galerie in Prinz-Max-Palais, Karlsruhe, **Germany**. For this occasion Deutsche Bundespost issued a special machine cancellation. Two such cancellation examples are shown in Fig. 5-2.1 ('Holomedia - Faszination in Licht und Ton' – [Holomedia - fascination with light and sound]. On the occasion of the '3e Colloque franco-allemand sur Les Applications de L'Holographie', a special, **November 15, 1991**, St Louis postal cancellation, **France**, was used (Fig. 5-2.2).

Fig. 5-2.1. German HOLOMEDIA cancellations.

Fig. 5-2.2. Cancel used for the French 1991 holography conference.

Fig. 5-2.3. Dennis Gabor IDAG'96 stamps.

On **June 5, 1996**, My Stamp Kft, Budapest, **Hungary**, issued a Cinderella stamp without a hologram. The picture on the stamp is a reproduction of a pulsed portrait hologram of Dennis Gabor (Fig. 5-2.3). The size of this no-value stamp is: 28 mm by 42 mm. These stamps were produced in a limited edition of 500 stamps for the 1996 holographic workshop 'IDGA'96' in Kecskemet, Hungary.

5-3. Dennis Gabor on stamps and FDCs

Dennis Gabor has been depicted on several postage stamps and FDCs. In addition to the Hungarian Gabor stamps featured in Figs. 3-1.7, 3-13.14, and 3-14.23, the following items have been issued.

Hungary issued on **November 16, 1995**, two stamps on the centenary of Nobel testament depicting Nobel Prize winners of Hungarian origin. The 100Ft-stamps honoring twelve Hungarian Nobel Laureates are shown in Fig 5-3.1. Among the listed ones is Dennis Gabor, the 1971 Physics Prize winner.

Fig. 5-3.1. The Hungarian Nobel Prize winners' stamps.

Republic of Guinea issued in **2008** a sheet with six 5000FG stamps honoring past winners of the Nobel Prize in Physics. In addition to Dennis Gabor (Fig. 5-3.2) the following physicists are featured on the sheet: James Chadwick, Ernest Lawrence, Lev Landau, Masatoshi Koshiba, and Vitaly Ginzburg. The stamp depicts a photo of Dennis Gabor and in the background Gabor receiving the 1971 Nobel Prize from the King Gustaf VI Adolf of Sweden.

Fig. 5-3.2. The Guinea Physics Nobel sheet and the Dennis Gabor stamp on it.

Fig. 5-3.3. The Dennis Gabor FDC with the Liberty Bell stamp.

USA issued on **June 5**, **2010**, a special FDC to honor Dennis Gabor, the inventor of Holography, who was born on June 5, 1900. The US forever first class 2007 Liberty Bell stamp is on the FDC. The FDC has a cachet photograph of a hologram portrait of Gabor. In addition Princess Leia from the 1977 'Star Wars' movie is also depicted on the envelope shown in Fig. 5-3.3.

Pre-paid envelopes of many Nobel Laureates were issued in **Spain** in **2013**. One of them features a photo of Dennis Gabor, the Hungarian 1971 Physics Nobel Prize winner, in front of a blackboard on the envelope. The illustration on the blackboard is a setup to record an off-axis transmission hologram. The envelope is shown in fig. 5-3.4.

Fig. 5-3.4. The Dennis Gabor photo on the prepaid Nobel Prize envelope issued in Spain.

5-4. Special items of philatelic interest

It is common the Post Authorities in countries issue albums with a collection of stamps issued during a calendar year. This is an annual event in **Germany** as described in Chapter 4. Hologram stamps produced only for a year book are unusual, which was the case in Germany. However only in 1999 Germany issued two definitive hologram stamps which were included in the 1999 Year Book.

Another country to mention is **Hungary**, with the limited-edition *Collection of Hungarian Stamps'90*. Although it covered the 1990 stamps, it included a hologram stamp issued in 1991 (**No. 7**) which was actually produced for the 1990 year book. The hologram stamp was based on a regular stamp issued during 1990, the 'Coat-of-Arms of the Republic of Hungary' stamp. The Hungarian album cover is shown in Fig. 5-4.1 and page 37 with the regular stamp and the hologram stamp in Fig. 5-4.2.

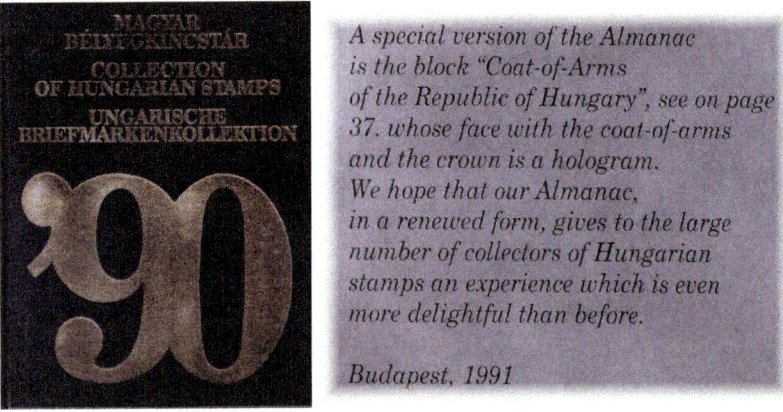

Fig. 5-4.1. The cover of Hungarian 1990 Year Book of stamps.

Fig. 5-4.2. Page (37) with the two stamps.

Fig. 5-4.3. The Deutsche Post *Phil Selection* Album.

Fig. 5-4.3. The ten-stamp hologram souvenir sheet included in the *Phil Selection* Album.

As mentioned in Chapter 3, Section 3-11, a special, large ten-stamp hologram souvenir sheet was issued on **October 8**, **1998**, in **Germany**. It was the Aquatic Warbler sheet which was included in the limited-edition (10,000) *Phil Selection* Album issued by Deutsche Post (Fig. 5-3.3). This beautiful 55-page publication contains detailed information about how postage stamps are designed and produced. It covers most of the techniques involved, including how holograms are manufactured and attached to stamps. The large 'Für die Wohlfartspflege' ten-stamp hologram sheet depicts two birds, two aquatic warblers (*Acrocephalus paludicola*) [in German: Seggenrohrsänger] is inserted in the album, shown in Fig. 5-4.4. The hologram stamp (denomination is 110+50 pF) is based on the conventional 1998 'Seggenrohrsänger' German stamp. The hologram sheet size is 210 mm by 105 mm and the stamp size is 35 mm by 35 mm. *Two aquatic warblers in the reed* appear in each hologram stamp on the sheet. 'Seggenrohrsänger', 'DEUTSCHLAND' and 'FÜR DIE WOHLFAHRTSPFLEGE' are also printed on the stamps. The hologram production process is described on two pages in the album (Fig. 5-4.5). Another hologram stamp is also included in this album which is the 'Wuppertal cable-railway' hologram stamp. This stamp appeared later in the ***2001 Year Book of German Stamps*** (see Fig. 4.3 in Chapter 4). The album page with this hologram stamp together with four regular stamps is show in Fig. 5-4.6. The master hologram was recorded by Irina Menz at Holographic Systems München GmbH and produced by Leonhard Kurz GmbH.

Fig. 5-4.4. The pages describing the hologram production process.

Fig. 5-4.5. The page with the 'Wuppertal cable-railway' hologram stamp.

Fig. 5-3.6. Chinese two-album set issued in 1999.

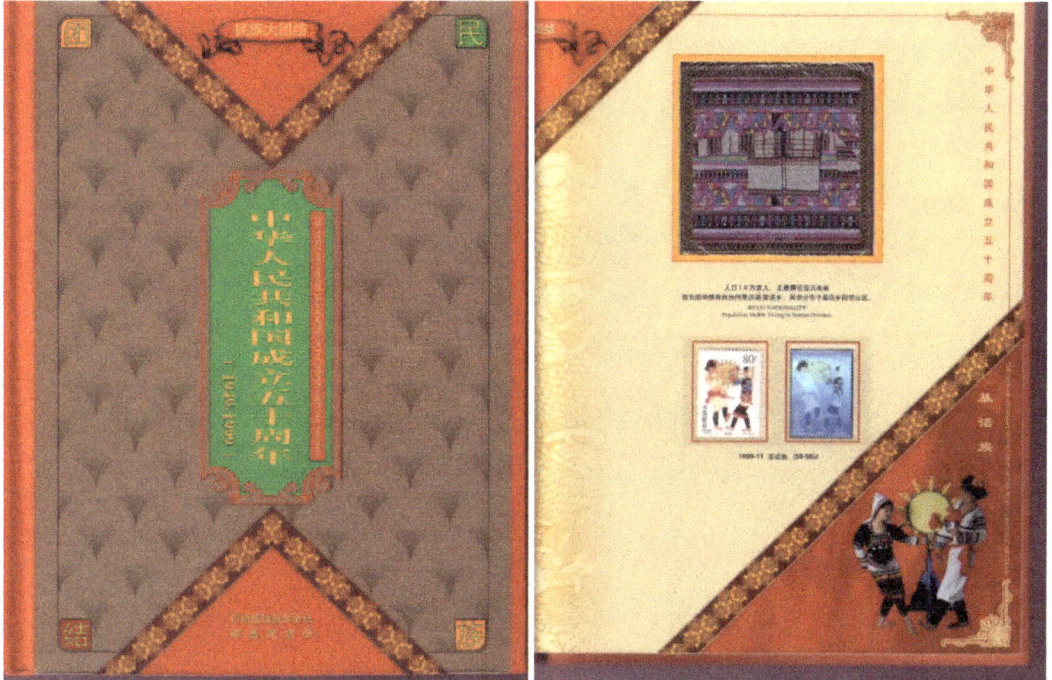

Fig. 5-4.7. The 'Chinese Ethnic Folk Groups' album cover and one page in the album.

Fig. 5-4.8. Three examples of the 56 Chinese hologram stamps. **Fig. 5-4.9.** Costume example.

People's Republic of China issued on **October 1, 1999**, a beautiful two-album collection of hologram stamps. The album features 56 stamps of different ethnic folk groups and a 50-year celebration of China 1949-1999. Fig. 5-4.6 shows the two-album set. The cover of one album and one two-stamp page in the album are shown in Fig. 5-4.7. The two 80-fen stamps, one conventional stamp and one hologram stamp, show *dancers from different ethnic folk groups*. Each page features one ethnic folk group with the corresponding two stamps and above them a miniature costume attached with a plastic cover over it. The left stamp is a conventional stamp and the one to the right is a holographic reproduction. Featured in Fig. 5-4.8 are three examples of the 56 different hologram stamps included in the album. One of the miniature costumes is shown in Fig. 5-4.9. The hologram stamps were produced on a very large sheet with all 56 stamps on the same sheet shown in Fig. 5-4.10. The stamps from the sheets were then used for the albums. The corresponding regular-stamp sheet, on which the hologram sheet was based, is shown in Fig. 5-4.11 and in Fig. 5-4.12 a description of each issued stamp. The stamps were design by Zhou Xiuqing and Jin Xiang. The album with the hologram stamps were produced at the National 5808 Factory in Taian, Shandong province.

Fig. 5-4.10. The sheet with the conventional 56 Chinese stamps.

Fig. 5-4.11. The sheet with the conventional 56 Chinese stamps.

(56-1)	汉族	Han Ethnic group	(56-29)	柯尔克孜族	Kirgiz Ethnic group
(56-2)	蒙古族	Mongolian Ethnic group	(56-30)	土族	Tu Ethnic group
(56-3)	回族	Hui Ethnic group	(56-31)	达斡尔族	Daur Ethnic group
(56-4)	藏族	Tibetan Ethnic group	(56-32)	仫佬族	Mulam Ethnic group
(56-5)	维吾尔族	Uygur Ethnic group	(56-33)	羌族	Qiang Ethnic group
(56-6)	苗族	Miao Ethnic group	(56-34)	布朗族	Blang Ethnic group
(56-7)	彝族	Yi Ethnic group	(56-35)	撒拉族	Salar Ethnic group
(56-8)	壮族	Zhuang Ethnic group	(56-36)	毛难族	Maonan Ethnic group
(56-9)	布依族	Bouyei Ethnic group	(56-37)	仡佬族	Gelao Ethnic group
(56-10)	朝鲜族	Korean Ethnic group	(56-38)	锡伯族	Xibe Ethnic group
(56-11)	满族	Manchu Ethnic group	(56-39)	阿昌族	Achang Ethnic group
(56-12)	侗族	Dong Ethnic group	(56-40)	普米族	Pumi Ethnic group
(56-13)	瑶族	Yao Ethnic group	(56-41)	塔吉克族	Tajik Ethnic group
(56-14)	白族	Bai Ethnic group	(56-42)	怒族	Nu Ethnic group
(56-15)	土家族	Tujia Ethnic group	(56-43)	乌孜别克族	Uzbek Ethnic group
(56-16)	哈尼族	Hani Ethnic group	(56-44)	俄罗斯族	Russian Ethnic group
(56-17)	哈萨克族	Kazak Ethnic group	(56-45)	鄂温克族	Ewenki Ethnic group
(56-18)	傣族	Dai Ethnic group	(56-46)	德昂族	De'ang Ethnic group
(56-19)	黎族	Li Ethnic group	(56-47)	保安族	Bonan Ethnic group
(56-20)	傈僳族	Lisu Ethnic group	(56-48)	裕固族	Yugur Ethnic group
(56-21)	佤族	Va Ethnic group	(56-49)	京族	Jing Ethnic group
(56-22)	畲族	She Ethnic group	(56-50)	塔塔尔族	Tatar Ethnic group
(56-23)	高山族	Gaoshan Ethnic group	(56-51)	独龙族	Drung Ethnic group
(56-24)	拉祜族	Lahu Ethnic group	(56-52)	鄂伦春族	Oroqen Ethnic group
(56-25)	水族	Shui Ethnic group	(56-53)	赫哲族	Hezhen Ethnic group
(56-26)	东乡族	Dongxiang Ethnic group	(56-54)	门巴族	Monba Ethnic group
(56-27)	纳西族	Naxi Ethnic group	(56-55)	珞巴族	Lhoba Ethnic group
(56-28)	景颇族	Jingpo Ethnic group	(56-56)	基诺族	Jino Ethnic group

Fig. 5-4.12. List of the 56 Chinese stamps included in the two albums.

A very large **Chinese** holographic souvenir sheet in a presentation folder was issued at the 22nd UPU Congress and China 1999 World Philatelic Exhibition. The folder 'THE WORLD AT THE SEA BOTTOM - CORAL REEF AND PET FISH' contains a holographic sheet, marked QXZ-2, and a normal souvenir sheet (Fig. 5-4.13). On the holographic sheet (size: 150 mm by 190 mm) there are eight stamps depicting fish and an additional stamp in the center, all printed in color. The large hologram area shows an *underwater scene with a coral reef and fish* (Fig. 5-4.14). The folder was produced by Guang Dong Tian Yi Cultural Co., Ltd and issued by Beijing Stamp Co. The folder was included in a set of three. Fig. 5-4.15 shows a stamp with a *blue* holographic background from another folder.

Fig. 5-4.13. Cover of Chinese stamp folder.

Fig. 5-4.14. Stamps with a holographic background.

Fig. 5-4.15. Chinese souvenir stamp with *blue* holographic background.

North Korea has issued several lenticular postage stamps but, so far, only one hologram souvenir sheet. On an overprinted Ryangchon Temple souvenir sheet, a small (16 mm by 21 mm) hologram is attached at the top of the sheet. The Ryangchon Temple is located in Rakchon-ri, Kowon County and South Hamgyong Province. This was a limited-edition (5000) sheet issued on **May 30, 2003**, which is very hard to find. The hologram which is of rather poor quality depicts the *temple building and the surrounding landscape*. The souvenir sheet, shown in Fig. 5-4.16, depicts the Taeung Hall on the 120-won stamp, surrounded by a dance and music painting in the Ryangchon Temple.

Fig. 5-4.16. North Korean souvenir sheet with hologram.

5-5. Australian overprinted booklets and souvenir sheets

In **2011 Australia** started to issue many overprinted versions of previously issued booklets and souvenir sheets. It was mostly issued for stamp exhibitions and to celebrate important events and achievements. Considering the large amount of such overprinted versions, only some of these issues are covered here. In addition to the overprinted issues, already covered in Chapter 3, Australia started to increase these issues in 2011. All of them are very limited-edition sheets or booklets. A limited-edition (150) special collector's folder on Royal Australian Air Force (RAAF) airplanes was issued on **February 22, 2011**. The stamps were issued to commemorate 90 years of RAAF. The special folder contains five numbered souvenir sheets with four airplane stamps featuring the following Air Force planes: F111, F/A 18F, Wedgetail, and C-17. The Wedgetail plane is covered with diffractive foil.

One of the most overprinted one is the twenty self-adhesive-5c-stamp booklet 'Fishes of the Reef' which was first issued on June 21, 2010. These overprinted booklets were issued in very limited editions, often only between 20 and 100. There are booklets with two different barcodes depending on if the booklet was sold through official post service or by philatelic outlets. On the back of the booklets the edition number is printed in red, silver or in holographic foil. Many, but not all, of the overprinted booklets (Fig. 5-5.1) with diffractive holographic *foil text* issued in 2012 and 2013 are listed here:

July 21, 2011 [50]:	CONGRATULATING QUEENSLAND'S MAROONS – 6TH CONSECUTIVE STATE OF ORIGIN WIN 2011
August 13, 2011 [100]:	"Z FORCE" Z SPECIAL UNIT REUNION Maryborough 13, 14, 15 August Official Souvenir
March 2, 2012 [75]:	50th Anniversary of the Issuance of Hong Kong Stamps HONG KONG STAMPEX 2012 2 – 4 March [+ Chinese lettering]
March 16, 2012 [75]:	*St. Louis Stamp Expo* March 16 – 18 2012 [with EXPO logo]
March 30, 2012 [50]:	LAKESHORE STAMP CLUB INC. ANNUAL STAMP EXHIBITION LAKESHORE 2012 Quebec, Canada
April 25, 2012 [50]:	126th Anniversary Remembering Our Heros ANZAC DAY 2012
April 27, 2012 [60]:	WESTPLEX 12 April 27 – 29, 2012 FORT ROSS [with this in Russian as well]
April 28, 2012 [75]:	PLYMOUTH STAMP SHOW Hellenic Cultural Center April 28 – 29, 2012 [+ Ship]
May 18, 2012 [75]:	ROCKY MOUNTAIN STAMP SHOW MAY 18 – 20 2012 *A Champion of Champions Philatelic Exhibition* [with Show Bell logo]
July 20, 2012 [75]:	*Minnesota Stamp Expo July 21, 12 & 23 2012* [text appears in a stamp with simulated perforation]
September 28, 2012 [50]:	INDYPEX 12 September 28 – 30 A World Series of Philately Show [Post diligence logo]
October 19, 2012 [40]:	Oklahoma City OKPEX 2012 October 19 – 20 [with OKPEX logo]
November 9, 2012 [20]:	San Jose Stamp Show FILATELICFIESTA 2012 November 9, 10 & 11
November 16, 2012 [20]:	126th Anniversary CHICAGOPEX 2012 November 16 – 18 [+ CHICAGOPEX logo]
November 30, 2012 [20]:	The Florida State Stamp Show FLOREX 2012 November 30 December 1 & 2 [with FLOREX logo]
January 2, 2013 [20]:	23rd Australian Scout Jamboree AJ2013 January 2 – 12 Maryborough QLD
January 18, 2013 [20]:	AMERISTAMP EXPO 2013 Louisville, Kentucky January 18 – 20 World Series of Philately
January 25, 2013 [20]:	SOUTHEASTERN STAMP EXPO Georgia, January 25-27 2013
February 1, 2013 [20]:	Sarasota National Stamp Exhibition World Series of Philately FLORIDA 1 – 3 2013 [alligator logo]
February 8, 2013 [20]:	SANDICAL 2013 World Series of Philately San Diego's Premier Stamp Show Feb 8.9.10
March 1, 2013 [20]:	Annual Texas Stamp Show TEXPEX World Series of Philately March 1 – 3 2013 [with TEXPEX logo]

HOLOGRAPHY AND PHILATELY

Fig. 5-5.1. Samples of the overprinted 'Fishes on the Reef' booklets and the holographic text on two of them.

311

In 2012 a very limited-edition (25) overprinted version were issued of the three-stamp sheet 'Stargazing the southern skies' which was first issued on August 25, 2008. It was issued to remember Neil Armstrong with this holographic overprint 'NEIL ARMSTRONG 1930 - 2012: ONE SMALL STEP'

In 2012 and 2013 other very limited-editions overprinted versions were issued. They were the four 60c-stamp sheet '50 Years World Wide Fund (WWF) for Nature'. This sheet, first issued on August 30, 2011, is the Australian Joint Territories Issue (No.125). Many, but not all, of the overprinted sheets with diffractive holographic *foil text* are listed here (Fig. 5-5.2):

March 16, 2012 [25]:	*St. Louis Stamp Expo* March 16 – 18 2012 [with Expo logo]
April 28, 2012 [25]:	PLYMOUTH STAMP SHOW Hellenic Cultural Center April 28 – 29, 2012 [+ Ship]
May 18, 2012 [25]:	ROCKY MOUNTAIN STAMP SHOW MAY 18 – 20 2012 *A Champion of Champions Philatelic Exhibition* [with Show Bell logo]
September 21, 2012 [25]:	Milcopex 2012 September 21 – 23 2012 By air & By Sea [with Air Plane and Ship]
November 16, 2012 [25]:	126th Anniversary CHICAGOPEX 2012 November 16 – 18 [+ CHICAGOPEX logo]
March 1, 2013 [25]:	Annual Texas Stamp Show TEXPEX World Series of Philately March 1 – 3 2013 [with TEXPEX logo]
November 16, 2013 [25]:	25th Anniversary BRISBANE BRONCOS 1988 - 2013 [+ BRONCOS Horse Head logo]

A similar sheet is the four 60c-stamp sheet '50 Years World Wide Fund (WWF) for Nature'. This sheet, the Australian Antarctic Issue (No.126), was first issued on August 30, 2011. Many, but not all, of the overprinted sheets with diffractive holographic *foil text* are listed here:

March 16, 2012 [25]:	*St. Louis Stamp Expo* March 16 – 18 2012 [with Expo logo]
April 28, 2012 [25]:	PLYMOUTH STAMP SHOW Hellenic Cultural Center April 28 – 29, 2012 [+ Ship]
May 18, 2012 [25]:	ROCKY MOUNTAIN STAMP SHOW MAY 18 – 20 2012 *A Champion of Champions Philatelic Exhibition* [with Show Bell logo]
October 19, 2012 [25]:	Oklahoma City OKPEX 2012 October 19 – 20 [with OKPEX logo]
February 1, 2013 [25]:	Sarasota National Stamp Exhibition World Series of Philately FLORIDA 1 – 3 2013 [alligator logo]

A similar sheet is the four 60c-stamp sheet '50 Years World Wide Fund (WWF) for Nature'. This sheet the Cocos Island Issue (No.127) was first issued on August 30, 2011. Many, but not all, of the overprinted sheets with diffractive holographic *foil text* are listed here:

March 2, 2012 [50]:	HONG KONG STAMPEX 2012 2 – 4 March [+ Chinese lettering]
March 16, 2012 [25]:	*St. Louis Stamp Expo* March 16 – 18 2012 [with Expo logo]
April 28, 2012 [25]:	PLYMOUTH STAMP SHOW Hellenic Cultural Center April 28 – 29, 2012 [+ Ship]
May 18, 2012 [25]:	ROCKY MOUNTAIN STAMP SHOW MAY 18 – 20 2012 *A Champion of Champions Philatelic Exhibition* [with Show Bell logo]
September 28, 2012 [25]:	INDYPEX 12 September 28 – 30 A World Series of Philately Show [Post diligence logo]
November 9, 2012 [25]:	San Jose Stamp Show FILATELICFIESTA 2012 November 9, 10 & 11

A similar sheet is the four 60c-stamp sheet '50 Years World Wide Fund (WWF) for Nature'. This sheet is the Christmas Island Issue (No.128) which was first issued on August 30, 2011. Many, but not all, of the overprinted sheets with diffractive holographic *foil text* are listed here:

March 2, 2012 [50]:   HONG KONG STAMPEX 2012 2 – 4 March [+ Chinese lettering]

March 16, 2012 [25]:   *St. Louis Stamp Expo* March 16 – 18 2012 [with Expo logo]

April 28, 2012 [25]:   PLYMOUTH STAMP SHOW Hellenic Cultural Center April 28 – 29, 2012 [+ Ship]

May 18, 2012 [25]:   ROCKY MOUNTAIN STAMP SHOW MAY 18 – 20 2012 *A Champion of Champions Philatelic Exhibition* [with Show Bell logo]

November 30, 2012 [25]:   The Florida State Stamp Show FLOREX 2012 November 30 December 1 & 2 [with FLOREX logo]

February 8, 2013 [25]:   SANDICAL 2013 World Series of Philately San Diego's Premier Stamp Show Feb 8.9.10

Fig. 5-5.2. Samples of two of the overprinted '50 Years World Wide Fund (WWF) for Nature'.

Fig. 5-5.3. Samples of two of the overprinted '50 Years World Wide Fund (WWF) for Nature'.

Other sheets are the two sheets issued for the 27th Asian International Stamp Exhibition which took place between November 11 and 15, 2011. One sheet is the single $1.60 Koala bear sheet (No.132). The other one is the single $1.65 Kangaroo sheet (No.133). Many, but not all, of the overprinted sheets with diffractive holographic *foil text* are listed here (Fig. 5-5.3):

April 25, 2012 [25]:	Remembering Our Heros ANZAC DAY 2012 [Sheet 132]
May 18, 2012 [25]:	PHILADELPHIA NATIONAL STAMP EXHIBITION MAY 18 – 20 2012 *A Champion of Champions Philatelic Exhibition* [with Show Bell logo] [Sheet 132]
July 20, 2012 [25]:	*Minnesota Stamp Expo July 21, 12 & 23 2012* [text appears in a stamp with simulated perforation] [Sheet 133]
January 2, 2013 [25]:	23rd Australian Scout Jamboree AJ2013 January 2 – 12 Maryborough QLD [Sheet 133]

The 'TECHNOLOGY - THEN & NOW' booklet was issued on February 7, 2012. The booklet has two sets of five different self-adhesive 60c stamps. An overprinted version (Fig. 5-5.4) has already been issued with diffractive holographic *foil text*:

September 21, 2012 [25]:	Milcopex 2012 September 21 – 23 2012 By air & By Sea [with Air Plane and Ship]

Fig. 5-5.4. The **MILCOPEX 2012** overprinted 'TECHNOLOGY - THEN & NOW' booklet.

Fig. 5-6.1. Polish "hologram stamp" coin.

5-6. Hologram stamps on coins

On **November 19, 2008**, a beautiful 10-zloty silver coin with a 'hologram stamp' on it was issued. Although it is not a real postage stamp, it is included here since it is of great philatelic interest. The coin was issued in commemoration of the 450th anniversary of postal services in **Poland**. The hologram on the face of the coin shows a stylized image of a *mounted post rider playing the trumpet*. The reverse side shows a stylized image of a 16th century post courier as well as a stylized fragment of a 17th century engraved copperplate with an image of an inn, and a larger image of a postal trumpet. It was on October 18, 1558, that King Sigismund II August (Zygmunt August) issued an official legal act on Polish postal services. That day is therefore recognized as the beginning of postal services in Poland. The first regular postal service ran from Cracow via Vienna and Graz to Venice. A letter took nine days to reach the addressee. A few years later postal services were established between Cracow and Vilnius. MAPPA POCZTOWA on the coin means a postal map, i.e. a map where postal carrier routes are marked. The coin (composition: 92.5% silver, size: Ø32 mm, weight: 14.14 g) is shown in Fig. 5-6.1.

Niue (an island country in the South Pacific Ocean) issued a silver coin with a hologram stamp on it in **2012**. It was the ELIZABETH II NIUE ONE DOLLAR coin. The "hologram stamp" on reverse depicts the *Space Station MIR, Vostok and Yuri Gagarin*. STARS FLIGHT is written on reverse. The hologram was produced by JSC Holography Industry in Minsk, Republic of Belarus. The coin (edition 5000) was engraved by Raphael David Maklouf (obverse) at the Lithuanian Mint in Vilnius. The coin (composition: 92.5% silver, size: Ø38.61 mm, weight: 28.28 g) is shown in Fig. 5-6.2.

Fig. 5-6.2. Niue "hologram stamp" coin.

CHAPTER 6
3D IMAGING THECHNIQUES, HOLOGRAMS AND HOLOGRAM STAMPS

This Chapter discusses briefly other 3D imaging techniques, such as, for example, lenticular images, which have been applied on stamps and FDCs (these techniques are sometimes wrongly referred to as holograms). It also describes the way in which hologram stamps should be illuminated in order to best view the recorded holographic image, and how to take photographs of hologram stamps. The Chapter contains in addition a presentation and examples of reported hologram errors, and missing or misplaced holograms on stamps or souvenir sheets.

HOLOGRAPHY AND PHILATELY

6-1. Postage stamps with other 3D images than holograms

This Chapter focuses on the way in which holograms should be illuminated for best viewing – something which is not always obvious to philatelists, unless they are also familiar with holography. Special techniques which must be applied when recording photographs of holograms will also be discussed in this Chapter. It is important to understand the nature of a holographic image in order not to confuse holograms with other 3D images, such as, for example, lenticular images, which are also used on postage stamps. A **_lenticular_** stamp is covered with a rather thick plastic raster (a plastic ribbed surface) gives the stamps a 3D depth effect (See Fig. 6-1.1). They can display 3D images as well as multiple images and images with animation. Bhutan Post has issued a lot of these stamps. A recent example of a lenticular stamp which was issued in the Netherlands on September 29, 2010, is shown in Fig. 6-1.2. This lenticular stamp features the shortest movie ever made (about one second long) by a Dutch director Anton Corbijn. The stamp was based on a 1951 classic Dutch stamp showing a girl posing in front of a windmill. The new stamp shows actress Carice van Houten. Depending on the angle from which the stamp is viewed, an animation occurs, where van Houten bites down on a man's middle finger. The stamp is made using lenticular printing, whereby a series of sequential images are superimposed on one another, enabling the picture to be seemingly transformed when changing the angle from which it is viewed. Corbijn shot 120 frames of film, of which 30 were used for the stamp.

On internet sites like eBay, lenticular stamps are often described with the help of words such as 'with hologram' or 'a hologram stamp', which is, of course, wrong. Normally, the image quality of lenticular stamps is not very high, and image resolution is poor.

Stamps covered with gold or silver foil are sometimes also described as holograms – which they are not – again something to be aware of when collecting hologram stamps. If the foil shows no light diffraction when properly illuminated, it is not a hologram stamp. One example of such a stamp is the OZONE stamp from Croatia, issued on September 16, 1999, which is often described as a hologram stamp. The "O" in the chemical ozone symbol O_3 on the stamp is only a circular piece of shiny foil. Another example is the 'Presidency of the Council of the European Union' sheet where the small map on the stamp is only a contour-cut piece of shiny foil. This stamp shown in Fig. 6-1.4 was issued on January 1, 2008, in Slovenia.

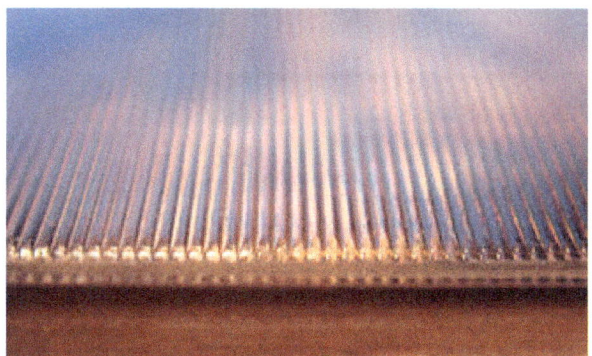

Fig. 6-1.1. Lenticular raster.

Fig. 6-1.2. Lenticular movie stamp.

Fig. 6-1.3. The OZONE stamp with shiny foil.

Fig. 6-1.4. A stamp with shiny foil.

Fig. 6-1.5. Italian anaglyph stamp.

Fig. 6-1.6. Hungarian anaglyph four-stamp sheet.

Fig. 6-1.7. Hungarian FDC with anaglyph stamp and cachet 3D image.

There are examples of other 3D techniques applied to postage stamps. For example, **anaglyph** images (red-cyan glasses are needed to view the image) as well as other types of stereo images. To the naked eye, the images are printed on top of each other. Traditionally, the image for the left eye is printed in red ink and the image of the right eye is printed in green ink or blue. Two anaglyph Globe stamps were issued in Italy on December 29, 1956, to commemorate the Nation's admission to the UN in 1956. One of the two stamps is shown in Fig. 6-1.5. Another very recent example of Hungarian anaglyph stamps are two sheets issued in the 'History of Hungarian Museums' series. One featured museum is the Lamp Museum in Zsámbék, which opened in 1979. Its collection of over one thousand lighting devices includes different oil lamps. A four-stamp anaglyph sheet is shown in Fig. 6-1.6 and in Fig. 6-1.7 the FDC with an anaglyph cachet 3D image of oil lamps. The other featured museum was the Calcite Crystal Museum in Fertőrákos. The two museum anaglyph sheets were issued on May 3, 2013.

Fig. 6-1.8. San Marino stereo-pair stamp.

Fig. 6-1.9. Stereoscope.

San Marino issued three **stereo pairs** of stamps with a stereoscope viewer on August 25, 2009. One sheet with one of the stereo pair of stamps is shown in Fig. 6-1.8. The stereoscope issued together with the stamps is shown in Fig. 6-1.9. Postal applications of the last two techniques are rare, but lenticular stamps are quite common. Cachet lenticular images on FDCs can also be encountered.

6-2. Illumination of and viewing hologram stamps

Techniques used for the recording and production of holograms are not covered here, and the interested reader is therefore advised to consult the list of references. [3-5] The nature of a holographic image is explained in the following.

Holograms are made by recording a very fine interference pattern in a high-resolution material, using laser beams. Upon illumination, the image in a recorded hologram is recreated by *light diffraction*. Most holograms used on stamps are of the embossed rainbow type. There are four main types of holograms found on postage stamps:

- 2D holograms made from 2D artwork, usually a transparency.
- 2D/3D holograms made from a stack of two-dimensional artworks, so that each layer is at a different distance from the film plane.
- 3D holograms made from solid 3D models.
- Computer-generated holograms and kinegrams.

The embossed hologram production process can be divided into three groups: *origination*, *electroforming* and *mass-replication*. The first step is the recording the master hologram on a *photoresist* plate using laser light. A photoresist plate for making hologram stamps is shown in Fig. 6-2.1. During the processing of the plate a relief pattern is created. This master plate is used to produce *nickel shims* with the relief pattern. This is accomplished during the second step, the electroforming process. The third step in the production process is embossing. In order to mass-produce copies of the master hologram, the production shim is mounted on a platen and repeatedly stamped into a web of material moving by at high speed. Holograms are most commonly embossed into hot stamping foil or laminating films (often aluminized PET) before final application. Each transfer creates a separate embossed hologram. To maximize yields, it is common to gang several images on one shim, so each transfer creates multiple holograms that can be die cut into separate units during the final converting and finishing steps. Rolls of these embossed holograms can be further processed and/or fed into hot-stamping machines or laminating machines, depending on the final application, for example, attached to the printed paper postage stamps.

Fig. 6-2.1. A photoresist plate for Chinese stamps.

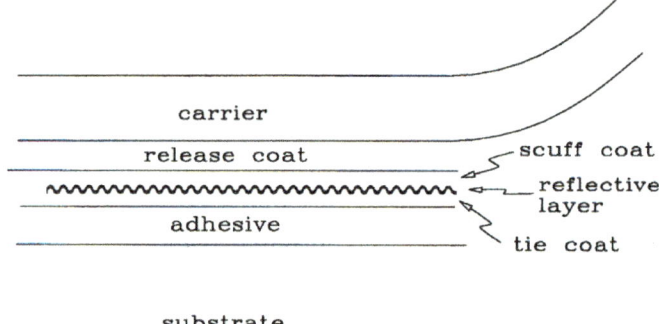

Fig. 6-2.2. A cross-section of a holographic hot-stamping foil.

It is important to be aware that a *reference beam* is used to record a hologram. In principle, the same reference beam is used to illuminate the hologram in order to view the image recorded in it. In order to obtain a faithful holographic image, correct use of the appropriate light source for the illumination of the hologram is of critical importance. The light used for the illumination of the hologram has to resemble that used for its recording. Without going into too many details, for effective viewing of a hologram stamp it is important that it be illuminated by a spotlight (scanners cannot therefore reproduce holographic images). The spotlight must be placed at a certain angle and distance in relation to the holographic stamp, since the quality and color of the image visible in the hologram will depend on how the hologram stamp is illuminated and viewed. To view a holographic stamp, a spotlight should be placed somewhere above the stamp, illuminating it at a 45 degree angle, as illustrated in Figure 6-2.1. Large diffuse light and multiple light sources are definitely not suitable for illuminating holograms, as illustrated in Fig. 6-2.2.

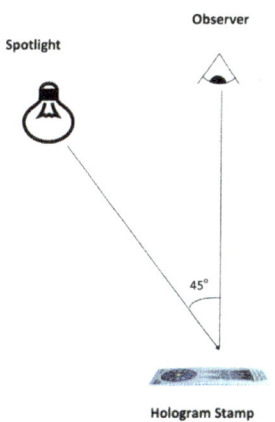

Fig. 6-2.1. Illumination and viewing a hologram stamp.

Fig. 6-2.2. Layman's diagram showing the importance of using a point source lamp to illuminate a hologram. Here we make an analogy to the shadow cast by a spotlight on a screen.
In (**a**) the spotlight emits light from a small point, resulting in a sharp image,
In (**b**) a large-area diffuse spotlight results in a diffuse image,
In (**c**) many spotlights illuminate the hologram, resulting in multiple images.

Some holograms on stamps contain more than one image. In this case in order to display the images stored in the hologram, the reference light may need to illuminate the hologram from different directions, for example, from above and from the side. An example is the two-channel Gabor hologram on the 2000 souvenir sheet (See Fig. 3-13.13) issued in Hungary (Fig. 6-2.3). Another example is the 1999 Australian Millennium hologram stamp where the viewer moves from left to right to see the transition from year 1999 to 2000 in the hologram (Fig. 6-2.4). More than two images can be recorded in a hologram, such as the images contained in the 1999 German stamp showing the approaching comet and the impact on the surface of Jupiter (see Fig. 3-12.51). Here the holograms were recorded with the same reference direction. When correctly illuminated and by observing the hologram from different directions, for example moving from left to right, the sequence of images is observed. A number of such hologram stamps have been issued, which is why it is important to understand how holograms of this type have to be illuminated for proper viewing.

Fig. 6-2.3. Gabor two-channel hologram.

Fig. 6-2.4. Australian two-channel hologram.

6-3. Photographs of hologram stamps

As already mentioned it is not possible to use scanners to reproduce hologram stamps, souvenir sheets and FDCs with cachet holograms. Since special illumination is needed for viewing a hologram, similar illumination is needed when taking photographs of hologram stamps. A correctly-illuminated rainbow holographic image is very bright. This means that a very high dynamic range has to be recorded when both the hologram and the printed parts around the hologram are to be reproduced. The human eye can easily adapt to a high contrast ratio, which means that both parts will look correct. Conventional or digital cameras cannot capture such a high dynamic range. To avoid this problem, as demonstrated in this book, separate photographs of the holograms have been taken, and are presented next to scanned reproductions of stamps or FDCs. This problem is demonstrated in Fig. 6-3.1 where the hologram is correctly recorded resulting in that the white paper around the hologram appears dark grey. In Fig. 6-3.2 the white paper is correctly recorded which means the hologram is now too bright (overexposed). Of course, this problem could be solved by using digital photo-editing software, so that both the hologram image and the surrounding areas appear correct which requires additional work.

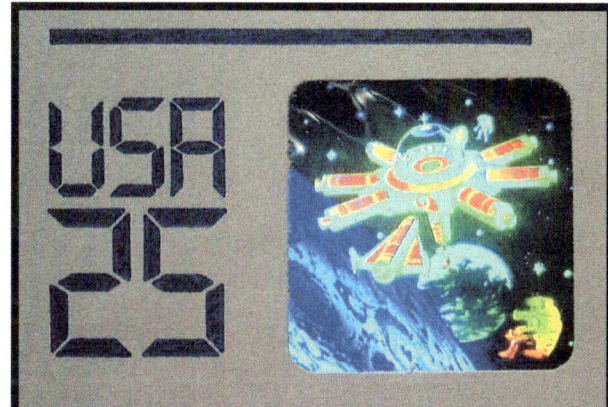
Fig. 6-3.1. Correct photograph of the hologram.

Fig. 6-3.2. Overexposed hologram photo.

6-4. Variations, errors, missing holograms

Described here are variations, errors, freaks, defects and other problems associated with holograms on stamps and hologram production, kiss-cutting, embossing, hot-stamping, etc. During the process of manufacturing holograms many steps are involved, where mistakes and errors can occur. Quality control of the finished hologram stamps should find and eliminate these stamps to reach the market. However, sometimes this process is not 100% efficient, and errors may reach philatelists and stamp collectors who happily try to get their hands on them.

6-4.1. Rainbow hologram color variations

It is important to discuss hologram color variations and errors with regard to postage stamps with holograms. First of all, the view of a holographic image depends on how it is illuminated. In the *rainbow embossed hologram*, the most often used type of hologram on postage stamps and souvenir sheets, the color of the image can show any of the rainbow colors. It makes therefore no sense to claim that the color of the image in a hologram stamp is "wrong". An illustration of color variations in a hologram stamp of the 1991 'Coat-of-Arms of the Republic of Hungary' is presented here. In Fig 6-4.1 the correct hologram image is shown (when the illumination and observation directions are correct). It is assumed that the hologram stamp should have the same appearance as the previously printed Hungarian stamp issued in 1990 with the same design (see Fig. 3-4.15 and Fig. 3-4.17). Fig. 6-4.2 illustrates different color variations of this hologram stamp depending on its illumination and observation angles.

Many recent stamps with holograms are using holographic foil with random and repeated patterns. The foil is often cut to form differently shaped figures which are attached to the stamps. Examples are the 2005 Jersey 'The Ugly Duckling' sheet with the holographic *faire* (Fig. 6-4.3) and the 2009 Portuguese 'Spectacle with hologram *lenses*' **(Fig. 6-4.4).** These examples show that the pattern within the hologram area **varies from stamp to stamp.** This is seldom the case in normal printed stamps, where all stamps in an issue are supposed to be identical. Any variation within an issue is regarded by philatelists as very interesting and such a stamp normally represents a high value to stamp collectors. As regards this type of hologram stamps, so many different stamps have been issued that it is impossible to list all of them here.

Fig. 6-4.1. Correct image.   **Fig. 6-4.2**. Color variations depending on illumination and observation directions.

Fig. 6-4.3. Hologram *Faire* variations.   **Fig. 6-4.4.** Hologram *Spectactle* variations.

6-4.2. Miss-cut holograms

A variation that often occurs in hologram stamps depends on how they have been cut out from the production sheets. This can vary depending on the tolerances within the production machines. In particular, variations in the 1991 'Canada in Space' hologram stamp have been reported. It should be noted that the hologram was produced larger than the final size used on the stamps. On the promotional folders the larger quadratic hologram was attached, as shown in Fig. 6-4.5. The TV-screen-shaped cut-out of holograms for stamps depends on the accuracy of this process. In some stamps the hologram image is cut so that the image appears higher than in other stamps where it appears lower, see Fig. 6-4.6. There are several other errors reported with regard to this particular hologram stamp. During the embossing process some defects can occur when a large amount of holograms is produced from the same nickel shim. Defects such as a 'black hole' and a 'black line' have been reported. 'Flight path' and 'meteor shower' are other variations or errors (small black dashes in blue background). In Fig. 6-4.7 the meteor shower variation is shown. Embossed holograms have sometimes errors like these marks or defects, and it is a question of whether they are really that interesting for a collector. Another example of a miss-cut hologram on a stamp is the 'Petronas Twin Towers' which is shown in Fig. 6-4.8.

Fig. 6-4.5. Large hologram.

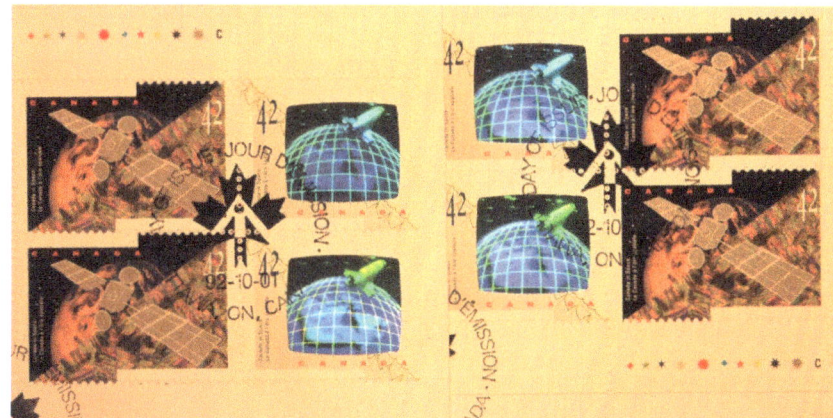

Fig. 6-4.6. High and low hologram images.

Fig. 6-4.7. Meteor shower variation.

Fig. 6-4.8. Miss-cut Petronas Twin Towers hologram.

Fig. 6-4.9. Upside down hologram on the Canada stamp.

6-4.3. Misplaced holograms on stamps

Another variation that can occur is a change in the exact *position* of the hologram on the printed stamp. For example, for the 1992 Canada Space stamp the following information was provided from the hologram producer Bridgestone Graphic Technologies Inc. responsible for the hologram mastering and production. "The holograms were produced on pressure sensitive material and were positioned on the congenitally printed stamps with a tolerance of +/- 1/64". Any larger variation in the position can therefore be regarded as an "error". There also one stamp reported with the hologram positioned upside down (Fig. 6-4.9). The 1991 Polish Phila Nippon butterfly souvenir sheets reveal serious errors in the position of the holograms (Fig.6-4.10). The 1998 duck stamps from Indonesia have several stamps with large hologram position variations (Fig. 6-4.11). None of the holograms on these stamps were supposed to be positioned so that they covered the ducks (see Figs. 3-11.11 and 3-11.12). There are also variations in the position of the attached holograms inside the three US envelopes. For example, the hologram image can be attached so that the image is positioned higher in some envelopes or slightly lower in others, as shown in Fig. 6-4.12. There are also envelopes with large errors in hologram position as shown in Fig. 6-4.13. A few of the 2000 US 'Space Achievement and Exploration' stamps have also been reported with errors or missing holograms. In addition, freaks have been reported. For example, a hologram or part of a hologram has appeared on a sheet which should have no such hologram. The US uncut souvenir sheets have had several such errors or freaks. One 'Landing on the Moon' souvenir sheet contained two $11.75 stamp holograms instead of one.

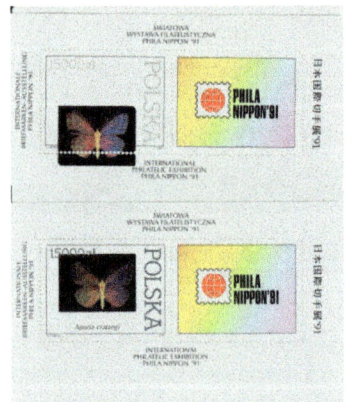

Fig. 6-4.10. Hologram position errors.   **Fig. 6-4.11**. Hologram position errors.

Fig. 6-4.12. Small hologram position variations.

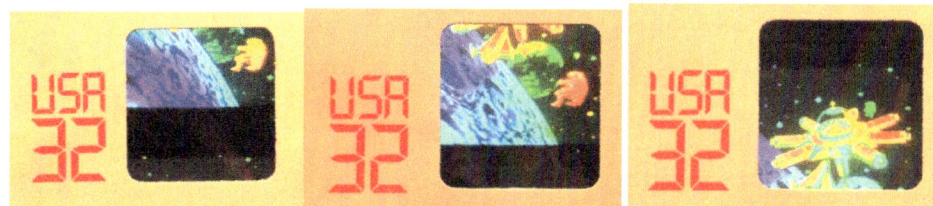

Fig. 6-4.13. Large hologram position errors.

6-4.5. Missing holograms on stamps

There are examples of stamps where a hologram is completely missing, for example, US envelopes without the inside hologram in the cutout (Fig. 6-4.14). When the first US hologram stationary was issued in 1991, the author ordered several hundred envelopes. In one box of 50 envelopes delivered from the US post office, one envelope had no hologram. As regards sheets with multiple stamps, several sheets with missing holograms have been found. In particular it seems that quality control of the 1992 Canada stamp sheets (See Fig. 3-5.23) was not very high. Quite a few sheets with one or more missing holograms have been reported, including a stamp sheet with all ten holograms missing. This sheet is shown in Fig. 6-4.15 with an authenticity certificate next to it. This sheet was listed in UNITRADE – Specialized Catalogue of Canadian stamps (2000 Edition) for CAN$ 25,000. More recently it has been listed for sale at City Stamp Montreal. You may ask how easily a hologram can be removed from a stamp. It is not impossible to do that. However, by a microscopic investigation of a stamp from which the hologram has been removed it is likely that broken paper fibers will be revealed. The hologram is attached to the stamp by hot-stamping, which means that if the hologram was removed an indentation in the paper should be visible. Caution is therefore advised, and an expert certificate is strongly recommended if one is about to invest in a stamp "without a hologram". Another certificate is reproduced in Fig 6-4.16 for a Canada sheet with the two top holograms missing.

Fig. 6-4.14. Missing US Space hologram.

Fig. 6-4.15. All ten holograms are missing on this Canada sheet with its certificate.

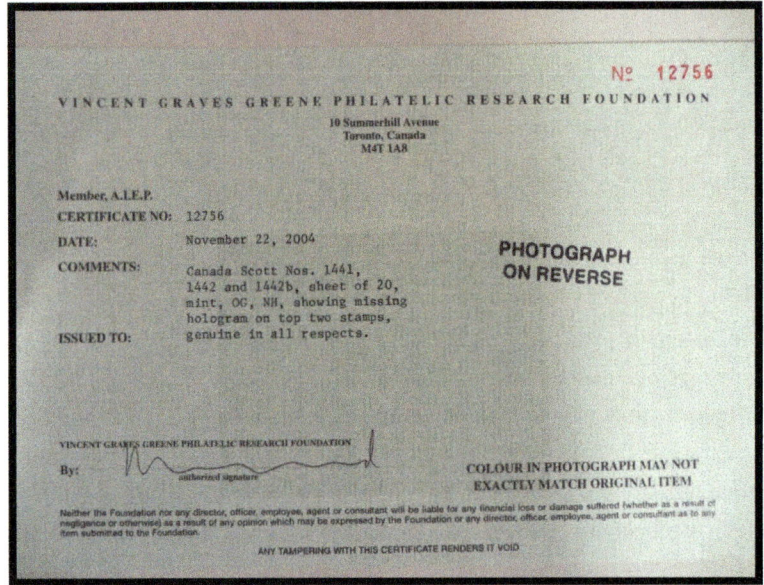

Fig. 6-4.16. Certificate for a sheet with the two top holograms missing.

6-5. Non-official hologram stamps

A few souvenir sheets with holograms issued in, for example, **Kyrgyzstan**, **Tajikistan** and **Turkmenistan** are not genuine. The two-sheet set which features a stamp with dogs and another with dinosaurs with a round hologram. The *scout emblem* hologram (Fig. 6-5.1) is attached to the area of the sheet between the stamps. The two Kyrgyzstan sheets are shown in Fig. 6-5.2. Note that these sheets were not officially issued by the respective countries and should not be regarded as philatelic hologram souvenir sheets. It is not clear by whom and why they were issued.

There are also sheets with what looks like stamps, which are not really postage stamps and should not be confused with real stamps. For example the KISS and STAR TREK sheets shown in Fig.6-5.3.

As already mentioned in regard to the Polish PHILA NIPPON '91'Butterfly souvenir sheet, an overprinted limited-edition private sheet was issued in 2000. This happened after that this block was withdrawn by the Polish Post in 1994 (See Fig 3-4.21 and Fig. 3-13.16). It is important to be aware of that not all stamps or souvenir sheets with holograms are officially issued by post authorities in different countries.

Fig. 6-5.1. *Scout emblem* hologram.

Fig. 6-5.2. The Dinousaurs and Dogs stamp sheets.

Fig. 6-5.3. The KISS and STAR TREK sheets.

Concluding Remarks

Over the period of about twenty-five years quite a few postage stamps, souvenir sheets and other philatelic items with holograms have been issued. The interest among philatelists in collecting such items has increased during the last few years. Initially the interest was created thanks to a few publications about stamps with holograms in philatelic journals. [41] For example, Komiensky's publication [42] is an early important contribution. At a holographic conference, *HOLOGRAPHY 2000,* in St. Pölten, Austria, in July 2000, the author presented a paper on holograms on stamps with the emphasis on the holographic images on the stamps. [43] A German booklet (three editions, two German and one English version by Schmitt [44-46] which lists postal holographic items is the only philatelic publication on the market before this book. There are some websites on hologram stamps which the reader may be interested to visit [47-49]. Some of the limited-edition holographic stamps are difficult to find, being therefore rather expensive. A missing hologram on a stamp or sheet is, on the other hand, extremely valuable.

References

[1]. S. F. Spira, "Photographica on postage stamps," *History of Photography* **3**, [No.1] (1979) pp.61-69
[2]. F. A. Miller, "A postage stamp history of optics," *Appl. Spectrosc.* **46** (1992) pp.1-15
[3]. Hariharan, *Basics of Holography*, Cambridge University Press, Cambridge (2002)
[4]. G. Saxby, *Practical Holography*, Third Edition, IOP Publishing Ltd, London (2004)
[5]. V. Toal, *Introduction to Holography*, CRC Press, London (2011)
[6]. "Brazil issues holographic souvenir sheet," *Linn's Stamp News* (December 4, 1989) p.95
[7]. "Simulated 3-D holographic postage stamp part of the design of new U.S. envelope," *Linn's Stamp News* (Oct. 23, 1989) p.1
[8]. "U.S. new issues: space station hologram envelope is launched," *Am. Philatelist* (Dec. 1989) p.1114
[9]. M. Hvidonov: "What's happening in Finland: hologram problems," *The Posthorn* (Nov. 1990) pp.167-168
[10]. "U.S. new issues: football hologram envelope issued," *Am. Philatelist* (Nov. 1990) p.986
[11]. *Techno-Thema,* Thematische Arbeitsgemeinschaft Technik und Naturwissenschaften, No. 61 (3) (2010) p.743
[12]. G. Griffith, "USPS announces seven stationery items: previous hologram design to be reused," *Linn's Stamp News* (Jan.13, 1992) p.1
[13]. "U.S. new issues: popular stamped envelopes released in new versions," *Am. Philatelist* (Febr. 1992) p.120
[14]. "New from Canada post: hologram stamp – Oct. 1," *The Canadian Philatelist* (Nov./Dec.1992) pp.529-53028
[15]. K. Scanlon, "Letter perfect: the, the science, the obsession behind the making of a Canadian postage stamp," *Equinox*, The Magazin of Canadian Discovery, No.65, (Sept./Oct. 1992), pp.63-71
[16]. L. McInnis, "Canada's hologram and other space stamps," *Linn's Stamp News* (March 22, 1993) p.20
[17]. L. Tauber, "Canadian space oddity," *Am. Philatelist* (Aug. 1999) p.748
[18]. D. McCarty, "Aland stamp Europe's best of 1997," *Linn's Stamp News* (July 19, 1999) p.16
[19]. D. Hatton, "World of new issues: Netherlands Antilles solar eclipse hologram," *Linn's Stamp News* (March 30, 1998) p.14
[20]. D. McCarty, "World of new issues: Lithuania issues its first hologram stamp," *Linn's Stamp News* (Nov. 9, 1998) p.58
[21]. D. McCarty, "World of new issues: Holograms from Indonesia, Czech Republic," *Linn's Stamp News* (Febr. 8, 1999) p.36
[22]. D. McCarty, "World of new issues: Czech hologram card honors stamp society," *Linn's Stamp News* (July 5, 1999) p.42
[23]. D. McCarty, "Dutch 'I Love Stamps' hologram," *Linn's Stamp News* (July 19, 1999) p.1
[24]. D. McCarty, "France issues first hologram at Philexfrance," *Linn's Stamp News* (July 5, 1999) p.14
[25]. D. McCarty, "World of new issues: New Caledonian sheet printed by five means," *Linn's Stamp News* (Aug. 23, 1999) p.28
[26]. D. McCarty, "Canada to issue hologram sheet," *Linn's Stamp News* (September 27, 1999) p.16
[27]. D. McCarty, "Canada prints sheets by three processes," *Linn's Stamp News* (Oct. 11, 1999) p.2
[28]. P. Martin, "The making of Canada's Millennium Keepsake, hologram stamp to soar," *Scott Stamp Monthly* (Oct. 1999), pp.68-70
[29]. D. McCarty, "World of new issues: Germany and others issue hologram stamps," *Linn's Stamp News* (Nov.15, 1999) p.16
[30]. D. McCarty, "Anyone may add photo to Australia's hologram stamp celebrating the Millennium," *Linn's Stamp News* (Nov. 8, 1999) p.1
[31]. D. McCarty, "Finland's program for 2000 includes Chinese puzzle sheet," *Linn's Stamp News* (Jan.

31, 2000) p.1

[32]. D. McCarty, "World of new issues: Hungary honors inventor of holography," *Linn's Stamp News* (Aug. 7, 2000) p.43

[33]. M. Baadke, "Hologram $11.75 Space Achievement stamps opens World Stamp Expo 2000 in Anaheim," *Linn's Stamp News* (June 26, 2000), p.1

[34]. M. Baadke, "Holographic stamps debut at Stamp Expo," *Linn's Stamp News* (July 24, 2000), p.18

[35]. D. McCarty, "World of new issues: new stamps welcome the third millennium," *Linn's Stamp News* (Jan. 1, 2001) p.44

[36]. *Techno-Thema,* Thematische Arbeitsgemeinschaft Technik und Naturwissenschaften, No. 64 (2) (2011) p.30

[37]. D. McCarty, "Innovative printing for British Nobel issue," *Linn's Stamp News* (April 9, 2001) p.14

[38]. "Erste Hologramm-Marke der Schweiz, Sondermarke 50 Jahre Rega" *Die Lupe, Das Briefmarkenmagazin* No. 1 (2002) pp.6-11

[39]. R. Murray, "A holographic portrait of Queen Elizabeth II", in *Advances in Display Holography*. Proc. 7th Int'l Symp.on Display Holography, River Valley Press (2006) pp. 155-164.

[40]. U. Schmitt, "Holograms on German prepaid parcel labels," *Linn's Stamp News* (Aug. 30, 1999) p.24

[41]. J. Mackay, "Holograms," *Stampmagazin* (February 1995), pp.85-87

[42]. M. Komiensky, "Holograms on stamps," *Scott Stamp Monthly* (December 1998), pp.39-42

[43]. H. I. Bjelkhagen, "Holography and philately: postage stamps with embossed holograms," in *HOLOGRAPHY 2000*, Proc. SPIE **4149** 12-31 (2000) pp.12-31

[44]. U. Schmitt, *Hologramme auf Postwertzeichen, Eine Übersicht zu hologrammen auf Briefmarken, Wertmarken, Fiskalmarken, Ganzsachen und Blockausgaben,* Taufkirchen/Vils (2000)

[45]. U. Schmitt, *Holograms on stamps, A handbook of holograms on postage stamps, pre-paid labels, postcards, postal stationary, stamp sheets and miniature sheets,* Taufkirchen/Vils (2001)

[46]. U. Schmitt, *Hologramme auf Postwertzeichen, Eine Übersicht zu hologrammen und holografischen Folien auf Briefmarken und Blockausgaben,* Taufkirchen/Vils (2007)

[47] http://philaquelymoi.blogspot.co.uk/2013/05/3d-holographic-stamps.html [Oct. 2013]

[48] http://www.hologramm-briefmarken.de [Oct. 2013]

[49] http://www.freewebs.com/hologramstamps/index.htm [Oct. 2013]

Table 1. Chinese New Year Stamp Presentation Folders with Holograms

Card No.	Date	Animal	Hologram size (mm)	Stamps, denomination	ID-number
1	1987-01-05	Rabbit	38 x 38	Set of 4, 0.08 Yuan	T.112, PZ-3
2	1988-01-05	Dragon	Ø50	Set of 4, 0.08 Yuan	PZ-8
3	1989-01-05	Snake	Ø60	Set of 4, 0.08 Yuan	PZ-12
4	1990-01-05	Horse	70 x 60	Set of 4, 0.08 Yuan	PZ-15
5	1991-01-05	Sheep	Ø50	Set of 4, 0.20 Yuan	T.159, PZ-19
6	1991-01-05	12 animals	31 x 26	Set of 12, no value	-
7	1992-01-25	Monkey	Ø50	2 sets of 4, 0.20/0.50 Yuan	1992-1, PZ-23
8	1993-01-05	Rooster	Ø50	2 sets of 4, 0.20/0.50 Yuan	1993-1, PZ-29
9	1994-01-05	Dog	Ø50	2 sets of 4, 0.20/0.50 Yuan	1994-1, PZ-35
10	1995-01-05	Pig	Ø48	2 sets of 4, 0.20/0.50 Yuan	1995-1, PZ-41
11	1996-01-05	Rat	Ø48	2 sets of 4, 0.20/0.50 Yuan	1996-1, PZ-46
12	1997-01-05	Ox	Ø48	2 sets of 4, 50/150 fen	1997-1, PZ-48
13	1998-01-05	Tiger	Ø48	2 sets of 4, 50/150 fen	1998-1, PZ-53
14	1999-01-05	Hare	Ø48	2 sets of 4, 50/150 fen	1999-1, PZ-59

Table 2-1. Postage stamps and souvenir sheets with holograms

No.	Issue date	Country	Type*	Size: S H* [mm]	Denomination	Edition	Perforation	Scott No.
1	**1988**-10-18	Austria	DS (8)	35x50 *21x17*	8 Schilling (Ats)	3.04M stamps	13½ : 13¾	1441
2	**1989**-10-14	Brazil	SS (3)	99x69/26x44 *25x20*	2, 3, 5 NCz$	200K blocks	10 ¾ : 11	2210 a-c
3	1989-12-03	USA	PS (1)	32x32 *32x32*	25¢	25M + 20M	imperf	U617
4	**1990**-01-19	Finland	DS (20)	26x36 *Ø15*	1.90 Fmk	1M sheets	13 : 13¼	810
5	1990-01-19	Finland	DS (20)	26x36 *Ø15*	2.50 Fmk	1M sheets	13 : 13¼	811
6	1990-09-09	USA	PS (1)	32x32 *32x32*	25¢	10.84M	imperf	U618
7	**1991**-11-15	Hungary	SS (1)	70x91/39x50.5 *32x48*	20 Forint (HUF)	13K sheets	11¼ : 11¼	3254
8	1991-11-16	Poland	SS (2)	38.5x50.5 *30x22*	15,000 Złoty (Zł)	2M blocks	12½ : 12½	3056
9	**1992**-01-21	USA	PS (1)	32x32 *32x32*	29¢	19.6529M	imperf	U625
10	1992-05-08	Finland	DS (15)	29.5x41 *13x18*	2.10 Fmk	1M sheets	K13 : 12¾	886
11	1992-05-08	Finland	DS (15)	29.5x41 *13x18*	2.90 Fmk	1M sheets	K13 : 12¾	887
12	1992-05-08	Finland	DS (15)	29.5x41 *13x18*	3.10 Fmk	1M sheets	K13 : 12¾	888
13	1992-10-01	Canada	DS (10+10)	32x26 *21x17*	42¢	5M stamps	13 : 13	1442
14	**1993**-03-26	San Marino	SS (3)	140x70/40x30 *Ø13*	2000 Lira	250K blocks	13¼ : 13¼	1280b
15	1993-05-06	Finland	4PC (1)	18x18 *18x18*	Int'l rate	-	imperf	-
16	1993-08-27	Mongolia	DS (4)	170x125/53x42 *35x25*	80 Möngö	-	K14 : 14¼	2139
17	**1994**-02-10	Guyana	DS(4)	108x125/36x54 *36x54*	GY$300	very limited	6 : 6	-
18	1994-02-10	Guyana	DS(4)	108x125/38x56 *38x56*	GY$300	very limited	imperf	-
19	1994-02-15	Hong Kong	PC (1)	29x31 *26x28*	96 HK¢	300K	simulated perf	23
20	1994-02-15	Hong Kong	PC (1)	29x31 *26x28*	1 HK$	300K	simulated perf	636
21	1994-07-05	Isle of Man	DS (10)	30.6x38 *23x30*	£5	300M	K14½ : 14¼	553c
22	1994-07-20	New Zealand	DS (10)	30x35 *18x25*	1.50 NZ$	732K	K12 : 12	1225
23	1994-08-08	Hungary	C (1)	30x30 *30x30*	100 Forint (HUF)	46.2K	simulated perf	-
24	1994-11-11	Bhutan	DS (1)	114x57/38x31 *29x22*	30 NU	50K	14¼ : 14¼	1101a
25	1994-11-11	Bhutan	DS (1)	114x57/38x31 *29x22*	36 NU	50K	14¼ : 14¼	1101b
26	1994-12-14	Tonga	BL (1)	39x29 *41x31*	T$2.00	5-10K	-	870m
27-35	**1995**-01-30	Finland	BL (8)	29x35.5 *18x14*	2.80 Fmk	800K	13 : 12¾	949-956a
36	1995-04-05	Australia	DS (10)	50x30 *oval 18x21*	A$1.20	-	14¼ : 14	1429
37	1995-04-05	Australia	DS (10)	50x30 *oval 18x21*	A$2.50	-	14¼ : 14	1430
38	1995-09-22	USA	PS (1)	32x32 *32x32*	32¢	20M	imperf	U639
39	**1996**-01-13	Malaysia	DS (1)	100x70/40x28.5 *20x35*	RM5.00	144K	14 x 14	577
40	1996-04-25	Hungary	SS (1)	90x129/32x25 *27x21*	200 Forint (HUF)	52.2K	-	2510

* DS = Definitive Stamp, MS = Miniature Sheet, SS = Souvenir Sheet, PS = Postal Stationary, PC = Postal Card, BL = Booklet, (stamps/sheet), C = Cinderella, OP = Overprinted, CCH = Contour-Cut Hologram or Foil, K= 1,000, M = 1,000,000.

** First figures: stamp size in mm (horizontal side x vertical side); Second figures: *hologram size in mm.*

Table 2-2. Postage stamps and souvenir sheets with holograms

No.	Date	Country	Type*	Size: S H* [mm]	Denomination	Edition	Perforation	Scott No.
41	1996-05-10	P. R. China	SS (1)	100x73/54.5x 40 Ø12	5 RMB.Y	30K	12 : 12	2448a
42	1996-06-09	Thailand	DS (25)	51x36 Ø20	3 Baht	5M	13½ : 13½	1671
43	1996-06-09	Thailand	SS (5)	185x123/51x36 Ø20	3 Baht	1M	13½ : 13½	1637a
44	1996-07-18	P. R. China	SS (1)	85x113/37x45 Ø12	3 RMB.Y	-	12 : 12	2530a
45	1996-08-12	Hungary	SS (1)	90x120/25x32 *21x27*	200 Forint (HUF)	20K	-	2510
46	1996-09-05	Australia	DS (10)	50x30 Ø20	45¢	-	14¼ : 14	1554
47	1996-09-05	Australia	DS (10)	50x30 Ø20	A$1.20	-	14¼ : 14	1555
48	1996-10-09	P. R. China	SS (1)	74/80/40x60 Ø12	3 RMB.Y	1M	11½ : 11½	1987a
49	1996-11-27	Hong Kong	PC (1)	25x40 *25x40*	1.30 HK$	-	simulated perf	244
50	1996-11-27	Hong Kong	PC (1)	25x40 *25x40*	2.00 HK$	-	simulated perf	369
51	1996-11-27	Hong Kong	PC (1)	30x30 *30x30*	1.80 HK$	-	simulated perf	554
52	1996-11-27	Hong Kong	PC (1)	25x40 *25x40*	5.00 HK$	-	simulated perf	442
53	1996-11-27	Hong Kong	PC (1)	40x27 *40x27*	5.00 HK$	-	simulated perf	610
54	1996-11-27	Hong Kong	PC (1)	25x40 *25x40*	1.00 HK$	-	simulated perf	416
55	**1997**-06-09	Åland	SS (1)	128x80/40x30 *12x15*	20 Fmk	300K blocks	12¾ : 13	137
56	1997-06-20	Ascension Island	SS(1)	130x90/25.5x38.5 *text*	£1	-	13¼ : 13¼	653a
57	1997-06-20	British Indian Ocean Territory	SS(1)	130x90/38.5x25.5 *text*	74p	-	13¼ : 13¼	160a
58	1997-06-20	Samoa	SS(1)	130x90/30.5x38.5 *text*	$2.50 (Tolar)	-	14¼ : 14¼	933a
59	1997-06-20	Tristan Da Chuna	SS(1)	130x90/25.5x38.5 *text*	60p	-	13¼ : 13	597a
60	1997-06-20	Falkland Islands	SS(1)	130x90/38.5x25.5 *text*	£1	-	14 : 14	607a
61	1997-06-20	British Antarctic Territory	SS(1)	130x90/ 38.5x25.5 *text*	£1	-	14 : 14	211a
62	1997-06-20	S. Georgia & S. Sandwich Islands	SS(1)	130x90/30.5x38.5 *text*	76p	-	14 : 14	211a
63	1997-06-20	St Helena	SS(1)	130x90/25.5x38.5 *text*	75p	-	13¼ : 13	691a
64	1997-06-20	Bahamas	SS(1)	130x90/25.5x38.5 *text*	70¢	-	14¼ : 14¼	860a
65	1997-06-20	Tuvalu	SS(1)	130x90/25.5x38.5 *text*	$2	-	14¼ : 14	739a
66	1997-06-20	Isle of Man	SS(1)	130x90/38.5x25.5 *text*	23p	-	13 : 13¼	-
67	**1998**-02-10	Grenada/ Grenadines	DS (4)	63x77/29x31 *28x34*	EC$1.50	-	13 : 13	2011
68	1998-02-10	Grenada/ Grenadines	DS (1)	85x52/52x64 *63x75*	EC$3.00	-	13 : 13	2012

* DS = Definitive Stamp, MS = Miniature Sheet, SS = Souvenir Sheet, PS = Postal Stationary, PC = Postal Card, BL = Booklet, (stamps/sheet), C = Cinderella, OP = Overprinted, CCH = Contour-Cut Hologram or Foil, K= 1,000, M = 1,000,000.

** First figures: stamp size in mm (horizontal side x vertical side); Second figures: *hologram size in mm*.

Table 2-3. Postage stamps and souvenir sheets with holograms

No.	Date	Country	Type*	Size: S H* [mm]	Denomination	Edition	Perforation	Scott No.
69	1998-02-26	Netherlands/Antilles	DS (1)	85x52/25x36 Ø12	750c	-	14 x 12¾	824
70	1998-10-08	Germany	SS(10)	210x105/35x35 *35x35*	110+50pf	10K	13¾ : 13¾	not listed
71	1998-09-10	Lithuania	DS (1)	55x86/40x30 Ø16	13 Litas (Lt)	60K	12 : 12	612
72	1998-10-19	Indonesia	DS (50)	42x25 Ø7.5	4000 rupiah (Rp)	1M	13½ : 12¾	1800
73	1998-10-19	Indonesia	DS (50)	42x25 Ø7.5	5000 rupiah (Rp)	1M	13½ : 12¾	1801
74	1998-10-19	Indonesia	DS (50)	42x25 Ø7.5	10000 rupiah (Rp)	1M	13½ : 12¾	1802
75	1998-10-19	Indonesia	DS (50)	42x25 Ø7.5	15000 rupiah (Rp)	1M	13½ : 12¾	1803
76	1998-10-19	Indonesia	DS (50)	42x25 Ø7.5	20000 rupiah (Rp)	1M	13½ : 12¾	1804
77	1998-10-19	Indonesia	SS (5)	207x105/42x25 Ø7.5	the five above	100K	13½ : 12¾	1805
78	1998-11-05	Grenada	DS (1)	63x77/53x63 *53x63*	EC$6.00	-	13 : 13	2786A
79	1998-11-05	Grenada/Grenadines	DS (1)	63x77/53x63 *53x63*	EC$8.00	-	13 : 13	2055A
80	1998-11-05	Guyana	DS (1)	63x77/53x63 *53x63*	GYD$300	-	13 : 13	3336A
81	1998-11-05	St Vincent/Grenadines	DS (1)	63x77/53x63 *53x63*	EC$8.00	-	13 : 13	2630
82	1998-11-09	France	C (1)	85x80 *25x30*	No value	-	imperf	not listed
83	**1999**-01-04	Czech Republic	PC (1)	- *14x8*	4 korona	-	-	-
84	1999-02-11	Hungary	SS (1)	105x76/45x30 *17x95*	1999 Ft (HUF)	200K	12¼ : 12¼	B247
85	1999-04-27	Kyrgyzstan	DS (1)	36x51 *30x40*	10 som	50K	13½ : 13½	123a
86	1999-04-27	Kyrgyzstan	DS (1)	36x51 *30x40*	10 som	50K	13½ : 13½	123b
87	1999-04-27	Kyrgyzstan	DS (1)	36x51 *30x40*	30 som	50K	13½ : 13½	123c
88	1999-04-27	Kyrgyzstan	DS (1)	36x51 *30x40*	50 som	50K	13½ : 13½	123d
89	1999-04-27	Kyrgyzstan	SS (4)x2	148x190/36x51 *30x40*	2x10, 30, 50 som	50K	13½ : 13½	123e
90	1999-05-06	The Netherlands	DS (1)	36x35 *15x11*	80 cent	1.7M	13¼ x 12¾	1025
91	1999-05-06	The Netherlands	DS (1)	36x35 *15x11*	80 cent	1.7M	13¼ x 12¾	1026
92	1999-05-06	The Netherlands	BL (5)	107x50/36x35 *15x11*	5x80 cent	1.7M	13¼ x 12¾	1026a
93	1999-05-17	Macau	SS (1)	138x90/40x30 *18x16*	8 ptcs	1.25M	12 x 12	984
94	1999-07-02	France	DS (25)	40.5x52 Ø15	6.70 Fr	3.36M	11¾ x 13	2732
95	1999-07-02	France	C (1)	80x85 *30x25*	No value	-	12½ : 12½	not listed
96	1999-07-02	New Caledonia	SS (5)	155x110/48x38 *25x30*	700 Fr	30K	13 : 13	831e
97	1999-07-02	Congo	DS (10)	290x170/40x52 *25x30*	300 Fr	-	13 : 13	1213
98	1999-07-02	Gabon	DS (10)	290x170/40x52 *25x30*	225 Fr	-	13 : 13	952

* DS = Definitive Stamp, MS = Miniature Sheet, SS = Souvenir Sheet, PS = Postal Stationary, PC = Postal Card, BL = Booklet, (stamps/sheet), C = Cinderella, OP = Overprinted, CCH = Contour-Cut Hologram or Foil, K= 1,000, M = 1,000,000.

** First figures: stamp size in mm (horizontal side x vertical side); Second figures: *hologram size in mm*.

Table 2-4. Postage stamps and souvenir sheets with holograms

No.	Date	Country	Type*	Size: S H* [mm]	Denomination	Edition	Perforation	Scott No.
99	1999-07-02	Guinea	DS (10)	290x170/40x52 *25x30*	750 Fr	-	13 : 13	1534c
100	1999-07-02	Ivory Coast	DS (10)	290x170/40x52 *25x30*	280 Fr	-	13 : 13	1043
101	1999-07-02	Niger	DS (10)	290x170/40x52 *25x30*	200 Fr	-	13 : 13	1040
102	1999-07-02	Senegal	DS (10)	290x170/40x52 *25x30*	240 Fr	-	13 : 13	1351
103	1999-08-20	Brazil	DS (1)	59x25 *25x10*	R$1.20	375K	11½ : 12	2722
104	1999-08-20	Brazil	SS (8)	161x150/59x25 *25x10*	R$120	375K	11½ : 12	2722
105	1999-08-21	Switzerland	SS (1)	105x70/45x54 Ø10	90c	-	12 : 12	1039a
106	1999-08-30	Malaysia	MS (1)	30.5x49.7 *22x42*	RM5	5M	14½ : 14.4	727
107	1999-10-01	Australia	MS (6)	30x25	45¢ , 50¢		14¼ : 14¼	1790
108	1999-10-12	Canada	DS (4)	42x42 *38x38*	46¢	9.27M	Imperf	1812
109	1999-10-12	Canada	SS (1)	42x42 *79x79*	46¢	300K	Imperf	1812
110	1999-10-14	Germany	DS (10)	55x32.8 *17x17*	110 + 50pf	25M	13¼ : 14	B858
111	1999-10-14	Germany	DS (10)	55x32.8 *29x18*	300 + 100pf	14M	13¼ : 14	B859
112	1999-11-01	Australia	DS (10)	(47) 30x30 *15x15*	45¢	-	14½ : 14	1798
113	1999-11-05	Australia	MS(6) OP	No. 107				
114	1999-11-05	Australia	MS(6) OP	No. 107				
115	1999-12-19	Macau	SS (1) OP	No. 93				984a
116	1999-12-31	Namibia	DS (1)	77/55/38x45 Ø27	9.00N$	30K	13½ : 13½	952
117	**2000**-01-01	Singapore	SS (4)	140x75/24x50 *text*	$1, $2, 60¢	100K	14¾ : 14	918a
118	2000-03-25	Australia	MS (6) OP	No. 107				(1790)
119	2000-05-30	Finland	SS (3)	120x80/14x25 *CCH*	3x3.50 Fmk	500K	13¾ : 13¾	1140
120	2000-06-13	Hungary	C (1) OP	No. 23				
121	2000-06-23	Monaco	DS (1)	41x30 *text*	€0.41/2.70F	-	13 : 13	2167
122	2000-06-23	Monaco	DS (1)	41x30 *text*	€0.69/4.50F	-	13 : 13	2168
123	2000-06-30	Hungary	SS (1)	35x35 Ø19	2000Ft (HUF)	100K	12 ; 12	3698
124	2000-07-07	Poland-private	SS (2) OP	No. 8		4K		not listed
125	2000-07-07	Mongolia	DS (1)	51x36 *42x24*	50₮	70K	13½ : 13½	2441
126	2000-07-07	Mongolia	DS (1)	51x36 *42x24*	100₮	70K	13½ : 13½	2441
127	2000-07-07	Mongolia	DS (1)	51x36 *42x24*	200₮	70K	13½ : 13½	2441
128	2000-07-07	Mongolia	DS (1)	51x36 *42x24*	250₮	70K	13½ : 13½	2441
129	2000-07-07	Mongolia	SS (4)x2	51x36 *42x24*	The above stamps x2	70K	13½ : 13½	2441
130	2000-07-07	USA	DS (1)	Ø92.1 Ø45.16	$11.75	1.695M	circular perf	3412

* DS = Definitive Stamp, MS = Miniature Sheet, SS = Souvenir Sheet, PS = Postal Stationary, PC = Postal Card, BL = Booklet, (stamps/sheet), C = Cinderella, OP = Overprinted, CCH = Contour-Cut Hologram or Foil, K= 1,000, M = 1,000,000.

** First figures: stamp size in mm (horizontal side x vertical side); Second figures: *hologram size in mm*.

Table 2-5. Postage stamps and souvenir sheets with holograms

No.	Date	Country	Type*	Size: S H* [mm]	Denomination	Edition	Perforation	Scott No.
131	2000-07-08	USA	DS (1)	184x127 *50x36*	$11.75	1.695M	10½ : 10½	3413
132	2000-07-11	USA	DS (2)	127x184 *50x36*	$3.20, $3.20	1.650M	10½ : 10½	3411
133	2000-07-13	USA	SS (15)	508x146	$38.50	305K	-	3409-3413
134	2000-10-03	Australia	SS (6)	166x73 *CCH*	6x45¢	-	14½ : 14	1914
135	2000-10-22	Australia	SS (6) OP	No.134				
136	2000-10-27	Åland	C (20)	146x210/24x28 *CCH*	None	20K		
137	2000-12-09	France	DS (1)	21.5x36 *CCH*	0.69/4.50Fr	4.05M	13 : 13¼	2795
138	2000-12-31	Hong Kong	DS (1)	28.5x33.5 *25x30*	HK$20	-	14.03 : 13.14	873
139	2000-12-31	Hong Kong	SS (1)	91x151 *40x135*	None	-	imperf	917
140	**2001**-01-08	Australia	DS (25)	35x26 *foil*	45¢	-	13.86 : 14.6	430
141	2001-01-08	Australia	DS (25)	35x26 *foil*	$1.35	-	13.86 : 14.6	431
142	2001-01-08	Australia	MS (2)	106x70/35x26 *foil*	45¢, $1.35	-	13.86 : 14.6	431a
143	2001-02-01	Australia	SS (6) OP	No. 134				(1914)
144	2001-04-24	Australia	DS (20)	30x30 (50) *15x15*	45¢	-	13.86 : 14.28	1955
145	2001-07-03	Belarus	DS (30)	28x30 Ø20	500r	200K	14¼ : 14	393
146	2001-09-01	Libya	SS(16)	146x205/31x42 *foil*	16x100 dirhams	-	13½ : 13½	1656R
147	2001-09-01	Libya	SS(1)	148x109/42x51 *16x13*	300 dirhams	-	13½ : 13½	1657
148	2001-09-01	Libya	SS(1)	148x109/42x51 *16x13*	300 dirhams	-	13½ : 13½	1658
149	2001-09-11	Kyrgyzstan	SS(4)x2OP	No. 89		16K		175
150	2001-10-02	Great Britain	DS (50)	35x37 *22x22*	65p	5M	14 : 14½	1998
151	2001-10-16	Åland	C (20)	146x210/24x29 *CCH*	None	20K		-
152	**2002**-03-12	Switzerland	DS (10)	40x32.5 *CCH*	SFr180	-	13 : 13½	1114
153	2002-08-21	Singapore	DS (8)	40.5x27.55 *CCH*	50¢	300K/each	13¼ : 13¾	1022
154	2002-08-21	Singapore	DS (8)	40.5x27.55 *CCH*	50¢	300K/each	13¼ : 13¾	1023
155	2002-08-21	Singapore	DS (8)	40.5x27.55 *CCH*	50¢	300K/each	13¼ : 13¾	1024
156	2002-08-21	Singapore	DS (8)	40.5x27.55 *CCH*	50¢	300K/each	13¼ : 13¾	1025
157	2002-08-21	Singapore	DS (8)	40.5x46.4 *CCH*	FLAO	300K/each	13¼ : 13¾	1026
158	2002-08-21	Singapore	DS (8)	40.5x46.4 *CCH*	FLAO	300K/each	13¼ : 13¾	1027
159	2002-08-21	Singapore	DS (8)	40.5x46.4 *CCH*	FLAO	300K/each	13¼ : 13¾	1028
160	2002-08-21	Singapore	DS (8)	40.5x46.4 *CCH*	FLAO	300K/each	13¼ : 13¾	1029
161	2002-09-01	Libya	SS(16)	146x202/31x42 *foil*	16x100 dirhams	-	13½ : 13½	1667R
162	2002-09-01	Libya	SS(1)	148x107/42x51 *16x13*	300 dirhams	-	13½ : 13½	1668

* DS = Definitive Stamp, MS = Miniature Sheet, SS = Souvenir Sheet, PS = Postal Stationary, PC = Postal Card, BL = Booklet, (stamps/sheet), C = Cinderella, OP = Overprinted, CCH = Contour-Cut Hologram or Foil, K= 1,000, M = 1,000,000.

** First figures: stamp size in mm (horizontal side x vertical side); Second figures: *hologram size in mm*.

Table 2-6. Postage stamps and souvenir sheets with holograms

No.	Date	Country	Type*	Size: S H** [mm]	Denomination	Edition	Perforation	Scott No.
163	2002-09-01	Libya	SS(1)	148x107/42x51 *16x13*	300 dirhams	-	13½ : 13½	1669
164	2002-10-09	Åland	C (20)	146x210/24x29 *CCH*	None	20K		-
165	2002-11-22	Romania	SS (2)	43.5x43.5 *CCH*	131000L (Lei)	39K	12.¾ : 12.¾	4553a
166	2002-11-24	Hong Kong	SS (25)	28x45 *CCH*	HK$1.40	-	13¼ : 13½	1018
167	2002-11-24	Hong Kong	SS (25)	28x45 *CCH*	HK$2.40	-	13¼ : 13½	1019
168	2002-11-24	Hong Kong	SS (25)	28x45 *CCH*	HK$3.00	-	13¼ : 13½	1020
169	2002-11-24	Hong Kong	SS (25)	28x45 *CCH*	HK$5.00	-	13¼ : 13½	1021
170	2002-11-24	Hong Kong	SS (8)	162x230/28x45 *CCH*	The above stamps x2	-	13¼ : 13½	1018-1021a
171	**2003**-03-02	Libya	SS(6)	148x117/51x42 *foil*	6x200 dirhams	-	13¼ : 13¼	not yet listed
172	2003-03-28	United Nations	DS (20)	36x50 *30x36*	70¢	910K	13¼ : 12¾	839
173	2003-07-03	Guernsey	DS (1)	160x82/36x36 *text*	£5	-	13 : 13	809
174	2003-08-10	Brazil	DS (1)	70x89/38x38 *28x33*	2.90R$	400K	11½ : 11½	2889
175	2003-09-23	Portugal	DS (1)	140x112/80x30 *13x80*	€2.50	90K	12 : 11¾	2577
176	2003-09-24	Australia	SS (6)	170x80/37x26 *CCH*	6x50¢	-	18.86 : 14.6	not listed
177	2003-10-01	Canada	DS(8)	110x260/Ø40 *CCH*	8x48¢	8x750K	imperf	1999B
178	2003-10-04	Australia	SS(6) OP	No.176				not listed
179	2003-10-10	Australia	SS(6) OP	No.176				not listed
180	2003-10-29	Macau	SS (1)	138x90/Ø38 Ø15	12.00ptcs	-	14	984
181	2003-11-11	Slovenia	DS (10)	41x28 Ø15	221 SIT tolar	120K	13 : 14½	537
182	2003-11-21	Australia	SS(6) OP	No.176				not listed
183	**2004**-01-08	Canada	DS (25)	30x40 *CCH*	49¢	8M	13 : 12½	2015
184	2004-01-08	Canada	DS (25)	30x40 *CCH*	$1.40	2.2M	13 : 12½	2016
185	2004-01-08	Canada	SS (1)	30x40 *CCH*	$1.40	1.7M	13 : 12½	2016a
186	2004-01-30	Canada	DS(25) OP	No.183		25K		2015
187	2004-05-01	Czech Republic	DS (10)	171x161/44x26 *14x8*	9 Kc	600K	11.9 : 11.2	3235
188	2004-05-05	Czech Republic	DS (6)	150x112/37.5x37.5 *14x8*	9 Kc	400K	11.2 : 11.2	3237
189	2004-10-09	South Africa	SS (1)	105x65/39x29 *CCH*	R12.05	25K	11¼ : 11¼	1343
190	2004-10-12	Australia	SS (10)	244x192 *foil*	10x50¢	-	13¾ : 14¼	not listed
191	2004-10-12	Australia	SS (10)	244x192 *foil*	10x50¢	-	14½ : 14	not listed
192	2004-12-05	Thailand	DS (1)	30x40 *CCH*	3 Baht	-	13 : 13	2154
193	2004-12-05	Thailand	DS (1)	30x40 *CCH*	3 Baht	-	13 : 13	2155
194	2004-12-05	Thailand	DS (1)	30x40 *CCH*	3 Baht	-	13 : 13	2156

* DS = Definitive Stamp, MS = Miniature Sheet, SS = Souvenir Sheet, PS = Postal Stationary, PC = Postal Card, BL = Booklet, (stamps/sheet), C = Cinderella, OP = Overprinted, CCH = Contour-Cut Hologram or Foil, K= 1,000, M = 1,000,000.

** First figures: stamp size in mm (horizontal side x vertical side); Second figures: *hologram size in mm*.

Table 2-7. Postage stamps and souvenir sheets with holograms

No.	Date	Country	Type*	Size: S H* [mm]	Denomination	Edition	Perforation	Scott No.
195	2004-12-05	Thailand	DS (1)	30x40 *CCH*	15 Baht	-	13 : 13	2157
196	2004-12-05	Thailand	SS (1)	132x190/30x40 *CCH*	3x3 Baht, 15 Baht	-	13 : 13	2157a
197	2004-12-20	Libya	DS(4)	150x132/60x51 *foil*	4 x 500 dirhams	-	13¼ : 13¼	not yet listed
198	**2005**-02-04	United Nations	DS (20)	50x35 *30x30*	20 x 75¢	360K	13 : 13	359
199	2005-04-02	Jersey	SS (1)	110x75/52x38 *CCH*	£2	-	13 : 13	1161
200	2005-05-04	Czech Republic	DS (6)	150x112/33x33 *14x8*	6 x 9 Kc	318K	11¼ : 11¼	3272
201	2005-05-26	Jersey	SS(1) OP	No.199				1161a
202	2005-05-31	Thailand	DS (20)	24x29 *CCH*	5 Baht	-	14¼ : 14¾	2176
203	2005-05-31	Thailand	DS (20)	24x29 *CCH*	5 Baht	-	14¼ : 14¾	2176
204	2005-05-31	Thailand	DS (20)	48x29 *CCH*	5 Baht	-	14¼ : 14¾	2176
205	2005-05-31	Thailand	DS (20)	48x29 *CCH*	5 Bhat	-	14¼ : 14¾	2176
206	2005-05-31	Thailand	SS (4)x4	199x210 *CCH*	8x5 Baht	1M	14¼ : 14¾	2176
207	2005-09-21	Italy	DS (4)	48x40/44x36 *CCH*	4 x €0.80	3M	Imperf	2689
208	2005-10-10	Åland	DS (40)	26x35.4 *26x8*	40 x 0.45€	450K	13¼ : 13	241
209	2005-11-02	Canada	BL (12)	160/70/24x24 *CCH*	12 x 50¢	40M	imperf : 8	2124
210	**2006**-02-04	United Nations	DS (20)	35x50 *30x35*	20 x CHF1.30	280K	13 : 13	451
211	2006-03-17	USA	DS (20)	40x31 *CCH*	20 x $4.05	-	11 : 11	4018
212	2006-03-17	USA	DS (20)	40x31 *CCH*	20 x $14.40	-	11 : 11	4019
213	2006-04-04	Jersey	MS (1)	150x100 *elliptic46x30*	£2	-	elliptic 13	1213
214	2006-05-25	Malaysia	SS (4)	100x70/70x35 *CCH*	4 x RM5	-	14 : 14	1093
215	2006-05-27	Thailand	SS(4) OP	No.206				2176e
216	2006-06-24	Thailand	SS(4)	178x90/47.5x30 *CCH*	4 x 20 Baht	100K	13 : 13	2234
217	2006-09-22	Iran	DS (40)	15x20 *15x20*	40 x 4400Rls	-	imperf	2919E
218	2006-09-22	Iran	DS (40)	Ø25 *Ø25*	40 x 5500Rls	-	imperf	2919F
219	2006-10-09	Åland	DS(40)	35.4x26 *4 stars*	40 x Domestic	450K	13¼ : 13	254
220	2006-11-16	Jersey	SS(1) OP	No.213				1213a
221	2006-11-16	Thailand	SS(4) OP	No.216				2234
222	2006-11-24	Philippines	DS (40)	40x30 *stars*	40 x 7	50K	14 : 14	3075
223	2006-11-24	Philippines	DS (40)	40x30 *stars*	40 x 20	49.8K	14 : 14	3076
224	2006-11-24	Philippines	DS (40)	40x30 *stars*	40 x 24¢	50K	14 : 14	3077
225	2006-11-24	Philippines	DS (40)	40x30 *stars*	40 x 26	50K	14 : 14	3078
226	**2007**-01-05	Canada	DS (25)	48x26 *CCH*	25 x 52¢	8M	13½ : 13½	2201

* DS = Definitive Stamp, MS = Miniature Sheet, SS = Souvenir Sheet, PS = Postal Stationary, PC = Postal Card, BL = Booklet, (stamps/sheet), C = Cinderella, OP = Overprinted, CCH = Contour-Cut Hologram or Foil, K= 1,000, M = 1,000,000.

** First figures: stamp size in mm (horizontal side x vertical side); Second figures: *hologram size in mm*.

Table 2-8. Postage stamps and souvenir sheets with holograms

No.	Date	Country	Type*	Size: S H** [mm]	Denomination	Edition	Perforation	Scott No.
227	2007-01-05	Canada	SS (1)	98x97 *CCH*	$1.55	700K	13½ : 13½	2202
228	2007-01-05	Peru	DS (1)	40x30 *5x5*	S2.00	-	14 : 13½	1541
229	2007-01-05	Peru	DS (1)	40x30 *5x5*	S2.00	-	14 : 13½	1542
230	2007-01-16	Peru	MS (1)	40x30 *text*	S8.50	-	13½ : 14	1545
231	2007-01-24	Finland	DS (1)	34.5x24.5 *34.5x24.5*	0.70€	1.5M	14 : 14	1276
232	2007-01-24	Finland	MS (2)	38x38/43x31 *CCH*	2x0.70€	350K	14 : 14	1280ab
233	2007-02-05	Peru	DS (1)	30x40 *5x5*	S2.00	-	14 : 13½	1551
234	2007-02-05	Peru	DS (1)	30x40 *5x5*	S2.00	-	14 : 13½	1552
235	2007-07-01	Hong Kong	SS (3)	130x90/30x60	3 x HK$10	-	13.33 : 13.33	1282
236	2007-07-07	Malaysia	MS (1)	120x70/50x38 *CCH*	RM5	-	13½ : 13½	1163
237	2007-08-03	Malaysia	MS(1) OP	No.236				
238	2007-10-02	Australia	SS (6)	160x90/26x46 *foil*	5x50¢ + $1	-	14 : 14¾	2878
239	2007-11-01	Canada	BL (12)	24x24 *holo stars*	12xDomestic (52¢+)	44M	simulated	2239a
240	2007-11-15	Chile	DS (80)	35x24 *holo stars*	80 x $250	50K	13 : 13	1488a
241	2007-11-15	Chile	DS (80)	35x24 *holo stars*	80 x $250	50K	13 : 13	1488b
242	2007-11-15	Chile	DS (80)	35x24 *holo stars*	80 x $250	50K	13 : 13	1488c
243	2007-11-15	Chile	DS (80)	35x24 *holo stars*	80 x $250	50K	13 : 13	1488d
244	2007-12-05	Thailand	SS(9)	40x39 Ø29	8x5 Baht, 80 Baht	1.3M	imperf	2334
245	2007-12-06	Australia	SS (6) OP	No.238				
246	2007-12-08	Australia	SS (6) OP	No.238				
247	2007-12-20	P. R. China	SS (1)	Penta shape *text*	6 yuan	-	13	3646
248	2007-12-27	Peru	DS (2)	40x30 *text*	2 x S3.00	-	13½ : 14	1613b
249	**2008**-01-18	Singapore	DS (1)	40x30 *CCH*	$5	-	13¾ : 13¾	1291
250	2008-01-18	Singapore	DS (1)	40x30 *CCH*	$10	-	13¾ : 13¾	1292
251	2008-01-18	Singapore	MS (2)	105x65/40x30 *CCH*	$5 + $10	-	13¾ : 13¾	1293
252	2008-01-23	Macau	DS (25)	35x35 *CCH*	25 x 10 MOP	350K	14.28 : 14.28	1239
253	2008-01-23	Macau	SS (1)	138x90/35x35 *CCH*	10 MOP	350K	14.28 : 14.28	1240
254	2008-06-01	Türkmenistan	DS (7)	Green 29x29 *29x29*	7 x ADGGOST	-	simulated	240-247
255	2008-06-01	Türkmenistan	DS (7)	Gold 29x29 *29x29*	7 x ADGGOST	-	simulated	248-257
256	2008-06-01	Türkmenistan	DS (7)	Silver 29x29 *29x29*	7 x ADGGOST	-	simulated	258-260
257	2008-06-05	Austria	SS (1)	35x42	3.75€	-	14 : 14	2131
258	2008-06-22	Romania	SS (2)	48x33 *CCH*	1.40L, 4.70L	17.6K	13½ : 13½	5056b

* DS = Definitive Stamp, MS = Miniature Sheet, SS = Souvenir Sheet, PS = Postal Stationary, PC = Postal Card, BL = Booklet, (stamps/sheet), C = Cinderella, OP = Overprinted, CCH = Contour-Cut Hologram or Foil, K= 1,000, M = 1,000,000.

** First figures: stamp size in mm (horizontal side x vertical side); Second figures: *hologram size in mm*.

Table 2-9. Postage stamps and souvenir sheets with holograms

No.	Date	Country	Type*	Size: S H** [mm]	Denomination	Edition	Perforation	Scott No.
259	2008-06-22	Romania	SS (2)	48x33 *text*	1.40L, 4.70L	500	13½ : 13½	5056b
260	2008-08-01	Thailand	SS (5)	125x170/30x49 *22x28*	3x5,10, 25 Baht	100K	13½ : 13½	2375
261	2008-08-01	Thailand	SS (1)	30x49 *22x28*	25 Baht	100K	13½ : 13½	2375var
262	2008-08-02	Thailand	SS (1)	30x49 *22x28*	25 Baht	100K	13½ : 13½	2375var
263	2008-08-03	Thailand	SS (1)	30x49 *22x28*	25 Baht	100K	13½ : 13½	2375var
264	2008-08-04	Thailand	SS (1)	30x49 *22x28*	25 Baht	100K	13½ : 13½	2375var
265	2008-08-05	Thailand	SS (1)	30x49 *22x28*	25 Baht	100K	13½ : 13½	2375var
266	2008-08-06	Thailand	SS (1)	30x49 *22x28*	25 Baht	100K	13½ : 13½	2375var
267	2008-08-07	Thailand	SS (1)	30x49 *22x28*	25 Baht	100K	13½ : 13½	2375var
268	2008-08-08	Thailand	SS (1)	30x49 *22x28*	25 Baht	100K	13½ : 13½	2375var
269	2008-08-09	Thailand	SS (1)	30x49 *22x28*	25 Baht	100K	13½ : 13½	2375var
270	2008-08-10	Thailand	SS (1)	30x49 *22x28*	25 Baht	100K	13½ : 13½	2375var
271	2008-08-02	Argentina	MS (1)	50x50 *CCH*	$4 ARS	-	14 : 14	2496
272	2008-08-08	P. R. China	SS (8)	200/120/44x33 *foil*	8 x 120 fen	-	13 : 13½	not listed
273	2008-08-09	Thailand	DS (10)	35x65 *CCH*	10 x 10 Baht	700K	13 : 13¼	2378
274	2008-08-09	Thailand	DS (10)	35x65 *CCH*	10 x 10 Baht	700K	13 : 13¼	2379
275	2008-08-09	Thailand	SS (2)	35x65 *CCH*	2 x 30 Baht	100K	13 : 13¼	2379a
276	2008-09-19	P. R. China	C (3)	180x85/50x38 *text*	No value	-	12 : 12	3664c
277	2008-10-09	Åland	DS (30)	33.35x33 *CCH*	30x0.55€	450K	13¾ : 13¼	280
278	2008-10-09	Åland	C (20)	146x210/24x20 *CCH*	None	14K	-	-
279	2008-12-08	Australia	SS(10)	156x215/26x37.5 *foil*	10x55¢	-	14.6 : 13.86	3006d
280	**2009**-01-09	Singapore	DS (1)	40x30 *CCH*	$5	-	13¾ : 13¾	1354
281	2009-01-09	Singapore	DS (1)	40x30 *CCH*	$10	-	13¾ : 13¾	1355
282	2009-01-09	Singapore	MS (2)	105x65/40x30 *CCH*	$5 + $10	-	13¾ : 13¾	1356
283	2009-03-02	Lichtenstein	DS (20)	32.5x32.5 *foil*	20 x 1.30 CHF	-	14 : 14¼	1432
284	2009-03-21	Romania	SS(2)	130x100/33x48 *CCH*	8.10 L 1.60 L	1K	14 : 14	5095b
285	2009-05-02	Indonesia	SS (3)	117x70/30x40 *foil*	3 x 30000 rp	300K	12¾ : 13½	2181
286	2009-05-06	Czech Republic	DS (6)	138x114/37.5x37.5 *14x8*	6 x 17 Kc	210K	11½ : 11½	3419
287	2009-06-30	Japan	DS (1)	31x38 *CCH*	80 yen	-	15 : 15	3125a
288	2009-06-30	Japan	DS (1)	31x38 *CCH*	80 yen	-	15 : 15	3125b
289	2009-06-30	Japan	DS (1)	31x38 *CCH*	80 yen	-	15 : 15	3125c
290	2009-06-30	Japan	DS (1)	31x38 *CCH*	80 yen	-	15 : 15	3125d

* DS = Definitive Stamp, MS = Miniature Sheet, SS = Souvenir Sheet, PS = Postal Stationary, PC = Postal Card, BL = Booklet, (stamps/sheet), C = Cinderella, OP = Overprinted, CCH = Contour-Cut Hologram or Foil, K= 1,000, M = 1,000,000.

** First figures: stamp size in mm (horizontal side x vertical side); Second figures: *hologram size in mm*.

Table 2-10. Postage stamps and souvenir sheets with holograms

No.	Date	Country	Type*	Size: S H* [mm]	Denomination	Edition	Perforation	Scott No.
291	2009-06-30	Japan	SS (4)	80x120/31x38 *CCH*	4 x 80 yen	-	15 : 15	3125
292	2009-07-23	Australia	SS(10) OP	No.279		200		not listed
293	2009-08-14	Ecuador	MS (2)	37x28 *CCH text*	2 x $3.00	6K	13½ : 13½	1972
294	2009-08-16	P. R. China	SS(1)	176x126/ Ø55 *text*	6 yuan	-	circular 13½	not listed
295	2009-08-31	Malaysia	MS (1)	30x40 *foil*	RM5.00	-	14 : 14	1265
296	2009-10-02	Portugal	DS (1)	30.6x40 *CCH*	0.80€	-	13 : 13	3159
297	2009-10-22	Great Britain	DS (10)	35x35 *20x20*	10 x 1st	-	14½ : 14½	not yet listed
298	2009-11-02	Canada	BL (12)	24x24 *spots*	Permanent	12M	10 : imperf	2344
299	2009-11-20	Switzerland	DS (20)	28x33 *star*	20 x 0.85CHF	-	13½ : 13¼	1364
300	2009-11-20	Switzerland	DS (20)	28x33 *star*	20 x 1.00CHF	-	13½ : 13¼	1365
301	2009-11-20	Switzerland	DS (20)	28x33 *star*	20 x 1.30CHF	-	13½ : 13¼	1366
302	2009-12-23	Ukraine	MS (6)	133x86/47x47x47 *foil*	1.50 to 3.30	100K	11½ : 11½	742
303	**2010**-01-02	Macau	DS (25)	35x35 *foil*	25 x 5 MOP	250K	14½ : 14½	1304
304	2010-01-02	Macau	SS (1)	138x90/35x35 *foil*	10 MOP	250K	14½ : 14½	1305
305	2010-01-08	Singapore	DS (1)	40x30 *CCH*	$5	-	13¾ : 13¾	1408
306	2010-01-08	Singapore	DS (1)	40x30 *CCH*	$10	-	13¾ : 13¾	1409
307	2010-01-08	Singapore	SS (2)	105x65/40x30 *CCH*	$5 + $10	-	13¾ : 13¾	1410
308	2010-01-18	South Africa	DS (1)	52x28 *foil*	SA small letter	-	14 : imperf	1401a
309	2010-01-18	South Africa	DS (1)	28x28 *foil*	SA small letter	-	14 : 14	1401b
310	2010-01-18	South Africa	DS (1)	28x39 *foil*	SA small letter	-	14 : imperf	1401d
311	2010-01-18	South Africa	DS (1)	80x40 *foil*	SA small letter	-	14 : imperf	1401c
312	2010-01-18	South Africa	DS (1)	80x40 *foil*	SA small letter	-	14 : imperf	1401e
313	2010-01-18	South Africa	MS (5)	120x80 *spots*	5 x SA small letter	-	14	1401
314	2010-01-28	Thailand	DS (1)	23x28 *spots*	3 Baht	-	13 :13	2477
315	2010-01-28	Thailand	DS (1)	23x28 *spots*	3 Baht	-	13 :13	2478
316	2010-01-28	Thailand	DS (1)	23x28 *spots*	3 Baht	-	13 :13	2479
317	2010-01-28	Thailand	DS (1)	23x28 *spots*	3 Baht	-	13 :13	2480
318	2010-01-28	Thailand	DS (1)	23x28 *spots*	3 Baht	-	13 :13	2481
319	2010-01-28	Thailand	DS (1)	23x28 *spots*	3 Baht	-	13 :13	2482
320	2010-01-28	Thailand	DS (6)	175x75/23x28 *spots*	6 x 3 Baht	-	13 :13	2477-82 BK1
321	2010-01-28	Thailand	BL (10)	243x70/23x28 *spots*	6 x 10 x 3 Baht	-	13 :13	2477-82 BK6
322	2010-04-28	Czech Republic	BL (10)	185x84/23x31 *14x8*	10 x A	-	15 : 16½	3450a

* DS = Definitive Stamp, MS = Miniature Sheet, SS = Souvenir Sheet, PS = Postal Stationary, PC = Postal Card, BL = Booklet, (stamps/sheet), C = Cinderella, OP = Overprinted, CCH = Contour-Cut Hologram or Foil, K= 1,000, M = 1,000,000.

** First figures: stamp size in mm (horizontal side x vertical side); Second figures: *hologram size in mm*.

Table 2-11. Postage stamps and souvenir sheets with holograms

No.	Date	Country	Type*	Size: S H* [mm]	Denomination	Edition	Perforation	Scott No.
323	2010-05-05	Czech Republic	DS (6)	146x112/33x33 *14x8*	6 x 17 Kc	204K	11¼ : 11¼	3452
324	2010-05-10	Malaysia	DS (1)	60x40 *Ø14*	5 MYR	-	14 : 14	in 1297
325	2010-05-10	Malaysia	SS (1)	110x80/60x40 *Ø14*	5 MYR	-	14 : 14	1297
326	2010-05-26	Czech Republic	BL (6)	147x72/44x55 *14x8*	6 x Z	-	14½ : 14½	3455a
327	2010-07-27	Great Britain	DS (10)	35x35 *20x20*	10 x 1st	-	14½ : 14½	not yet listed
328	2010-09-06	France	DS (1)	30x40 *CCH*	0.75€	4.7M	13 : 13	4959
329	2010-09-06	France	DS (1)	40x30 *CCH*	0.58€	4.7M	13 : 13	4960
330	2010-09-06	France	DS (1)	40x30 *CCH*	0.95€	4.7M	13 : 13	4961
331	2010-09-06	France	DS (1)	40x30 *CCH*	0.58€	4.7M	13 : 13	4962
332	2010-09-06	France	SS (4)	110x160/30x40 *CCH*	6.88€	1.65M	13 : 13	4962a
333	2010-10-09	Nigeria	DS (1)	25x40 *Ø6*	₦20	10M	12¼ : 12½	822
334	2010-10-09	Nigeria	DS (1)	25x40 *Ø6*	₦30	10M	12¼ : 12½	823
335	2010-10-09	Nigeria	DS (1)	24.5x40 *Ø6*	₦50	10M	12¼ : 12½	825
336	2010-10-09	Nigeria	DS (1)	24.5x40 *Ø6*	₦50	10M	12¼ : 12½	824
337	2010-10-09	Nigeria	DS (1)	24.5x40 *Ø6*	₦120	10M	12¼ : 12½	829
338	2010-10-09	Nigeria	DS (1)	40x24.5 *Ø6*	₦90	10M	12¼ : 12½	827A
339	2010-10-09	Nigeria	DS (1)	24.5x40 *6x6*	₦20	10M	13 : 13	822A
340	2010-10-09	Nigeria	DS (1)	24.5x40 *6x6*	₦50	10M	13 : 13	827
341	2010-10-09	Nigeria	DS (1)	24.5x40 *6x6*	₦50	10M	13 : 13	826
342	2010-10-09	Nigeria	DS (1)	24.5x40 *6x6*	₦50	10M	13 : 13	not yet listed
343	2010-10-09	Nigeria	DS (1)	40x24.5 *6x6*	₦30	10M	13 : 13	not yet listed
344	2010-10-09	Nigeria	DS (1)	40x24.5 *6x6*	₦100	10M	13 : 13	828
345	2010-10-20	Czech Republic	BL (10)	186x84/23x30 *14x8*	10 x A	-	15 : 16½	3473 BK
346	2010-10-20	Singapore	DS (1)	26x37.5 *CCD*	55¢	-	14.40 :14.62	1454
347	2010-10-20	Singapore	DS (1)	26x37.5 *CCD*	55¢	-	14.40 :14.62	1455
348	2010-10-20	Singapore	DS (1)	26x37.5 *CCD*	55¢	-	14.40 :14.62	1456
349	2010-10-20	Singapore	DS (1)	26x37.5 *stars*	55¢	-	14.40 :14.62	1457
350	2010-10-20	Singapore	DS (1)	26x37.5 *CCD*	1st or $1.10	-	14.40 :14.62	1458
351	2010-10-20	Singapore	DS (1)	26x37.5 *CCD*	1st or $1.10	-	14.40 :14.62	1459
352	2010-10-20	Singapore	DS (1)	26x37.5 *CCD*	1st or $1.10	-	14.40 :14.62	1460
353	2010-10-20	Singapore	DS (1)	26x37.5 *stars*	1st or $1.10	-	14.40 :14.62	1461
354	2010-10-20	Singapore	SS (8)	210x148/26x37.5 *CCD*	4x$1.10 + 4x55¢	-	14.40 :14.62	1462

* DS = Definitive Stamp, MS = Miniature Sheet, SS = Souvenir Sheet, PS = Postal Stationary, PC = Postal Card, BL = Booklet, (stamps/sheet), C = Cinderella, OP = Overprinted, CCH = Contour-Cut Hologram or Foil, K= 1,000, M = 1,000,000.

** First figures: stamp size in mm (horizontal side x vertical side); Second figures: *hologram size in mm*.

Table 2-12. Postage stamps and souvenir sheets with holograms

No.	Date	Country	Type*	Size: S H** [mm]	Denomination	Edition	Perforation	Scott No.
355	2010-11-04	Switzerland	DS (20)	28x33 *star*	0.85 CHF	-	13½ : 13¼	1403
356	2010-11-04	Switzerland	DS (20)	28x33 *snow crystal*	1.00 CHF	-	13½ : 13¼	1404
357	2010-11-04	Switzerland	DS (20)	28x33 *star*	1.40 CHF	-	13½ : 13¼	1405
358	2010-12-31	Ukraine	MS (6)	132x86/47x47x47 *foil*	3x1.50 +3x2.00	-	11½ : 11½	813
359	**2011**-01-01	Taiwan	MS (4)	*160x87/30x30/24x48 foil*	2x$5 + 2x$25	800K	13½ : 13½	3975
360	2011-01-05	Macau	DS (5)	35x35 *CCH*	5 MOP	250K	13.25 : 13.25	1332a-d
361	2011-01-05	Macau	SS (1)	138x90/35x35 *CCH*	10 MOP	250K	14.28 : 14.28	1334
362	2011-02-09	Czech Republic	BL (10)	186x84/26x30 *14x8*	10 x A	-	15 : 16½	3486a BK
363	2011-05-04	Czech Republic	BL (10)	186x84/26x30 *14x8*	10 x A	-	15 : 16½	3498a BK
364	2011-05-04	Czech Republic	DS (6)	146x112/33x33 *14x8*	6 x 20 Kc	192K	11¼ : 11¼	3499
365	2011-06-01	Romania	SS (2)	119x112/33x48 *stars*	0.5 L + 8.10 L	9K	13 : 13	not yet listed
366	2011-07-07	Japan	DS (10)	127x187/31x38 *CCH*	10 x 80 Yen	4M	13 : 13	3343
367	2011-07-27	Great Britain	DS (10)	35x35 *20x20*	10 x 1st	-	14½ : 14½	not yet listed
368	2011-07-28	Japan	DS (10)	188x127 *spots*	10 x 80 Yen	3M	13 : 13	not yet listed
369	2011-08-05	Kyrgyzstan	SS(8) OP	No.89				384
370	2011-08-31	Czech Republic	DS (6)	122x79/54x33 *14x8*	6 x E	-	11½ : 11½	3508a
371	2011-10-05	Czech Republic	BL (10)	186x84/26x34 *14x8*	10 x A	-	15 : 16½	3512a
372	2011-11-10	Taiwan	SS (1)	100x60/70x35 *text*	$25	800K	13¼ : 13¼	not yet listed
373	2011-10-13	United Nations	DS (2x8)	200x100/32x40 *spots*	4x0.62€,4x 0.70€	100K	13 : 13	505, 506
374	2011-10-13	United Nations	DS (2x8)	200x100/32x40 *spots*	4x0.98, 4x1.40CHF	88K	13 : 13	544, 545
375	2011-10-13	United Nations	DS (2x8)	200x100/32x40 *spots*	4x$0.44, 4x$0.98	92K	13 : 13	1035, 1036
376	2011-10-17	Peru	SS (1)	80x114/30x40 *text*	S10	100K	14 : 14	1798
377	2011-11-01	Canada	BL (12)	160x72/24x24 *spots*	12 x Permanent	27M	13½ : 13½	2491a
378	2011-11-15	Antigua & Barbuda	DS (12)	182x133/40x30 *foil*	12 x 65¢	-	13 : 13	3177
379	2011-11-15	Liberia	DS (12)	182x133/40x30 *foil*	12 x $18	-	13 : 13	2779
380	2011-11-15	Guyana	DS (12)	182x133/40x30 *foil*	12 x $50	-	13 : 13	4092
381	2011-11-15	Grenada	DS (12)	182x133/40x30 *foil*	12 x 65¢	-	13 : 13	3838
382	2011-11-15	Grenada Carriacou & Petite Martinique	DS (12)	182x133/40x30 *foil*	12 x 65¢	-	13 : 13	not listed
383	2011-12-01	Russia	DS (9)	138x138/37x37 *text spots*	9 x 20 RUB	567K	11¼ : 11¼	7325
384	**2012**-01-05	Macau	DS (25)	35x35 *CCH*	5 MOP	250K	14½ : 14½	1356a

* DS = Definitive Stamp, MS = Miniature Sheet, SS = Souvenir Sheet, PS = Postal Stationary, PC = Postal Card, BL = Booklet, (stamps/sheet), C = Cinderella, OP = Overprinted, CCH = Contour-Cut Hologram or Foil, K= 1,000, M = 1,000,000.

** First figures: stamp size in mm (horizontal side x vertical side); Second figures: *hologram size in mm*.

Table 2-13. Postage stamps and souvenir sheets with holograms

No.	Date	Country	Type*	Size: S H* [mm]	Denomination	Edition	Perforation	Scott No.
385	2012-01-12	Malaysia	SS (1)	115x99/50x60 CCH	RM5	20K	13¾ : 14	1379
386	2012-01-12	Brazil	DS (24)	25x59 Ø18	1.60 BRL	300K	12 : 11½	3208
387	2012-04-03	Australia	MS (2)	105x70/26x37.5 text	60¢, $2.35	-	14.6 : 13.86	3677a
388	2012-04-20	Ecuador	MS (1)	90x70 (38x28) text	$4.00	7K	13 : 13½	2056
389	2012-04-20	Ecuador	MS (1)	90x70 (38x28) text	$4.00	7K	13 : 13½	2057
390	2012-04-27	P. R. China	DS (1)	28x55 foil	1.20 yuan	-	13 : 13	3993
391	2012-04-27	P. R. China	DS (1)	28x55 foil	1.20 yuan	-	13 : 13	3994
392	2012-04-27	P. R. China	DS (1)	28x55 foil	1.20 yuan	-	13 : 13	3995
393	2012-04-27	P. R. China	DS (1)	28x55 foil	1.20 yuan	-	13 : 13	3996
394	2012-04-27	P. R. China	SS (8)	166x148/28x55 foil	8x1.20 yuan	-	13 : 13	3996a
395	2012-06-01	Jersey	DS (10)	37.5x51 29x39	£10	-	13¼ : 13¼	1590
396	2012-06-04	Kiribati	DS (1)	42.5x28 text Ø4.5	0.50 AUD	-	14 : 14	991
397	2012-06-04	Kiribati	DS (1)	42.5x28 text Ø4.5	0.75 AUD	-	14 : 14	992
398	2012-06-04	Kiribati	DS (1)	42.5x28 text Ø4.5	1.00 AUD	-	14 : 14	993
399	2012-06-04	Kiribati	DS (1)	42.5x28 text Ø4.5	2.50 AUD	-	14 : 14	994
400	2012-06-18	Malaysia	SS (1)OP	No.385				
401	2012-06-20	Czech Republic	DS (20)	298/210/30x23 13x13	20 x E	-	12 : 12	3542
402	2012-06-20	Czech Republic	DS (20)	298/210/30x23 13x13	20 x A	-	12 : 12	3541
403	2012-06-20	Czech Republic	DS (20)	298/210/23x30 13x13	20 x A	-	12 : 12	3540
404	2012-06-25	Ukraine-Poland	SS (3)	110x90/30x57.4 22x22	3x13.80	30K	12½ : 12½	not yet listed
405	2012-07-06	Japan	DS (10)	127x187/29x37 CCD	10 x 80 yen	4M	13 ; 13	3449
406	2012-08-01	Ecuador	MS (1)	126x69/55x35 text	$3.00	7K	13 : 13½	2069 (gold)
407	2012-08-01	Ecuador	MS (1)	126x69/55x35 text	$3.00	7K	13 : 13½	2069a (silver)
408	2012-08-01	Ecuador	MS (1)	126x69/55x35 RED	$3.00	7K	13 : 13½	2069b (red)
409	2012-08-12	Thailand	SS (9)	150x180/40x40 text	8x5 baht, 80 baht	700K	imperf	2705i
410	2012-08-29	Great Britain	DS (10)	35x35 20x20	10 x 1st	-	14½ : 14½	not yet listed
411	2012-09-05	Czech Republic	BL (6)	244x79/30x23 14x8	6 x A	-	11½ : 11½	not yet listed
412	2012-09-18	Australia	MS(5)	170x80/35x35 CCH	3x60c,$1.65,$2.35	500	imperf	not listed
413	2012-09-26	P. R. China	DS(1)	30x40 CCH	1.20 yuan	-	13½ : 13½	not yet listed
414	2012-09-26	P. R. China	DS(1)	30x40 CCH	1.20 yuan	-	13½ : 13½	not yet listed
415	2012-09-26	P. R. China	SS(1)	96x126/40x86 foil	6 yuan	-	13 : 13½	not yet listed
416	2012-09-27	Great Britain	DS (10)	35x35 20x20	10 x 1st	-	14½ : 14½	not yet listed

* DS = Definitive Stamp, MS = Miniature Sheet, SS = Souvenir Sheet, PS = Postal Stationary, PC = Postal Card, BL = Booklet, (stamps/sheet), C = Cinderella, OP = Overprinted, CCH = Contour-Cut Hologram or Foil, K= 1,000, M = 1,000,000.

** First figures: stamp size in mm (horizontal side x vertical side); Second figures: *hologram size in mm*.

Table 2-14. Postage stamps and souvenir sheets with holograms

No.	Date	Country	Type*	Size: S H* [mm]	Denomination	Edition	Perforation	Scott No.
417	2012-09-27	Malaysia	DS (1)	30x40 *CCD*	0.60sen	-	14 : 14	1421
418	2012-09-27	Malaysia	DS (1)	30x40 *CCD*	0.60sen	-	14 : 14	1422
419	2012-09-27	Malaysia	DS (1)	30x40 *CCD*	0.60sen	-	14 : 14	1423
420	2012-09-27	Malaysia	DS (1)	30x40 *CCD*	0.60sen	-	14 : 14	1424
421	2012-09-27	Malaysia	DS (1)	30x40 *CCD*	0.60sen	-	14 : 14	1425
422	2012-10-05	Czech Republic	BL (10)	185x84/30x23 *14x8*	10 x A	-	14 : 14	not yet listed
423	2012-11-05	Luxembourg	DS (12)	140x190/38x38 *stars*	12x0.60+0.05CHF	-	13 : 13	not yet listed
424	2012-11-05	Luxembourg	DS (12)	140x190/38x38 *stars*	12x0.85+0.10CHF	-	13 : 13	not yet listed
425	2012-11-19	Malaysia	SS (1)	120x90/70x45 *hearts*	RM5	-	14 : 14	1438
426	2012-11-24	Nigeria	DS (1)	40x24.5 *6x6*	₦50	-	13 : 13	not yet listed
427	2012-11-24	Nigeria	DS (1)	24.5x40 *6x6*	₦50	-	13 : 13	not yet listed
428	2012-11-24	Nigeria	DS (1)	24.5x40 *6x6*	₦50	-	13 : 13	not yet listed
429	2012-11-24	Nigeria	DS (1)	40x24.5 *6x6*	₦120	-	13 : 13	not yet listed
430	2012-12-01	Malaysia	SS(1)OP	No.425				
431	2012-12-12	Taiwan	SS (4)	140x95/50x30 *CCH*	NT$12	800K	14 : 13¼	4082
432	**2013**-01-03	Macau	DS (5)	35x35 *CCH*	5 MOP	250K	13.25 : 13.25	not yet listed
433	2013-01-03	Macau	SS (1)	138x90/35x35 *CCH*	10 MOP	250K	14.28 : 14.28	not yet listed
434	2013-02-05	Malaysia	MS (1)	73x100/30x50 *foil*	5RM	-	14 : 14	not yet listed
435	2013-04-10	Czech Republic	BL (25)	185x84/30x23 *13x13*	25 x A	-	14 : 14	not yet listed
436	2013-04.30	Curaçao	SS (2)	120x80/35x35 *foil*	2 x 1000c	-	13¼ : 14	not yet listed
437	2013-05-02	Czech Republic	BL (6)	185x84/37x37 *14x8*	6 x 25Kc	-	12 : 12	not yet listed
438	2013-05-11	P. R. China	DS (16)	182x162/33x33 *foil*	16 x 1.20 yuan	-	13½ : 13	not yet listed
439	2013-05-11	P. R. China	SS (8)	185x160/33x33 *foil*	8 x 1.20 yuan	-	13½ : 13	not yet listed
440	2013-05-29	Czech Republic	BL (10)	185x84/33x26 *14x8*	10 x A	-	11½. : 11½	not yet listed
441	2013-06-10	Czech Republic	BL (25)	185x84/30x23 *14x13*	25 x A	-	14 : 14	not yet listed
442	2013-06-26	Czech Republic	BL (10)	185x84/33x54 *14x8*	10 x E	-	11½ : 11.½	not yet listed
443	2013-07-05	Japan	DS (10)	127x187/29x37 *CCD*	10 x 80 yen	5M sheets	13 ; 13	not yet listed
444	2013-08-14	Hungary	SS (3)	155x140/40x40 *foil*	3 x 600Ft (HUF)	10K	13 : 13	not yet listed
445	2013-08-23	Singapore	SS (2)	102x81/31.5x48 *foil*	2 x $5	2K	13 : 13	not yet listed
446	2013-08-26	Israel	SS (12)	160x160/30x30Ø45	8 x 2₪. (ILS)	-	13 : 13	not yet listed
447	2013-09-04	Czech Republic	BL (8)	244x79/56x34 *14x8*	8 x A	-	15 : 15	not yet listed

* DS = Definitive Stamp, MS = Miniature Sheet, SS = Souvenir Sheet, PS = Postal Stationary, PC = Postal Card, BL = Booklet, (stamps/sheet), C = Cinderella, OP = Overprinted, CCH = Contour-Cut Hologram or Foil, K= 1,000, M = 1,000,000.

** First figures: stamp size in mm (horizontal side x vertical side); Second figures: *hologram size in mm*.

Table 2-15. Postage stamps and souvenir sheets with holograms

No.	Date	Country	Type*	Size: S H** [mm]	Denomination	Edition	Perforation	Scott No.
448	2013-09-04	Czech Republic	BL (8)	244x79/56x34 *14x8*	8 x E	-	15 : 15	not yet listed
449	2013-09-04	Czech Republic	BL (8)	244x79/56x34 *14x8*	8 x A	-	15 : 15	not yet listed
450	2013-10-22	Peru	SS (1)	*80x100/30x40 text*	$10.00	5K	13½ : 13.½	not yet listed
451	2013-10-22	Peru	SS (1)	*100x80/30x40 text*	$10.00	5K	13½ : 13.½	not yet listed
452	2013-12-04	Japan	DS (10)	*127x187/28x36 CCD*	10 x 80 yen	5M sheets	13 : 13	not yet listed
453	2013-12-20	Nigeria	DS (1)	*40x24.5 6x6*	₦50	5M sheets	13 : 13	not yet listed
454	2013-12-20	Nigeria	DS (1)	*40x24.5 6x6*	₦120	5M sheets	13 : 13	not yet listed

* DS = Definitive Stamp, MS = Miniature Sheet, SS = Souvenir Sheet, PS = Postal Stationary, PC = Postal Card, BL = Booklet, (stamps/sheet), C = Cinderella, OP = Overprinted, CCH = Contour-Cut Hologram or Foil, K= 1,000, M = 1,000,000.

** First figures: stamp size in mm (horizontal side x vertical side); Second figures: *hologram size in mm*.

Table 3. Hologram stamps issued by country

COUNTRY	NO.	ISSUE DATE	TYPE & DENOMINATION
Åland	55	1997-06-09	Souvenir sheet 20Fmk
	136	2000-10-27	Souvenir sheet No value
	151	2001-10-16	Souvenir sheet No value
	164	2002-10-09	Souvenir sheet No value
	208	2005-10-10	Definite stamp 0.45€
	219	2006-10-09	Definite stamp Domestic
	277	2008-10-09	Definite stamp 0.55€
	278	2008-10-09	Souvenir sheet No value
Antigua & Barbuda	378	2011-11-15	Definitive stamp 12x65¢
Argentina	271	2008-08-02	Miniature sheet $4
Ascension Island	56	2007-06-20	Souvenir sheet, £1
Australia	36	1995-04-05	Definitive stamp $1.20
	37	1995-04-05	Definitive stamp $2.50
	46	1996-09-05	Definitive stamp 45¢
	47	1996-09-05	Definitive stamp 1.20
	107	1999-10-01	Miniature sheet 45,50¢
	112	1999-11-01	Definitive stamp 45¢
	113	1999-11-05	Definitive stamp 45¢
	114	1999-11-05	OP Miniature sheet 45,50¢
	118	2000-03-25	OP Miniature sheet 45,50¢
	134	2000-10-03	Souvenir sheet 45¢
	135	2000-10-22	OP Souvenir sheet 45¢
	140	2001-01-08	Definitive stamp 45¢
	141	2001-01-08	Definitive stamp $1.35
	142	2001-01-08	Miniature stamp 45¢,$1.35
	143	2001-02-01	OP Souvenir sheet 45¢
	144	2001-04-24	Definitive stamp 45¢
	176	2003-09-24	Souvenir sheet 50¢
	177	2003-10-01	OP Souvenir sheet 50¢
	178	2003-10-04	OP Souvenir sheet 50¢
	179	2003-10-10	OP Souvenir sheet 50¢
	182	2003-11-21	OP Souvenir sheet 50¢
	190	2004-10-12	Souvenir sheet 50¢
	191	2004-10-12	Souvenir sheet 50¢
	238	2007-10-02	Souvenir sheet 50¢,$1
	244	2007-12-06	OP Souvenir sheet 50¢,$1
	245	2007-12-08	OP Souvenir sheet 50¢,$1
	279	2008-12-08	Souvenir sheet 55¢
	292	2009-07-23	OP Souvenir sheet 55¢
	387	2012-04-03	Miniature stamp 60¢,$2.35
Austria	1	1988-10-18	Definitive stamp 8Ats
	257	2008-06-05	Souvenir sheet 3.75€

COUNTRY	NO.	ISSUE DATE	TYPE & DENOMINATION
Bahamas	64	2007-06-20	Souvenir sheet 70¢
Belarus	145	2001-07-03	Definitive stamp 500r
Bhutan	24	1994-11-11	Souvenir sheet 30NU
	25	1994-11-11	Souvenir sheet 36NU
Brazil	2	1989-10-14	Souvenir sheet 2,3,5NCz$
	103	1999-08-20	Definitive stamp 1.20R$
	104	1999-08-20	Souvenir sheet 1.20R$
	174	2003-08-10	Souvenir sheet 2.90R$
	386	2012-01-12	Definitive sheet 1.60R$
British Antarctic Territory	61	2007-06-20	Souvenir sheet £1
British Indian Ocean Territory	57	2007-06-20	Souvenir sheet 74p
Canada	13	1992-10-01	Definitive stamp 42¢
	108	1999-10-12	Definitive stamp 46¢
	109	1999-10-12	Souvenir sheet 46¢
	177	2003-10-01	Definitive stamp 48¢
	183	2004-01-08	Definitive stamp 49¢
	184	2004-01-08	Definitive stamp $1.40
	185	2004-01-08	Souvenir sheet $1.40
	186	2004-01-30	OP Souvenir sheet $1.40
	209	2005-11-02	Block 50¢
	226	2007-01-05	Definitive stamp 52¢
	239	2007-11-01	Block 52¢
	298	2009-11-02	Block Permanent
	377	2011-11-01	Block Permanent
Chile	240	2007-11-15	Definitive stamp $250
	241	2007-11-15	Definitive stamp $250
	242	2007-11-15	Definitive stamp $250
	243	2007-11-15	Definitive stamp $250
China P. R.	41	1996-05-10	Souvenir sheet 5Yuan
	44	1996-07-18	Souvenir sheet 3Yuan
	48	1996-10-09	Souvenir sheet 3Yuan
	247	2007-12-20	Souvenir sheet 6Yuan
	272	2008-08-08	Souvenir sheet 1.20Yuan
	276	2008-09-19	Souvenir sheet 1.20 Yuan
	294	2009-08-16	Souvenir sheet
	438	2013-05-11	Definitive stamp 1.20Yuan
	439	2013-05-11	Souvenir sheet 8x1.20Yuan
Congo	97	1999-07-02	Definitive stamp 300Fr
Curaçao	436	2013-04-30	Suvenir sheet 2x1000c
Czech Republic	60	1999-01-04	Postal card 4 korona
	Many different cards with the same hologram issued after this date		
	187	2004-05-01	Definitive stamp 9Kc
	188	2004-05-05	Definitive stamp 9Kc

HOLOGRAPHY AND PHILATELY

COUNTRY	NO.	ISSUE DATE	TYPE & DENOMINATION
Czech Republic (cont.)	200	2005-05-04	Definitive stamp 9Kc
	286	2009-05-06	Definitive stamp 17Kc
	322	2010-04-28	Definitive stamp A
	323	2010-05-05	Definitive stamp 17Kc
	326	2010-05-26	Definitive stamp Z
	345	2010-10-20	Definitive stamp A
	362	2011-02-09	Definitive stamp A
	363	2011-05-04	Definitive stamp A
	364	2011-05-04	Definitive stamp 20Kc
	370	2011-08-31	Definitive stamp E
	371	2011-10-05	Definitive stamp A
	401	2012-06-20	Definitive stamp E
	402	2012-06-20	Definitive stamp A
	403	2012-06-20	Definitive stamp A
	411	2012-09-05	Definitive stamp A
	423	2012-10-05	Definitive stamp A
	435	2013-04-10	Definitive stamp A
	437	2013-05-02	Definitive stamp 25Kc
	440	2013-05-29	Definitive stamp A
	441	2013-06-10	Definitive stamp A
	442	2013-06-26	Definitive stamp E
	447	2013-09-04	Definitive stamp A
	448	2013-09-04	Definitive stamp E
	449	2013-09-04	Definitive stamp A
Ecuador	293	2009-08-14	Miniature sheet $3
	388	2012-04-20	Miniature sheet $4
	389	2012-04-20	Miniature sheet $4
	405	2012-08-01	Miniature sheet $3
	406	2012-08-01	Miniature sheet $3
	407	2012-08-01	Miniature sheet $3
Falkland Islands	60	2007-06-20	Souvenir sheet £1
Finland	4	1990-01-19	Definitive stamp 1.90Fmk
	5	1990-01-19	Definitive stamp 2.50Fmk
	10	1992-05-08	Definitive stamp 2.10Fmk
	11	1992-05-08	Definitive stamp 2.90Fmk
	12	1992-05-08	Definitive stamp 3.10Fmk
	15	1993-05-06	4 Postal cards Int'l rate
	27-35	1995-01-30	Booklet 2.80Fmk
	119	2000-05-30	Souvenir sheet 10.50Fmk
	231	2007-01-24	Definitive stamp 0.70€
	232	2007-01-24	Miniature sheet 2x0.70€
France	82	1998-11-09	Souvenir sheet No value
	94	1999-07-02	Definitive stamp 6.70Fr
	95	1999-07-02	Souvenir sheet No value
	137	2000-12-09	Definitive stamp 4.50Fr
	328	2010-09-06	Definitive stamp 0.75€
	329	2010-09-06	Definitive stamp 0.58€
	330	2010-09-06	Definitive stamp 0.95€
	331	2010-09-06	Definitive stamp 0.58€

COUNTRY	NO.	ISSUE DATE	TYPE & DENOMINATION
Gabon	98	1999-07-03	Definitive stamp 225Fr
Germany	70	1998-10-08	Definitive stamp 110 + 50pf
	110	1999-10-14	Definitive stamp 110 + 50pf
	111	1999-10-14	Definitive stamp 300 +100pf
Great Britain	150	2001-10-02	Definitive stamp 65p
	297	2009-10-22	Definitive stamp 10x1st
	327	2010-07-27	Definitive stamp 10x1st
	367	2011-07-27	Definitive stamp 10x1st
	410	2012-08-29	Definitive stamp 10x1st
	416	2012-09-27	Definitive stamp 10x1st
Grenada	78	1998-11-05	Definitive stamp EC$6
	381	2011-11-15	Definitive stamp 12x65¢
Grenada Carriacou & Petite Martinique	382	2011-11-15	Definitive stamp 12x65¢
Grenada/Grenadines	67	1998-02-10	Definitive stamp 1.50EC$
	68	1998-02-10	Souvenir sheet 3.00EC$
	79	1998-11-05	Definitive stamp 8EC$
Guinea	99	1999-07-02	Definitive stamp 750Fr
Guyana	17	1994-02-10	Definitive stamp 300$(GYD)
	18	1994-02-10	Definitive stamp 300$(GYD)
	80	1998-11-05	Definitive stamp 300$(GYD)
	380	2011-11-15	Definitive stamp 12x$50(GYD)
Hong Kong	19	1994-02-15	Postal card 96¢
	20	1994-02-15	Postal card HK$1
	49	1996-11-27	Postal card 1.30$
	50	1996-11-27	Postal card 2.00$
	51	1996-11-27	Postal card 1.80$
	52	1996-11-27	Postal card 5.00$
	53	1996-11-27	Postal card 5.00$
	54	1996-11-27	Postal card 1.00$
	138	2000-12-31	Definitive stamp HK$20
	139	2000-12-31	Souvenir sheet No value
	166	2002-11-24	Souvenir sheet HK$1.40
	167	2002-11-24	Souvenir sheet HK$2.40
	168	2002-11-24	Souvenir sheet HK$3
	169	2002-11-24	Souvenir sheet HK$5
	170	2002-11-24	Souvenir sheet HK$1.40-$5
	235	2007-07-01	Souvenir sheet HK$10
Hungary	7	1991-11-15	Souvenir sheet 20Ft
	23	1994-08-08	Souvenir sheet 100Ft
	40	1996-04-25	Souvenir sheet 200Ft
	45	1996-08-12	Souvenir sheet 200Ft
	84	1999-02-11	Souvenir sheet 1999Ft
	120	2000-06-13	Souvenir sheet 100Ft
	123	2000-06-30	Souvenir sheet 2000Ft
	444	2013-08-14	Souvenir sheet 3x600Ft

HOLOGRAPHY AND PHILATELY

COUNTRY	NO.	ISSUE DATE	TYPE & DENOMINATION
Indonesia	72	1998-10-19	Definitive stamp 4000rp
	73	1998-10-19	Definitive stamp 5000rp
	74	1998-10-19	Definitive stamp 10000rp
	75	1998-10-19	Definitive stamp 15000rp
	76	1998-10-19	Definitive stamp 20000rp
	77	1998-10-19	Souvenir sheet
	285	2009-05-02	Souvenir sheet 30000rp
Iran	217	2006-09-22	Definitive stamp 4400Rls
	218	2006-09-22	Definitive stamp 5500Rls
Isle of Man	21	1994-07-05	Definitive stamp 5£
	66	1997-06-20	Definitive stamp 23p
Israel	446	2013-08-26	souvenir sheet 12x2 ILS
Italy	207	2005-09-21	Definitive stamp 0.80€
Ivory Coast	100	1999-07-03	Definitive stamp 280Fr
Japan	287	2009-06-30	Definitive stamp 80yen
	288	2009-06-30	Definitive stamp 80yen
	289	2009-06-30	Definitive stamp 80yen
	290	2009-06-30	Definitive stamp 80yen
	291	2009-06-30	Souvenir sheet 4x80yen
	366	2011-07-07	Definitive stamp 10x80yen
	368	2011-07-28	Definitive stamp 10x80yen
	405	2012-07-06	Definitive stamp 10x80yen
	443	2013-07-05	Definitive stamp 10x80yen
	452	2013-12-04	Definitive stamp 10x80yen
Jersey	199	2005-04-02	Souvenir sheet £2
	201	2005-05-26	OP Souvenir sheet £2
	213	2006-04-04	Miniature sheet £2
	220	2006-11-16	OP Miniature sheet £2
	395	2012-06-01	Definitive stamp £10
Kiribati	396	2012-06-04	Definitive stamp 0.50AUD
	397	2012-06-04	Definitive stamp 0.75AUD
	398	2012-06-04	Definitive stamp 1.00AUD
	399	2012-06-04	Definitive stamp 2.50AUD
Kyrgyzstan	85	1999-04-27	Definitive stamp 10som
	86	1999-04-27	Definitive stamp 10som
	87	1999-04-27	Definitive stamp 30som
	88	1999-04-27	Definitive stamp 50som
	89	1999-04-27	Souvenir sheet 10/30/50som
	149	2001-09-11	OP Souvenir sheet
	369	2011-08-05	OP Souvenir sheet
Liberia	379	2011-11-15	Definitive stamp 12x$18
Lichtenstein	283	2009-03-02	Definitive stamp 1.30CHF
Lithuania	71	1998-09-10	Definitive stamp 13Lt

COUNTRY	NO.	ISSUE DATE	TYPE & DENOMINATION
Libya	146	2001-09-01	Souvenir sheet 100dirhams
	147	2001-09-01	Souvenir sheet 300dirhams
	148	2001-09-01	Souvenir sheet 300dirhams
	161	2002-09-01	Souvenir sheet 100dirhams
	162	2002-09-01	Souvenir sheet 300dirhams
	163	2002-09-01	Souvenir sheet 300dirhams
Luxembourg	423	2012-11-05	Definitive stamp 0.65CHF
	424	2012-11-05	Definitive stamp 0.95CHF
Macau	93	1999-05-17	Souvenir sheet 8ptcs
	115	1999-12-19	OP Souvenir sheet 8ptcs
	180	2003-10-29	Souvenir sheet 12.00ptcs
	252	2008-01-23	Definitive stamp 10MOP
	253	2008-01-23	Souvenir sheet 10MOP
	303	2010-01-02	Definitive stamp 5MOP
	304	2010-01-02	Souvenir sheet 10MOP
	360	2011-01-05	Definitive stamp 5MOP
	361	2011-01-05	Souvenir sheet 10MOP
	384	2012-01-05	Definitive stamp 5MOP
	432	2013-01-03	Definitive stamp 5MOP
	433	2013-01-03	Souvenir sheet 10MOP
Malaysia	39	1996-01-13	Souvenir sheet 5.00RM
	106	1999-08-30	Souvenir sheet 5.00RM
	214	2006-05-25	Souvenir sheet 5.00RM
	236	2007-07-07	Miniature sheet 5.00RM
	237	2007-08-03	OP Miniature sheet 5.00RM
	295	2009-08-31	Miniature sheet 5.00RM
	324	2010-05-10	Definitive stamp 5.00RM
	325	2010-05-10	Souvenir sheet 5.00RM
	385	2012-01-12	Souvenir sheet 5.00RM
	397	2012-06-18	OP Souvenir sheet 5.00RM
	417	2012-09-27	Souvenir sheet 0.60sen
	418	2012-09-27	Souvenir sheet 0.60sen
	419	2012-09-27	Souvenir sheet 0.60sen
	420	2012-09-27	Souvenir sheet 0.60sen
	421	2012-09-27	Souvenir sheet 0.60sen
	425	2012-11-19	Souvenir sheet 5RM
	430	2012-12-01	OP Souvenir sheet 5RM
	434	2013-02-05	Souvenir sheet 5RM
Monaco	121	2000-06-23	Definitive stamp €0.41
	122	2000-06-23	Definitive stamp €0.69
Mongolia	16	1993-08-27	Souvenir sheet 80Möngö
	125	2000-07-07	Definitive stamp 50₮
	126	2000-07-07	Definitive stamp 100₮
	127	2000-07-07	Definitive stamp 200₮
	128	2000-07-07	Definitive stamp 250₮
	129	2000-07-07	Souvenir sheet 50-250₮
Namibia	116	1999-12-31	Souvenir sheet 9.00N$

HOLOGRAPHY AND PHILATELY

COUNTRY	NO.	ISSUE DATE	TYPE & DENOMINATION
Netherlands/Antilles	69	1998-02-26	Souvenir sheet 750ct
(The) Netherlands	90	1999-05-06	Definitive stamp 80cent
	91	1999-05-06	Definitive stamp 80cent
	92	1999-05-06	Booklet 5x80cent
New Caledonia	96	1999-07-02	Souvenir sheet 700Fr
New Zealand	22	1994-07-20	Definitive stamp 1.50NZ$
Niger	101	1999-07-03	Definitive stamp 200Fr
Nigeria	333	2010-10-09	Definitive stamp ₦20
	334	2010-10-09	Definitive stamp ₦30
	335	2010-10-09	Definitive stamp ₦50
	336	2010-10-09	Definitive stamp ₦50
	337	2010-10-09	Definitive stamp ₦120
	338	2010-10-09	Definitive stamp ₦90
	339	2010-10-09	Definitive stamp ₦20
	340	2010-10-09	Definitive stamp ₦50
	341	2010-10-09	Definitive stamp ₦50
	342	2010-10-09	Definitive stamp ₦50
	343	2010-10-09	Definitive stamp ₦30
	344	2010-10-09	Definitive stamp ₦100
	426	2012-11-24	Definitive stamp ₦50
	427	2012-11-24	Definitive stamp ₦50
	428	2012-11-24	Definitive stamp ₦50
	429	2012-11-24	Definitive stamp ₦120
	453	2013-12-20	Definitive stamp ₦50
	454	2013-12-20	Definitive stamp ₦120
Peru	228	2007-01-05	Definitive stamp $2
	229	2007-01-05	Definitive stamp $2
	230	2007-01-05	Miniature sheet $8.50
	233	2007-02-05	Definitive stamp $2
	234	2007-02-05	Definitive stamp $2
	248	2007-12-27	Definitive stamp $3
	376	2011-10-17	Souvenir sheet $10
	450	2013-10-22	Souvenir sheet $10
	451	2013-10-22	Souvenir sheet $10
Philippines	222	2006-11-24	Definitive stamp $7
	223	2006-11-24	Definitive stamp $20
	224	2006-11-24	Definitive stamp $24
	225	2006-11-24	Definitive stamp $26
Poland	8	1991-11-16	Souvenir sheet 15000zł
	124	2000-07-07	Private OP issue 15000zł
Portugal	175	2003-09-23	Definitive stamp €2.50
	296	2009-10-02	Definitive stamp €0.80
Romania	165	2002-11-21	Souvenir sheet 131000L
	258	2008-06-22	Souvenir sheet 1.40, 4.70L
	259	2008-06-22	Souvenir sheet 1.40, 4.70L
	284	2009-03-21	Souvenir sheet 8.10, 1.60L
	365	2011-06-01	Souvenir sheet 0.50, 8.10L

COUNTRY	NO.	ISSUE DATE	TYPE & DENOMINATION
Russia	383	2011-12-01	Definitive stamp 20RUB
Samoa	58	2007-06-20	Souvenir sheet $2.50
San Marino	14	1993-03-26	Souvenir sheet 2000Lira
Singapore	117	2000-01-01	Souvenir sheet 1$,2$,60¢
	153	2002-08-21	Definitive stamp 50¢
	154	2002-08-21	Definitive stamp 50¢
	155	2002-08-21	Definitive stamp 50¢
	156	2002-08-21	Definitive stamp 50¢
	157	2002-08-21	Definitive stamp FLAO
	158	2002-08-21	Definitive stamp FLAO
	159	2002-08-21	Definitive stamp FLAO
	160	2002-08-21	Definitive stamp FLAO
	249	2008-01-18	Definitive stamp $5
	250	2008-01-18	Definitive stamp$10
	251	2008-01-18	Miniature stamp 5$+$10
	280	2009-01-09	Definitive stamp $5
	281	2009-01-09	Definitive stamp $10
	282	2009-01-09	Miniature sheet $5+$10
	445	2013-08-23	Souvenir stamp 2x$5
Slovenia	181	2003-11-11	Definitive stamp 221SIT
South Africa	189	2004-10-09	Souvenir sheet R12.05
	308	2010-01-18	Definitive stamp SA
	309	2010-01-18	Definitive stamp SA
	310	2010-01-18	Definitive stamp SA
	311	2010-01-18	Definitive stamp SA
	312	2010-01-18	Definitive stamp SA
	313	2010-01-18	Miniature sheet SA
St Helena	63	1997-06-20	Souvenir sheet 75p
St Vincent/Grenadines	81	1998-11-05	Definitive stamp EC$8
S Georgia & S Sandwich Islands	62	1997-06-20	Souvenir sheet 76p
Switzerland	105	1999-08-21	Souvenir sheet 90c
	152	2002-03-12	Definitive stamp CHF1.80
	299	2009-11-20	Definitive stamp CHF0.85
	300	2009-11-20	Definitive stamp CHF1.00
	301	2009-11-20	Definitive stamp CHF1.30
	355	2010-11-04	Definitive stamp CHF0.85
	356	2010-11-04	Definitive stamp CHF0.85
	357	2010-11-04	Definitive stamp CHF1.40
Taiwan	359	2011-01-01	Miniature sheet 2x$5 + 2x$25
	372	2011-11-10	Souvenir sheet $25
	431	2012-12-12	Souvenir sheet NT$12

HOLOGRAPHY AND PHILATELY

COUNTRY	NO.	ISSUE DATE	TYPE & DENOMINATION
Thailand	42	1996-06-09	Definitive stamp 3 Baht
	43	1996-06-09	Souvenir sheet 3 Baht
	192	2004-12-05	Definitive stamp 3 Baht
	193	2004-12-05	Definitive stamp 3 Baht
	194	2004-12-05	Definitive stamp 3 Baht
	195	2004-12-05	Definitive stamp 15 Baht
	196	2004-12-05	Souvenir sheet 3, 15 Baht
	202	2005-05-31	Definitive stamp 5 Baht
	203	2005-05-31	Definitive stamp 5 Baht
	204	2005-05-31	Definitive stamp 5 Baht
	205	2005-05-31	Definitive stamp 5 Baht
	206	2005-05-31	Souvenir sheet 8x5 Baht
	215	2006-05-27	OP Souvenir sheet 8x5 Baht
	216	2006-06-24	Souvenir sheet 20 Baht
	221	2006-11-16	OP Souvenir sheet 20 Baht
	244	2007-12-05	Souvenir sheet 8x5, 80 Baht
	261	2008-08-01	Souvenir sheet 35 Baht
	262	2008-08-02	Souvenir sheet 35 Baht
	263	2008-08-03	Souvenir sheet 35 Baht
	264	2008-08-04	Souvenir sheet 35 Baht
	265	2008-08-05	Souvenir sheet 35 Baht
	266	2008-08-06	Souvenir sheet 35 Baht
	267	2008-08-07	Souvenir sheet 35 Baht
	268	2008-08-08	Souvenir sheet 35 Baht
	269	2008-08-09	Souvenir sheet 35 Baht
	270	2008-08-10	Souvenir sheet 35 Baht
	273	2008-08-09	Definitive stamp 10 Baht
	274	2008-08-09	Definitive stamp 10 Baht
	275	2008-08-09	Souvenir sheet 30 Baht
	314	2010-01-28	Definitive stamp 3 Baht
	315	2010-01-28	Definitive stamp 3 Baht
	316	2010-01-28	Definitive stamp 3 Baht
	317	2010-01-28	Definitive stamp 3 Baht
	318	2010-01-28	Definitive stamp 3 Baht
	319	2010-01-28	Definitive stamp 3 Baht
	320	2010-01-28	Definitive stamp 3 Baht
	321	2010-01-28	Block 10x3 Baht
	409	2012-08-12	Souvenir sheet 8x5, 80 Baht
Tonga	26	1994-12-14	Booklet 2.00T$
Tristan Da Chuna	59	1997-06-20	Souvenir sheet 60p
Tuvalu	65	1997-06-20	Souvenir sheet $2
Türkmenistan	254	2008-06-01	Definitive stamp 7xADGOST
	255	2008-06-01	Definitive stamp 7xADGOST
	256	2008-06-01	Definitive stamp 7xADGOST
Ukraine	302	2009-12-23	Miniature sheet (1.50-4.48)r
	358	2010-12-31	Miniature sheet 3x1.50r+3x2.00r
	404	2012-06-25	Souvenir sheet 2x13.80r

COUNTRY	NO.	ISSUE DATE	TYPE & DENOMINATION
United Nations	172	2003-03-28	Definitive stamp 70¢
	198	2005-02-04	Definitive stamp 75¢
	210	2006-02-04	Definitive stamp CHF1.30
	373	2011-10-13	Definitive stamp 0.62, 0.70€
	374	2011-10-13	Definitive stamp 0.98,1.40Fr
	375	2011-10-13	Definitive stamp $0.44, 0.98
United States	3	1989-12-03	Postal envelope 25¢
	6	1990-09-09	Postal envelope 25¢
	9	1992-01-21	Postal envelope 29¢
	38	1995-09-22	Postal envelope 32¢
	130	2000-07-07	Definitive stamp $11.75
	131	2000-07-08	Definitive stamp $11.75
	132	2000-07-11	Definitive stamp $3.20,$3.20
	133	2000-07-13	Souvenir sheet $38.50
	211	2006-03-17	Definitive stamp $4.05
	212	2006-03-17	Definitive stamp $14.40

Table 4. Hologram producers

Listed here are the companies which produced the holograms for the first and later many of the postage stamps and souvenir sheets issued around the world. Recently some of the companies have been bought or merged with other producers of security holograms. Today there are only a few large companies responsible for producing OVDs and document security holograms, including holograms for postage stamps.

3D AG
Lättichstr. 4a, CH6342 Baar, Switzerland
http://www.3dag.ch

American Bank Note Holographics Inc.
now: **OpSEC**.
1600 Stout Street, Ste 800, Denver, CO 80202, USA
http://www.opsecsecurity.com

API Holographics
Astor Road, Eccles New Road
Salford, Manchester, M50 1BB
England (UK)
http://www.api-group.com

Applied Holographics plc
now: **OpSEC**
40 Phoenix Rd., Washington,
Tyne & Wear, NE38 0AD, England (UK)
http://www.opsecsecurity.com

Crown Roll Leaf Inc.
91 Illinois Ave., Paterson, NJ 07503, USA
http://www.crownrollleaf.com

Czech Holography s.r.o.
now: **Optaglio s.r.o.**
Technology Park Řež Hlavni 326
25068 Husinec - Řež, Czech Republic
http://www.optaglio.cz

De La Rue Holographics
De La Rue House, Jays Close, Viables, Basingstoke, Hampshire
RG22 4BS, England (UK)
http://www.delarue.com

DuPont Holographics Inc.
1750 north 800 West, Logan UT 84321, USA
http://www.authentication.dupont.com

Holografica Produções Ltda
Rua Barão de Jaguará 980, Cambuci, CEP 01520 Brazil

Holographic Systems München GmbH.
now: **Dausmann Holographics GmbH**
MelchiorHuberStr. 25, 85652 Ottersberg, Germany
http://www.dausmann-holographics.de

Hologram.Industries (Now Surys)
22, ave. de l'Europe, Bussy-Saint-Georges,
F-77607 Marne-la-Vallée, Cedex 3, France
http://www.surys.com

Hologram Kft
Szerb u. 17-19, H1056 Budapest, Hungary
http://www.hologram.hu

HSM Polska SP z.o.o.
ul. Porzeczkowa 8, PL50416 Wrocław, Poland
http://www.hologram.pl

Kolbe-Coloco Spezialdruck GmbH.
Im Industrigelände 50, PF 1254
D33775 Versmold/Westf, Germany
http://www.kolbe-coloco.com

Leonhard Kurz GmbH. & Co. KG
Schwabacher Str. 482, D90763 Fürth, Germany
http://www.kurz.de

Light Impressions Int'l Ltd.
5 Mole Business Park 3, Leatherhead
Surrey KT22 7BA, England (UK)
http://www.lightimpressions.co.uk

Light Impressions Inc. USA
now: **New Light Industries, Ltd.**
9715 W. Sunset Highway
Spokane, WA 99224, USA
http://www.nli-ltd.com

Optaglio Limited OK
Basepoint Business Centre
Caxton Close, East Portway Industrial Estate
Andover, SP10 3FG, Hampshire, England (UK)
http://www.optaglio.com

OpSEC USA.
1600 Stout Street, Ste 800, Denver, CO 80202, USA
http://www.opsecsecurity.com

OVD Kinegram AG
Zählerweg 12, CH-6301 Zug, Switzerland
http://www.kinegram.com

Table 5. Hologram stamp printers

Listed here are the main companies which print banknotes and postage stamps. They have also produced many of the hologram stamps. Some companies, such as **De La Rue** in England, can in-house, produce both the holograms as well as print the final postage stamps. In most cases the holograms are produced by any of the companies listed above and delivered to a security printer for producing the finished product. Many of the hologram stamps issued around the world have been produced by the main security printers located in Europe, except for stamps issued in Canada and USA.

ABnote North America
225 Rivermoor Street
Boston, MA 02132, USA
http://www.abnotena.com

American Banknote Corporation
(ABnote Corporate)
2200 Fletcher Avenue
Fort Lee, NJ 07024
http://www.abnote.com

ANY Security Printing Company PLC
(*Former* **State Printing House**)
Halom u. 5, 1102 Budapest, Hungary
http://www.any.hu/en/

Bundesdrukerei GmbH
Oranienstrasse 91, D-10969 Berlin, Germany
http://www.bundesdruckerei.de

Canadian Bank Note Company, Ltd.
Canadian Bank Note Company, Limited
145 Richmond Road, Ottawa, ON K1Z 1A1, Canada
http://www.cbnco.com

Cartor Security Printing
Avenue Rowland Hill
Z I Gutenberg, F-28240 La Loupe, France
http://www.cartor.com

Giesecke & Devrient GmbH
Prinzregentenstrasse 159
D-81677 Munich, Germany
http://www.gi-de.com

Gravure Choquet Inc.
8777 Champ d'Eau, Montréal, QC H1P 3M3, Canada
http://www.hotstamping.ca

Hungarian Banknote Printing Company
(Pénzjegynyomda Co)
1055 Budapest, Markó str. 13-17.
http://www.penzjegynyomda.hu

Joh. Enschedé Security Print
Oudeweg 3, NL-22031 CC Haarlem,
The Netherlands
http://joh-enschede.nl/en

Lowe-Martin Group
400 Hunt Club Road
Ottawa, Ontario, Canada K1V 1C1
http://www.lmgroup.com

Southern Colour Print
1 Turakina Road , Dunedin, New Zealand
http://www.scolour.co.nz

Thai British Security Printing Public Co. Ltd
41/1 Soi Wat Suan Som, Poochao-Saming Prai Road,
Samrongtai, Phrapradaeng, Samutprakarn 10130, Thailand
http://www.tbsp.co.th

Walsall Security Printers Ltd
Midland Road, Walsall WS1 3QL, England (UK)
http://www.wsp.co.uk

2013-2016 Issues

3-26. Additional holographic stamps and souvenir sheets issued in 2013

Ecuador issued on **June 21, 2013,** the '50 Years Scout Group #14 La Salle Guayaquil' stamps the US$1.00 hologram stamps were issued in sheets of 20 stamps. A total of 80,000 stamps were issued.

3-27. Holographic stamps and souvenir sheets issued in 2014

Czech Republic continued to issue booklets and stamp sheets with the security hologram (shown in Fig. 3-22.15) attached.

Singapore issued on **January 3, 2014,** China Lunar Year Horse Hologram limited-edition S$16.80 souvenir sheet. It was made using offset lithography with high reflective index transparent hologram with morphing effect.

Hong Kong issued on **January 23, 2014,** the 'Heart-Warming' stamps and sheelets.

Hungary issued on **February 25, 2014,** the limited-edition (10,000) 'Hungarian Saints and Blesseds II'. The offset printed special edition has a shiny surface, because the offset printing method was supplemented with so-called diffraction film printing.

Indonesia issued on **April 1, 2014,** a souvenir sheet with a hologram. It was a re-issue of the first 'Netherland Indies Stamp' first issued on April 1, 1864 - to commemorate this 150th Anniversary. The 40,000 numbered sheets were printed in France by Cartor. A certificate of Authenticity is signed by Mr. Baudi Setiawan, Director of POS Indonesia and Mr. Ian Brigham, Directort of Cartor.

Thailand issued on **April 13, 2014,** 'Zodiacs of Sun Sign' stamps in sheets of twelve different 3 Bath stamps.

Canada issued on **Friday June 13, 2014,** a set of five stamps titled 'Haunted Canada', which highlighted some of Canada's more infamous spooky stories; the stamps have been printed with a holographic image along with the words *Haunted Canada* in English and French which can be seen when the stamp is tilted at a slight angle. A souvenir sheet of five stamps, a booklet of ten stamps and an uncut press sheet were issued.

Belgium issued on **July 7, 2014,** the '200th Birth Anniversary of Adolphe Sax' souvenir sheet.

Japan issued on **July 7, 2014,** the 'Tales from the Stars Series Part 1' series of nine stamps. Only at the top of the sheet there is a hologram of *stars in the sky* and *a telescope*. On the stamps there is silver printing only.

Argentina issued on **August 11, 2014**, a souvenir sheet the 'PhilaKorea 2014'with red holographic foil. The stamp exhibition took place at Gangnam, Seoul's business district, between August 7 and12, 2014.

Hungary issued on **August 25, 2014**, the 'Repatriation of the Sevaso Treasure's commemorative HUF 3,000 stamp sheet to mark the repatriation of the Sevso treasure. An imperforate edition with red numbering was released and produced by the banknote printing company Pénzjegynyomda using embossed and diffraction film printing and UV ink. 6,000 of the special imperforated sheet were printed.

Australia issued on **August 26, 2014**, the 'Impressions - Southern Lights, Circular Minisheet' in a special folder, with only 500 issued.

Hungary issued on **September 9, 2014**, 'The Fauna of Hungary' stamps. Printing technique: offset printing and diffraction film printing in the case of the HUF 405 and 445 denominations. Printed by Pénzjegynyomda.

Åland issued on **October 9, 2014**, the €0.70 'Little Christmas Fairy Tale Image' hologram stamps. Designed by Emelie Hage and printed by Southern Colour Print in a quantity of 300,000.

Philippines issued on **October 16, 2014**, the souvenir sheet 'Quezon City Memorial Circle'. 8,000 sheets were printed.

Malaysia issued on **November 5, 2014**, a 'World Youth Stamp Exhibition 2014' souvenir sheet. The stamp exhibition took place in Kuala Lumpur between September 1 and 6, 2014.

Peru issued on **November 5, 2014**, the 'Prehistoric animal, insects' sheets, *Sycorax peruensis* (Fossils).

New Caledonia issued on **November 6, 2014**, 'Swallowtail Butterfly (Papilio montrouzieri) stamp.'

Spain issued on **November 11, 2014**, Christmas (Navidad) stamps with gold holographic foil. The Class A stamp bears the image of a stained-glass window. It is accompanied by the message "Merry Christmas" written in the four official languages spoken in Spain. Cold foil was added to the stamp to accentuate the colors and give greater depth to the stained-glass image. The Class B stamp is presented in mini-sheet format, made up of six equal stamps joined together to form a Christmas tree. This issue brings the novelty of thermal ink, a substance that gives the impression that the stars shine when you slide your fingers over them.

Nigeria issued on **November 27, 2014**, a set of seven stamps with holograms of the seven 'Seven Civilian Heads of State that have ruled Nigeria between 1914 and 2014'. The square hologram, which has been used on the stamps from Nigeria before, consists only of a piece of *diffracting foil*. It is attached to the circular perforated ₦50 stamps.

Malaysia issued on **December 3, 2014,** a souvenir sheet on the occasion of the 'Malaysia World Youth Stamp Exhibition 2014' which was held between December 1 and 6, 2014, at the Kuala Lumpur Convention Centre (KLCC). A special miniature sheet featuring the Hibiscus was released on the third day of the exhibition.

3-28. Holographic stamps and souvenir sheets issued in 2015

Czech Republic continued to issue booklets and stamp sheets with the security hologram (shown in Fig. 3-22.15) attached.

Finland issued on **January 19, 2015**, synchronized skating hologram stamp 'The World championship skating team Marigold on ice'.

Jersey issued on **February 18, 2015**, a £5 hologram stamp. The new definitive stamp depicts the 'Crest of Jersey'. The hologram stamp was issued in minisheets of four and incorporates three different holographic effects as well as micro printing. The hologram stamp with micro printing was created by Kurz, Germany, and printed by Cartor Security Printing, France.

Hong Kong issued on **March 17, 2015**, a set of special stamps on the theme of 'Astronomical Phenomena', featuring seven astronomical phenomena – Solar Eclipse, Meteor Shower, Comet, Saturn's Ring Tilt Variation, Sunspot, Moon-Planet Conjunction and Lunar Eclipse along with a $20 sheetlet with a 3D hologram Stamp of the *Moon* to give the Moon a life-like appearance.

Canada issued stamps on **April 13, 2015**, of five prehistoric animals that once roamed Canada. The stamps have been treated with holographic foil and multilevel embossing to create a 3D effect on the souvenir sheet only and not on the booklet. The stamps are Permanent Stamps for domestic mail value. A souvenir sheet of five stamps, a booklet of ten stamps and uncut press sheet with holographic foil and multilevel embossing.

P.R. China issued on **June 13, 2015**, the 'Thanks Dad - China Father's Day' stamps and a souvenir sheet.

Hungary issued on **August 7, 2015**, the limited-edition (10,000) 'Hungarian Saints and Blesseds III' The offset printed special edition has a shiny surface, because the offset printing method was supplemented with so-called diffraction film printing.

Thailand issued on **August 14, 20015**, 26 Bath 'Emerald Buddha' special souvenir sheet. The stamps show the Emerald Buddha wearing the three sets of gold clothing.

Canada issued on **September 14, 2015**, which features five permanent (Domestic) stamps in the 'Haunted Canada Stamp Series', each depicting a hair-raising ghostly tale from across Canada, printed in six color ink with a holographic foil finish.

Japan issued on **September 23, 2015**, the 'Tales from the Stars Series Part 2' series of nine stamps. At the top of the sheet there is a hologram of *stars in the sky* and *a telescope.*

Hungary issued on **November 10, 2015**, 'Christmas Stamp with hologram foil' as well as a Christmas miniature sheet of four stamps with hologram foil on borders.

Philippines issued on **December 5, 2015**, the 'Philippine Daily Inquirer: 30 Years' P30 commemorative stamps.

3-29. Holographic stamps and souvenir sheets issued in 2016

Czech Republic continued to issue booklets and stamp sheets with the security hologram (shown in Fig. 3-22.15) attached.

Finland issued on **January 22, 2016**, a special holographic stamp featuring a *winter ice crystal* printed on a holographic foil which reflects all colors of the spectrum when light hits the foil in all angles and gives glimmer effect as in ice crystals.

Japan issued on **January 22, 2016**, the 'Tales from the Stars Series Part 3' series of nine stamps. At the top of the sheet there is a hologram of *stars in the sky* and *a telescope*.

Indonesia issued on **May 5, 2016**, a souvenir sheet with special stamps printed as a 3D hologram stamp to commemorate the 66 years of the Diplomatic Relations between Indonesia and Thailand. One of the stamp features a Mural painting from the Emerald Buddha temple in Thailand while the other stamp features the paintings of Kamesan. The stamps are self adhesive.

Spain issued on **June 30, 2016**, a set of four-stamps featuring Dinosaurs - The Europelta, The Pelecanimimus, The Proa and The Turiasaurus. Different 3D techniques were used including holographic ink used for the *Pelecaniminus* dinosaur stamp.

Canada issued on **September 8, 2016,** the third edition in the 'Haunted Canada series' in time for Halloween with a miniature sheet of 5 domestic permanent stamps printed with holographic foil finishing.

Croatia issued on **September 9, 2016**, an 11.00 kuna stamp with a hologram. It was for the Croatian Post's 25-Year Anniversary of issuing postage stamps of the Republic of Croatia. The particularity of the hologram postage stamp is that the number 25, the central motif of the hologram – is presented in kinetic 3D effect in nano-gravure. In this technique the number seems convex, as 3D object, above the basic hologram surface although it is entirely flat and on it a rainbow spectrum can be seen. Post-horns on postage stamps are realized in real 3D effect which creates the impression of depth beneath the basic hologram surface.

CPSIA information can be obtained
at www.ICGtesting.com
Printed in the USA
LVOW06s1546160617
538407LV00049B/1981/P